Faithful Magistrates and Republican Lawyers

Studies in Legal History

Published by the University of
North Carolina Press in association with
the American Society for Legal History

EDITOR Morris S. Arnold

EDITORIAL ADVISORY BOARD

John D. Cushing
Lawrence M. Friedman
Charles M. Gray
Thomas A. Green
Oscar Handlin

George L. Haskins
J. Willard Hurst
S. F. C. Milsom
Joseph H. Smith
L. Kinvin Wroth

Faithful Magistrates and Republican Lawyers

Creators of Virginia Legal Culture, 1680–1810

by A. G. Roeber

The University of North Carolina Press *Chapel Hill*

© 1981 The University of North Carolina Press
All rights reserved

Library of Congress Cataloging in Publication Data
Roeber, A G 1949–
  Faithful magistrates and republican lawyers.
  (Studies in legal history)
  Bibliography: p.
  Includes index.
  1. Law—Virginia—History and criticism.
2. Courts—Virginia—History. 3. Judges—Virginia—
History. 4. Lawyers—Virginia—History. I. Title.
II. Series.
KFV2478.R63   349.755   80-19524
ISBN 978-0-8078-9766-9 (pbk.)

TO MY PARENTS

Contents

Preface	xi
Abbreviations	xiii
Introduction	xv
1. Justices and Lawyers in England, 1680–1714	3
2. Justices and Lawyers in Virginia, 1680–1720	32
3. Court Day and Its Critics, 1720–1750	73
4. Country Justice Besieged, 1750–1774	112
5. Republican Lawyers, 1774–1790	160
6. The Impact of the District Courts on the Country, 1790–1805	203
7. The Legacy of Court and Country in Virginia Legal Culture	231
Bibliography	263
Index	283

Tables

1. Sample of Lawyers, 1660–1700   54
2. Barristers and Attorneys in Virginia, 1699   55
3. Some Members of the Williamsburg Bar, 1700–1750   101
4. Barristers, General and County Court Attorneys, and Inns of Court Members on County Benches in the Tidewater, 1750–1770   123
5. General Court Examiners of Prospective Lawyers, 1732–1772   124
6. Ratio of Lawyers to Population in Eight Tidewater Virginia Counties, 1740–1770   129
7. Grand Jury Presentments, 1720–1750   141
8. Grand Jury Presentments, 1750–1770   142
9. Courts and Grand Juries Missed, 1750–1770   143

MAP

Virginia Counties, 1740–1780   33

CHART

The Courts of Virginia, 1705–1810   2

Preface

It is a pleasant obligation to acknowledge those people and institutions that helped to bring this study to its completion. Many research trips to Virginia were made incomparably more pleasant than they might have been by the hospitality of Michael and Genevieve McGiffert and Howard E. White. I decided to pursue the historian's craft under Mike McGiffert's tutelage at the University of Denver; I am pleased to acknowledge him as a colleague and friend as well as a former mentor. Philip J. Schwarz of Virginia Commonwealth University graciously extended hospitality while I was in Richmond. George M. Curtis III of the John Marshall Papers, Thad Tate and his colleagues at the Institute of Early American History and Culture, and staff of the libraries at the College of William and Mary, the Virginia State Library, Colonial Williamsburg, and the University of Virginia were kind and courteous. I am grateful to them all.

Dr. Edward M. Riley, now retired as director of the research department of Colonial Williamsburg, made the resources of his department available and research more pleasant through the Grant-in-Aid Program, for which I am thankful. Nancy Merz, Harold Gill, and the staff of the department have been highly instrumental in aiding my work, as has Edward Ayres of the Southside Historical Sites Foundation and Gerald R. Mullin of Sacramento State. Stanley N. Katz offered me sage advice on the perils of studying colonial legal history and has responded generously to requests for criticism of the manuscript. Colleagues at Princeton and Brown read the manuscript and made useful suggestions, especially David Underdown, James M. Banner, Jr., Wesley Frank Craven, and, in a particularly incisive and encouraging manner, John M. Murrin, from whom I have learned just how much his notion of "anglicization" informed my own interpretation of colonial legal history. Charles T. Cullen, now editing the Jefferson Papers at Princeton, read the thesis while serving as editor of the Marshall Papers and contributed many hours of discussion and suggestion about the chapters dealing with the early republic.

Gordon S. Wood directed the dissertation from which the book has grown. I first laid hold of Clifford Geertz's work in Wood's seminar and have learned much under his criticism and encouragement. I hope that he, Geertz, and Rhys Isaac will discover that I profited from their suggestions and attempts to aid me in unraveling the "webs of significance" that made up Virginia's legal culture.

A National Endowment for the Humanities Fellowship administered through the American Antiquarian Society immensely aided the speedy completion of this project and the initiation of a second. To Marcus McCorison, John Hench, Bill Joyce, Nancy Burkett, and their staff, I am deeply grateful. Other scholars at the Society during 1978–79 made many useful suggestions and comments, especially James Beard, George Billias, and particularly Gloria L. Main. Parts of the book were delivered as papers at the Columbia University Seminar and at Princeton's Shelby Cullom Davis Center for Historical Studies. I am particularly indebted to the participants in the Davis Center seminar and especially to Lawrence Stone, who invited me and who has generously supported my work.

Win Thrall at Lawrence University did the final work on the map, for which I am grateful.

Personal friends helped in their own ways and in degrees far beyond the level of scholarly encouragement. Bruce Tucker, Conrad Wright, Walt Conser, Rudy and Joy Favretti, and especially John, Suzanne, and Anna Larson are more intimately bound up with this book than they know—or perhaps they know all too well.

My largest debt is to Patricia Stutzman-Roeber for being a firm but gentle critic and a patient spouse who has managed an alternately aspiring and despairing historian, his interminable requests for readings of drafts, and her own career into the bargain. The book is dedicated to two people who encouraged a love of books in a son who might have spent his time less profitably were it not for their direction.

Appleton, Wisconsin
June 30, 1980

Abbreviations

DAB   Alden Johnson et al., eds., *Dictionary of American Biography*, 20 vols. and index (New York: Charles Scribner's Sons, 1928–37).

EJCV   H. R. McIlwaine et al., eds., *Executive Journals of the Council of Colonial Virginia*, 6 vols. (Richmond: Virginia State Library, 1925–66).

Hening   William Waller Hening, *The Statutes at Large: Being A Collection of all the Laws of Virginia, From the First Session of the Legislature, in the Year 1619*, 13 vols. (Richmond and Philadelphia, 1809–23).

JVHB   H. R. McIlwaine et al., eds., *Journals of the Virginia House of Burgesses, 1619–1776*, 13 vols. (Richmond: Colonial Press, E. Waddey Co., 1905–16).

JVHD   Virginia General Assembly, *1776–1860, House of Delegates Journal, 1776–1790*, 4 vols. (Richmond: Samuel Shepherd, Thomas W. White, 1827–28).

PRO: CO   Public Record Office: Colonial Office. Colonial Records Project, Colonial Williamsburg Foundation.

Shepherd   Samuel Shepherd, *The Statutes at Large of Virginia, October 1792 to December 1806*, 3 vols. (Richmond, 1835).

VCSP   William P. Palmer et al., eds., *Calendar of Virginia State Papers and Other Manuscripts*, 11 vols. (Richmond, 1875–93).

VMHB   *The Virginia Magazine of History and Biography*.

VSL   The Virginia State Library Archives.

WMQ   *The William and Mary Quarterly*.

Because of space limitations and the need to keep the length of footnotes as short as possible, all prosopography of justices and lawyers, unless otherwise noted, should be assumed to have been compiled from the following sources: Earl Gregg Swem, *The Virginia Historical Index*, 2 vols. (Roanoke, Va., 1934); Lyon G. Tyler, ed., *The Encyclopedia of*

Virginia Biography, 5 vols. (New York, 1915); Horace Edwin Hayden, *Virginia Genealogies* (Wilkes-Barre, Pa., 1891); *Northern Neck of Virginia Historical Magazine* (1951–); H. R. McIlwaine, ed., "Justices of the Peace of Colonial Virginia, 1757–1775," *Bulletin of the Virginia State Library*, 14 (April, July, 1921): 43–149.

All legal terms cited or explained are as defined in *Black's Law Dictionary: Definitions of the Terms and Phrases of American and English Jurisprudence, Ancient and Modern*, by Henry Campbell Black, M.A., revised fourth edition (St. Paul, Minn.: West Publishing Co., 1968).

Introduction

When the seventeenth-century Englishman Roger Green reflected on the problem facing the young colony of Virginia, he suggested that it would flourish only with "*Careful tending under* faithful Teachers and Magistrates."[1] Virginia took Green's analysis to heart. Between the Restoration of the Stuart monarchy and the American Revolution, the Old Dominion developed a self-perpetuating county magistracy that dominated every aspect of the province's life through the structural mechanism of the county court. Under the "careful tending" of its faithful magistrates, Virginia did flourish during the eighteenth century and during that flowering came to be considered the most English of all the North American British colonies.

In an essay published almost thirty years ago, Charles S. Sydnor suggested that Virginia's justices rode out the Revolution with their powers and prestige intact; their county court was still the first step on the "road to power" that it had been during the colonial period. Much has changed in the posture of the historical profession in the years since Sydnor published his influential monograph entitled *Gentlemen Freeholders: Political Practices in Washington's Virginia*.[2] Recent scholarship in history and cultural anthropology has advanced new concepts about the role of ideas in cultural development. Scholars may once have seen ideas as mere reflections or "rationalizations" of changes that occur at a deeper, more "real" socioeconomic level of society. But now, most agree that concepts operate as an integral part (neither "above" nor "after the fact") of a cultural system. Rather than regard ideas as reflections, or even deceptions, advanced to "explain" social or cultural change, we do better to consider how an apparent institutional, rhetorical stasis that once sprang from and made sense to the participants of a vibrant, working culture can also obscure from later generations the deep cultural reorientation that was occurring. Such reorientations often manifest themselves in confused attempts by participants to reconcile new challenges and demands with old values and habits of thought, often with surprising, unpredictable,

---

1. *Virginia's Cure*, 3:10–11.
2. Reprinted as *American Revolutionaries in the Making*.

paradoxical results. No wonder, then, that so much of our sense of history is cast in an ironic mode.[3]

Though we labor to respect the integrity of the subjective meaning historical persons placed on their actions and lives, we are seldom content with that elusive task. If the consequences of actions performed long ago seem to speak to concerns of the historical investigator about his own time and culture, we usually suggest that the study of history is still instructive, at least in some sense. No social or intellectual historian operating under Weberian, Marxist, or structuralist categories has solved the classic dilemma of doing justice both to the integrity of the past and to its perceived significance for his contemporary audience. Yet it is always helpful in sorting out various perspectives as a reader of history to follow E. H. Carr's advice: to know what history you are reading, know your historian.[4]

The study of professional lawyers and lay justices necessarily raises certain questions that cannot be ignored. Whether there is such a phenomenon as "modernization" or "professionalization" in law and society is by now an old debate, though one rather belatedly joined by historians. Most of us eschew the notion that as historians we should erect models, draft laws of history, or subscribe to transhistorical theory to the detriment of the immediate, historic moment. Yet while the historian recognizes the insoluble qualities of epistemological dilemmas, he cannot write without reference to a particular perspective. There is no reason to hide the fact that this book is in some respects about the professionalization of law and the modernization of society.

Gordon Wood was shrewdly prophetic when he suggested that no purely "ideational" history would erase the accomplishments of the Progressive historians in American social history. Yet the task of a later generation of social or cultural historians is complex: to describe what

---

3. See chapter 3 in particular for Clifford Geertz's influence on historians trying to interpret ritual actions, rhetorical and visual symbols that guide and change societies and cultures. I avoid using the word "ideology" in describing the "world view" of rural nonliterate Anglo-Americans, since the term often seems to convey the sense of intentional subscription to preconceived programs. "In politics firmly embedded in Edmund Burke's golden assemblage of 'ancient opinons and rules of life,' the role of ideology, in any explicit sense, is marginal. In such truly traditional political systems, the participants act as . . . men of untaught feelings. . . . The function of ideology is to make an autonomous politics possible by providing the authoritative concepts that render it meaningful, the suasive images by means of which it can be sensibly grasped" (Geertz, *Interpretation of Cultures*, p. 218).

4. On the difficulties posed by various theories employed to do justice to subjective and objective meaning in the area of law, see Unger, *Law in Modern Society*; Carr, *What is History?* pp. 26, 48.

looks very much like the phenomenon sociological theorists call modernization without prescribing that process as inevitable, rational, scientific, liberal, or progressive. The crosscurrents and contradictions and what was lost in this process of modernization have to figure in our understanding nearly as prominently as the qualities that clearly predominated. Few of us would care to write history as the record of those who won, the chronicle of past triumphs.[5]

What follows, however, is in part narrative history, a straightforward recounting of what happened to Virginia's legal culture during more than a century of change. That tale contains some rather interesting surprises, and perhaps our capacity to relish those oddities and quirks in the human past says a good deal about why we still study a legal system that has passed from the scene. Yet even this narrative treatment, the simple chronology of Virginia legal history traced in this book, shows clearly that law did get more complex, that lawyers proliferated, and that print culture spread throughout a formerly oral and largely nonliterate plantation society. Gradually, a specialized knowledge of the law and the self-concept that accompanied that realization did dawn in the minds of Virginia attorneys. But until the middle of the eighteenth century no one talked about "modern" society, or even about law as a "science" or a "profession." The mode in which Virginians thought, the way they made sense of their world, utilized a different rhetoric, a more ancient lexicon.

Reading the letters, pamphlets, and newspapers of the late seventeenth and early eighteenth centuries, no one doing Anglo-American history can escape the conclusion that individuals interpreted events according to their identification with one of two opposing traditions—"Court" and "Country." These terms were not purely political, nor were they notions that people in everyday life read or heard of and then adopted in self-conscious fashion. Rather, they sprang out of the lived experience and inherited culture of English life. They were used for partisan political purposes, to be sure, by office seekers that John Morrill identifies as "Court" and "Official Country," but at the simplest level Court and Country expressed the "webs of significance" that made sense of the cultural experience of Englishmen. In order to do justice to the self-understandings of justices and lawyers, it has seemed to me imperative to follow the course of these terms in Virginia legal history, precisely be-

---

5. For the distinction between "legal honoratiores" and "legal rationalizers" advanced by Max Weber, see Rheinstein, ed., *Max Weber on Law*. A brilliant example of fruitful insights gained from tilling Weberian ground is Little, *Religion, Order, and Law*. On the issue of modernization, see Brown, *Modernization*; Henretta, "'Modernization'"; Wood, "Rhetoric and Reality."

cause that history was so intimately bound up with, and indebted to, British culture.[6]

As is usual in human affairs, the divisions were not always logical or consistent, and Anglo-Virginians were often confused about whether they wanted to be Court people or Country people. Most who were exposed to the choice probably would have opted for the best of both worlds. A deep-seated ambivalence among many of the gentry about the values of localism, simplicity, and deference to natural superiors existed because of the constant, beckoning allure of the cosmopolitan, luxurious, refined atmosphere of the Court. The literature on Court and Country is immense. But little of it has heretofore been related to the growth of colonial legal culture.

I was led to believe that Court and Country were vitally important aspects of the developing legal culture of Virginia by the intriguing remarks of J. G. A. Pocock. In his book *The Machiavellian Moment* he identified Virginia as a colony particularly Country-oriented in self-concept and practice. It struck me as odd that the "legal humanism" transferred from England to Virginia could speak through defenders of common law about law being a vibrant species of activity whose main purpose was "one of preserving, refining and transmitting the usages and customs that made . . . England" and Virginia what they were.[7] The question was which "usages and customs" were preserved, and even more important, how did a Country commonwealth get led into a revolution by lawyers? A lawyer, as Pocock has ably demonstrated, was commonly perceived by the Country as an enemy of virtue: "Like the soldier . . . and stockjobber, who corrupts by interposing himself in a virtue which all men should practice equally."[8] Here, then, was the central paradox that belied a simple, "progressive" view of the "professionalization" of law in Virginia. Was it possible that the Country tradition not only informed true Whigs like Thomas Jefferson, the lawyer, but also inspired anti-lawyer sentiment in Virginia? If so, how could one resolve this apparent contradiction?

The generally accepted view of the local courts of Virginia is that espoused by Sydnor and some of his students—that not much happened to change the quality of legal culture, the self-concept of lawyers, or their

---

6. The best introduction to concepts of Court and Country is Zagorin, *Court and Country*. On the use of Country rhetoric by ambitious politicians, see Morrill, *Revolt of the Provinces*.

7. Pocock, *Machiavellian Moment*, pp. 9–21, 341. On Virginia's Country tradition, see ibid., pp. 515–32.

8. Ibid., p. 475.

reputation in the eyes of other Virginians after the Revolution. Sydnor remarked on the peculiar quality of southern life about which he spoke in his essay "The Southerner and the Laws,"[9] seeking an answer to the question why residents of the southern states seemed to put their trust in local, personal arrangements. Why did the South tend to neglect or shun more formal, regular avenues of redress through the rigorous application of statutory and procedural norms?

Part of Sydnor's insight has been vindicated, I think, by my attempt to follow up some of his suggestions about the need to look carefully at local institutions and public rituals. But profound change *did* occur in Virginia, change that Sydnor said remarkably little about. Precisely because lawyers as a profession were coming into their own in the years just prior to the Revolution, practitioners of the law molded and gave direction to that great event. Jefferson and George Wythe began in their revisal of the laws of 1776–79 to assault the local, customary institutions of Virginia. How did the lawyers manage to bring off their reforms and convince their Country neighbors that lawyers make good republicans? How did the reforms of the lawyers succeed, and how did they yet continue to be hedged in by the deep cultural traditions of local life? What is the legacy of the debate between Court and Country for Virginia, and the nation, in the nineteenth and twentieth centuries?

These are the questions this study seeks to probe, arguing along the way that deep-seated cultural and institutional change was in process long before the American Revolution gave an added spur and vigor to those changes. The lawyers of Virginia managed to execute an impressive series of reforms between 1776 and 1790 on the structure of courts, the definitions of power, and the priorities that the new republic would honor. Virginia did not enter the antebellum period with its myths of a collective, local agrarian past ready-made and universally believed. Nor did the gentry subscribe to revolution because they were slaveowners who could appreciate the meaning of the words "slavery" and "freedom," the ingenious, but tenuous, conclusion advanced by Edmund S. Morgan.[10] The legacy of Court-Country battles included stalemate about the issue of slavery, and much else besides. If the tense, uneasy truce later brought about devastating consequences for Virginia, the compromises were still nearly unavoidable. The relationship of law to slavery was not the only ambivalent aspect of the template of ideas and persons that have created Virginia's, and the nation's, legal culture.

---

9. Sydnor, "Southerner and Laws."
10. E. S. Morgan, *American Slavery*, pp. 363–87.

Faithful Magistrates and Republican Lawyers

The Courts of Virginia, 1705–1810

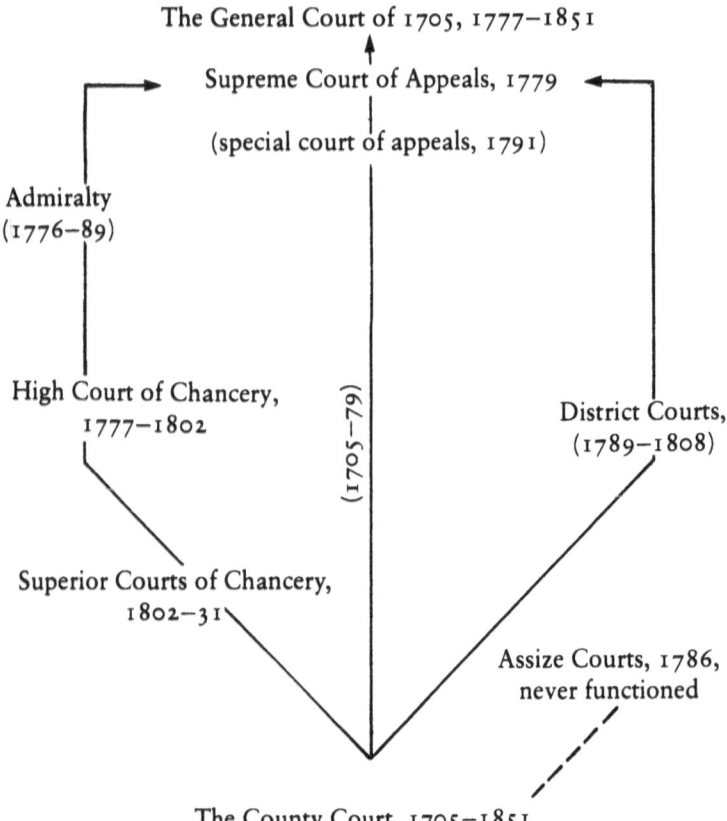

Hustings Courts: Williamsburg, 1722; Norfolk, 1736; Richmond, 1782; Alexandria, 1791

Source: Adapted, with additions, from Thomas Jefferson Headlee, Jr., "The Virginia State Court System, 1776– : A preliminary Survey of the Superior Courts of the Commonwealth with Notes Concerning the Present Location of the Original Court Records and Published Decisions" (typescript, Virginia State Library, 1969).

Chapter 1
Justices and Lawyers in England, 1680–1714

That Estate of Men which be Called Worshipful
—SIR THOMAS ELYOT, *The Book Named the Governor*

In 1749 a former county justice named Henry Fielding published a very long novel entitled *A History of Tom Jones, a Foundling*. Among the many character studies worked into the tale, none is more memorable than that of Squire Western, the country justice. Drawn from Fielding's own memories of the county bench, Western epitomized the qualities of the independent country gentry. "The great are deceived," wrote Fielding, "if they imagine they have appropriated ambition and vanity to themselves." Western, the petty tyrant of his county, was a man whose arrogant self-importance was nonetheless rendered admirable by his sturdy defense of virtuous independence. Remonstrating with him over a decision, his sister cattily observed that a London magistrate would never have ruled so. Western responded with the classic dictum of the Country justice: "Like enough," he cried. "It may be so in London; but the law is different in the country."[1]

By Fielding's day the bucolic independence of the country gentry had become part and parcel of the mythology of England. In another novel, *Joseph Andrews*, Fielding had already captured the nature of the vertically organized social order over which the gentry supposedly still presided. Society was divided into ranks that later generations would call "classes." But in Fielding's day the nature of social relationships was thought of as a "picture of dependance like a kind of ladder." In a famous passage, Fielding summarized the patronage relationships of the greater and lesser residents of the counties in this way:

> Early in the morning arises the postillion, or some other boy . . . and falls to brushing the clothes, and cleaning the shoes of John the footman, who . . . applies his hands to the same labours for Mr Second-hand the squire's gentleman; the gentleman . . . a little later in the day, attends the squire; the squire . . . attends the levee of my

1. 1:126, 290.

3

lord ... my lord himself is seen at the levee of the favourite, who after his hour of homage is at an end, appears himself to pay homage to the levee of his sovereign. Nor is there perhaps, in this whole ladder of dependance, any one step at a greater distance from the other, than the first from the second: so that to a philosopher the question might only seem whether you would chuse to be a great man at six in the morning, or at two in the afternoon.[2]

A curious combination of feisty independence of mind, landed rank, and deference to one's social superiors made English country life what it was. Yet by the eighteenth century social reality in the counties was not a simple picture of rural gentlemen presiding over their dependents. From the mid-seventeenth century on, policies of the central government disrupted the independence of many localities, imposing a greater degree of control on the counties than before. Moreover, one of the areas where this change intruded most strongly was in the courts of law. Imagine the chagrin of a proud Western when berated by Judge Hyde at the Hereford winter assizes in 1663. To the assembled gentry the judge acidly ordered that "if there be any lawyer a justice of peace sitting on the bench ... the rest of the justices ought to acquiesce to his judgment and opinion therein, and not (as is commonly practised) put [it] to the vote of many ignorant justices on the bench according to their fancy and opinion."[3]

Such an incident illustrates, as well as any, the changes that occurred as a more professional brand of law was brought into the counties. Understandably, the gentry was not always pleased with such orders, and even less so because its own character and composition were changing at this very moment. Just as the aristocracy of England had begun to lose political and social power to the gentry in the early seventeenth century,[4] so by the end of that century the old gentry itself was declining. Justices of the peace were no longer simply local squires, nobles, and landowners. England by the 1690s was embarked on a mercantile adventure, and the rise of merchants swung the balance of monied power once and for all out of the hands of the old landed gentry. New men—merchants—began sitting on the county benches, much to the chagrin of older families. Despite the picture drawn by Fielding and others the independence of the gentry in dealing with county problems from the bench of Quarter Sessions was seriously circumscribed by 1714. That circumscription was part of a larger story which involved a nation in the struggle between

2. P. 159. See also Perkin, *Origins of Modern English Society.*
3. Quoted by Cockburn, *History of English Assizes*, p. 171.
4. Stone, *Crisis of the Aristocracy.*

local traditionalism and national cosmopolitanism. The law became one of the central arenas in which very different notions of what the law was, and what men who were officers of the law ought to be doing, battled for supremacy throughout England from the local to the national level. Moreover, the proper notion of what law was, was itself intimately bound up with cultural definitions of what society and social relations along the "ladder of dependence" were supposed to be like.

The ladder of dependence that Fielding described defined the proper social relations of Britons in the county and the nation at large. Yet in any society social relations and the norms that govern conduct are never merely personal, one-to-one concerns. One of England's boasts, that England was "a nation of laws, and not of men," was a truism for some, a saw for others, and an empty bit of rhetoric in the opinion of yet others. But in so saying, Englishmen who subscribed to this notion were suggesting that not arbitrary power but the predictable and equitable application of law—ancient, customary, common law—determined the fate of an Englishman. Whether the administration of laws actually *was* equitable and fair is not the concern here. However, one can scarcely begin a discussion of justices of the peace and lawyers in any culture without also considering law, and especially what Englishmen thought the law was.

Law is broadly defined as a species of social control. But this positivist, utilitarian description of what laws *do* does not in fact satisfactorily convey understanding of what "law" *meant* for seventeenth-century Englishmen. The common law was the pride of those Englishmen who were fond of comparing their country's customs and ancient institutions with those of more despotic and less happy nations. But besides familiarity with customary law or chancery decisions where discretion held out some hope for redress when remedies at law failed, most Englishmen (even the humblest) were also aware of statutory laws defined by Parliament, other kinds of law that governed through church courts and procedures, and above all these the king, the fountain of justice in the realm. The proper relationship between the various types of law and whether the king was above or subject to an even "deeper" or "higher" law would be hammered out in the controversies that wracked seventeenth-century England. Beyond all of the specific areas and types of law most Englishmen, like most descendants of medieval rural European society, had a sense that laws of whatever sort, though made by men, ought to reflect in some measure the laws of God. Nothing would be more erroneous than to suggest that the law, whether in the Country or elsewhere during the late seventeenth century, had already been disconnected from this notion, inherited from the classical, and more especially, the medieval discussion of natural law.[5]

To the modern student, thoroughly schooled in the dicta of legal realism and convinced by Justice Holmes's statement that the law is not "some brooding omnipresence in the sky," such transcendent notions of what the law was, or was supposed to be, seem remote. To the casual observer it may seem that the daily routine of affairs in county life had little to do with the lofty theories of the Schoolmen or of the constitutional theorists of the day.[6] Yet, too vigorous a pursuit of such hardheaded attitudes risks impugning the integrity of a local community's sense of itself. For precisely because they were geographically and mentally distant from the centers of power and novelty, Country justices clung to older notions of societal relationships and the awesome quality of the law in spite of, even in defiance of, vast social, economic, and demographic changes.

While these changes were taking place, a remarkably backward-looking search for a usable past and an attachment to a traditional definition of the law characterized the mentality of local Englishmen. The most widely used publication for justices of the peace in the 1680s illustrated this. Published in 1681 as an update of Michael Dalton's *Countrey Justice* (1618), Richard Chamberlain's *Complete Justice* continued to advocate that the law be considered a species of activity very much like that carried on by the church—both were designed to secure the peace. Whether for peace of spirit and soul or for peaceable relations with others, the "Government of this Kingdom consists of two parts, vizt. first the Laws Ecclesiastic for the peace of the Church, and Laws Civil, or Temporal, for the peace of the Land."[7] The emphasis on peaceable relations in the kingdom reflected both St. Augustine's claim that peace was the precondition for all other civilized action and England's bloody recent past.

A clear notion of what law is was expressed by Chamberlain's section entitled "A Compendious Charge to be given at the Quarter Sessions." In this piece, Chamberlain reveals a very astute mind at work, one which saw how closely the peace of the county depended not merely on control and punishment but on the internal reformation of character through

---

5. On the idea of "higher" or "fundamental" law, see Gough, *Fundamental Law*; Little, *Religion, Order, and Law*, pp. 167–217; Corwin, *'Higher Law' Background*; the medieval concepts are best represented by Aquinas's *Summa*, questions 90–97, in Parry, ed., *Thomas Aquinas*, pp. 1–116.

6. Holmes's aphorism was delivered in *Southern Pacific Co. v. Jensen*, 224 U.S. 205, 222 (1917).

7. Chamberlain, *Complete Justice*, p. 470.

education and work. Chamberlain suggested to his justices that doing justice under the laws was no simple matter: "Now seeing *Justitia est duplex* viz. The punishing part, and the preventing Justice, the premisses only touching the former, therefore the conclusion shall point something at the latter, with a direction how it may be effected. We find by experience, that it is not frequent punishment that prevents offences; *praestat cautela, quam medela*, it is better preventing, than redressing offences." The county justices, Chamberlain believed, should recognize that preventative justice lay in three things: first, education of youth, "which ought to be by instruction in the knowledge of Religion, and by learning some Trade in their tender years, so as there should not be an idel person, or a Beggar, according to the Scripture, Deut. 15. 4"; second, the justices needed to enforce the already sufficient laws against idleness; third, justices ought to refrain from pardoning too frequently, "which make many offend in hope. This preventing Justice is better than punishing Justice; as obedience is better than sacrifice; for in sacrifice we do but repent of sin, but in obedience we prevent sin; and it is better preventing than repenting sin."[8]

The persistence of the idea that offenses against the laws of God and society were sin marks one of those important areas in which Squire Western's dictum held some truth—the law continued "different in the country." The precise expression of that sense of being different, however, was quite complex. Gradually, a devotion to old-fashioned virtues, a sense of sin, and a dedication to doing one's duty to God and one's betters and dependents were acknowledged by seventeenth-century Englishmen as the special preserve of the Country.

During the seventeenth and eighteenth centuries, the terms "Court" and "Country" acquired political definitions as catchall terms denoting groups alternately in and out of power. But the original meaning of the words derived less from politics than from a cultural understanding of what was right and wrong with life in Albion. Court and Country were symbols that summoned up a host of associations by which the user could identify what he believed in, who his friends or his enemies were, and what made his world intelligible and significant. As Perez Zagorin points out, Nicholas Breton's tract *The Court and the Country* (1618) identified the Country as "the symbol of simplicity and wholesome pleasures based on religion and respect for tradition." The definition of a Country man was one who not only stood for time-honored values and institutions but also served his "country" (originally this meant his

---

8. Ibid., p. 485. On the use of Chamberlain and Michael Dalton's *Countrey Justice* in Virginia, see Bryson, *Census of Law Books*, pp. xvii, 44, 46.

county) out of a sense of duty and public spirit. This sense of duty, and the moral, religious tenor of private life that presumably informed and nourished the sense of duty, the Country called "virtue." This term was also a verbal symbol, combining fairly secular notions of civic duty borrowed from the Renaissance with more squarely Christian notions of moral behavior and obedience to the law, even while depending through faith alone on the promise of the gospel. If the Country never bothered to define precisely the sources and implications behind its notion of virtue, that was hardly surprising. They did not seem vague to one raised in the Country tradition.[9]

The Country did know, precisely, what virtue was not. To identify the threats to virtue and the source of imminent doom they pointed to the Court. When the gentleman of Parliament in 1625 called himself "neither

9. Zagorin, *Court and Country*, p. 34. The term "virtue" is vexatious because of the various concepts that this word connotes. Various exegeses of the term reveal two or three sources for the word in opposition thought. In *Machiavellian Moment* (see index under virtue) Pocock distinguishes between private and public virtue. Private virtue consisted of the moral, religious habits of mind and behavior derived from the Christian ethical tradition. Public virtue was more generally associated with the Renaissance word *virtù* and conjured up public-spiritedness and civic duty, but with courageous, managerial skill behind public action. Wood, in *Creation of the American Republic*, agrees with Pocock on the two-sidedness of the "virtue" endorsed by opposition writers. Public virtue in the people consists of deference to natural leaders, who are engaged in selfless service to the public good. Presumably, private virtue is the wellspring from which public virtue should issue (p. 69). In the present study, this dual concept of virtue is assumed. Critics of lawyers, when attacking a lack of virtue, meant both that lawyers were lacking in private morality because their advancement depended on other men's sorrow and that they were devoid of public virtue because of the artificial nature of their calling and their incapacity to work for the public good. Stourtz, in *Alexander Hamilton* (pp. 63–64), reviews three types of virtue: (1) Christian norms of fear of God, brotherly love, and humility; (2) wisdom, knowledge of how to design a state best suited to public life and peace; and (3) passion for the public good, related to (2) but modern in its emphasis on "passion" rather than on intellect or spiritual qualities. Fiering, "Benjamin Franklin," pp. 199–223, suggests three sources: (1) Platonic knowledge; (2) Judaeo-Christian conversion or change of heart to follow moral precepts; and (3) the concept of habit as the source of "behavioral change." These definitions roughly correspond to Stourtz's. In any event, classical and Christian concepts seem to have been easily combined into one for the Country. Private morals and public-spiritedness are inextricably intertwined. More "modern" apologists disagreed and denigrated the importance of private morality in the promotion of public good, hence Bernard de Mandeville's famous dictum "private vices, public benefits." With regard to the law and especially the judiciary, constitutional thought in the seventeenth century could not conceive of a separate "branch" of government but only the "magisterial" power. Hence the dangers to public and private virtue in the law tended to be seen as stemming from the corruption of law by tyranny. On the belated recognition by republican theorists of the value a judiciary might play in their defense of virtue, see Wood, *Creation of the American Republic*, pp. 453–63.

Courtier nor Lawyer but a plaine Countrey Gentleman," his symbolic identity was immediately clarified for his listeners. The Court was associated with the monarchy and with those of nobility and their minions who did the bidding of the Stuarts. This aspect of the definition never completely disappeared, and it was still quite viable when Virginians in 1776 revived it with a rather piquant use against otherwise Whig Britons. But in the interim the writing of republican theorists during and after the Civil War—especially that of Harrington—had changed the definition in other aspects. By the late seventeenth century the "Whigs" under Lord Shaftesbury were reaching back into Harringtonian thought to justify their ideas and excoriate the political faction of "Tories" under Lord Danby. The added notion used by these "neo-Harringtonians" was that the Court represented "corruption," which threatened the independent thinking, action, and care of dependents by the Country gentry. The abuse of the natural relationships on the ladder of dependence was a crime that the Court excelled in committing, according to Whig writers. Whether by buying the support of a person in Parliament or by suborning the judiciary by placing loyal favorites on the bench, the Court destroyed the possibility for sober, thoughtful action by men whose rightful duties and virtues on behalf of dependents and the nation was short-circuited. The means of buying men came, the Country said, from new, mercantile wealth.[10]

Ironically, even as the Whigs refined this definition, they themselves came to power, and the original, cultural definitions of Court and Country reemerged. Never really political identification tags, the terms Court and Country increasingly meant those who exercised power and aggrandized new wealth and those who berated and scorned them for so doing. The dilemma of Country partisans who sought to perpetuate their ancient and reformist ideas was simple and discouraging. As Pocock says: "They could not take office without falsifying their own ostensible values."[11] By the late seventeenth century, then, Court and Country were terms with political overtones but not terms synonymous with either "Whig" or "Tory" factions in English political life.

The Glorious Revolution of 1688–89 ended the overt threat of monarchic Court dominance and appeared to guarantee a limited monarchy in the Protestant line, but the troubles of the Country were far from

---

10. Zagorin, *Court and Country*, p. 35. On the evolution of the terminology and issues raised by Harrington, see Pocock, *Machiavellian Moment*, pp. 406–22.

11. On the dilemma of Country officeholders, see Pocock, *Machiavellian Moment*, p. 409. See also his "Machiavelli, Harrington, and English Political Ideologies" and *Ancient Constitution*.

over. Indeed, between 1690 and 1714 the death knell rang for the old-fashioned, pastoral England, so lovingly described by the Augustan poets, the England whose virtue, long since departed, was so eloquently mourned by the Scriblerians and the grandest apologist of the ancien régime, Henry St. John, Lord Bolingbroke. Even as John Locke and other Whig theorists justified revolution in the defense of property and liberty, the rise of mercantile entrepreneurs helped to dissolve the ability of the gentry to act responsibly toward their dependents. The tradition of natural law came to be used in a perverse way to terrorize the hapless poor, caught between traditional social relationships and occupations and the less personal, less agrarian future toward which Britain was now committed. Protests against the success of a Whig Court presided over by Sir Robert Walpole and the Pelham-Holleses had little genuine impact. By the time Fielding wrote inexorable economic and social change had long since altered British rural life.[12]

Why, then, the continued paean to a supposed "golden age" of English virtue? What role did the gentry who ruled the counties from the bench as justices of the peace play in this on-going criticism of modernity, and why did the Country see lawyers as the allies of the enemy—the Court, increasingly composed of the mercantile clique whose interests Whig policies protected? Most important, what implications did this cultural battle between Court and Country hold for the transplanted Englishmen returning from Virginia for education and trade at the end of the seventeenth century? The answers to these questions lie in the nature of county law and in what the gentry sitting as justices of the peace actually did. The shrinking sphere of influence left them by the legal reforms of the Commonwealth and Restoration periods must be understood if we are to appreciate the potency and the nature of the myth of the Country tradition.

Court and Country competed for adherents and existed side by side in England, and Anglo-Americans returning to England in the 1680s and

12. The Revolution Settlement did not completely settle the issue of whether judges were independent of magisterial tyranny. By the Act of Settlement judges in England sat *quamdiu se bene gesserint* instead of *durante beneplacito*, as formerly. See Maitland, *Constitutional History*, pp. 312–13. For the colonies, this issue seemed all the more pressing by 1761, since after that date all judges sat at pleasure and not during good behavior. See Labaree, ed., *Royal Instructions*, 2:366–68. In England, popular dislike of judges and lawyers continued a common theme in literature and art. See, for example, Hogarth's famous drawings *The Bench* and *Royalty, Episcopacy and Law*. On the concept of virtue among the Augustan literateurs, see Kramnick, *Bolingbroke and His Circle*. The perversion of natural law precepts by propertied Whig theorists, shearing away the moral obligations toward inferiors, is perceptively treated by Macpherson in *Political Theory of Possessive Individualism*; Olafson, ed., *Society, Law and Morality*, pp. 1–24, 117–48. On the impact

1690s encountered a culture straining against the developments of trade, mercantile success and international political importance. In a very real sense the Country tradition played a singular role both for Englishmen "at home" and for those from Virginia. The tradition was at once myth and reality. As reality, it was rooted in a rural, agrarian experience that was immediately familiar to Virginians. As myth, it represented the way in which insecure Englishmen grounded themselves in a more familiar past while entering the future. One can argue that the adoption of an old-fashioned mode of thought merely facilitates change while denying that change is happening. But the invocation of Country notions had a more potent legacy than that. By 1714, at least for Englishmen in Virginia, county life and the Country tradition represented the reality far more ably than did a rapidly changing, mercantile Britain herself.[13]

In both England in 1689 and Virginia in 1776 the defense of Country virtues was led by lawyers. This paradox—the allies of the Court fashioning the instruments by which the Country fought to vindicate its ideas—can only be understood in Virginia by first reviewing what happened between justices and lawyers in England.

Justices and the Country

"Courteous Reader, The great Antiquity of Justices of Peace in this Kingdom . . . and the . . . continuing their Authority hitherto; speaks both the Utility and Necessity of that weighty Office: how it hath been established and rendered more ample and extensive by the grave wisdom of our Law-Makers." So wrote Chamberlain to the purchasers of his 1681 manual, *The Complete Justice*. No one would have quarreled with him, but some might well have quoted William Lambarde's 1581 query: "How many Justices, thinke you, may now suffice (without breaking their backes) to bear so many, not loads, but Stacks of Statutes, that have . . . been laide upon them?" The duties of the local justices were indeed broad, and perhaps a concern over the local squires' inability to live up to all their duties prompted the central government during the course of the seven-

---

on English social conditions of the defense of property without moral and political restraint, see Hay, "Property, Authority and the Criminal Law," pp. 17–63; E. P. Thompson, *Whigs and Hunters*.

13. The term "myth" is used here in a very precise sense to mean that sense invoked by a culture seeking to root itself in the past while undergoing severe change. This largely unconscious act of placing certain subjects beyond discussion reveals their essential meaning: they cannot be substantially altered without destroying the very sense of the world they convey. See Cohen, "Theories of Myth"; Halpern, "'Myth' and 'Ideology'"; Kirk, *Myth*.

teenth century to direct justices toward overseeing administrative and petty criminal matters alone. Civil causes had never been the chief concern of the Courts of Quarter Sessions, and felonies that involved the possible taking of life or limb were dealt with not only at sessions but at the meetings of the Courts of Assize. In former days justices had exercised the power to execute felons. By the Restoration, however, this practice was dying out, and its demise was urged upon the local courts by the lawyers and judges of Westminster, who preferred to consider such grave causes at the procedurally more rigorous sessions of assizes. There the judge exercised full sway, and local considerations would work neither for nor against a putative felon.[14]

Justices of the peace were theoretically appointed by the king, the source of all law and magistracy in the realm. In practice the lord chancellor exercised this patronage power. In every county the lord lieutenant acted as the custos rotulorum, recommended names to be added to the Commission of the Peace to the Chancery, and suggested men who might be left off the list if he felt them incompetent or politically unsympathetic to the crown. A local bishop, a group of justices, even a single powerful noble acting as a justice might exercise his patronage over the commission. No less an authority than Sir Edward Coke had opined that the Commission of the Peace constituted "such a forme of subordinate government for the tranquillity and quiet of the Realm, as no part of the Christian world hath the like, if the same be duly executed."[15]

The due execution of the office involved those men elevated by patronage to the bench to oversee the affairs of the county. Between fifteen and twenty justices sat at the quarter sessions meetings, which were ordained by statute to sit four times a year in the weeks following Epiphany (January 6), Easter, the Translation of St. Thomas the Martyr (July 7),

---

14. Chamberlain, *Complete Justice*, introduction. Lambarde's query is quoted in Allen, ed., *Essex Quarter Sessions*, p. ix. On the decline of capital punishment imposed by quarter sessions, see Cockburn, *English Assizes*, pp. 89–90, 97.

15. *Fourth Part of the Institutes*, p. 170. On the justices, their duties, and their relationship to higher authority, see Glassey, "Commission of the Peace," pp. 15–17, 33–40; Barnes, *Clerk of the Peace*; Moir, *Justice of the Peace* and *Local Government in Gloucestershire*. Moir finds a wide variety of wealth and occupation of eighteenth-century justices; assizes imposed close supervision; few lawyers sat on the benches; most magistrates attempted to be conscientious in attendance and in their duty regarding poor relief. See also Dowdell, *A Hundred Years of Quarter Sessions*. The clerk of the peace in some counties was the officer who acted in place of the custos. The lord lieutenant was chief military officer of the county, responsible for mustering its defense; as custos, he was also chief civil officer. This man was often senior magistrate of the Quorum; he was usually presiding justice of the county, hence Chancery's determination to keep a man sympathetic to the reigning monarch in this position. See Webb and Webb, *English Local Government*.

and St. Michael's Day (September 29). Although leet courts still met in the towns of England and courts baron still functioned under the eye of the nobles, in fact by the 1660s the quarter sessions court had become the central legal institution of the county. In the fifty-two counties of England and Wales the old "hundreds" or divisions within the county had become the sessional divisions of individual groups of justices. By a means which no one can account for, so-called "petty sessions" were often held during the year in these divisions when the Court of Quarter Sessions was not sitting.

Eventually, the Privy Council formally directed justices to hold "divisional" sessions to investigate petty nuisances. No jury trials or offenses requiring a grand inquest could be dealt with here. But these local sessions did appoint two or more overseers of the poor and look over their accounts, deal with unlicensed alehouses, investigate reputed parents of bastard children, control servants trying to leave their employers, and punish forcible entry and riots, idle women, the killing of game or stealing of eggs, and rather more serious crimes like rick burning. The justices had as their officers of enforcement the undersheriff, the high bailiffs of hundreds, franchises, and liberties, and deputy-sheriffs or "foot" bailiffs. By 1689 the sheriffs, high bailiffs (or town constables formerly appointed by the court leet of a village or town) were appointed for one-year terms by quarter sessions to hold the "County Court" or Sheriff's Court. Small debts under forty shillings could be recovered here, and outlawry still declared against malefactors. The high sheriff, appointed by the crown, ordinarily did not bother with these sessions, but instead directed his attention during his year in office to the affairs of the quarter sessions of the peace.

Technically, justices could not refuse to sit at the sessions for their counties, although in practice it was becoming increasingly difficult by the 1660s to get nobles and the greater gentry to serve. By statute a justice had to be of the county where he sat, possess an estate of not less than £20 per year (quite a large sum in 1439 when the law was passed [18 Henry 6, c. 11, secs. 1 & 2]), and take out his writ of *dedimus potestatem*, which empowered him to act. He did this by going before the clerk of the peace, taking the oath of office, and paying the required fees, a ceremony which was largely neglected and seldom enforced. Apparently, an English justice (unless a peer of the realm) was to be paid four shillings a day for attendance, but only eight justices could be so paid. An Elizabethan Statute of Labourers gave five shillings a day out of fines imposed, but it is not known to what extent justices actually were paid from such sources in the seventeenth and eighteenth centuries. By 1791 stipendiary, or paid, justices had become the norm in Middlesex County, but the rule for the country at large was that justices served for no fee, or at best, for next to nothing.[16]

The convening of that court was an occasion of high spectacle and drama in every shire town four times a year. Yet by 1689, of the supposedly three thousand justices in England and Wales, only about seven hundred to eight hundred responded to the writ of *venire facias* directed to the sheriff. A total of fifteen days was allotted to the justices who did sit for summoning jurors by the various writs. The quarter sessions opened with a solemn procession, the justices escorted by the sheriff and bailiffs to the shire hall where the clerk of the peace read the writ of summons and produced both the lists of jurors and officials ordered to attend and the calendar of prisoners. Once roll was called and fines for nonattendance were imposed, the justices were handed the inquisitions, recognizances, and examinations, juries were sworn, and a charge delivered to the juries. Meanwhile, the clerk of the peace compiled the names of the jurymen for the foremen, and bills of indictment were drawn up to be considered by the Grand Inquest of the County. While the grand jury deliberated, the justices appointed a county treasurer, inspected accounts, assessed wages for laborers and servants, and fixed the prices for ale and beer sold in the ordinaries. Usually the court adjourned for a short time at this point, and after convening again the grand jury's bills were heard and petit jury trial of minor offenders commenced. Felony was supposed to be considered first, but in practice these serious crimes and their supposed perpetrators were handed over to the Courts of Assize. Against lesser offenders processes were called, and if no voluntary appearance was forthcoming, a writ of *capias* was issued, followed by writs, as necessary of *sicut alias capias, exegi facias*, and finally, all else failing, outlawry.[17]

The four days usually spent at quarter sessions wound their way from petty criminal matters through defendants pleading not guilty and traversing their indictments. Usually the justices ordered a defendant who contested his indictment to appear at the next court and to enter a recognizance against his appearance. Turning next to those cases held over from previous sessions, the justices listened as defendants' lawyers argued their causes. The last day of sessions was devoted to administra-

16. This summary taken from Webb and Webb, *English Local Government*. One should note Robson's caveat: the Webbs were rather hard on local justices in their recounting of the shortcomings of county institutions. See *Attorney in Eighteenth Century England*, p. 108.

17. Webb and Webb, *English Local Government*, pp. 303–21; Allen, ed., *Essex Quarter Sessions*, pp. ix–xxxii.

tive matters. These duties of the justices centered about the enforcement of the poor laws, and included licensing itinerant beggars, returning those unable to work to their place of birth, and trying to distinguish between "sturdy beggars" and the "impotent poor," sending the former to prison and requesting information from the overseers of the poor on the latter. Every parish was to provide funds to the overseers with monies levied against every freeholder or occupant of property in the parish. From this fund children, the able-bodied unemployed, and the aged and infirmed were supposed to benefit. Other parishes in the hundred could be assessed to make up the rate for a parish too poor to pay for its indigents. And, if an able-bodied laborer would not work, justices after the 1590s were empowered to commit him, and disorderly persons, mothers of illegitimate children, and vagabonds, to the house of correction.[18]

This round of duties, which was seen to four times each year, provided a chain of information and a common linkage among the various elements in the ranked social order. Anyone who attended the sessions certainly learned the latest gossip and the crises, scandals, and novelties that had occurred in the county. Yet the gradual but inexorable growth of central control over legal affairs from the Tudor period onward meant that quarter sessions were bound closely to the Courts of Assize, not only in the types of cases heard but also by a large degree of oversight. Moreover, as Assizes increased in significance, quarter sessions necessarily diminished as a central spectacle and a place where information was retailed. The sessions were still important, of course, but the trials at the six circuits of assizes were far more dramatic. The judges from the king's bench at Westminster sat on those circuits, which grouped the counties together by contiguity. To these sessions came felons, on trial for their lives. Procedurally, assizes were far more strict than sessions, and the judges did not hesitate to order grand juries to refrain from searching statutes to find reasons to indict and to resist the temptation to independent actions of any sort. On the other hand a felon standing trial was hampered by rules that allowed no defense witnesses, prohibited perjury charges from being leveled, and forbade counsel in felony and treason cases. Although by 1760 some judges in assizes did informally allow lawyers to answer questions of fact for an accused felon, not until 1836 was counsel allowed in all cases of felony. Assize sessions also dealt with some of the same petty crimes that occupied quarter sessions, and the

---

18. Overseers of the poor were particularly hated for harsh and unfeeling attitudes, which the justices were supposed to moderate and reprove. See Webb and Webb, *English Local Government*, pp. 65–66; Allen, ed., *Essex Quarter Sessions*, pp. xviii–xxi.

16 *Faithful Magistrates and Republican Lawyers*

local justices of the peace who sat on the grand jury at assizes were quick to take notes for their own later use from the methods displayed by the professional judges of this superior court.[19]

Assizes were the courts where civil causes were often heard, brought to this relatively local spot by writ, thus saving the litigants the arduous journey to London to argue their causes before one of the three common law benches there. The Restoration period was notoriously litigious, and the judges of assizes regularly sat as a *nisi prius* court, deciding with a jury those actions brought from exchequer, common pleas, and king's bench by writ of *postea*. The bulk of these cases dealt with debt, ejectment, and trespass. Action on the case was the outstanding single cause heard, and an occasional assumpsit rounded out the causes which were largely matters of dispute over contracts and debts. In these cases the bystanders could see one of the most striking differences between assizes and quarter sessions, for civil causes were technically involved and notoriously expensive, and for both reasons, local residents watched with awe and suspicion the arguments and machinations of the lawyers.[20]

Lawyers and the Court

To speak of "lawyers" in England is, of course, somewhat inexact. Throughout English history men functioned as officers of the court at various levels of law, doing some of the work one now associates with the word "lawyer." By the Restoration the two levels of lawyers known today in England were clearly distinguishable—barristers and solicitors. Barristers were graduates of the Inns of Court, and only they were permitted to plead a cause within the bar. Solicitors prepared the cause and conducted business outside of court, but they could not plead. In actual fact one should also distinguish between solicitors and attorneys, although the distinction was becoming blurred by the seventeenth century. The law of 1605, which attempted to curb abuses among attorneys, lumped them together with solicitors, who had begun as assistants to

---

19. Cockburn, *English Assizes*, pp. 122–29, 170–71. Assizes also dealt with common nuisances and petty causes that quarter sessions had failed to settle. See ibid., p. 97; Allen ed., *Essex Quarter Sesssions*, pp. xxii–xxiii.

20. Ibid., pp. 134–87. Civil causes were also handled in some localities by so-called Courts of Conscience or Courts of Requests. These courts presided over cases involving small debts; jury trial was not allowed; the court was not a court of record and issued summary judgments. How widespread its use was is difficult to ascertain. See Winder, "Court of Requests."

attorneys but whose name has come to include both of the old offices. In both instances the duties of those officers were confined to drawing up papers and preparing the cases of their clients, and indeed, clerical work was the strength of those gentlemen, who often became the clerks of the peace in the counties. When they did so, they were forbidden to practice, but could and often did get partners to do their casework for them. The barrister, on the other hand, worked largely in the Courts of Assize rather than in the county and was better educated than his solicitor. When he appeared as a local gentleman sitting on the bench, he represented something of a threat to the rustic gentry at quarter sessions. It was no mere accident of language that these men were graduates of the "Inns of Court." The proximity of the Inns to the king's court was purposeful, and Temple Bar and the area surrounding it quickly became synonymous with the legal profession, whose antiquity and perhaps ambiguous reputation Spencer conjured up when he wrote:

> Those bricky towers
> The which on Themees brode aged back doe ride,
> Where now the studious lawyers have their bowers,
> There whilom wont the Templar Knights to bide,
> Till they decayed through pride.[21]

Far from being proof of having been a "studious lawyer," attendance at the Inns had become by the early seventeenth century a means of polishing rough Country sons of the gentry into Court gentlemen. Indeed, the aristocracy's sons acquired their sophistication at the Inns from the 1580s until the 1630s. The Inns were well known for the revels and masques intended to prepare the gentleman for life as the king's servant at court. Legal learning at these institutions was pursued seriously during Tudor and early Stuart monarchies, but declined sharply thereafter. By the Restoration the Inns had resumed their notoriety as centers of cosmopolitan taste and revelry, but examinations for the call to the bar had become a fiction. Questions were put to the student in stock words; readings and exercises were abandoned after 1680. If they intended to practice, most serious students of the law learned by reading for two or three years in a barrister's chambers. Attendance at the Inns was the prerogative, at first, of the sons of the aristocracy and, by the Restora-

---

21. Quoted in Pearce, *History of the Inns*, p. 43. See Hurst, *Lincoln's Inn*, pp. 9–10, 28–29. The best scholarly treatment is Prest, "Legal Education" and *Inns of Court*. Prest is now at work on the Inns in the eighteenth century. See also Stone, *Crisis of the Aristocracy*, pp. 310–31.

tion, of those of the greater gentry, for little money was ever spent on scholarships for poor applicants.²²

Barristers who did go into practice made their living in circuit work at assizes. In those courts they found the litigation open to them in a less authoritarian atmosphere than in criminal causes where judges ruled with a heavy hand. It was probably the close relationship of barristers to the judges of Westminster at assizes that had prompted Judge Hyde to suggest that local justices heed the superior opinions of a barrister sitting on their bench. Such advice was not very palatable to local squires, probably not even to those lucky enough to be able to send a son to the Inns for learning and polish. Even more so, attorneys and solicitors were viewed by gentry and people alike as a vile species, bent on making money from other men's woes. Local justices had to be on their guard with these lawyers, for they could be reprimanded for high-handed behavior upon a writ of *supersedeas*, and a writ of *certiorari* could remove the proceedings of a county decision to a higher court. But more often, local squires feared the troublesome attacks that were spurred on by local solicitors, who might well object, for example, to a justice's handling of unlicensed alehouses. Despite his good intentions, as one contemporary reported, "he finds himself surrounded with numbers of pettifogging attorneys and solicitors, who watch his steps, and if there happens the least flaw in the method of drawing up and managing the proceedings, he finds himself obliged to attend a certiorari in the King's Bench."²³

Moreover, despite the vagaries of constitutional government in the seventeenth century under Stuart and Commonwealth the local gentry continued to hold lawyers in low esteem, be they Cavaliers or Roundheads. Antilawyer sentiment was a tradition in English life and lore and had been so since Geoffrey Chaucer's day, at least. The Englishmen of the seventeenth century maintained that tradition precisely because those individuals who practiced law were identified as belonging to the Court interest. As John Morrill has demonstrated, local squires were not fooled by the use of anti-Court rhetoric by men ambitious for power. Despite the reforms proposed under the leadership of Commonwealth lawyers seeking to put their own house in order, no very noticeable improvement in public opinion regarding lawyers was forthcoming. Indeed, so fearful of the public's attitude were lawyers that some ten years after the end

22. Hurst, *Lincoln's Inn*, pp. 310–31. On the rise of lawyers and print culture in general, see Bouwsma, "Lawyers and Early Modern Culture."

23. On the barristers at assizes, see Cockburn, *English Assizes*, pp. 143–48. The complaint against attorneys is from the essay *Distilled Liquors the Bane of the Nation* (1736), cited in Webb and Webb, *English Local Government*, p. 336.

of the Commonwealth they panicked when confronted with what they thought was imminent slaughter.[24]

Into the palace yard near the Courts there galloped one morning a mad cow. Those inside the building saw only the swords drawn in the yard, and some paranoid barrister shrieked that the Fifth Monarchy men had come to murder the lawyers en masse. The resulting pandemonium that gripped the fleeing serjeants and hastily disrobed barristers speaks most eloquently of the continuing, uneasy relationship between lawyers and the nation.[25] This is all the more remarkable given the attempts of many lawyers during the Puritan ascendancy to effect major legal reforms, including the abolition of Star Chamber and a concerted attack on the chancery court, perhaps inspired by John Selden's well-known, acid remark "Equity is a roguish thing, depending on the Chancellor's foot."[26]

Despite the alliance of many lawyers with Parliament against the claims of Stuart prerogative in the ship-money controversy and the attack on those courts that seemed to undermine the common law, most lawyers joined the royalist cause when the crisis finally broke. In one of the many paradoxical turnings of history, royalist lawyers found it a simple trick to argue that they were the real champions of the limitations that common law imposed on Englishmen and that the more radical sectarians like the Levellers, the Puritan faction, and the Parliament forces at large represented usurpation and tyranny. Initially, of course, in the early seventeenth century opposition to lawyers had sprung from the Stuart court itself against Sir Edward Coke and his allies, who seemed all too ready to put the common law in the way of the king's prerogative. But by the end of the century that opposition had been rendered irrelevant by the events of 1688–89, and no one continued the attacks of the extremist sects of the Revolution. Once the Restoration had been accomplished, no one seriously challenged the legal profession, nor had anyone brought forward serious proposals for much-needed reforms. Despite the appalling

---

24. Resentment of greedy attorneys' abuse of the poor laws resulted in a ban in Worcester excluding attorneys from the office of guardian of the poor. See Ward, *English Land Tax*, p. 88. Note the *OED* etymology of the word "pettifogger" (cf. "Fogger") suggesting the connection to the Augsburg House of Fugger, which used devious means of financing on a small scale. The association of attorneys with sharp business practices was well fixed in English lore by the seventeenth century. See below.

25. Recounted in Veall, *Popular Movement for Law Reform*, p. 177.

26. Selden, *Table Talk*, p. 52. Prall, *Agitation for Law Reform*, pp. 128–30, discusses radical antilawyer sentiment, which revived old memories of Wat Tyler's sacking of Inner Temple and the advice of Dick and Jack Cade: "The first thing we do, let's kill all the lawyers," and "Now go some and pull down the Savoy; others to the inns of court; down with them all" (*Henry VI, Part II*, act 4, scenes 2, lines 83–84, and 7, lines 1–3).

lack of real learning going on at the Inns, no one suggested that these private societies should be challenged to improve their performance of duties to the public. Neither were there any regulations to control the swarms of ambitious solicitors excluded from the Inns. By a statute of 1729 (2 Geo. 2, c. 23) a start was made in reforming the latter branch of the legal profession, and by 1739 the "Society of Gentlemen Practisers in the Courts of Law and Equity" established fees for services, set requirements for training, and prescribed for disciplinary actions against unscrupulous lawyers. The reforms were late in coming and did little to change the negative attitude of most Countrymen about the legal profession.[27]

In the end the Whig lawyers of the Restoration era managed to salvage part of their reputation only because they came down on the right side of the constitutional crisis of 1688–89. It is tempting to think that those eminent barristers and judges who played so important a role at that time had a clear notion of what they were about. More probably they were as insecure as their Tory opponents as to what the future should hold. Beyond the desire to keep a Catholic from succeeding to the throne the Whig lawyers were not entirely sure of themselves. Events proved, nonetheless, that in order to consolidate the gains of the Revolution, support for William and Mary had to be guaranteed at all levels of English life. The resistance of the nonjuring bishops, Jacobite sentiment among the overtaxed lesser gentry, hatred of the new era from Catholic families of the North, and resentment of the mercantile wealth that increasingly characterized membership in the Whig party—all these developments which threatened the Revolution demanded swift attention. Almost against their own political instincts, which had been to prevent greater power from being exercised by the king, the Whig lawyers instituted their own program of centralization. The importance of the Protestant victory that took place at Westminster apparently held the attention of the nation while systematic purges of the Tory faction from county benches solidified the power and influence of Whigs and their lawyer allies throughout Britain. Various purges of the bench had occurred in previous reigns, often signifying not incompetence or malfeasance but merely displeasure with a sitting justice who harbored sentiments felt to be inimical to the interest of the present monarch or one of his powerful ministers. But the late Stuart and early Hanoverian period was peculiarly characterized by routine purgation: "Every component of the courts [was] an instrument of public propaganda as each party strove to use the voice of the law to broadcast a political message."[28]

27. Prall, *Agitation for Law Reform*, pp. 45–48; Abel-Smith and Stevens, *Lawyers and the Courts*, p. 231.
28. Landau, "Gentry and Gentlemen," pp. 45–50.

Here, as much as anywhere else, was the basis for the Augustan laments for the pastoral life that had existed relatively free from conflict, in which a local hegemony flourished under the beneficent squirearchy of the shire. The contemporary spectacle of squalid vendettas and forced placement of Court Whigs on the local benches embittered the Country, which yearned for a lost Elizabethan consensus led by an independent landowning gentry free from the continual interference of Westminster lawyers and politicians. Whether the supposed "golden age" ever existed precisely as it was memorialized is at least dubious. As the history of the seventeenth century courts makes clear, the independence of local sessions had already shrunk since the reign of Elizabeth. Horizons had necessarily expanded beyond the county boundaries since those days. But it cannot be doubted that the events that transpired between the Exclusion Crisis of 1678 and the final collapse of Tory opposition in 1714 left profound doubts in the minds of many Britons about the quality and direction of the new era. The legal, constitutional defense of that era was justified by the ascendant Whigs' invocation of Coke's proclamation that a "fundamental" law existed to fence in James I's claims to the prerogative. The notion of an "ancient" constitution and king-in-parliament sovereignty did little to allay the suspicions of ordinary Britons that "the artificial reason and judgment of the law" used by lawyers and defended by Coke was simply a cunning artifice useful to a sly band of grasping attorneys.[29]

Unfortunately for Countrymen who hoped for a genuinely powerful political opposition, Whig lawyers sought to limit the king by conservative means to promote libertarian ends symbolically represented by the Magna Charta and tangibly exploited by lawyers and merchants. To this turn of events the Tories could make no adequate response. By definition the Tory party, whether led by the Earl of Danby under Charles II or directed by Oxford and Bolingbroke under Anne, was committed to the supremacy of the Anglican church, the royal prerogative, and a patriarchal notion of the king as the fountain of all justice. By the mid-1680s the Tories were embarrassed by James II's attempt to justify first a dispensation and then a wholesale suspension of the penal statutes against Papists and Dissenters. Unable to countenance such an attack on the Elizabethan Settlement the Tory lawyers watched in dismay as the offen-

29. Conclusions about the relationship of law to political and ideological crises of the late seventeenth century are perilous. No adequate study exists relating English legal history to important cultural and political developments. But see Nenner, *By Colour of Law*. On the manipulation of opinion about the legality of the Revolution of 1688–89, see Schwoerer, "Propaganda in the Revolution." On the historiography of the late Stuart era, see Johnson, "Politics Redefined." Coke's dictum is cited by Corwin in *"Higher Law" Background*, p. 39, from Prohibitions del Roy, 7 Co. 63–65 (1609).

sive of the Court floundered in the trial of the "Seven Bishops" in 1688 and ended in James's flight and removal. Despite a brief resurgence under Anne, the Tories began a long slide from national prominence that ended in the Hanoverian Settlement of 1714. Yet tainted with Jacobitism at the national level, a peculiar remnant of Toryism persisted in the institutional forms of English life at the local level. This was peculiarly so in the justices of the county, who now more than ever clung to the virtues of the Country persuasion, or as Isaac Kramnick has called it, "Bolingbrokeian ideology."[30]

Historians should not be misled into assuming that cultural conflict did not exist at the local level, because the records of politics there seem rife with petty squabbles worth hardly more than passing acknowledgment. The local justice in England was materially affected by the larger constitutional and legal issues. His office was made highly sensitive, both because he represented the ancient Country tradition at the local level and because the redefinition or continuation of his proper role was hotly contested between Whigs and Tories. Despite cautions advanced by scholars over the precise nature of "party" or "interest" recent local studies make it clear that the ideological quarrels of English politics and culture extended to the benches of quarter sessions and gradually blunted those institutions, and with them the potency and centrality of local culture in English life at large.

The transformation of the notion of what a justice of the peace was is the key to understanding the tenacity of those who clung to the Country persuasion. The declining fortunes of the lesser gentry of England between 1640 and 1740 gave persuasive power to the image of virtuous country gentlemen threatened by Whigs, whose policies swallowed up more of the independent gentry's ancestral lands each year. Lord Bolingbroke epitomized the resentment of the smaller landed gentry against the Whigs, especially Robert Walpole.[31] Local gentlemen could not be content even to sneer from a distance at the Whigs, for the county bench itself was now stacked with appointees of the new regime. The sight of these vulgar "placemen," the "jobbers" who did the bidding of a corrupt, mercantile Whig Court, evoked a disgust expressed in the refusal of many local gentlemen to sit upon the bench. The hated "Robinocracy" of

30. My views of party and ideology conform largely to those outlined in Plumb, *Growth of Political Stability*; however, see also Walcott, "Idea of Party"; Rubini, *Court and Country*, pp. 15–20; Foord, *His Majesty's Opposition*; Holmes, *British Politics*; Speck, *Tory and Whig*; Walcott, *British Politics*. On the purgation of the benches by the Whigs, see Landau, "Gentry and Gentlemen," pp. 88–163. On the role of lawyers in the 1680s, see Landon, *Triumph of the Lawyers*.

31. Kramnick, *Bolingbroke and His Circle*, pp. 56–63.

Walpole came to symbolize the declining fortunes not only of the Country gentleman but of the office of justice of the peace itself. Very early on, Tory opponents surmised that the Whigs considered the justice to be an extension of the burgeoning central government. Theoretically, of course, the Country could hardly argue with this, since a justice was quite literally "His Majesty's Justice of the Peace." But practically, the Country persisted in believing that the justice was an independent guardian of the virtue and traditional vertical social relations deemed essential to the nation's welfare.

Unfortunately, Country writers never came up with a political plan that would overcome the corruption that they believed was destroying what little virtue still remained in the land. Instead, they gave expression to their frustration and local dismay by writing against Court policy wherever they encountered it, directing most of their barbs at the rising "new men" placed by the Court in powerful positions. In their comments on life at the local level Bolingbrokeians or Country writers left no doubt of their hatred for the groups of men they perceived to be allies of the Court, and foremost among these were the lawyers.

One of Fielding's early efforts, *The Justice Caught in his own Trap* (1730), was a vitriolic satire aimed at the "trading justices," those men of "mean degree" who came from a business or mercantile background and used their office for personal gain. They refused to enforce the laws against vice, thereby making the bench impotent, and they protected themselves from criticism or revenge by alliance with the Whig Court. In 1717, *The Perjuror* had identified the source of corruption in local courts as not the justice, "an old fellow, qualified with ill nature and avarice." The real villain in the piece was usually his clerk, "some broken attorney (for they make the best clerks) . . . and for their honesty they are generally on a par." Other popular ballads and plays echoed variations on the theme perhaps first sounded in 1707 in the anonymous pamphlet *An Attorney, Proposals Humbly Offered to the Parliament*. . . . This effective satire lampooned the ambitions of "every little pitiful tradesman, that can just make up enough money to put his son out clerk . . . for making him a lawyer." Country balladeers played on this theme, and their lament for the virtuous past scorned the grasping, sordid spirit of the age by querying:

> Lord what a broking advocate is this?
> He was some squir's scrivenor, that hath scrapt
> Gentilitie out of aturney's fees.³²

32. In addition to Kramnick, see the discussion of Fielding's satire and contemporary ballads in Robson, *Attorney in Eighteenth Century England*, pp. 144 (fn. 5), 174–77. That

These excoriations of lawyers and mercantile ambition that sullied the Country benches by allying the corruption of the Court with the expansion of trade had little real effect. The landowning gentry, who by the 1720s groaned under Walpole's taxation schemes, might well have thought that theirs was a lost cause. But these partisans of the Country, though pitifully weak as a force in British politics, scored a victory of sorts, with lasting consequences, with Englishmen who had engaged in the adventure of colonizing England's oldest overseas plantation. Virginia had remained stubbornly loyal to the House of Stuart, and upon the monarchy's restoration the colony reestablished ties and its sons began returning home in the 1680s and 1690s for education, trading alliances, and observation. What these colonials saw and how they absorbed elements from both Court and Country traditions would have a profound impact on the subsequent history of Virginia's legal culture.

Court, Country, and Colonials

Between 1680 and 1714 some of the wealthiest and most eminent sons of Virginia went to London to represent their families' and their colony's trading interests. Moreover, men like William Byrd II, John Carter, and Benjamin Harrison were not in England merely to secure a favorable connection for the export of their tobacco and to arrange for credit with London merchants. Those native Virginians also attended the Inns of Court. Despite the desuetude into which those venerable institutions had fallen, they were nonetheless the acknowledged centers of cultural, intellectual, and literary life in London. Living at the Inns, hobnobbing with the social elite, pursuing favorable trading deals in the coffeehouses, the Virginia provincials imbibed an atmosphere clearly scented with "courtly" habits, tastes, and interests.[33]

In his later years, William Byrd yearned for this excitement and the cosmopolitan surroundings of his London years and found the comparative, if grand, solitude of his country house at Westover stifling. A country

---

many people regarded the lawyer-merchant combine as inimical to the poor can be seen in the Middlesex grand jury presentment against Bernard Mandeville for his *Essay on Charity and Charity Schools* in 1723. Despite the offended paternalism of the jurors and justices and the political machinations involved, the presentment stands for a genuine horror at Mandeville's suggestion that charity schools be abolished since they raised the poor above their station, thus reducing the labor force. See Speck, "Bernard Mandeville."

33. That Byrd was delighted with the Court and was reluctant to pursue a Country lifestyle advocated by the far wealthier and more influential Robert Carter is the subject of an excellent study by Shaviro, "Carters and Byrds in Colonial Virginia."

house was what Virginians of "quality" aspired to, all the while aping the latest fashions and habits of London, where the greater gentry migrated during the "season." The grafting of London fashion and language onto Virginia, which Hugh Jones noticed in 1720, was due partly to the anxiety any provincial feels when he compares his rustic habits to the sophistication of someone from a center of power and culture. And Byrd revealed in a particularly instructive letter to an English friend that his own attendance at the Inns of Court and the patronage society of the Court were reconciled only with difficulty with his Virginia instincts, even though Virginians such as he had tried to become as cosmopolitan as possible. Writing in 1741 to Major Francis Otway, Councillor Byrd explained in somewhat apologetic terms his "creolian notions" in objecting to a "placeman" proposed for office in Virginia. The brother of the dean of Canterbury, one Head Lynch, had been put forward as worthy to assume the duties of clerk of the Naval Office of York River. Byrd explained carefully that such offices had always been filled by native-born Virginians. The colonists, including himself, felt uneasy at having such a place filled by patronage appointment from London, not from Williamsburg. Clearly, some of the Country opposition to patronage power exercised by London Court figures still remained with Byrd.[34]

His powerful fellow councillor Robert "King" Carter made a similar statement exemplifying this odd mixture of Court and Country attitudes. As treasurer of the colony, Carter was responsible for the positions of quite a number of Virginians who filled lesser posts and were his dependents. Yet he too strenuously differentiated his views from those of the Court when his son, while in England, met John Randolph. Suggesting that Randolph sported more sumptuous clothing than he did, John Carter felt insulted and suspected that Randolph had spoken ill of him. The "King" in Virginia huffed in reply, "His principles and mine are of a very different nature: a rank Tory, a proud, humble parasite, a fawning sycophant to his patron, with all the other requisites to a servile courtier. These are as much reverse to my nature as white is to black. . . . From whence you may conclude there is very little familiarity between us." Byrd, more enamored of cosmopolitan airs, disagreed with Carter about Randolph and exulted to Philip Ludwell in 1718 about "Jack Randolph, whome we have got call'd to the bar before his time."[35]

For all his courtly exercise of patronage, Carter remained a Country-

---

34. Jones, *Present State*, pp. 71, 80. Byrd to Major Francis Otway, Feb. 10, 1740/41, *Correspondence*, 2:577–79; Byrd to Sir Charles Wager, Feb. 17, 1740/41, Ibid., p. 582. On the absence of placemen in Virginia, see J. T. Main, *Upper House*, 5–43.

35. Robert to John Carter, July 13, 1720, p. 8. Byrd to Philip Ludwell, Jan. 31, 1717/18, *Correspondence*, 1:310.

man, as he indicated in another letter. When a particularly delicate case came up involving a large sum of money, Carter was annoyed that the litigant "feed . . . all the lawyers [who] are of any value in the country. How far the strength of lungs may go in bewildering a court and worrying poor men out of their rights, I can't tell." Even Byrd himself, though bored with local affairs and decidedly prolawyer in sentiment, wrote in a decidedly sardonic vein to his cousin in 1736 about the death of two of Virginia's most famous attorneys of the day. Recently, Byrd reported, Virginia had suffered "a rot amongst our General Court lawyers, Holloway dyed here, & Hopkins in England, & made room at the bar for 2 other orators to succeed them."[36]

The most eminent and wealthy sons of Virginia who joined the governor's Council in Williamsburg were clearly dedicated to at least some of the attributes of the Country and, at the same time, could not resist the attraction they felt for the atmosphere of the Court. Wealthy men in a relatively fragile social environment in Virginia, they were anxious to secure the added assurance of English education and connections to undergird a pedigree of very recent creation. Yet living in a rural environment, they also wondered from time to time if the excitement of the city, the pursuit of law and commerce, and the acquisition of cosmopolitan airs were really goals compatible with Country virtue. Perhaps that ambivalence explains why William Byrd II's father resignedly informed William Blathwayt in 1697 about "my son who being resolved to follow the law & settle in the Temple now returnes for England," and why he did not and finally returned to Virginia.[37]

What that ambivalence signified is perhaps best understood if one recalls that the second definition of "Court" made by the Country and leveled against their opponents concerned what corruption did to social relations. Men situated along the ladder of dependence that Fielding described were bound in the normal course of affairs by reciprocal bonds. Eminence in the world proceeded not so much from the possession of wealth as from the proper utilization of it and how one deported oneself in the execution of public duties. Traditionally, public service, and the fame that went with it, and deference to others along the ladder of dependence marked the man of civic virtue and were their own rewards. Theorists of the seventeenth century only gradually came to the conclusion that the pursuit of wealth was an acceptable use of the passionate

---

36. Robert to John Carter, July 13, 1720, *Letters*, p. 9; Byrd to his cousin Daniel Horsmanden, suggesting that Horsmanden come to Virginia to replace Holloway and Hopkins (he never did), Feb. 25, 1735/36, *Correspondence* 2:475.
37. William Byrd I to Blathwayt, Apr. 29, 1697, *Correspondence*, 1:178–79.

nature of the eminent gentleman. Far more preferable than the mere accumulation of lucre or the indulgence of sexual prowess was the pursuit of fame and honor.[38]

If the pursuit of wealth was endorsed and made respectable by political theorists, that solution to the problem of reconciling a trading spirit with the definition of what constituted a gentleman was acceptable only to the firmly committed Courtier. Virginians living in late-seventeenth-century London imbibed sentiments that were still attempting the reconciliation between past and present. It is no great surprise that Virginians carried away with them a mixture of Court and Country attitudes, for a reconciliation that placed lawyers and merchants together in defense of old-fashioned values was precisely the accomplishment (if not the conscious intent) of the preeminent lawyer of seventeenth-century England.

Sir Edward Coke has been the subject of an immense literature, most of it seeking to understand the relationship of this curious figure to the enormous social, economic, and jurisprudential change that swept over England in the 1600s. Most scholars agree by now on the ambiguous nature of Coke's own intentions in his arguments favoring the liberation of economic and legal affairs in England from royal control. Most probably the lawyers of Coke's day were as confused as anyone else about how to reconcile needed economic and legal growth with royal and landed conservative prerogatives. What Coke hit upon, perhaps in all sincerity, was the notion that the "ancient constitution" of English rights demanded a more limited role for the king than James I was willing to concede. Moreover, lawyers were to Coke like so many protectors of law, which was itself "more than the measure of reason. It [was] . . . the measure and source of virtue as well."[39]

Coke bequeathed a tortured legacy to later generations of Whig admirers because while seeming to wrap his arguments in medieval precedent and ancient custom, the eminent jurist was heavily involved in political and economic schemes that appear startlingly modern and Court-like. By the 1630s the common lawyers of England had become some of the largest investors in the trading companies of their day. Moreover, because lawyers had had the benefit of education and refinement, "the highest public offices went to those who had been trained to think

---

38. On the arguments that defended aggrandizement as a respectable goal for gentlemen, see Hirschman, *Passions and Interests*; Crowley, *This Sheba, Self*; Pocock, *Machiavellian Moment*, pp. 423–505. On the struggle to reconcile agrarian principles with trade and cosmopolitan values, see Liddle, " 'Virtue and Liberty.' "

39. Little, *Religion, Order, and Law*, p. 177; White, *Edward Coke*.

clearly, could analyze a situation, draft a minute, know the technicalities of the law, and speak a foreign language."[40]

While a changing and expanding social order clearly favored lawyers and merchants, it is also true that, like any rising elite, lawyers and merchants made themselves palatable by the appeal to custom and the past and, at the same time, indispensable to the expansion of trade and commerce. Inevitably, the two groups were bound by common interest, and the ties were forged even more solidly in the alliance of the Parliament forces in the controversies of the 1620s and 1630s. By the end of the century Whig magnates who sat as the Lords of Trade and Plantations called upon the legal talent of the nation for advice and management of a burgeoning mercantile venture, one which far exceeded anything Coke could have imagined when he began his attacks on crown monopolies.

The Virginians returning to the Inns and the merchant exchanges in the 1680s had little choice but to ally themselves with what was a Court interest, one which favored more than anything else the controlled and predictable pursuit of mercantile interests on behalf of the nation. Unfortunately, as any farmer can tell any banker or merchant, Dame Agriculture is seldom seduced by the promise of rational production or liberal marketing opportunity. Tobacco planters nevertheless trimmed their sails to fit the needs of a mercantile age as best they could, given weather, colonial status, and a rather odd identity as merchant-farmers. Even if attracted by the ideas of London merchants and barristers with whom they studied, socialized, and traded, even the greatest remained rural gentlemen. In the meantime the cultural definition of what constituted Court and Country continued to evolve. By the early eighteenth century the Country writers had refined the tools by which they ferreted out Court corruption. In a fashion disturbing to the American planter, Country writers of the Augustan age made clear the idea that corruption and Court subversion centered about the threat of a standing army, the pursuit of commerce, and an increased specialization of function in society—all developments manipulated by Court dispensers of patronage. Instead of selfless public service, the Court advocated "the ego's pursuit of satisfaction."[41]

Virginians returning to England between 1680 and 1714 squirmed uncomfortably as they wrestled to reconcile Country theory with Virginia's trading, speculating, commercial practices. Thus, when Carter proclaimed in 1720 that "politics I hope I have done with for the rest of my days," he did so out of disgust with fellow Virginians, some of whom

40. Stone, *Crisis*, pp. 303–4. On the new merchants' investments in Virginia in 1650, see Breuner, "Commercial Change."
41. Pocock, *Machiavellian Moment*, p. 487.

he believed "are ready to sacrifice all that's dear to us, provided they may have a small share in the honor and the profit and swim glib in the tide of favor." Far better the fate of "Poor Nat Burwell," Carter thought, who though sick and failing, "left his place" in the colonial Council, eliciting from the "King" the conclusion, "'Tis well he can live without it, and may all honest men be able to do so."[42]

Despite the vast mercantile affairs of Carter, Byrd, and other Virginians this ambivalence about success and the tantalizing atmosphere of power and culture that emanated from the Court, this delicate balancing of Court and Country sentiment, had to continue, because the pursuit of wealth for its sake alone could not be approved without abandoning a key point of Country identity. Carter summarized the outlines of the Virginia Countryman's position in 1721 in a letter to his agent William Dawkins. Incensed at what he believed to be an arrogant tone in Dawkins's letters to him, Carter reprimanded the Briton and in the process revealed the Court-Country tension present among the great families of the colony. Carter made certain that Dawkins should never consider "looking upon me as one of your dependents and inferiors." The true nature of virtue and deference, Carter expostulated, lay not in wealth, but in more substantial social relationships. How then, he asked, could Dawkins use him "with the language that was hardly fit for your footman?" Carter both anxiously defended his rank, which was of recent origin, and posed in a simple, Country style by stating, "I was your master's equal and all along have lived in as good rank and fashion as he did ... and am old enough to be your father, not to mention any more reasons that justly give me a title to your deference." Country deference was dependent as much on paternal-filial—that is, familial—relationships as on mere differences in wealth. The source of much evil in the world, the Virginian went on, was that there were too many and "too great lovers of this world. ... The thoughts of having a little more white and yellow earth than our neighbours would not puff us up with so much vanity and insolence, nor make us so uneasy when we meet with plain dealing," if we were men of unaffected character.[43]

42. Robert Carter to Micajah and Richard Perry, July 14, 1720, *Letters*, p. 6; Carter to William Dawkins, July 15, 1720, ibid., p. 30.

43. Carter to Dawkins, Feb. 23, 1720/21, ibid., pp. 80–82. To his son, Carter wrote in 1720 that education was not for one's own sake but that one should return to his "country fitted for your duty to your God and neighbours" ([no date given], ibid., p. 1). To friends in England caring for the orphans of Colonel Ralph Wormeley, Carter expressed the same sentiments that the allures of cosmopolitan society might give Virginians "a disrelish to their [occupations here] all their Lives after & make ye Drudgery of Virginia a trade too mean for their thoughts." Since the younger Ralph Wormeley's "fortune promises him no other yn a Virginia Life," care had to be taken since "too much finery, and too much

Since trade and the dangers of corrupt patronage undermined true Country virtue and paternal care for one's dependents, Carter and other Virginians tried to keep their distance, though they could hardly refrain from business and commerce and remain colonial planters. The other great nemesis of Country virtue in the public sphere—the standing army—Virginians met in their own way. The county militia of Virginia became, by the early 1700s, one of the hallmarks of county life. In their assumption of titles such as "Colonel," "Major," and "Captain" the planters were not so much indulging militarism as indicating their dedication to a homegrown variety of vigilance. In this way they scorned the corruption endemic in a professional soldiery, as every good Countryman scorned the interposition of specialized elites who subjugated natural relationships between superiors and dependents to their own selfish interests. Here again, as Carter explained to Governor Spotswood in 1720, the key in a Country colony to natural and successful relationships lay in personal, face-to-face relationships, not in a reliance upon "professional" military training. In seeking to carry out Spotswood's appointments for military officers, Carter pointed out that the dependent subalterns "will go near to refuse unless they knew who were to be their captain." Recognizing the importance the militiamen placed on personally knowing their leaders, Spotswood and subsequent governors had little choice but to follow the advice of local leaders like Carter, who suggested that the governor delay filling several commissions until Carter himself came to Williamsburg. As he wrote, "When I wait upon you at the General Court, I shall inform myself who may be the properest persons to have them."[44]

The provincial gentry of less than ancient lineage obviously had no objection to turning a profit. Perhaps the vigorous pursuit of trade, fame, and public eminence was permissible, Virginians hoped, if reconciled with Country virtue. Leaders of the colony lived in rural settings and admired the English gentry, whose virtue, though endangered, was praised in fulsome eloquence by the Scriblerians and Bolingbroke. William Byrd II and Robert Carter had no choice but to ape many of the attributes of the Court. But the colony as a whole identified with the Country.

The Country spirit surfaced in dramatic fashion between 1680 and

---

pockett money, raises in young ffolks such opinions of their Estates that they hardly know how to take up when they come to be their own Masters.... Those Boys that wore the finest close and had ye most money in their pocketts still went away with the least Learning in their heads" (Letters of Robert Carter, July 15, 1702, to Francis Lee; July 6, 1705, to Thomas Corbin; July 6, 1705, to Francis Lee, from the Lancaster County Clerk's Office, reprinted in *WMQ*, 1st ser., 17–18 [1908–10]: 252–64).

44. Carter to Alexander Spotswood, Aug. 12, 1720, *Letters*, p. 43; no date, ibid., p. 51.

1720 over the issue of courts and lawyers because of fears that the Virginia bench and bar would become the tool of corrupt Court patronage. Moreover, most of the county gentry of Virginia never got the chance to go back "home" for education and social polishing. The adaptation to a Country style of thought was simple for them because it fit nicely with their lived experience and their self-interest. They repeatedly refused to endorse the growth of a genuine legal "profession" that would threaten the control of the county exercised by the ordinary planters, and they had ample reason to perceive lawyers in Virginia as allies of a Court circle that had begun to grow up around the capital in Jamestown.

The best cultural and institutional guarantor of Country thought and habits of virtue in the counties was the traditional office of justice of the peace. The county court became the instrument of consolidation by which Virginians protected the independence of the local gentry. The justices reigned supreme—over all county officials save one. The appointment of clerks to the courts remained a prerogative of the governor, and it was in the offices of the county clerks that the fledgling legal profession of Virginia eventually grew and prospered. During the seventeenth and early eighteenth centuries, however, the gentry of Virginia resolved to rely on the ancient office of justice of the peace to secure their liberty and their social and political power. As the Virginia statute said, justices would be of "the most able, honest, and judicious persons of the county," and like their ancient forbears in England, members of "that Estate of Men which be Called Worshipful."[45]

45. County justices were referred to as "judicious persons" in the statute of 1661–62. See Hening, 2:69–70.

Chapter 2
Justices and Lawyers in Virginia, 1680–1720

For out of the old fields must come the new Corn
—WILLIAM FITZHUGH,
quoting Geoffrey Chaucer "Parlement of Foules"

William Fitzhugh, Stafford County lawyer and planter, could not have chosen a more apt phrase than this epigram from Chaucer to illustrate the issue that would set justices and lawyers at odds in Virginia. When he suggested to client Major Richard Lee that Virginians had to seek the proper bases and applications of the law in England's "old fields," he was repeating a phrase that had been one of the favorite dicta of that hero among common law advocates, Sir Edward Coke. Country justices, of course, believed as much as anyone in the ancient and "immemorial" nature of common law and in the rights of property, liberty, and rightly constituted authority. Attorneys like Fitzhugh (and Coke as well) represented a different species of law, one whose characteristics can be divined by a close look at Chaucer's saw, which both lawyers quoted:

> For out of old feldes as men seyth
> Cometh al this newe corn from yer to yere
> And out of olde bokes in good feyth
> Cometh al this newe science that men
>   lere.[1]

The identification of lawyers with "olde bokes" and a "newe science," which they believed only professionals could rightly direct, set attorneys on a collision course with the lay gentry of the counties from 1680 to 1720. The planter-justices had had to fight too long and hard to establish their own legitimacy in a fractious, insecure social order to consider abdicating their power and prestige to a cadre of men whose skills might easily be employed by a central government in Jamestown. Not surprisingly, the legal culture of Virginia was to be shaped by social

---

1. The verse is from Chaucer's "Parlement of Foules," lines 22–24. Fitzhugh was obviously using a phrase that by his day had passed into common parlance. On Coke's fondness for the line, see Knafla, *Law and Politics*, p. 124. I am indebted to Richard Spear for aid in tracking Fitzhugh's quotation.

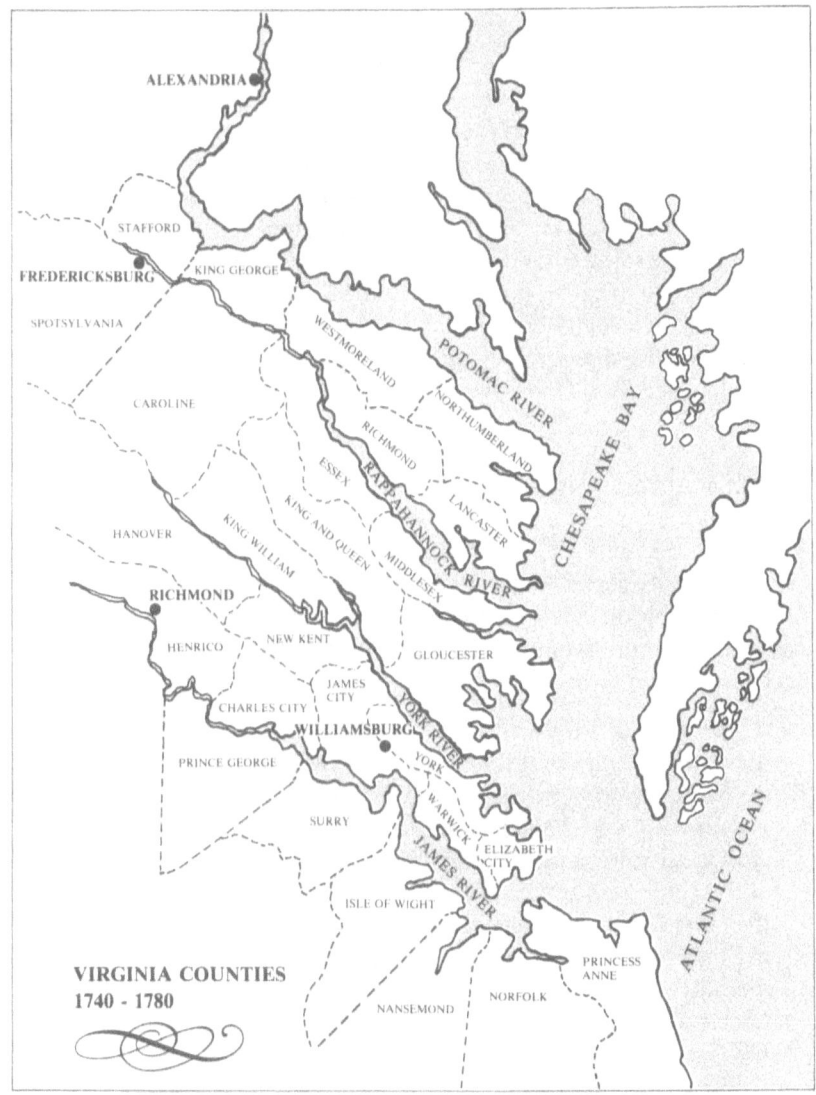

**VIRGINIA COUNTIES
1740 - 1780**

Copyright © 1981 The University of North Carolina Press
Map by Win Thrall

and political developments in the culture at large. The proper definition of the law in Virginia could emerge only when social and economic controversies over property and authority had been settled. Once the social ladder of dependence began to show some signs of stability, the boundaries of authority and the precise nature of the office of justice of the peace could be resolved. The lay definition of law, and the exclusion of a professional class of legal experts from the rule-making process by which authority governed, confirmed Virginia in a Country way of thinking. The resolution of those issues took the better part of forty years and involved a struggle which can best be appreciated as part of the process by which social, economic, and legal institutions came to shape the ideas of Virginians about authority, property, and the liberties of Englishmen.

English Planters and Virginia's Social Order

The central dilemma of Virginians in the seventeenth century had always been easily stated—and unsuccessfully resolved: how to be as English as possible in alien surroundings. A descendant of one of these seventeenth-century families reviewed the goals and characteristics of his ancestors in these terms:

> The pride of Virginia had so long been a topic of discourse in the other colonies that it had almost grown into a proverb. Being the earliest among the British settlements . . . having been soon . . . drawn . . . to the dignity of a government immediately under the crown, advancing rapidly into wealth from her extensive territory and the luxuriant production of her staple commodities, the sons of the most opulent families trained by education and habits acquired in England and hence perhaps arrogating some superiority over the provinces not so distinguished, she was charged with manifesting a cons[c]iousness that she had more nearly approached the British model.

Such an attitude, characteristic of the colony, Edmund Randolph concluded, "readily diffused itself among the individuals who were members of it."[2]

Yet Randolph was speaking of the glory of Virginia in the eighteenth century. The imitation of English values and life-styles there had been a

2. Randolph, *History of Virginia*, p. 177.

tortuous process, accomplished only at great cost. The colony, which boasted the earliest settlements, could by 1680 point to very little real continuity with the days of 1607. A merciless mortality rate, conflict with native Americans, the vagaries of the Commonwealth period, and a chronic shortage of labor unsettled the colony. Moreover, transplanted Englishmen encountered conditions that, even after these other matters had been settled, presented them with further evidence that Virginia was not yet England, and probably never would be. Even in the eighteenth century the by then stable social order resembled England's only remotely. Between 1695 and 1720 England's agricultural production increased markedly, probably by about 11.4 percent. Yet by 1700 between 70 and 75 percent of cultivable land was held by landlords, and the plight of small tenants, including rentiers of a £20 holding, was very bad. Moreover, the local shires in England increasingly fell under the guidance of "clerical magistrates," as the absentee gentry spent more and more time in London. In all these respects conditions in Virginia were utterly unlike those in England.[3]

For example, even as late as the 1660s Virginians were not particularly deferential in their attitudes toward the gentry. Moreover, the presence of indentured servants and enslaved Africans presented peculiar problems. The value of a ranked, vertical social order, one that closely resembled England's, was still unquestioned among transplanted Anglo-Americans. The struggle to weld social and political power into an authoritative whole, however, depended in great degree upon securing the trust and deference of the large numbers of indentured servants and freeholders who occupied property in numbers far in excess of anything England's elites ever dreamed of. The problem of achieving gentry rank and meriting the deference of one's neighbors was demonstrated in October 1662 in York County Court. William Hatton was brought into court by the churchwarden of Hampton Parish "for abuseing severall Justices of this County calling them Coopers, Hogg trough makers, Pedlars, Cobblers,

---

3. On population and mortality, see E. S. Morgan, *American Slavery*, appendix 1; Craven, *White, Red, and Black*, pp. 10–17; E. S. Morgan, "Headrights and Head Counts"; Menard, "Immigration to the Chesapeake" and "Immigrants and Their Increase"; D. B. Smith, "Mortality and Family." On the rate of growth in England, see Brenner, "Agrarian Class Structure"; Cooper, "In Search of Agrarian Capitalism," who notes that English agrarian capitalism was not the "pursuit of profit and economic rationality," since landlords were "investing in authority and a social system ... and ... [were] more interested in maximizing their returns in that direction than in the pursuit of profit" (p. 65). The same seems to be true in colonial Virginia, except where the availability of cheap lands interfered, creating both a labor problem and difficulties in the definition of social rank.

tailors, weavers & saying they are not fitting to sit where they doe sit." Although Hatton subsequently apologized, the incident highlighted the nature of the social problem in Virginia life.[4]

No clear-cut answer to the problem of determining who should defer to whom was immediately available. But gradually, part of the problem was resolved by the "unthinking decision" by which Virginians allayed potential unrest among white indentured servants and, in the process, bequeathed an agony-filled legacy to later generations. Between 1660 and 1680 black Virginians were bound to perpetual and hereditary servitude. Intermarriage between ranks of the servant population, across racial lines, was forbidden.[5]

The problem of securing deference to recently arrived "gentlemen" was paradoxically made more intractable precisely because of the availability of that hallowed, precious commodity that in England had always been assumed to be a guarantor of both authority and order, and liberty as well—land. Everyone somehow knew then, as they do now, that "land law was the kernel and core of common law."[6] In the minds of Englishmen real property might theoretically be under the sway of supreme magistracy—the king—and his regality was certainly considered, in the words of one scholar, to be "grounded in the soil." Yet the ancient, customary, and "immemorial" mythology surrounding the common law of England forbade a complete surrender of property and liberties to magistracy and authority. Ironically, "the institution of property had its roots in the *Ius Gentium*: in Law therefore which flowed out of the pure Law of Nature without the aid of the State, and in Law which was when as yet the State was not. Thence it followed that particular rights which had been acquired by virtue of this Institution in no wise owed their existence exclusively to the State."[7]

In England, of course, the six species of land tenure of medieval origin were not only gradually modified but grew up alongside of towns, guilds, and trades of various sorts. In an ancient society with a diversified economic base and a correspondingly complex social order, the vertical organization of the culture evolved with various occupations slotted into the appropriate ranks, promoting the traditional deference of servants to superiors. Many Englishmen in England and in Virginia prescribed the

---

4. York County Orders, Oct. 24, 1662.
5. Jordan, *White over Black*, pp. 44–91; E. S. Morgan, *American Slavery*, pp. 295–337.
6. Friedman, *History of American Law*, p. 202.
7. On the "immemorial" and customary nature of common law, see Pocock, *Ancient Constitution*, pp. 30–54. On property and natural law, see Gierke, *Political Theories*, p. 80, and *Natural Law*, p. 295 (fn. 44). On private property as an entity over which the sovereign power retains "eminent domain," see Dietze, *Magna Carta and Property*.

same blueprint as the cure for Virginia's social and economic ills. To their frustration social and economic reality in Virginia had, since 1613, been molded not by guildhalls and towns but by the discovery by John Rolfe and others that the streets of Jamestown made excellent cleared ground for the growing of tobacco. The "stinking weed" was the foundation upon which the "Empire built on Smoke" of the London Company of Virginia came to rest. Tobacco and the black labor needed to cultivate it remained at the center of economic life in the colony during all of the seventeenth century and much of the eighteenth. Virginians admitted that the staple did not provide the diversified economic base necessary to promote a properly ordered dependent society. But geographic conditions and profit encouraged tobacco's cultivation in Tidewater Virginia. The action of the burgesses in 1660 ordering in each county "one or more Tanhowses, and that they provide Tanners, Curryers and shoemakers" to alleviate "an unavoydable ruine" due to the "Incertaine vallew of tobacco" made no difference. The economic base of the society remained what it had been, and the possession of real property devoted to the planting of tobacco became the basis on which political, social, and legal authority in the area would be based for a very long time to come.[8]

There are five areas within the boundaries of eastern Virginia where broad rivers empty into the tidal waters of Chesapeake Bay. In the eighteenth century the Eastern Shore was largely a peninsula to itself, cut off from the center of population, culture, and politics by the bay and oriented toward the West Indies in trade and social concerns. Though connected to the rest of mainland Virginia, the Southside, from the James River south toward the Dismal Swamp area, harbored first Puritans and in later years Baptists and other religious and social dissenters from the dominant culture of Virginia. Population drifted from east to west here, and settlers seldom regarded a trip to Williamsburg necessary, even to patent lands. The remaining three regions of the Tidewater were the nucleus of everything that the colony would later be noted for. The "Peninsula," the area between the James and the York, was the center of government and was the oldest area of settlement. The "Middle Peninsula," between the York and the Rappahannock, was similar to the Peninsula in character, geography, and county life. The "Northern Neck," on the other hand, between the Rappahannock and the Potomac,

---

8. On the varieties of land tenure in England, see Maitland, *Constitutional History of England*, pp. 23–39. On the tension between social and political power, see Bailyn, "Politics and Social Structure." On diversification, see Rainbolt, *From Prescription to Persuasion*. The 1660 statute is in Kukla, ed., "Some Acts Not in Hening." On Virginia's failure to create towns conducive to a diversified socioeconomic structure, see Rainbolt, "Absence of Towns."

was the domain of the lord proprietor. Sparsely settled, it was dominated by fewer families, but these were some of the wealthiest, most aristocratic, and genuinely "Cavalier" gentry families of the colony.

From east to west the Tidewater stretched up the broad winding waters for one hundred miles. On the James in the 1740s the enterprising William Byrd II laid out the plots of ground that would become Richmond City at the "Falls." The fall line ran northward through Hanover and Caroline counties, both created by increased settlement by the late 1720s, and ended on the shores of the Potomac in King George. Stafford sprawled to the north and west, and as the river bent sharply to the north toward its sources, settlement thinned. During the next forty years expansion into Piedmont areas and further up the Potomac increased rapidly, but the political, social, and legal culture of Virginia would be determined largely by the families who lived east of the fall line and between the Potomac and the James Rivers.[9]

Life between the rivers was dominated by a concern for one item—tobacco. Despite attempts by the government in London to force a diversified economic system on Virginia planters, the allure of the sot-weed was irresistible. By the 1720s diversification had ceased to be an issue, although many Virginians still agreed that the effects of the tobacco culture were pernicious. By the 1760s a thriving grain trade was flourishing in the Tidewater and over the mountains in the Valley. In the early 1770s, the Assembly awarded £100 to John Hobday for his invention "of a machine which pressed out the wheat with ribbed cylinders put into circular motion by horses." Yet tobacco was to remain the central economic variable in Virginia because land was cheap and readily available, demand was high, and, though lands might have been distributed more equitably to favor further increases in population, only large tracts of tobacco land "could command money for the planter."[10]

In a colony where land was abundant it was no wonder that, as one scholar observed, "nearly every white male Virginian was a planter of sorts." Where Maryland residents paid a 4s. quitrent on their lands, Virginians were obligated to pay about 1s. per 100 acres. Maryland deeds in the 1720s averaged about 158 acres; a typical Virginia deed during the same period totaled around 487 acres. Virginia tobaccos were highly

9. The geographical divisions used here are fairly standard. See, for example, E. S. Morgan, *American Slavery*, p. 410. On the Southside, see Nicholls, "Origins of the Virginia Southside"; Kelly, "Economic and Social Development." On the Eastern Shore, see Ames, *Studies of the Virginia Eastern Shore*; Ames, ed., *County Court Records*.

10. Randolph, *History of Virginia*, pp. 202, 216; Rainbolt, *From Prescription to Persuasion*, pp. 142–71. On the grain trade, see Klingaman, "Development of Virginia's Coastwise and Grain Trade"; Gill, "Wheat Culture in Colonial Virginia."

valued in Europe. The Oronoco, a bright-leafed, hot-smoking variety grown in the Northern Neck areas, sold largely to Germany and northern countries. Sweet-scented, a milder and more highly valued variety, was sold to the French and English from sources along the James and York rivers and the shore of the Potomac. Between 1713 and 1730 Virginia tobacco prices languished at about 1 3/4d. per pound, exclusive of duty. The reexport price brought 4d., but the cost of shipping to London in the 1720s and 1730s was between £6 and £8 per ton of tobacco. Although the tobacco hogsheads had to weigh 950 pounds net weight, some were much larger; this was to the merchants' advantage, as a contemporary observer wrote, "because four hogsheads, whatsoever their weight be, are esteemed a tun, and pay the same freight."[11]

Although practically everyone in Virginia was a planter of sorts, distinct ranks were discernible among them, largely determined by the exigencies of the marketing system. This system contributed materially to the growth of a paternalist order in which a patron-client relationship was established between greater and lesser planters, a system not noticeably threatened until the 1750s and the intrusion of the Scottish factors from the great Glasgow houses on the Virginia economy.

There were essentially three methods of trade in the Chesapeake. One was the practice of selling tobacco to independent merchants, who then marketed the tobacco. Although the number of independent merchants grew in Virginia after 1720, the other two methods were far more important and widespread. From the 1740s the supercargo-store system was the most widely used method in Virginia for the export and marketing of tobacco. In this method collection points were established, where large amounts of tobacco were stored until a massive shipment was arranged with a London or a Glasgow firm. Increasingly, in the last half of the eighteenth century, factors—representatives of British firms—contracted with planters for their tobacco and arranged shipment with the large houses overseas.[12]

But for the early years of the century the most important method of tobacco dispersal and marketing was shipment through planter-consignors. The consignment system dominated Virginia tobacco marketing not only because it was a logical way of getting a crop to market but because it fit well into a society which understood vertical relationships, from patron to client, from master to servant, from free whites to black slaves. A

---

11. Sutherland, *Population Distribution*, pp. 204–5; Carman, ed., *American Husbandry*, pp. 159–62; Gray, *History of Agriculture*, 1:214–18. On planter occupation, see Risjord, "Virginians and the Constitution," p. 623.

12. Price, *France and the Chesapeake*, 1:663.

lesser planter brought his tobacco to a wealthier, larger planter, who agreed to ship the smaller grower's crop to overseas markets. Virginia's great planters established business contacts with tobacco merchants in London, who agreed to sell the crop and, in return, indicate to the Virginians how much credit they had against which they could purchase English goods or pay off debts. The greater planter at home in turn could indicate to his lesser neighbors how much they in turn owed him, how much credit they had, and how much he would charge for the use of his docks, storage houses, and the small implements, textiles, and other sundries that the planter-consignor sold in his "store" on the large plantation.[13]

By the practice of shipping goods, selling implements, and extending credit to lesser planters, the planter-merchants of Virginia established what came to be known as book-debt. The ledgers of the large plantations contained the accounts of lesser men and their financial standings with the master of the plantation. By the 1730s, since more than half of Virginia's tobacco was marketed by consignment, the influence and importance of the consignor was obviously great. The relationship between consignor and consignee was one based on personal contact and a certain bond of trust; moreover, nearly everyone in Virginia was in debt to everyone else for small as well as large sums. It is difficult for one to understand today how such an informal, personal network of political economy must have worked, for it contradicted the models of efficiency and industry by which modern, technological society is run.[14]

The "tissue of debt" that enmeshed all of Virginia's planters sprang from two sources. One was the need of the largest planters to keep up the appearances of gentility by which they distinguished themselves as men of quality and standing. A second source, however, and an equally important one, was the fact that the informal nature of relationships and the extension of credit so necessary to the consignment system made it utterly impossible for anyone to know at a given time precisely what he was worth. Given the lack of specie and the predominance of credit dealings, indebtedness affected the most tightly run financial operation, because no one could predict with certainty when his own debtors would pay him, or when he would be able to pay his own creditors.

The continual problem of debt causes and the inconvenience attendant upon arguing with neighbors over amounts due prompted the House of Burgesses to action in 1732. The planter-merchants finally had a statutory basis upon which to rest the "Method for proving Book Debts." The

13. Land, ed., *Bases of Plantation Society*, pp. 99–145; Rosenblatt, "House of John Norton and Sons."
14. Gray, *History of Agriculture*, 1:435–36. By 1776 only one-quarter of the colony's crop was on consignment due to the rise of the Scottish factors; see below.

new law observed the growing number of debt causes and the prevalence of the practice among the planter-merchants of merchandising necessary implements to their consignees on credit. Yet "no body is privy thereto but the buyer and seller," and since legal evidence of such a transaction was lacking, acrimonious charges swirled over the question of whether debts had been contracted and, if so, how such were to be proven. The new statute attempted to remedy this problem by stating that the planter-merchant or the storekeeper could produce in court his own ledger as evidence of debt and that such a ledger was lawful evidence, *"provided nevertheless,* That the defendant shall be at liberty to contest the plaintiff's evidence."[15]

Even such a summary view of the economic and social relationships spawned by the tobacco marketing system indicates why property and authority came to be consolidated in the hands of the greater planters. The debtor-creditor relationships of the culture and the necessity of doing business at the only genuinely public meeting place of a rural society meant that the justices of the peace in the county courts were bound to become powerful shapers of the legal culture of the colony. The elaborately differentiated and diversified economy of England was never replicated in Virginia, but the relatively homogeneous nature of a rural, agricultural society nevertheless promoted a Country style of action and thought, defining the nature of law and its administration in the courts. By the 1680s the law and the courts, like the socioeconomic character of Virginia, were assuming a definitive, normative character.

English Law and Virginia Culture

As early as 1618 the great charter of Virginia referred to the necessity of a government characterized by "Majestracy and just Laws." In those early years the orderly rule of legitimate authority in Virginia fell on the commanders of the plantations, who acted in various capacities. By 1624 civil suits for less than the value of one hundred pounds of tobacco and petty offenses were dealt with in Charles City and Elizabeth City corporations by a monthly court presided over by the commanders and others commissioned by the governor and Council. Between 1624 and 1634 the expanding population of the colony necessitated the creation of more "monthly" courts, and in the latter year the Assembly divided the colony into eight counties whose monthly courts were designed to replicate England's Quarter Sessions of the Peace. Virginia's local courts dealt

---

15. Hening, 4:327–29.

with the administrative details and petty criminal matters of county life. Prior to 1634 the Quarterly Court at Jamestown had heard all cases for the original counties, whose territory was now divided into eight shires. Former commanders of plantations were in 1634 succeeded by commissioners of the monthly courts; former marshals now became sheriffs. The monthly courts adopted the name "county courts" in 1643, but their function remained what it had always been—to provide easy access to the law in Virginia's spreading settlements. During this period Virginia justices also exercised a power that English justices had—that of passing the death sentence on felons. But in 1656 a statute forbade this, saying, "Wee conceive it no ease nor benefit to the people to have their lives taken away with too much ease." Acknowledging a departure from English precedent, the burgesses stated that their society was different and that "wee cannot with safety follow the example" of England.[16]

Gradually, the range of the powers exercised by Virginia justices came into focus. A single magistrate could dispense summary justice in any cause involving less than twenty shillings or two hundred pounds of tobacco. A constable enforced the justice's orders, and each justice shared a precinct of his county with at least one other. In each county the monthly court comprised at least eight justices, four of whom were of the "Quorum," more learned in the law, largely because they were the senior members who had sat the longest on the commission. Two justices out of court could sign probates of wills and letters of administration of estate and close ordinaries for violating the Sabbath. But outside of the sitting court justices could not deprive a person of his liberty or proceed "against his person" on suspicion or allegation, except on suspicion of murder or theft.[17]

When all the justices sat in court, their jurisdiction over criminal matters resembled that of English magistrates. Petty crime was reported on information from individuals, churchwardens of the parishes, or the presentments of the grand jury. The "grand inquest" of the county met at least once a year, in April and December from 1662 to 1705 and thereafter until the 1780s in May and November. By the seventeenth century

---

16. On the early history and evolution of the courts, see Craven, *Southern Colonies*, pp. 167–70; Billings, ed., *Old Dominion*, pp. 69–103. On felony jurisdiction, see Billings, "Some Acts Not in Hening," p. 71. The 1656 statute (Hening, 1:397–98) repeals an act passed in 1652 giving local courts life and death powers under a commission of oyer and terminer, with one member of the Council sitting with them. Apparently the statute was intended to help reduce a backlog of pending criminal causes. Until the 1690s this power was very occasionally vested in justices with regard to felons in general, but by that time was restricted in most cases to slave trials only. I am indebted to Warren Billings for discussing this issue with me.

17. On court duties, see Porter, *County Government*.

English justices were urged to turn over felons to the Court of Assize; in Virginia by 1705 statute law had formalized a late-seventeenth-century practice whereby justices sat as an examining or "called" court to determine if an accused white man should be sent to the General Court to stand trial as a felon. Petty offenses, consisting for the most part of quarrels, assaults, profane language, sexual misconduct, drunkenness, siring and giving birth to bastards, and petty theft, were dealt with by the justices. Slaves accused of felony were tried at Jamestown before 1692; after that date they were tried by the justices sitting under a commission of oyer and terminer issued to them and to whatever additional residents the governor thought fit to aid them on the bench. Each separate trial required a particular commission to the justices, a practice that changed in 1765 when the power was vested permanently in the magistrates.[18]

Administrative matters were as important as petty criminal concerns. In newly settled counties the roads, bridges, and ferries had to be maintained and their overseers appointed by the court. Rates to be charged in the ordinaries were regulated; the tax, or "levy," of the county was set each year. Justices recorded deeds of land and oversaw the proper administration of estates, the transfers of land titles, and the care of the orphans, the aged, the physically disabled, and the mentally incompetent. Since Virginia did not develop church courts, in 1645 the justices assumed ecclesiastical duties as well, overseeing probate and administration of wills and the settlement of legal separations and divorces. Widows who remarried were privately examined before waiver of the right of dower was allowed to guarantee that forfeiture of a deceased husband's estate was not being done under the coercion of the new spouse. Essentially, these duties devolved upon the gentlemen who sat on the local benches because the fledgling social order could not support the diversification of legal duties and prerogatives into the many types of courts that England had developed over the centuries.[19]

Of those many courts England had developed three to hear cases at

18. Until "called" court sessions were formally adopted in 1705 (Hening, 3:390), local courts were bound to hold criminals until they could be transported to Jamestown and, later, Williamsburg, since after 1656 justices did not, as a rule, try and sentence felons. See the 1658 Charles City example cited by Billings in *Old Dominion*, p. 100. The 1705 statute made official what had become common practice in the late seventeenth century. On the use of oyer and terminer power to try slaves, see the text of the 1692 law in Hening, 3:102–3.

19. Hening, 1:302–3 (1645). The text of the law seems to imply that the decision to give over probate of wills, appraisements, inventories, and accounts to local court jurisdiction and to invest them with equity powers stemmed from the pragmatic judgment that Jamestown was too far away for most Virginians to use the high court there. A reception statute passed in 1661–62 (Hening, 2:69–71) empowered a Virginia justice (first called a justice of peace here) to do whatever an English justice could do in or out of sessions.

common law (king's bench, exchequer, and common pleas) and a separate Court of Chancery to hear pleas in equity in cases in which a remedy at law seemed impossible. Virginia justices of the peace exceeded their English cousins' powers in this area, for the colonial justice heard causes at law and, after 1645, in chancery as well. Petty suits of less than forty shillings had been heard in England at the Sheriff's Court, but in Virginia any cause involving less than ten pounds sterling (1705) came under the jurisdiction of the justices. The ease of moving from law to equity guaranteed a kind of informality, which aided colonists in arguing their own causes in court, but procedurally that ease was anathema to English lawyers, who very soon came to dislike the local courts in which they practiced when they arrived in Virginia. Indeed, many of them liked the General Court very little better.[20]

That august body, composed of the governor and his Council, sat at Jamestown, and later Williamsburg, as the supreme court of the colony. By 1642 the General Court had decreased the meeting of local courts to six times a year, so large was the volume of suits, and the court ordered the justices to give special attention to preventing the "many chargeable suits tending to the molestation and ruine of divers poor men for pettie and trivial debts." In this way the General Court hoped to cut down on the number of appeals, for appeals went from the justice to the monthly (county) court, to the General Court (not formally so-called until 1683), and thence to the Assembly. Appeal to the Assembly, however, would be stricken from Virginia's procedures following the upheavals of Bacon's and the Plant Cutters' rebellions. Thereafter, the crown decided that the General Court would be the highest court of Virginia; appeals could be carried to the Privy Council in rare instances involving more than one hundred pounds sterling. Only one attempt was made in the colonial era

---

20. The resort to equity in Virginia's colonial courts deserves a study in depth. The statute (Hening, 1:303–4 [1645]) stated that Virginians could stop a cause at law before it went to a jury and at that time demand relief in equity. If the justices saw no relief in equity, the bill was remanded back for trial at law. The person having a complaint could force the appearance by subpoena of the person or persons named in the bill and these individuals had to answer the complainant's petition in the court sitting as one of chancery. Injunctions were used in the local courts, but specific performance for transfer of real property appears to have been rare. The increase of local court powers stemmed largely from the phenomenal growth rate. Despite high mortality among the unseasoned, Virginia's population rose from a mere 5,200 in 1634, when the local courts were formally established, to 8,000 in 1644, right before the expansion of jurisdiction to include equity and ecclesiastical court duties, and to 25,600 by 1662. By 1680 population had reached 40,000 and by 1699 had risen to approximately 62,800 people in twenty counties. See E. S. Morgan, *American Slavery*, p. 404. The 1705 law setting the sums involved in cases over which justices had jurisdiction is in Hening, 3:289.

to erect an intermediate circuit court system to keep the governor and Council more tightly in control of local justices and to cut down the volume of appeals to the General Court. Between 1634 and 1663 the governor and councillors sat on circuit, but the three meetings a year of the General Court prohibited such travels. Abandoning the idea of a circuit, the General Court itself began to sit but twice a year, hoping to discourage planters from flooding it with more causes.[21]

Between 1660 and 1680 a sifting process began which defined who would sit on the local courts and on the Council. Allied by marriage and wealth and enjoying the special favor of Governor William Berkeley, a coterie of gentlemen emerged in those years who would dominate Virginia's local and provincial life. Those justices and burgesses now attempted to control the former jostling for position that had characterized earlier years (and their own behavior). After the abandonment of circuit courts in 1662 the Council may have felt that Virginians were coming too often to complain in Jamestown against local justices. Hence, the Council in 1673 decided to pay justices a salary to encourage gentlemen to do their office, authorizing a levy on each litigant who failed to win his suit. In Middlesex County the justices defended themselves when this new law was put into effect, pleading that the salary of five hundred pounds of tobacco and fodder for their horses was needed to defray expenses. Public outcry, however, forced the repeal of the act and forcefully demonstrated that aggrandizement on the part of this increasingly narrow elite group of justices could not be aided by public taxes.[22]

21. On the need to cut down the number of petty cases, see Hening, 1:224, 273; Chumbley, *Colonial Justice*, pp. 55–64, 68–69 (on appeals); Smith, *Appeals to the Privy Council*, table 1, p. 668. The issue of circuit duty by councillors is somewhat complex. Originally Council members resident in their counties sat with the local courts. In 1642 and 1648 local justices were instructed that Council members could sit with them, as could the governor himself. In 1662 the statute (Hening, 2:64–65) creating circuits on which two councillors sat to hear complaints of partiality or injustice leveled against local magistrates also specified that the councillors could not sit in the circuit including their place of residence. The inconvenience of riding the circuits led to a repeal (Hening, 2:179 [1662]). See Bruce, *Institutional History*, 1:496–99. For an example of the circuit judges on a local bench, see "Itinerary Judges," *WMQ*, 1st ser., 25–26 (1916–18): 29–30.

22. Billings argues persuasively that between 1660 and 1676 access to the local bench was restricted and that the definition of rank and the exclusion of many men from magisterial positions helped spark Bacon's Rebellion. See his "Virginia's Deploured Condition" and "Growth of Political Institutions," pp. 225–42. On the rebellion, see Washburn, *Governor and the Rebel*, pp. 60–75, which tends to support Berkeley's policies. Apparently no matter what policy was followed—cutting down the number of justices or increasing it—factionalism and jealousy were the result. See the statute (Hening, 2:21 [1660–61]) cutting down the magistrates' number from fifteen to eight, since so many justices "hath rendered the place contemptible and raysed factions," and Berkeley's opinion that drawing the

In fact, the absence of a salary was no impediment to men bent on consolidating wealth, rank, and authority in local Virginia life. Multiple office holding, a practice encouraged by the burgesses to hold local worthies to their duty, guaranteed that the gentry who served as unpaid justices could make a tidy sum by serving in other positions simultaneously. It was quite common for justices to be coroners, sheriffs, escheat masters, public notaries, and attorneys all at the same time during the late seventeenth century. In 1642–43 a sheriff was allowed to charge 10 pounds of tobacco for each arrest made, 10 for each peace bond, 10 for each subpoena, 4 for each summons to court that he delivered, and 20 for each whipping delivered. The coroner's fee for viewing a corpse was 133 pounds of tobacco. Elaborate fee scales were set up for various services performed by a clerk. Of these offices the one most carefully guarded by the gentry was that of sheriff. It quickly became the practice in Virginia for the office of sheriff to revolve through the Commission of the Peace, descending through the ranks in order of the date one ascended to the bench. The sheriff's office guaranteed an income of sorts to the justice, and once one's year-long term of office as sheriff ended, the court regularly asked its officer of enforcement back onto the bench again as a justice of the peace.[23]

Multiple office holding persisted well into the eighteenth century, even among families that no longer needed the income. One of the most burdensome of those offices was that of overseer of the roads. Failure to perform that duty satisfactorily brought a presentment from the grand jury and a fine from the court. Yet the justices themselves often acted as overseers. The reason, of course, was that even if they themselves did not

---

Council and local commissioners (justices) from only a few families of many members "is [so] dishonqrable to their wisdome and reputacon, that the Generall amendment of this is most necessary though it bee knowne the particular wilbee envious," signaling Berkeley's ill-fated attempt to decrease factionalism by cutting the numbers of men within the few families who held public office. See Kukla, ed., "Some Acts Not in Hening," p. 96. Part of the reaction against Berkeley's recent favoritism toward a tighter elite can be found in the 1676 laws. With respect to the courts, under the June Assembly's direction the appointment of county court clerks was given over to the justices, and Council members were forbidden to vote while sitting in the county courts, especially on the collection of the levy since only the justices, and not the councillors, were answerable for those actions (Hening, 2:355, 358). Those acts were repealed by royal proclamation. The clerkship was reinstated as the patronage preserve of the governor and colonial secretary. A new law, however (Hening, 2:390 [1676–77]), though upholding the right of a councillor to vote in the local courts, did add that the councillor is "equally liable and responsible with every other justice of the peace for all such acts or orders of court, he shall at the tyme of such sitting with the court give his vote and assent to."

23. Hening, 1:265–67; repealed, ibid., 2:325. For details, see Bruce, *Institutional History*, 1:502–4; *VMHB* 78 (1899–1901): 185.

do a particularly able job, the office was theirs to bestow on another member of the family or a dependent tenant. That patronage power in a social order that valued a ranked order was important, for the justice could illustrate his patriarchal eminence in the assignment of such duties. The only significant office not under the justices' control was that of county clerk. That official was appointed by the secretary of the colony, whose office in Williamsburg served as the training ground for county clerks, and eventually for county lawyers.[24]

For these last-named creatures, the gentry harbored deep suspicions. Clearly, the accumulation of offices, property, wealth, and, hence, authority, both social and political, meant that the local leaders of the Tidewater had a vested interest in preventing a widespread and potentially uncontrollable legal profession from developing. From a pragmatic standpoint it was essential that attorneys be only gentlemen whose rising stars shed luster on the magisterial elites in the counties. As late as the 1670s justices appointed by Sir William Berkeley could be demoted by him as well, and being left off the commission dealt a devastating blow to a planter's public image as a gentleman of consequence. Therefore, the strict control of who might become a lawyer was all the more imperative.[25]

---

24. Bruce, *Institutional History*, 1:590, 600, 604. Coroners' fees were first forbidden then instituted (Hening, 2:324 [1674]; ibid., p. 419 [1677]; ibid., 4:503 [1736]). The sheriff was one of the justices. A revolving order passed the office on from year to year (Hening, 2:21, 78). Scales for fees can be found throughout the volumes of statutes. Laws against multiple officeholding were passed in the eighteenth century, but applied only to sitting members of the House of Burgesses. Thus, Hening, 4:292–93 (1730) prohibits sheriffs from being burgesses and exempts burgesses from serving as sheriffs; Hening, 6:185 (1748) prohibits tobacco inspectors from being burgesses while in office and for two years thereafter. The concern over "placemen," who might be bribed into compliance with Court policies, obviously motivated those laws. Their passage attests to the success of the local gentry by the 1730s in securing their social and political position firmly enough not to need multiple offices as had their ancestors. For an example of earlier officeholding and resultant problems, see Tyler, *Encyclopedia*, 1:139–40, on John Lear, staunch supporter of Berkeley and object of a bitter attack in a county court petition because of his offices as justice, county court clerk, escheat master, notary public, and surveyor while his brother David was sheriff. By 1680, Lear was presiding justice of his county and soon thereafter Council member, trustee of the college, and collector for the lower district of James River.

25. Fishburne, "Office of Secretary of State"; A. M. Smith, "Virginia Lawyers." Quitt, "Virginia House of Burgesses," argues that the number of disputed elections to the House between 1680 and 1706 demonstrates the resentment of people increasingly excluded from the local centers of power, the county courts. That confirms Billings's contention that nobody before 1676, and few people thereafter, sat in the House who was not also a justice. See Quitt's observations at p. 194 (fn. 1). He also believes that the 1730 place act was not significant since many burgesses resigned to become sheriffs rather than continue to sit, indicating that local office (and salary) was more important to some than sitting in Wil-

Furthermore, since the laws that *were* passed regulating the licensing of attorneys brought revenue into the governor's hands, a natural, and deepening, anxiety spread among the gentry that lawyers might easily become the partisans of a governor's, or "Court," party. If the Court in Jamestown were able to control the practice of attorneys, who could predict how favor and lucre might combine to unsettle the jealously guarded ranks of the local gentry? The House of Burgesses, however, saw to it that no such alarming developments occurred. In 1643–44 a licensing act specified that the attorney had to be licensed before the local and Quarter (General) Court. He could practice only in one local court. (Men who had letters of procuration from England and who represented English merchants and investors were exempted.) In 1645 the mercenary attorney act expelled all lawyers who were aggrandizing fortunes by charging fees in petty suits. The licensing act was repealed and a 1647 law reconfirmed this, allowing only that the court could appoint a person to represent the defendant. Justices could serve as attorneys in such causes, but clerks, sheriffs, undersheriffs, or commissioners (justices) could plead only in another court, never in the one where they were officers, except on behalf of a poor person or when granted a general power of attorney for someone out of the colony. In the latter case a justice had to give security, and if the court ruled that he was bringing an unjust suit, he was liable for costs and damages. In 1656 a new law provided that the governor and Council could appoint lawyers for the Quarterly Court and justices for their local courts, after attorneys took a prescribed oath. A year later a law clarified the intent of the 1656 law by expressly forbidding attorneys to take fees for their services under penalty of five thousand pounds of tobacco.[26]

Upon the Restoration Virginia's local elites (increasingly defined as those families upon whom Berkeley's favor was bestowed) seemed to be operating in conjunction with the governor; little Country opposition was possible or conceivable as long as the justice-burgesses of Virginia got on reasonably well with a governor like Berkeley. Nor was there much reason to fear that lawyers as a distinct class or group of men might interfere in the social and political order of the colony. Between 1660 and 1680, however, resentment over Berkeley's preferential treatment of certain families and his reluctance to press a vigorous war against the Indians finally sparked Bacon's Rebellion. In the aftermath men who had formerly been members of the "Greenspring Faction" and loyal to

---

liamsburg. The House unsuccessfully tried to punish members who accepted a sheriff's appointment before the House rose from sitting (pp. 187–88).

26. The acts regarding attorneys are in Hening, 1:275–76, 302, 313, 349, 419, 482–83, 523; ibid., 2:81–82, 478–79, 498. The text of the 1656 lawyer's oath has not survived.

Berkeley's rather aristocratic policies suddenly found themselves confronted with governors who were not of one mind with some of the recently favored gentry of Virginia. For the first time, and for a very long time thereafter, the issue of what role lawyers should play in Virginia's culture and who should control them assumed a new importance. The political confrontation between successive governors Culpeper, Howard, and Nicholson and the justice-burgesses swept the issue of lawyers into a maelstrom of Court versus Country issues. The results of that conflict left no doubt about the determination of the local gentry to keep the legal profession out of Virginia's public life.[27] As the political and social character of the colony emerged from the conflict between the governor-Court party and burgess-Country partisans, the legal culture of Virginia was inevitably fashioned in the image of the social order as a whole.

The struggle began in 1680 as part of a larger crisis. While Berkeley was away in England defending his draconian methods of handling former rebels, his deputy Henry Chicheley was prevailed upon to convene an Assembly. Under an act passed by the burgesses attorneys were allowed to practice and take fees for their work, but had to be licensed by the governor after studying for a year with someone already an attorney. In practical terms this meant the attorney general in Jamestown or one of the eminent men practicing there, like William Fitzhugh who had arrived in Virginia in 1674, boasting (probable) training in Ireland. This new law pointedly stated, however, that every man was still allowed to plead his own cause in a county court of the General Court.[28]

The Assembly, which had been called in late 1679, was still sitting when it learned that Thomas Lord Culpeper was to be the new governor of Virginia. Arriving May 10, 1680, Culpeper immediately set about trying to follow his instructions, which were that he obtain fixed salaries for officials. The new law regarding attorneys passed the burgesses in June and apparently generated no controversy at that time. An attorney from Gloucester County, however, decided that a record of the proceedings should be printed. John Buckner employed John Nuthead to

27. Quitt, "Virginia House of Burgesses," p. 226, concludes that lawyers were seldom burgesses, but believes Virginians encouraged legal learning, citing Bruce, *Institutional History*, 1:569, about the "society" at Jamestown favored by William Fitzhugh. Bruce's opinion on the early legal 'profession" (pp. 561–69) is shared by Richard Beale Davis who thinks that by the 1680s a "profession" of law is clearly in evidence. My own interpretation falls between this one and Daniel Boorstin's. Boorstin believes no profession of law existed before the 1750s. See Davis, *Intellectual Life in the Colonial South*, 3:1601–9; Boorstin, *Americans*, pp. 195 ff.

28. The following account of the political controversies relies heavily on Wertenbaker, *Virginia under the Stuarts*, pp. 195–259; Craven, *Southern Colonies*; R. L. Morton, *Colonial Virginia*; Quitt, "House of Burgesses."

print the laws for him and planned to resort to the proceedings in the course of his legal work. He eventually had to appear before Culpeper and post bond in the amount of £100, promising not to print any more of the statutes, but in the meantime, far more serious problems beset the colony and boded ill for the future of the legal profession.[29]

The burgesses had little opportunity to consider whether their new governor would use the licensing act wisely in choosing attorneys because he remained in Virginia only a very brief time. Culpeper hastened aboard ship in August and sailed from the muggy exile of the Chesapeake to the more invigorating climate at Court. While he was away during 1681, the chronically depressed tobacco prices in the colony stirred up sentiment among the planters that an assembly be convened to pass a cessation act under whose provisions less tobacco should be planted. Acting in Culpeper's place and against the Council's advice, Chicheley convened the Assembly in the spring, only to receive an order from England that no assembly should sit until November when Culpeper was to arrive. The plant-cutting riots were the result. On November 10 a lawful Assembly did convene, and one of its first acts was to repeal the 1680 law that provided for the licensing of attorneys.

The repeal was arguably motivated by ruinous financial conditions that made it inconvenient, to say the least, to pay 500 pounds of tobacco in the General Court or 150 pounds in the counties for each lawyer's fee taken by licensees. Yet the burgesses were quite probably and properly in a resentful mood as they reflected that in the midst of their financial misery a royal governor (and not a very faithful one at that) should be able to collect fees for licensing lawyers and, moreover, to control access to the profession. Their negative impression of Culpeper's handling of public affairs was not alleviated by his hasty and selfish actions.

After arriving in November and prosecuting the instigators of the Plant-Cutters' Rebellion, Culpeper set about clearing the docket in the courts. By February 1683, Buckner had been hailed before the Council and forbidden to print laws of the Assembly "until his Majesty's pleasure be known." Robert Beverley, Sr., former clerk of the House and practicing attorney, had been removed from office in 1678 for protesting Colonel Herbert Jeffreys's seizure of the Assembly's records following the draconian measures the vengeful Sir William Berkeley instituted against the defeated Baconians. Culpeper now confirmed Beverley's incapacity to hold public office, upheld the attorney's disbarment as well, and canceled all sums voted to the hapless former clerk by the Assembly, which had

29. On Buckner's reprimand, see *EJCV*, 1:39, 493. This incident marks the first public recognition of the relationship between lawyers and book print. Its cultural ramifications are discussed in chapters 3 and 4.

continued to support the Country leader. Though Beverley escaped with his life, he and fellow Gloucester County leaders had the ghastly lesson of Court power driven home when another leader of the late rebellion, Black Austin, was hanged in front of the county courthouse. Culpeper informed his superiors: "Having Dispatched the Generall Court last April (notwithstanding the Great Arreare of old Causes, and that the Criminal ones took up halfe the time) In fewer days and with speedier Justice than ever was yet practiced there before, and I hope as Good, since none would appeale . . . there appeared a universall satisfaction."[30]

Culpeper's report was, of course, that of a victorious Court leader. Upon his return home (without the king's permission), Culpeper was removed from office and Lord Howard Effingham was dispatched to Virginia. There he discovered that the Country, though bruised, was far from defeated.

Effingham was made governor in September 1683 but did not arrive until February 1684. By April the burgesses were convened again and were stunned by the announcement that from henceforth they were forbidden to hear appeals of legal causes from the General Court. Only the Privy Council now stood above the governor and councillors of Virginia. The fact that Philip Ludwell, one of the Berkeley Greenspring Faction, had appealed to the Assembly after trial for his contempt of Colonel Jeffreys had alerted the crown to the old Virginia practice. Part of the tightening of Court control on Virginia by the 1680s was the suppression of the Assembly's role as the court of last resort in the colony.[31]

A second aspect of an ascendant Court policy was the proclamation read by Effingham on June 19 in accord with instructions from the king that the 1680 law providing for the licensing of lawyers was to be reinstated. Following so closely on the constitutional issue, the argument over

30. "Culpeper's Report on Virginia in 1683," *VMHB* 3 (1896): 236 (from the MacDonald manuscripts, VSL). On the creation of a Court party and policy and the defeat of the Country, see Webb, *Governors-General*, 329–435. For details on Robert Beverley, see ibid., pp. 364–68, 413–14, 418. On Black Austin's fate, see ibid., p. 417. See also *EJCV*, 1:36, 55, 509.

31. Craven, *Colonies in Transition*, pp. 154–57, and Webb, *Governors-General*, pp. 364–66. Webb's otherwise excellent account of the rise of a Courtier party seems to me to exaggerate the defeat of the Country. For an important corrective, see Bailey, *Popular Influence*, 1–19. Bailey points out that petitioning was the major source of legislation for the late seventeenth and all of the eighteenth century, thereby raising questions about the notion of Court "prescription" for Virginia policymaking, the thesis advanced by John Rainbolt and Edmund Morgan. The vast majority of colonial laws sprang not from government initiatives but from popular petitions; see pp. 55–60. As events from 1690 to 1730 indicate, I would argue, the Country in Virginia was perhaps unique in the colonies for its ability to subvert the Court power and policies Webb ably explicates. See below.

bestowal of licenses on attorneys defined the Court-versus-Country terms under which control of the profession of law would proceed. Appealing to the crown, the burgesses asked for a restitution of appellate jurisdication to the House and a repeal of the reinstitution of the 1680 licensing law. The 1684 mission of Thomas Milner and William Sherwood on behalf of the House to Secretary Jenkins succeeded only in displeasing the new monarch, James II, who informed Effingham that he was highly displeased with the two clerks who had circumvented the governor after Effingham refused to forward the petitions of the House. For their parts, Sherwood and Milner were turned out of "all imployments to their great damage and disgrace." The treatment given to the England-born and trained attorney Sherwood and Beverley's disgrace indicated to the Country just how real their fears of Court domination of the profession were.[32]

Those fears were exacerbated during the next few years by Effingham's rapacious aggrandizement of his own fortune through an aggressive insistence that each jot and tittle of the law be executed. Attorney General Edmund Jenings, though a Court figure, obliquely but incisively gave voice to his Country fellows' unstated resentments when he asked for a raise in salary. Formerly, he said, he was not even obliged to be in regular attendance at the General Court. But "whereas ... the Employment of yor Petitionr ... hath much encreased by reason of the Strict Inquiry & inspection of ye Breach & ye due execution of ye Laws ... ,"[33] a higher salary for the attorney general was needed. Presumably, Jenings was overworked in some degree as well because, as one contemporary French observer noted, the councillors were "men of parts, but ... not necessarily educated in the law. They sit officially in their boots and swords."[34] As Effingham's tenure came to a close, the governor's control of the legal profession and the increase in the volume of cases seemed to point to a victory for the Court in Virginia.

In 1689, however, the Glorious Revolution seemed to some Country

32. Sherwood was an attorney who practiced in Virginia after beginning his career in England; Milner was clerk and resident of Nansemond, speaker of the house from 1691 to 1693, and a planter of note. I have been unable to determine conclusively whether he practiced law actively. For details on the Sherwood-Milner mission, see Wertenbaker, *Virginia under the Stuarts*, pp. 242–43. Beverley's deprivation of office in 1686 resulted from his role in the port bill controversy. During that same crisis the House lost its power of naming the clerk of the house. Ibid., pp. 248–52.

33. *VMHB* 5–6 (1897–99): 398–99 (1692).

34. [Durand of Dauphine,] *Frenchman in Virginia*, p. 51. One wonders at Durand's observation: "It is a common law country. The laws are so equitable that there are almost no lawsuits" (p. 96). Presumably, he meant few formal suits involving attorneys. Court records indicate that property, debt, and assault disputes were quite numerous.

partisans to augur a chance to restate the grievances of the House concerning control of the lawyers and the curtailment of representative privileges. Led by the erstwhile Greenspring leader Philip Ludwell, the burgesses successfully petitioned William and Mary to repeal the reinstatement of the 1680 licensing act. Consulting the attorney and solicitor generals, king, queen, and Council accepted their advice that "in as much as the said Act of Assembly is represented as inconvenient and prejudicial to that Colony they humbly offer their Opinion that the same be repealed." In July 1690 the governor proclaimed the repeal of the 1680 licensing act, and in 1692 the crown specifically asked for confirmation that the repeal had been effected. From 1690 to 1732 no law regulated the licensing of practitioners of the law in Virginia. Speaking for the Country but led by men who had at least one foot in the Court while employing Country rhetoric, the burgesses had apparently wrested control over the legal profession from the hands of the governor and Court.[35]

There continued to be lawyers in Virginia during the period 1690 to 1732, nonetheless. Their precise number, function, and public reputation one shall probably never know (see table 1). The fluid and ill-defined boundaries between offices and occupations of "planter," "lawyer," "merchant," and so on, are eloquent testimony to the persistence in real life of one of the cherished theoretical points of the Country persuasion—the independent man doing for himself and his dependents, rather than submit to the artificiality imposed by a "professional" who seeks to insinuate himself between the proper relationships of deference and obligation in society. If the profession of law in the counties survived between 1690 and 1732, it did so because the men in practice *were* primarily gentlemen-planters, or because a few were England trained and valuable in the running of the government, particularly at Jamestown and Williamsburg. Of the thirty-one names of attorneys on a surviving civil list (see table 2), fully one-third (ten) were residents of York and James City counties and an additional four came from the Stafford-Westmoreland area, where the business of the lord proprietor of the Northern Neck provided ample room for lucrative practice.

Yet the existence of an arguably able bar in late-seventeenth-century Virginia did not produce a stable and socially distinct class of attorneys which survived into the eighteenth century. Two factors conspired against such an evolution. One was mortality and movement out of the country, and the second was a related reluctance of gentlemen to see their sons identified as lawyers when they could just as easily be perceived primarily as landed gentlemen. This latter anxiety was, of course, the result of the

35. On the disputes and eventual success of the House in repealing the 1680 law, see *EJCV*, 1:61–62, 116, 120, 270, 500–501, 521.

TABLE 1. *Sample of Lawyers, 1660–1700*

YORK–JAMES CITY:
William Sherwood
John Holcroft
Thomas Ballard
James Bray
John Page
Daniel Parke
Robert Smith
Edward Chilton
Hugh Owen
William Hockaday
Francis Willis

HENRICO:
Thomas Bushrod
Bartholomew Fowler
James Cocke
Benjamin Harrison
William Glover
John Everett

MIDDLESEX:
William Leigh
Robert Peyton
Peter Beverley
Thomas Gregson

Sampson Darell
Thomas Stapleton
Robert Beverley, Sr.

OLD RAPPAHANNOCK:
Denis McCarty
Joshua Davis

John Waters
Richard Robinson

ESSEX:
Denis McCarty

James Boughan

RICHMOND: Arthur Spicer

STAFFORD: Anthony Bridges

William Fitzhugh

WESTMORELAND:
Simon Robins
Alexander Webster
Gerard Fowke
William Payne
Valentine Peyton
Gerard Lowther
George Brent

Sigismund Massey
William Horton
John Newton
Lewis Markham
Willoughby Allerton
Robert Brent

Source: Bruce, *Institutional History*, 2:570–87.

Justices and Lawyers in Virginia, 1680–1720   55

TABLE 2 *Barristers and Attorneys in Virginia, 1699*

BARRISTERS:[a]

John Clayton
Benjamin Harrison

ATTORNEYS: (with county of residence when known)

Lancelot Bathurst (Essex)
Mathew Kemp, Jr. (Middlesex)
William Fitzhugh (Stafford)
Edmund Jennings (York)
Charles Turner (James City or New Kent)
Robert Beverley (James City)
George Brent (Stafford)
James Gaylor (Westmoreland)
Robert Bradley (James City)
Charles Holden (Northampton)
Edward Hill (Charles City)
William Sedgwick (York)
Richard Clarke (James City)
Peter Wall
William Sherwood (James City)
Richard James (James City)
William Leigh (New Kent)
Edward Harrison
William Thompson (Westmoreland)
William Evans
Hugh Owen (York)
Joseph Stiles
Robert Colles
Robert Playton (Gloucester)
Ambros Clare (James City)
Thomas Clayton (James City)
Malachy Thruston (Norfolk)
Philip Howard
John Lear (Nansemond)
Jonothan Wilkinson (Accomac?)
William Harrison (Prince George)

Source: *VMHB* 1 (1892): 251–52, which gives attorneys in practice at 1699; shortly thereafter, Fitzhugh, Brent, Sherwood died.
 a. Barrister here means an active practitioner who had attended the Inns or was invited to join. Clayton had attended; Harrison may have, but only briefly, since he is listed as a Middle Templar of 1697 and by December 1698 was clerk of the Council. Edward Chilton had left Virginia by this date; neither Stevens Thomson nor William Byrd II was returned from the Inns yet; and Henry Perrott, the first Virginian to attend the Inns (Gray's, 1674), apparently never practiced before the bar. Two lists which name Virginians invited to join the Inns should be used with great caution, since an invitation to join does not indicate attendance, or a call to the bar and later practice. See E. Alfred Jones, *American Members of the Inns of Court*; J. G. de Roulhac Hamilton, "Southern Members of the Inns of Court," pp. 278–79.

inherited prejudice of the Country against professional occupations in a rural, dependent social order.

It is rather remarkable that men like Fitzhugh, George Brent, Arthur Spicer, Sherwood, Edward Chilton, Henry Hartwell, and several other attorneys of note had all died or left the colony by 1705. Moreover, their sons (when they had sons) did not succeed them in practice but instead went to England to receive genteel education in polite learning and either settled there or became noted as Virginia planters. Burgesses, justices, and occasionally councillors, none ever practiced law.[36] To appreciate fully why such eminent practitioners in the law either discouraged their progeny from becoming identified as a Virginia lawyer or urged extensive English training as the only appropriate mode of entry into the law, one needs to recall that a split had long since been obvious between the partisans of the Country and the Court. For the latter English training, familiarity with book print and print culture in general, and deep immersion in English precedent and common law procedure tied them mentally to the Court—to Jamestown, to cultured society, to the excitement and arguments before the superior court. To the Countryman, of course, such high-flown arguments seemed to come from precisely that shameless sort of fellow who would easily become the pawn of a powerful governor or councillor, to the detriment of the Country interest. This interest held the view that the law should be kept simple and direct and under the firm hand of the local gentry who sat as justices of the peace.

In 1666, Secretary of the Colony Thomas Ludwell had explained to officials in London the workings of the General Court. This court, he wrote, was one "wherein as greate care is taken to make the Lawes and pleadings upon them easy & obvious to any mans understanding as in other parts they doe to keep them a mystery to the people." Ludwell described the limitations on pleadings where both plaintiff and defendants were "kept within the first Limmitts of Ye Merritts of their cause

---

36. Bruce, *Institutional History*, 1:570–87, concludes that attorneys tended to cluster around Jamestown and in York County, in other words, near the General Court and the county courts most likely to use their services. See also Shammas, "English-Born and Creole Elites," pp. 282–92, on the percentage of English émigrés returning to England. Darrett and Anita Rutman are finding in Middlesex County that informal handling of a neighbor's business often led to a de facto transformation of a planter into a practicing attorney. Still, no self-conscious identity of attorneys-of-fact as members of a "profession" can legitimately be advanced for the period 1680–1720 except for rare instances, usually in cases in which the person was an England-trained immigrant, like Fitzhugh. Bruce also concurs in the opinion that Governor Howard wanted to continue licensing in order to bring in monies for himself. For an example of a governor licensing an attorney just before 1690, see Bruce, *Institutional History*, 1:567 (fn. 3) (Surry County, 1685).

and Judgm[ents] pas secundum alegata et probata & References are rarely obtayned but upon very just grounds."[37]

When Robert Beverley II wrote his *History and Present State of Virginia* in 1705, he continued this explanation of the Country style, despite the fact that he himself was a sometime lawyer. Beverley noted with satisfaction that in the county and General Court "every one that pleases, may plead his own Cause... there being no restraint in that case, nor any licensed Practitioners in the law." Yet Beverley entered a *monitum* about the General Court, sniffing the air for Courtly odors as he sourly observed: "They us'd to come to the merits of the cause, as soon as they could without Injustice, never admitting such impertinences of Form and Nicety, as were not absolutely necessary: and when the substance of the case was sufficiently debated, they us'd directly to bring the suit to a decision. By this Method all fair Actions were prosecuted... and all the tricking, and foppery of the Law happily avoided." Now, however, Beverley believed that cosmopolitan airs were creeping into the business of the General Court, for the greater gentry came as much "to see Fashions, as to dispatch their particular Business."[38]

Barristers and attorneys who practiced at the General Court (most of them England born and trained), had a very different view of Virginia law. They were highly critical of the informality of procedure, and they made no secret of their low regard for the gentry justices and even the councillors who sat as judges in the General Court, whom they considered so many provincials. Court prejudices in favor of more learning, the spread of print culture, and a greater reliance on precedent and proper forms in drawing writs were expressed by more than one attorney in late-seventeenth-century Virginia. Arriving in Virginia in 1674, William Fitzhugh immediately began to demonstrate his superiority to other planters who lacked the benefits of such education. His correspondence with other lawyers and planters was stuffed with references to precedent and citations from Coke's *Institutes*. Asked to satisfy curiosity on abstruse points of the law, he condescendingly replied that an answer would require "rather a small treatise than a letter fully to discourse upon."

Hobnobbing with other lawyers and the great planters of Stafford County and the Northern Neck, Fitzhugh was adamant in his insistence

---

37. Thomas Ludwell letter, from the Winder Papers, *VMHB* 5 (1897): 57. The "very just grounds" were in case of sickness of the parties or where evidence or papers from England were needed. Judgments, "*secundum* ...": according to what is alleged and proven, without resort to pleading errors in form.

38. Beverley, *History and Present State*, pp. 255, 258, 259. On Beverley's Country style of living, see Alexander, ed., *Journal of John Fontaine*, entry for Nov. 15, 1715, p. 86.

that understanding of the common law was "the only guide, & which is only to be learn'd out of antient Authors, (for out of the old fields must come the new Corn)." Of course such learning could only be obtained from study in England, and both that study and the need to pay close attention to precedent was "contrary to the opinion of the generality of our Judges & practi[c]ers of the Law here."[39] Fitzhugh argued proficiently before the General Court, joining forces with fellow attorney Robert Beverley, Sr. (whom he also defended after the plant-cutter riots in 1682–84), for Ralph Wormeley in a complicated cause involving traverse of an escheat. Fitzhugh's abilities and his own comments about the "generality" of lawyers and judges in Virginia make it clear that he was the exception, not the norm, in seventeenth-century legal expertise.[40]

Fitzhugh was joined in his censures and negative views of the informal and unlearned nature of law learning in Virginia by another attorney. Although Robert Beverley II believed by 1705 that the General Court had become enmeshed in the "foppery" of law, a prominent lawyer of the time disagreed. Moreover, the Country gentlemen sitting on the county benches would not have been pleased had they been able to read a description of themselves written by this Virginia barrister in 1697. Edward Chilton, a former attorney general and coauthor with James Blair of *The Present State of Virginia and the College*, spelled out the low regard in which county justices were held by trained lawyers in his chapter the "Administration of Justice." Chilton informed Englishmen that in Virginia all causes "belonging to Chancery, King's Bench, Common Pleas, Exchequer, Admiralty, and Spirituality, are decided altogether in one and the same Court." After also describing the official role of the county courts, Chilton entered an aside on the quality of the magistrates:

> These County Courts having always been held by Country Gentlemen, who had no Education in the Law, it was no Wonder if both the Sense of the Law was mistaken, and the Form and Method of Proceedings was often very irregular; but of late the Insufficiency of these Courts has been much more perceiv'd and felt that [than?] in former Times, while the first Stock of *Virginia* gentlemen lasted, who having had their Education in *England*, were

39. Fitzhugh, *William Fitzhugh*, pp. 24–26; Fitzhugh to Thomas Clayton, Apr. 7, 1679, ibid., p. 73; Fitzhugh to Major Richard Lee, May 15, 1679, ibid., p. 66.

40. Ibid., pp. 88–89, 152–60. Traverse of an escheat involved the denial of Wormeley's claims to the tenure of certain lands he held or claimed to hold under the law of descents, an area of English law that Fitzhugh prided himself on knowing thoroughly. See his explication of certain points of it to Beverley, Sr., Sept. 11, 1679, ibid., pp. 68–70.

a great deal better accomplish'd in the Law ... that [than?] their Children and Grand-children, who have been born in *Virginia*, and have had generally no Opportunity of Improvement by good Education, further than that they learned to read, write, and cast Accompts, and that but very indifferently.[41]

Besides the insults offered to the present generation of planter gentry, Chilton's remarks also included his own Court notions that law, if it were to be learned and practiced at all, needed to be studied professionally in London. The crude state of legal procedure was not confined to the counties, in Chilton's opinion. The informal nature of law had infected the General Court itself, where proceedings were "disagreeable to the Laws of *England*, and very irregular. Original and judicial Writs run not in the Name of the King, but resemble Warrants made by Justices of the Peace. There are no formal Declarations there, Petitions are made use of in their stead; neither is there any Method observed in Pleading."[42] Chilton's censures on the lack of knowledge among Virginians on how to draw original writs and his horror at county sheriffs making arrests without writs from the courts reveal that the level of sophistication in Virginia legal practice was lower than most lawyers thought permissible for the transaction of legal business.

In such an atmosphere, when a lawyer arrived from England, he had an open field and able opportunity to display his arrogance, a trait which seemed to characterize many General Court lawyers, as John Randolph recalled in 1734. Writing of the deaths of John Holloway and William Hopkins, Randolph reviewed Holloway's career. That lawyer arrived in Virginia in 1705 and settled in Williamsburg after an unsuccessful career in speculation had failed to increase his income, first augmented by his attorneyship at Marshalsea Court. Fleeing disaster, Holloway went "first to Maryland and afterwards hither." Randolph felt that Holloway's ability was rather poor in ejectment cases, particularly, and that the unscrupulous attorney continually drew notes up for special verdicts: "He would state naked Circumstances of Facts only, and leave to the Court to collect the Matter of Fact out of them; so that upon such Verdicts we have had many tedious Debates.... Against this I could never prevail." Nevertheless, Randolph concluded, "his reputation was such, that he was universally courted, and most People thought themselves obliged to him, if he would engage of their Side upon any Terms; and he really thought so himself. This gave him great Opportunities of exacting

41. Farish, ed., *Present State*, pp. 44–45. The work was not published until 1727.
42. Ibid., pp. 47–48.

excessive Fees.... It was impossible to be blind to [his] Imperfections. He died little lamented in the 69th year of his age."[43]

Of Hopkins, Randolph wrote that he "became a very ingenious Lawyer and a good Pleader," unlike Holloway, who "practised with much Artifice and Cunning, being thoroughly skilled in Attorneyship." But even Hopkins had a great "Desire of Dipping into al Kinds of Knowledge, wherein he had a great Deal of Vanity." Randolph mourned his passing, nevertheless, as "a Loss to this poor Country, which is not like to abound (at present at least) in Great Geniuses."[44]

Randolph's observation was surely shared by the governor, who came twice to Virginia between 1690 and 1705 and upon his second departure, left an even more embittered legacy of Court-Country hostility to his hapless successors. Francis Nicholson's contempt for homegrown legal abilities gradually emerged in the late 1690s and finally resulted in the recall petition of 1703, which summarized his tyrannical behavior and high-handedness by which "he endeavors mightily to make parties, and foment Divisions in the Country." As a judge of the General Court, Nicholson was accused of "gross & visible partiality in most cases of his friends or Enemies, abusing the Council at the barr, & often hectoring his fellow judges, if they happen to differ in opinion from him." Employing a favorite Country term, the petitioners scornfully noted that the governor "sends for his creatures from the Country & gives directions to the Sheriff to put them upon the Grand Jury and tampers with these Juries to procure flattering encomioums of himself.... He often makes particular entries contrary to the opinion of the rest of the Court, & in very abusive and reflecting terms."[45]

The vitriolic nature of the 1703 petition was due in part to an incident which probably involved the Harrison family. Benjamin, Sr., sat as a councillor during Nicholson's tenure and was the father of Benjamin, Jr., a Middle Templar and clerk to the Council, who was soon to become attorney general. The old attorney Bartholomew Fowler had assumed office in 1698, shortly before Nicholson arrived, but had resigned because of ill health and his own admitted lack of experience on September 4, 1700. After that date no formal appointment was forthcoming from the crown for a new attorney, but the young Harrison agreed to prose-

43. "Two Old Lawyers," in *Virginia Historical Register and Literary Advertiser* 1 (1848): 119–23. From John Randolph's Breviate Book, the original of which was apparently lost; this excerpt had been the property of George Wythe and was given to the Virginia Historical Society by John Page in 1834.
44. Ibid., p. 123.
45. "A Memoriall Concerning the Mal-administration of his Excelly Francis Nicholson, Esqr., Her Ma'ties Lieut. and Governour Generall of Virginia," *VMHB* 3 (1896): 374–80.

cute cases for the crown and to tender legal opinions to the Council. Nicholson's behavior, however, guaranteed that the Harrisons would turn against him, for "he values not how arbitrary & illegal his commands are. If the ordinary attorney for her ma'tie will not undertake his designs as being against Law he employs others that will." Here again, the implied threat of a corrupt Court manipulating a compliant profession was pointed out, but with reference to a specific incident. "Upon an Attorney General [almost surely Harrison, Jr.] declining one of his comands as being against Law, he took him by the collar & swore by God that he knew of no Laws we had & that his comands should be obeyed without hesitation or reserve."[46]

The young Harrison had resigned his post as clerk of the Council on June 12, 1700, to work full time on a general revisal of the laws. Nicholson must have expressed his contempt for the young lawyer's abilities to the Board of Trade, since those gentlemen wrote back in November 1702 that they recognized native legal talent to be inept and the business long and tedious but that Nicholson should nevertheless encourage the revisers. "But if there be absolute need that our Attorney General or any other such considerable Officer be sent from hence, you must in the first place take care that competent provision be made for their support and advise us of it; for it is not to be imagined that any man of Learning and parts fit for such employments will leave their Native Country without good assurance of such provision for them in America."[47]

By March 1703, Nicholson seemed to be hectoring Harrison for not being a "man of Learning and parts fit for such employments." Asked to deliver an opinion as to who could administer public oaths, Harrison reported that all public officers could swear people to their respective oaths, depending on the matters cognizable by the officer in question. Nicholson demanded a citation from the specific laws of England and Virginia that Harrison claimed to be relying on, an odd request from a man who had so often in the past indicated his disregard for Virginia statutes.[48]

---

46. Ibid., p. 379. On Harrison and Fowler, see *EJCV*, 1:397; ibid., 2:87, 105–6, 111, 304–5, 307.

47. Board of Trade to the Governor of Virginia, Nov. 4, 1702, *VMHB* 23 (1915):393. But as Shammas points out, in one previous letter at least, Nicholson (grudgingly?) admitted that Harrison was an able attorney. See Shammas, "Benjamin Harrison," p. 169, citing Nicholson to Board of Trade, Dec. 2, 1701, PRO: CO 5/1312, fol. 19.

48. *EJCV*, 2:304–5, 307. Nicholson had managed to alienate both Divinity and Law from his cause due to his infatuation with Lucy Burwell. The senior Harrison's daughter was married to Commissary Blair, and Blair and the Harrisons were on good terms with the

Undoubtedly it was Nicholson's high-handed ways that inspired the son of the deposed clerk-attorney Robert Beverley to maintain anonymity when he published *An Essay upon the Government of the English Plantations on the Continent of America* in 1701. The Country flavor of the essay "By an American" was especially pointed in Beverley's cautions against a too powerful governor who might easily corrupt the administration of justice. Virginia's judiciary, the essay argued, was alarmingly weak because there were no independent judges who were able to tell where English law took precedence or where colonial practice was to be favored. Beverley, who joined in the censures of Nicholson in this essay, signed an affadavit to the Council's memorial in 1703, and in 1705 censured Court policies in his *History and Present State of Virginia*, was echoing the concerns of Nicholson's Council. Besides Harrison, the wealthy but remarkably sober Robert Carter censured Nicholson, joined by Commissary James Blair and Philip Ludwell, the son of the old Greenspring agitator. None of these men was truly trained in the law, nor were Mathew Page and John Lightfoot, though the latter had been nominated for the post of attorney general in 1670. Beverley joined James Wallace, James Moody, George Luke, and the Reverend Stephen Fouace in signing the affadavits against Nicholson.[49]

There were many grounds for complaint, but surely one of them, as Beverley remarked in his essay,[50] was that because of the absence of

---

Burwells and the Reverend Stephen Fouace, minister to that family. For details, see R. L. Morton, *Colonial Virginia*, 1:376–92.

49. *VMHB* 3 (1896): 414; Williams, "Anglo-Virginia Politics."

50. Louis Wright believes that the author was Beverley or William Byrd II. Virginia White Fitz, "Ralph Wormeley," pp. 586–95, argues against Beverley's authorship, asserting that he had been nothing but a clerk by 1700; that the man who wrote the essay was in poor health, while we know of no sickness afflicting Beverley; and that the author was a well-educated Whig in political matters who exhibited respect for Nicholson. Given the context of the essay, Nicholson's treatment of the Council and the General Court, and his powerful influence at home, it seems doubtful that the author of the essay believed much would have been gained by making a personal attack on Nicholson. Beverley's legal training under his father gave him ample access to Whig political views, legal expertise, and friendship with the Harrisons. Use of government records would not have been difficult. Wormeley's authorship is still a real possibility. I disagree with White's analysis of the *History*, which she claims contains no objective, analytical content. With due regard for the very different purposes and audiences toward which each piece was directed, I suggest that the style and tenor of argument in both is, in fact, remarkably similar. Shammas argues for Benjamin Harrison's authorship in her article "Benjamin Harrison." I certainly concur with Shammas that Harrison had ample reason to desire a better court system. Despite Harrison's difficulties with Nicholson (see below), I remain convinced of Beverley's authorship, though Harrison would be my own second choice for the composer of the essay.

independent judges of learning, "we are too often obliged to depend upon the Crooked Cord of a Judge's Discretion, in Matters of the greatest Moment and Value." The most urgent remedies proposed by the essay concerned the removal of the judiciary from the governor's prerogative, a point urged again and again. Beverley argued that in each colony the supreme court of judicature should be established on the basis of *quam diu se bene gesserint* (good behavior) rather than at the pleasure of the crown and governor (*durante bene placito*). Those ideas were interspersed with warnings about "placemen" and corrupt governors who, Beverley felt, would never seek further preferment in England through virtuous administration unless the crown itself took the necessary steps to enforce the needed reforms.[51]

The consistent hallmark of the Country was stamped on the essay by its firm argument for an independent judiciary. Yet the author made no plea for a "professional" cadre of judges and lawyers, set apart from the rest of society. Like so many Country apologists, Beverley's concern was oriented less toward the lack of procedurally sophisticated law (though he did lament that, too) and more toward demands for strict enforcement of laws against blasphemy, swearing, profaneness, cursing, and Sabbath breaking. Only a virtuous (i.e., Country) judiciary could secure enforcement of these laws and the peace of Virginia, and such judges would not come, in Beverley's opinion, from the ranks of Virginia's governors and councillors.

Beverley's choice of anonymity was prudent as he broached this last point. Hostility to Governor Nicholson gave Beverley's essay an added degree of meaning for Virginians, who by 1703 attempted to remove the General Court judgeships from the control of the governor and to place them instead in the persons of independent judges to be appointed for prescribed periods of office. Before the issue could be argued in full, the Board of Trade killed the notion.

The issue of independent judges was not confined to the General Court magistrates. In 1705 a new governor, Edward Nott, set about a plan to demonstrate his prerogative by appointing justices of the peace himself, which under the laws of the colony he was entitled to do. The Burwell-Ludwell factions in both House and Council, however, opposed him on this point, insisting in a new bill that five councillors had to concur in appointments to the county benches. Nott bowed to the advice of his superiors in London, who upheld his undoubted right to appoint justices but suggested that a wise governor always heeded the opinions of his

51. Wright, ed., *Essay*, pp. 23, 39–40, 50, 52–53.

councillors. Since no assemblies were held between 1705 and 1710, some people were perhaps lulled into thinking that the issue was settled. It was not.[52]

When Hugh Jones wrote his *Present State of Virginia* in 1724, the issue of judges, justices, and lawyers was still a hot topic and had been at the center of controversy since the arrival of Alexander Spotswood as the governor of Virginia in 1710. Jones delicately opined that for promulgation of religious values and enforcement of the laws against vice the county courts should be relied on, for "the people hate the very name of the bishop's court," and the Country had to be assured that "here would be no innovation in the proceedings." Trade patterns had established London speech, London manners, and London habits of sophistication in Williamsburg, Jones noted. But the British should note, he warned, that the planters, while "apt to learn, yet . . . are fond of, and will follow their own ways, humours, and notions, being not easily brought to new projects and schemes." Spotswood had to learn that unpleasant truth the hard way, especially in regard to the Country's hostility to Court control of justices, judges, and lawyers.[53]

For the first three years of his administration, Spotswood appeared to be consolidating successfully the legal culture of Virginia under a centrally controlled, anglicized plan administered by himself. In 1710 the new Assembly passed a law that formally erected the county courts on lines that they would have for the next sixty years. The duties, powers, and obligations of the justices were outlined, summarizing the evolution of this vital institution in the counties of Virginia. Spotswood noted with approval the 1705 law that had set up the General Court and defined its duties for the eighteenth century, and he moved to improve upon another 1705 statute which had specified the procedures for "called courts," where county justices examined suspected felons before sending them to Williamsburg for trial. By proclamation in 1710, Spotswood guaranteed the writ of *habeas corpus* to all nonfelony prisoners and for all nontreasonable offenses. In 1711 the governor further consolidated the queen's power and presence in all Virginia by engineering an order in the Council on June 13 which provided for deputy queen's attorneys in all county courts to prosecute the interests of the crown, the deputies to be "such Practitioners in the Law attending the several County Courts (where the Attorney Genll. cannot be present) as the Governor shall

---

52. On anti-Nicholson feeling and the events surrounding the debate over judges, see Rankin, *Criminal Trial Proceedings*, pp. 20–22. On the controversy with Nott, see Williams, "Political Alignments," pp. 81–82, where he discusses the fears among county residents of a fledgling "governor's party."

53. Jones, *Present State of Virginia*, pp. 112, 118, 121–22, 20, 21.

think fitt." Responding to instructions from home, Spotswood extended the sitting of the General Court beyond its usual two terms in April and November. In addition, the governor and councillors from henceforth sat in June and December as a Court of Oyer and Terminer, to speed up processes and prevent prisoners from languishing in the public gaol in Williamsburg. Taken as a whole, Spotswood's performance seemed to augur well for a more streamlined judicial establishment in Virginia. Yet confrontation and crisis were the hallmarks by which Virginians remembered his administration.[54]

Modest events sometimes signal, even if they do not immediately cause, more momentous consequences. Spotswood's signal to his critics was a warning to the county courts in 1710. To the local gentry, Spotswood sent the notice "I have received Complaints of great delays in the administration of Justice through the County Courts' Neglecting to meet on the days appointed for holding the Same & the Justices refusing upon frivolous pretences to Sitt when Mett." The governor ordered sheriffs to notify him of courts not held and of the justices not sitting and to inform him of their excuses. Causes were to be docketed and those pending for over six months forwarded to the General Court for scrutiny. Such eminently sensible regulations did not sit well with the gentry of the Country, and the gentlemen made known their displeasure with the Court's interference in their affairs in a controversy that began, not over the law, but over the regulation of tobacco.[55]

The governor probably thought, in all sincerity, that his proposals in support of the 1713 tobacco act would improve Virginia's export commodity, raise the price obtained in England, and, at the same time, prevent people in the colony from paying public debts with trash tobacco. Under the governor's program the tobacco agent who examined the crop gave each man a certificate, surrendered the inspected tobacco for immediate shipment, and posted a bond of two thousand pounds for his job. Fees and a prorated salary of five shillings per hogshead or 8 percent of tobacco handled brought the agent a handsome revenue of two hundred and fifty pounds, and since officials were appointed by the governor, the Country immediately cried "patronage" and "corruption." So bitter was the criticism of the new measure that when elections had to be called at the death of Queen Anne in 1714 only sixteen of the fifty-one incumbent burgesses survived the wrath of the Country. The new Assembly was

54. This account of the Spotswood years differs only in certain particulars from Dodson, *Alexander Spotswood*; Dowdey, *Virginia Dynasties*. On the streamlining of procedure, see *EJCV*, 3:276; Hening, 3:287–302, 389–92, 504–16; Rankin, *Criminal Trial Proceedings*, pp. 25–36; *EJCV*, 3:255.

55. York County Orders, May 21, 1711.

elected to oppose the governor and his schemes, and by 1718 the tobacco law was dead. But that confrontation was merely the opening salvo of a war between Court and Country, which quickly turned to the old issues of judges, justices, and lawyers, and their places in the legal culture of Virginia.[56]

Spotswood had actually removed one justice, Nicholas Meriwether of New Kent, for stirring up the people against the tobacco law. Petitions flooded into Williamsburg against the new law in 1714–15, but were rejected. Convinced that it had a mandate to oppose the governor and to rule Virginia, the new Assembly very nearly ended in alienating not only governor and Council but the local county gentry as well. So much confusion and so many charges and countercharges swirled about governor, House, and Council between 1714 and 1719 that the lines of battle still look confused today. The important consequence, however, was clear: by 1719 the local gentry had clearly demonstrated that no one—not the governor, the Council, or even the House—had the right to dictate to them in their capacity as gentlemen justices of the peace.

The local justices were attacked by the new House in 1714 because many of the elections had been contested, and no doubt accusations were exchanged about whether the burgesses elected were of the "Country" or the "governor's party." No simple identification links those members of the gentry who were attacked by the House. George Marable of James City, an old opponent of Spotswood, was left out of the commission in 1712 for "misbehaving." George Eskridge, attacked by John Cottrell, had formerly been assigned a headright by this man, his neighbor, in Northumberland, and their quarrel may have been the result of nothing more than petty local jealousy. Leonidas Dodson has theorized that the local justices were on the side of the governor because they were his appointees, but this seems unlikely. In fact, the local justices were as annoyed with high-handed behavior on the part of the House in reprimanding local authorities as they were with the governor's laws. Unexpectedly, they soon received help from the governor himself.[57]

In 1715 the House was reprimanded by the Council and governor for pursuing local justices who contravened the burgesses' instructions by refusing to send up whatever propositions and grievances local citizens decided to proffer to the Assembly. In a strange and decidedly

---

56. On the tobacco law provisions and resulting controversy, see Hemphill, "Virginia and the English Commercial System," chapters 2 and 3 and pp. 152–57; Dodson, *Alexander Spotswood*, pp. 50–55, 117–27.

57. Dodson, *Alexander Spotswood*, pp. 117–20, discusses the old rivalries between the governor and some House members. Marable's name was ordered dropped from the Commission of the Peace in 1712. *EJCV*, 3:316.

un-Country fashion the House insisted that justices had to send up everything that residents presented to them. Governor and Council were annoyed because the House began considering the grievances that were coming in without consulting the executive and his advisers. Siding with the justices, Spotswood pointed out that the local magistrates were not mere tools of the House and that historically their office included the obligation to use discretion in certifying or rejecting grievances that were presented. The Council agreed with this point and reprimanded the House for its pretensions and failure to support Spotswood when he asked for money to defend the frontiers.

By 1716 the governor and Council thought that they could discern the reason for the burgesses' insistence that all grievances be presented to them, and to them alone. According to the Council the petitions against tobacco agents and the government's frontier policies and protests against Spotswood's insistence that heretofore concealed lands be evaluated and tithes collected on them were receiving an added potency because of the machinations of an insidious group. The Council pointed out in September 1715 that propositions and grievances were indeed being sent up without certification by the justices of the peace. Far from representing the sober opinions of the yeomanry and planters, as the House pretended, the petitions were in fact the work of "divers persons" who had presumed "to practice as Attorneys in the Courts of this Colony without being qualifyed with a sufficient knowledge in the Laws . . . & by their evil practices amongst the ignorant & illiterate people . . . in order to persuade the Vulgar into an opinion of their Capacity as well to direct the State in making new laws as to Interpret the old . . . have taken upon them to frame Scandalous & Seditious papers under the Title of Grievances to this Assembly; & by their insinuations procured thereto the Subscriptions of diverse unwary people." To prevent such disruptions the Council ordered the justices to take notice that no one was allowed to practice law unless he was approved of by the governor and Council and the justices themselves. The old issue of lawyers, justices, and the Country persuasion was back at the heart of Virginia's public concerns, largely because no effective law controlled persons who wished to earn their livings as lawyers.[58]

Between 1690 and 1716, however, legal business had had to be done, not only for Virginians, but for merchants abroad as well. While the letter of proxy remained in use throughout that period and well beyond

---

58. Dodson, *Alexander Spotswood*, pp. 127–31; *EJCV*, 3:411. Unfortunately, though Bailey, in *Popular Influences* (p. 55), points out Spotswood's subsequent intemperate speech against petitions promoted by attorneys, he sheds no light on the nature of these petitioners.

1750, some men did in fact earn their livings as lawyers. Until 1716, Spotswood had not made any attempt to control the process by which lawyers were to come forward for examination prior to practicing. The September order in Council, however, prodded at least two attorneys, Henry Holdcraft and Godfrey Pole, to submit petitions to the governor, noting "your Hono'rs Order Whereby all persons are forbidden the practise of the Law as Attorneys untill they obtain your Hono'rs Approbation." Holdcraft nervously pointed out that he had been serving as king's attorney in James City and New Kent, "and for that your Petitioner hath a large Family & little besides his practise to maintain them, Your Petitioner humbly begs your Hono'rs will approve of your petitioner to practise as formerly." Perhaps Holdcraft thought that his James City connection would ally him in the governor's mind with George Marable. He need not have worried; both he and the recently arrived Pole were approved by the Council.[59]

In December 1715 the Council decided that a law should be drawn up that would provide for licensing of lawyers in the future. According to the proposed law a prospective attorney would have to prove sufficient knowledge of the laws of England and Virginia to the Council, swear loyalty to the crown, and present a testimony from the local justices of his decent behavior and living. Attorney General John Clayton, attorney John Holloway, and the old Country skeptic Robert Beverley were to draw up the oath, and these three were to constitute the examining board before which lawyers would appear. However, the noble idea came to naught. In May 1716 the committee's opinion was referred to a full council meeting and died. No regulation of lawyers was forthcoming, and nothing was done about forcing justices to attend their courts or sheriffs to collect quitrents and tithes on hidden lands. Instead of a law regulating lawyers, the governor and Council had to settle in 1718 for a modest bill setting fees for county lawyers at 15 shillings of 150 pounds of tobacco and for General Court practitioners at 50 shillings or 500 pounds.

In 1715 the governor had tried to show himself a friend of the Country by ordering that the form of the Commissions of the Peace be altered for the future. Before that date the justices had received their commissions in the governor's name. From henceforth, after his name the words "By virtue of the power & authority to me given as Commander in Chief of this His Majesty's Colony & Dominion" were to be inserted. Spotswood had dissolved the House of Burgesses in late 1715 after delivering a withering speech in which he practically accused the arrogant House of

59. "Miscellaneous Colonial Documents," *VMHB* 17 (1909): 147–52.

conspiring against the dignity of government by promoting "the Giddy Resolves of the illiterate Vulgar in their Drunken Conventions." The Council had sided with the governor up to this point, noting their disapproval of House conduct right before censuring the "vulgar" attorneys. But Spotswood had overreached himself in hectoring and then dissolving the House, and his allies in the Council and what friends he had made in the counties by defending the justices now deserted him.[60]

Spotswood tried to consolidate his position with the Country by circulating a petition to the justices of the county courts noting that since the House had denied the discretionary, judicial nature of the office of the justices, the burgesses could not therefore expect the county courts to exercise a legislative function and levy taxes for burgess salaries. The governor proposed to bring this issue into the General Court and was dismayed when the Council begged off, pointing out that they would have to sit as judges and could therefore not advise him on the matter. The issue was never raised, for Spotswood discovered that Country opposition thinking had infected his Council as well as the county courts. Reconvened in 1718, the burgesses prudently sniffed the wind from the Country and allied themselves with the local justices by passing a bill giving the courts the power to suspend county clerks. The clerks were under the patronage power of the secretary of the colony, but the power to suspend them was the governor's, and Spotswood beat back this attack from the House. His real concern by 1718, however, was the Council, because those gentlemen who sat with him had finally broken with his policies on the issue of courts, judges, and an independent judiciary.[61]

The controversy over the Courts of Oyer and Terminer is generally well known, and only the bare facts need be reviewed here. What is

---

60. *EJCV*, 3:419, 420, 425–26; Hening, 4:59. Dodson discusses the governor's intemperate speech to the House in *Alexander Spotswood*, pp. 129–31. See also *JVHB*, pp. 166–70.

61. *EJCV*, 3:413. See R. L. Morton, *Colonial Virginia*, 2:455–62, on the truculence of the burgesses, their refusal of a postmaster general of America, Spotswood's veto of their bill forbidding such a post, and the House's attempt to give justices the power to suspend their clerks. Clerks for the county courts were trained in the colony secretary's office, at their own expense, under bond, and for seven years received no compensation. At the end of their tenure, the clerk of the General Court, who actually took care of the details of the secretary's office, passed on their ability, and they were then placed in a county post or continued under the General Court clerk for wages. Many of the clerks became practicing attorneys in courts other than the ones in which they were clerks, and even those who never practiced often trained young men in the counties who wished to become attorneys. See Heaton, "Littleton Waller Tazewell's Sketch," pp. 61–64 and 129–35 on his grandfather Benjamin Waller, who began his luminous career under the patronage of Secretary John Carter.

significant, and not as generally recognized, is the impact Country rhetoric had on men whose true loyalties were only vaguely similar to those of the lesser gentry of the counties. When Spotswood claimed that he could appoint anyone he chose to sit on the oyer and terminer sessions of the court in Williamsburg, the Council disagreed; only councillors were allowed to sit, for both General and Oyer and Terminer courts owed their existence to the councillors who were judges there. The governor and the councillors sent representatives to London to defend themselves against opposing charges.

The Council's representative, William Byrd II, writing to his superiors, the Ludwell faction of the Council, revealed just how much the eminent gentry of Virginia who sat in Williamsburg dreamed of being the aristoi of that colony and how much they dreaded to be thought Courtiers because of their ambition. When Colonel Edmund Jenings continued to serve on the Court and failed to sign the Council's remonstrance against Spotswood, Byrd struck out at him, snidely labeling him a Court toady by referring to "that mean sycophant Col. Heartless the only counciller that woud set in the court of O[yer] and T[erminer] in that linsey woolsey commission. He is a worm fit only to be trod upon, a spaniel to be beat into any compliance." Byrd's use of Country terms was somewhat ingenuous, however, for in the same letter he proposed his plan by which the Council would be maintained as a "Supream Court of Chancery, for which they were to retain their salary of three hundred and fifty pounds a year." The possibility that such a court might be dominated by the governor kept Byrd from referring the plan to the Council of Trade, even though Lord Chief Justice Sir Thomas Parker approved of the idea. Byrd's reluctance to press the issue stemmed not so much from any Country notions about the value of an independent judiciary as from his realization that the Council was opposed to losing the perquisites of office in the General Court. Byrd explained that he would not oppose the Council but could not help but comment "upon the absurdity of mens judging of matters of law which they did not understand, which every body knows is the case of most of us councellours." Byrd's Court attitudes revealed themselves also in his explanation that he only thought to keep money in Virginian hands by paying judges with quitrents and that his deep-seated hope was "that it would encourage gentlemen to breed up their sons to the study of the law, in hopes of arriveing at such profitable employments."[62]

62. On the oyer and terminer controversy, see Dowdey, *Virginia Dynasties*, pp. 249–68; Dodson, *Alexander Spotswood*, pp. 170–73; R. L. Morton, *Colonial Virginia*, 2:469–75; Byrd to Philip Ludwell about Jenings, Sept. 24, 1717, *Correspondence*, pp. 304–5.

Despite Byrd's predilection for London society and his hopes that Virginia would develop a more cosmopolitan character and breed its own sons to the law, the controversy over the Courts of Oyer and Terminer did little to change the nature of the law and the courts in Virginia and even less to foster the growth of a genuine legal profession. By 1720, Spotswood had been vindicated when the home government upheld his right to appoint anyone he wished to the court. But the governor had learned his lesson from this fight and magnanimously assured the Council that only they would be judges in future. Spotswood's realization of what had occurred was indicated in his letter home when he wrote "all private Resentments are Abolished . . . and no more Invidious Distinctions left of Governor's and Country's Partys."[63]

Spotswood had failed to ally the local justices with him against the House, and the Council had won a victory of sorts in forcing him to bow toward its own appropriation of Country opposition rhetoric. But the real winners in all of this were the local justices of the peace, who had proved that the shires were immune from domination by House, Council, or governor. From henceforth, whenever the tune of Country sentiment was piped, the entire colony danced to the independent airs of the county gentlemen.

In 1729, Virginia finally obtained a governor who understood the cultural milieu into which he was expected to fit. Sir William Gooch shrewdly divined the nature of Virginia's legal culture and, in seeking support for his first important piece of legislation—the Tobacco Act of 1730—cast his fortune and his identity with the Country, assuming the nom de plume of "Justice Love-Country," a choice of name that was hardly accidental. In the 1720s, Gooch learned, Country courts of justice were self-perpetuating institutions free of central control and absolutely dominant in county life. Lawyers were unlicensed, relatively scarce, and unneeded in the counties where gentlemen looked after each others' legal affairs. Justices presided over courts that passed father to son, uncle to nephew, in a succession that publicly informed the county of the rank of the sitting justices of the peace.

The law in the Country was patriarchal and perhaps not exactly what Fitzhugh had had in mind when he wrote of Virginia's need to emulate England in building up the colony's legal culture. Country law was not illiterate law; yet the law rested not only on the printed knowledge gleaned from manuals, statute books, and opinions but also on years of experience learning what it meant to be a junior justice in the Commis-

---

63. Spotswood to Secretary Craggs, May 20, 1720, *Official Letters of Alexander Spotswood*, 2:341.

sion of the Peace. In contrast with the formal, learned, and technical law advocated by Court lawyers in Williamsburg, the monthly meetings of the local courts in Tidewater Virginia during the eighteenth century were characterized by a kind of drama that confirmed the notion that, indeed, "the law was different in the country."

Chapter 3
Court Day and Its Critics, 1720–1750

The law is different in the country.
—HENRY FIELDING, Squire Western in *Tom Jones*

Despite the fact that lawyers, justices, and the law became entangled in politics between 1680 and 1720, Court and Country cultures made those politics inevitable, and were not the result of them. To get behind the political controversies of Virginia's public life, to understand what made Court and Country vivid experiences and not mere rhetorical expressions for Virginians, requires a close look at the law in action.[1] In 1745 a correspondent wrote the editor of the *Virginia Gazette* that "Law is a dead Letter, and lives only in the due Administration thereof."[2]

What the law was and how it was to be administered, according to what principles and to the understanding of which officers, was the heart of the debate between Country justices and Court lawyers. Probably at no time was every justice wholly persuaded of the superiority of the county courts' procedures and traditions. Certainly, some lawyers recognized that better procedural techniques and more elaborate pleadings did not always result in better justice. But when one compares the actions of court day in the Country with the proposals, arguments, and complaints of the lawyers of the period, one discovers a distinct sense of two very different worlds, which contemporaries referred to as Court and Country. Court and Country constituted different modes of perceiving the world, and hence the law.

Local Law and Social Standards

Virginians of the mid-eighteenth century lived in a world that was both formal and familiar. The tension produced by exchanges between formal and familiar styles enabled the propertied, patriarchal gentlemen justices of the peace and the county residents over whose legal affairs they presided

---

1. Part of this chapter appeared in article form as Roeber, "Authority, Law, and Custom."
2. *Virginia Gazette*, Oct. 3–10, 1745.

once a month, every month, to define social rank, mutual obligation, and shared values. To do this the law itself had to share the formal and familiar qualities of Virginia life. Clearly, power and authority belonged to the propertied, and the body of rules that was Virginia law constituted the dimensions and boundaries of conduct, obligation, and order. The authoritative and customary institutions that the Old Dominion had inherited from England were celebrated in public statements such as the one Sir William Gooch made to the General Court grand jurors in 1730. Informing them that they should see to the safety of their community, Gooch reminded the jurors that ancient procedures and laws were only as good as the "execution of them, is *punctual* and *exact*."[3]

Virginians concurred. A writer to the *Virginia Gazette* argued for the regular enforcement of law, since "the Laws of *England* are our best Inheritance, the Ties of harmonious Society, and Defence of Life, Liberty, and Property. . . . *English* Law (from Antiquity not to be traced) hath preserved it's Purity, and Certainty," and "this Purity, and Certainty of Law, hath been transmitted to us."[4] Virginians participated in discovering the meaning of law—ancient, formal, but customary. The degree of participation varied, depending on their social distance from the authorities who dominated the center of power that was the courthouse. In a semiliterate society, it was not in printed opinions of authors but in ritual actions, in the face-to-face, familiar meetings in the courthouse, that the reality of law unfolded in a formal setting modulated by routine and repetition.[5]

The key that unlocks the meaning of court day is *action*—action that proceeded as a kind of dramatic play, whose setting we can reconstruct from contemporary records. Certain "acts" in this cultural pageant are especially worthy of our attention, for they informed Virginians where they stood in society, what obligations they had to social superiors and

---

3. "A Charge to the Grand Jury," in Wroth, *William Parks*, p. 33.

4. *Virginia Gazette*, Oct. 3–10, 1745. Virginians like William Beale appealed to antiquity and custom in the local courts even in defiance of English custom and common law prohibitions. See Richmond County Orders, June 4, 1739, in which Beale defended his right to stop up a public way, "setting forth that he and his ancestors here for a Long time Enjoyed the conveniency of keeping gates upon the severall roads Leading through his land without which he could not have the benefit of a pasture."

5. The concepts and analysis in this chapter depend heavily on Geertz, *Interpretations of Cultures*, pp. 3–32, and "Centers, Kings, and Charisma." On ritual action in a world of oral communication, see Ong, *Presence of the Word* and *Interfaces of the Word*. On the literacy rate in Virginia, see Lockridge, *Literacy*, pp. 77–78, 90, 93, who argues that at best two-thirds of able-bodied white males may have been literate in Virginia; after 1750 the increase in the rate may have begun to stagnate. On personal meetings in an oral culture, see Goffman, *Presentation of Self*, *Behavior in Public Places*, and *Interaction Ritual*.

inferiors, and what constituted the accepted norms of social conduct. Those norms were defined not merely by authority and power but by communal sanction. The oath of the justice told the county that he must "do equal right, to the poor, and to the rich," and do so with "cunning, wit" (that is, intelligence and skill), and "power." As the Virginia correspondent to the *Gazette* observed, law lives only in its administration, and it is particularly in four select but similar patterns of action that we begin to glimpse the interplay of authority and custom within the theater of court day. The acts to watch are (1) contempt of court, (2) settlement of debt cases, (3) the meeting of the grand jury, and (4) the use of the court by the nonpropertied. In these four acts we see mirrored the justices' attempts to "do equal right to all manner of people, great and small, high and low, rich and poor ... without favour, affection, or partiality," and according to their rank and station.[6]

The principals of the drama, in which the entire county played a part, were His Majesty's gentlemen justices, the planters who had risen from humble and fractious seventeenth-century antecedents and who by the 1720s were secure in their rank and claim to deference. Familial pedigrees had for the most part been established a generation or two earlier. The justices included both elite magnates and lesser squireens, allied by marriage, who as a rule handed down their seats from father to son, from uncle to nephew.[7]

6. Hening, 3:508–9. The method used quantifies the most numerous types of action in twelve Tidewater county courts, analyzing such actions as symbolic, ritualized summations of key cultural concepts such as deference, hierarchy, dependence, and property. On action as text, see Ricoeur, "Model of the Text"; Merton, "Unanticipated Consequences"; Schutz, "Concept and Theory Formation" and "Common-Sense and Scientific Interpretation." The twelve counties analyzed here are York, Henrico, Warwick, Charles City, Middlesex, Essex, Caroline, Lancaster, Richmond, Westmoreland, King George, and Northumberland.

7. Inventories of justices at death, sampled for the various counties, reveal a wide range of wealth, but every member's personal wealth was counted in hundreds of pounds, current money. Courts were kept running by groups of faithful magistrates, for example, three Randolph brothers in Henrico and Taylors, Taliaferros, and Buckners in Caroline. Great magnates sat irregularly: the Corbin, Beverley, and Baylor families in Caroline were allied by marriage to the above named faithful magistrates, but sat infrequently. The same was true of the Carters and Byrds in their counties, with the exception of the highly conscientious Landon Carter in Richmond. On Caroline, see Campbell, *Colonial Caroline*, p. 349. Campbell found no justice who owned fewer than one thousand acres. Family connection and tradition, however, were just as important. In York, Thomas Barber, whose family had served on the bench since the 1650s, refused to sit, and the court ordered the sheriff to go and plead with him. When he died, his total inventory was only £105 10s. York Orders, Mar. 19, 1710/11, May 18, 1713. Barber's fellow justice Robert Reade owned twenty-two slaves and two indentured mulattoes, with other chattels. York Orders, May 18, 1713. King George justice William Strother's personal estate was valued at £858 19s. 3½d. King George Inventories, 1721–44. At the other end of the spectrum were men like Augustine

The act of passing on a seat to a junior member of the family also meant that the public rank of the assembled bench was visibly proclaimed, according not only to the degree of propertied wealth possessed but to age as well. The rank of the justices was immediately obvious, since the Commission of the Peace named the senior justices of the Quorum first. Quorum justices were regarded as more learned in the law than their associates because of their experience; the counties came to rely on them as customary leaders. These stalwarts were essential to the functioning of the court: at least one of them had to be present for a lawful court to sit. Deference to the grey locks of the colony's patriarchy encouraged the courts to press the governor into appointing even aged men like Francis Thornton, who had refused one commission already, "alledging that he was Sickly and uncapable," and Leonard Hill, who declined "because he is now antient & thinks himself uncapable." Lancaster County mourned the loss of Edwin Conway in 1752 when he refused to sit after serving forty years. The seventy-one-year-old justice retired "for that his Sense of hearing is much impaired and he is far advanced in Years." As late as 1787, Essex County pointed out to the governor the necessity of nominating two mature men, even though the loyalty of one of them to the Revolution had been questionable. Since John Upshur and James Edmondston could no longer sit, the next two most experienced justices were essential because "they . . . as senior magistrates would keep more Order and decorum in Court."[8]

Property, family, and experience were important, but literacy in a largely aural culture also set the bench apart from the county folk. Yet both the unlearned folk and the learned gentry had a common cultural experience. From the fragmentary literary remains of the gentry one senses that literacy was coupled in their minds with familiar wisdom. Since barristers, attorneys-at-law, and even attorneys of fact who were not also gentlemen were scarce in Virginia before 1750, the gentlemen justices took a peculiar

---

Washington, whose personal inventory in the King George Inventories read: July 1, 1743, £824 8s. 3d., including twenty-seven slaves and surveyor's instruments in that county; in Westmoreland, June 28, 1743, £409 10s. 8d.; and in Stafford, £287 8s. Washington's rank would have been comparable to that of James Burwell of York, whose inventory totaled forty-two slaves and other servants, as well as a personal estate worth £2,386 18s. 10d. York Orders, Mar. 16, 1718.

8. On the value of older men, see Fischer, *Growing Old in America*, and his disagreements with Lawrence Stone in "Growing Old: An Exchange." See also Stone, *Family, Sex and Marriage*, pp. 58–60, 403–4, 125–218. For the Virginia examples cited, see York Orders, July 21, Aug. 19, 1719; on Conway, see Lancaster Orders, June 19, 1752, and Hayden, *Virginia Genealogies*, pp. 238–44; on Essex, see justices to Gov. Randolph, Mar. 27, 1788, VCSP, 4:417–19.

pride in their literate, if homely, legal ability. As one planter observed, "It is a shame for a gentleman to be ignorant of the laws of his country and to be dependent on every dirty pettifogger," but highly "commendable . . . for a gentleman of independent means, not only [not] to stand in need of mercenary advisers, but to be able to advise his friends, relations, and neighbors of all sorts." Justice Landon Carter aptly defined the proper use of literate knowledge when a lawyer accused him of not knowing how to bring a suit to trial. The feisty colonel retorted that "it pleased me to find a Gentleman Pique himself on a little Mechanical knowledge. . . . Attorneys were always lookt upon as so many Copyers and their Knowledge only lay in knowing from whom to Copy properly."[9]

Such an attitude helps to explain the lack of a licensing law for attorneys in Virginia from 1690 to 1732. The rarity of these professionals even after that latter date until 1750 enabled the justices both to sustain their singular authority and to deal in direct, familiar terms with the people and the cases before them whether civil or petty criminal causes. As the eighteenth century dawned, the county court enforced a host of statutes purposefully broadly drawn to give the justices wide-ranging discretionary powers over nearly every aspect of local life.[10]

Court day began with a summons to the assembled crowd. Standing in the door of the courthouse, the deputy clerk or undersheriff issued an archaic bidding that coupled the formal, authoritative bench—the locus from which power emanated—with the familiar gatherings on the piazza, on the green, in the nearby ordinary: "Oyez, Oyez, Oyez, silence is commanded in the court while his Majesties Justices are sitting, upon paine of imprisonment. All manner of persons that have any thing to doe at this court draw neer and give your attendance and if any one have any plaint to enter or suite to prosecute lett them come forth and they shall be

---

9. Charles Carroll of Doughregan Manor to Charles Carroll of Carrollton, Oct. 16, 1759, *Unpublished Letters*, pp. 33–34; quoted in Davis, *Intellectual Life in the Colonial South*, 3:1588; Greene, ed., *Diary of Landon Carter*, pp. 92–93.

10. My survey of called courts for the period 1730–50 reveals that Caroline held twenty-one examinations resulting in only nine people being sent to Williamsburg, on charges of horse stealing, breaking and entering, and theft. The remainder were found not guilty or were summarily punished (at times at their own request) or bound over to the grand jury session to await a bill of indictment. Likewise, in King George County, thirty examinations sent eighteen culprits to Williamsburg, primarily for burglary but also for murder, forgery, and accidental shooting. Twenty-five were whipped, fined, found not guilty, or remanded to the grand jury on a lesser charge. In York, twenty-four sessions examined twenty-nine people, sent fifteen to Williamsburg for theft and murder, one for forgery, one unspecified, and dealt with another dozen in the county. Slave trials under the commission of oyer and terminer were consistently fewer in number in all counties than called courts. See below.

heard. God Save the King." By this means were all bidden to "draw neer" to those gentlemen justices who sat with tricorns on their wigs before the uncovered ranks of society.[11]

The dramaturgy of this opening spectacle was not less effective for being humbler than its counterpart in England or, for that matter, in the General Court of the colony. There was no preliminary sermon, no formal procession from parish church to shire hall, no parade of judicial gowns or gold-laced coats, no tipstaffs leading the way. Yet justices in Virginia could expect the deference due them as "beings of a superior order," in the words of Devereux Jarratt, who recalled from boyhood that "when I saw a man riding the road, near our house, with a wig on . . . I would run off." In those times, he believed, "such ideas of the difference between *gentle* and *simple* were . . . universal among all of my rank and age." The vivid visual symbols of propertied "quality" were awesome—even frightening—outside the context of court day. Within the setting of the courtroom county folk heard the well-defined rules according to which justice was to be done in return for their deference. The oath sworn by each justice in order of seniority defined and limited authority's obligations in public, oral fashion. No magistrate was permitted to serve as counsel in a cause before him unless a man needed representation and could not afford an attorney; all proceedings, whether taken before one justice or before the whole bench, would be public and recorded—print culture would operate for the simple as well as for the gentle; and no justice was allowed any "fee, gift, or gratuity, for any thing to be done by virtue of [his] office." The rule-making quality of law limited the otherwise illimitable power of the gentlemen justices but demanded deference from the ruled, while assuring them of familiar and regular administration of the law, applied with "cunning, wit, and power."[12]

As we examine the ritual actions of court day, we must place ourselves upon the set or stage where the drama took place. The courthouse was located at a crossroads near the center of the county, on a green with a tavern or ordinary close at hand. By the 1720s the old wooden frame courthouses were giving way to new buildings that were the boasts of the shires. Most of the new Tidewater courthouses were patterned after models first developed at the colonial capital in Williamsburg. A Virgin-

---

11. The "stile" for calling the court is in Hening, 2:59–60, 72. Forms used for swearing jurors and officers and those cited herein for the conducting of business are drawn from one of the most common manuals of the day, *The Office of the Clerk of Assize*. Colonial courts adapted such treatises to local conditions. See Parker's *Conductor Generalis*, modeled on Burn's *Justice of the Peace*.

12. *Life of Devereux Jarratt*, p. 14. On General Court ritual and appointments, see Rankin, *Criminal Trial Proceedings*, pp. 63–87.

ian riding up to the courthouse beheld a public meeting place that was markedly superior to his own home dwelling. Most Virginia houses in the early eighteenth century were still of the English puncheon type, susceptible to termites and rotting. A contemporary described for a London correspondent the house of a neighbor, which he said was a "Shell of a house without Chimney or partition, & not one tittle of workmanship about it more than a Tobacco house work."[13]

The courthouse, on the other hand, was an impressive place. Outside, the county standard flew in the morning air, and as coaches and horsemen arrived and gentlemen took early draughts in the ordinary, the red brick of the courthouse on its green stood in sharp contrast to the surrounding wood. Viewed from the entry side, the courthouse presented an arcaded loggia of five rounded arches and a flagged pavement. This porch was usually occupied by servants, slaves, and smallholders, who milled about, hawked wares, quarreled, or listened to the proceedings inside. The arcaded piazza had recently become an integral part of public symbolism and display in Virginia and was used to connect the large main houses of the greater planters to lesser buildings or "dependencies." The dependent nature of the lesser orders of society who occupied these piazzas was ratified in the architecture of the courthouse, just as the interior of that building signified that it was particularly the place of authority, formality, and power.[14]

On entering the courthouse proper, the spectator saw to his immediate right and left the two rooms reserved for the deliberations of the jury. But his attention was drawn quickly to the point from which the action of court day sprang. The social ranking of the county was confirmed as he walked the length of the building, gazing at portraits of members of the royal family and colonial officials hung in ascending order of significance along the side walls. The wall above the bench was dominated by the king's arms, and immediately below the royal emblem were arrayed the seats of the gentlemen justices. The seats were arranged behind the bench, which was raised above the floor at least one foot and sometimes three. A jury box stood directly below the bench. Clerk, deputy king's attorney, and sheriff each had a place within the bar, and the walls of that space were wainscoted, while the interior of the public area was whitewashed

---

13. Fitzhugh to Nicholas Hayward, Jan. 30, 1686, *William Fitzhugh*, pp. 203, 208 (fn. 4).

14. On courthouse architecture and the evolution of a public style of display in plantation and government buildings, see Whiffen, *Public Buildings*, pp. 50, 152–61, and "Early County Courthouses"; Nichols, "Palladio's Influence"; Watkins, *Cultural History*, pp. 115–22. On contemporary houses and their evolution, see Forman, *Virginia Architecture*.

and plastered. The county's perception that the bar was a place somewhat apart from the larger room was moderated by the architectural device of a "neat Mondillion Cornice all round the whole" room.[15]

Not a little imposing, the scene was nonetheless a familiar one. County residents marked the rhythm of their communal lives by the events that unfolded there. As winter ended in March, courts convened after the inclement weather that often forced cancellations of sessions in December and January had ended. Suits were brought, and freeholders were notified to be on hand in May to sit as participants in the "grand inquest" of the county. Public claims and grievances were often settled in the spring. The grand jury met in May, for summer sessions wilted in the merciless heat and humidity of the low country. In September cooler weather and the ripening of crops occasioned constables' complaints of farmers tending "seconds" or inferior stalks of tobacco. Every fourth year in that same month the vestries "beat the bounds" of the parishes and made a return of their processioning to the court. Orphans' estates were inquired into in late autumn, and the county gathered again in November for another biannual examination of petty sins and misdemeanors. In December the county levy was laid. Punctuating this yearly cycle were the called courts and oyer and terminer sessions, whose meetings were infrequent and, though important, mere reflections of the monthly gatherings of the county court. On those regular, repeated occasions, in particular, we can observe the law in action.[16]

Act 1. Authority and Deference: Contempt of Court

Court sessions opened to a medley of affairs. The justices estimated the age of slaves brought in for public record of tithable status, appointed

15. Lancaster Orders, Aug. 8, 1740. On Elizabeth City's old 1693 courthouse, see Sweeny, "Gleanings from the Records of (Old) Rappahannock County and Essex County Virginia"; Campbell, *Colonial Caroline*, pp. 125–27; Adams, *Courthouse in Virginia*. On the concept of "otherness" or "noumenal" space set aside from the "phenomenal" familiar world, see Otto, *Idea of the Holy*, pp. 65–68; Eliade, *Images and Symbols*; Beane and Doty, eds., *Myths, Rites, Symbols*. See also Berger, *Sacred Canopy*; Berger and Luckmann, *Social Construction of Reality*. That ritual actions in a legal context should be viewed as a species of quasi-religious definition of life in semiliterate cultures can be seen in Turner, *Ritual Process* and *Dramas, Fields, and Metaphors*; Gluckman, *Judicial Process among the Barotse* and *Ideas in Barotse Jurisprudence*; Fallers, *Law without Precedent*; Bohannan, *Justice and Judgment*.

16. The cycle was dictated by statutes drawn by burgesses who had been justices and would be again when they finished their terms of office or were turned out. See Greene, "Foundations," pp. 485–506. Four-fifths of the members during this era were former justices. Of the thirty-nine lawyers Greene identifies, twenty-eight sat after 1745—another index of the growing importance of lawyers after 1750.

road surveyors, and heard cases docketed from earlier sessions. The formal anthems of the king's law were intoned over a continuo line of scuffling and murmuring. Flies buzzed in and out of open doors and windows. Other sounds intruded from the courthouse porch and the nearby ordinary, where business transactions and peddlers' hawking competed for attention with racehorses pounding across the green. Inside, the court directed the action to the keeping of the king's peace.

That peace was interrupted from time to time by Virginians clearly not intimidated by gentry authority to such a degree that they remained silent. Like the hierarchical culture itself their obstreperous behavior was graduated in seriousness, as was the response of the court. The collective identity of the justices was routinely invoked whenever someone challenged their dignity. Always referring to themselves as "this Court," the justices carefully guarded their authority. When Allen Hawthon came into the room with his hat on, the justices noted that such an act "appeared to this Court an Insolent behaviour." Hailed before the bench, Hawthon, "readily acknowledging his fault & humbly Begging pardon for the same," was able to satisfy the justices that he had not meant to affront them. Predictably, they declared that they were "well satisfied" and "it is therefore ordered he be released out of Custody paying fees." Hawthon was reminded of his inferior rank, and the justices confirmed their authority. He was called upon to explain and apologize; the court thereupon administered a minimal correction. Hence, on such ritual occasions, face-to-face meeting with authority took place within carefully circumscribed limits, according to commonly accepted linguistic exchanges.[17]

The intensity of such encounters naturally varied with the grossness of the offense and the rank of the offender. Culprits were treated firmly but in the light of the justices' recognition of the temptations of the nearby tavern. Magistrates were used to hearing a person confess that his behavior stemmed from "being much in drink." The court was thus only temporarily startled by Richard Patterson "by his Looking in at the Court and Speaking out a Loud 'Come here You Dogs and Fight.'" Fined twenty-nine shillings and put in the stocks until the court rose, he was remanded to the sheriff's custody and ordered "before the court Tomorrow Morning (when perhaps he may be sober)." Another planter, through his vivid, albeit vulgar, language, threatened the natural order of society from his "appearing Drunk and Insolent by his bidding Benjamin Weeks undersheriff Kiss his Arse in the face of the Court." Though fined for his behavior, three weeks later "the said Davis came now into Court in a very submissive manner and asked pardon for the high offence he

17. Westmoreland Orders, July 31, 1728.

had been guilty of & promises for the future to take care never to be guilty of an offense of the Like nature." The court's formulaic response graciously proclaimed to all that "this Court being willing to Show & grant Compassion etc. do therefore retract their said order" that Davis be fined.[18]

Planters and lawyers who questioned the integrity of the court's decisions could expect a higher penalty for their outrages. Richard Lowe had to pay five pounds current money, which was not remanded, for saying that the sheriff, justices, and clerk were rogues for charging him more than his taxable status allowed, "which Impudent, base, false, and scandalous Speeches were fully proved against him . . . by Sundry Witnesses." William Kennan, one of the few attorneys appearing in the county courts during this era, paid the same sum for asserting the court had made "a Roguish order in favor of one Moses Self in a Suit." Similarly, when John Bolling, a former justice, a Burgess, and a wealthy Henrico planter, came into court and behaved "himself after a very rude manner to the Justices by calling them Puppies and calling on God to damn them together with other misdemeanours," he was taken into custody and fined.[19]

Yet the court knew where custom and social convention set limits on authority's use of the law. Its treatment of two important but distinct groups of men guilty of the same sort of "contempt" signaled this recognition to the county. When a new Commission of the Peace appeared under the governor's hand, the sitting justices sent the sheriff out into the February weather to the tavern, requesting that the new nominees appear in court. Several did, but the court sent the sheriff out again. He returned to report that five of the gentlemen were still in the ordinary and, when asked why they would not come in and swear, he stated that "the Reason they gave him was they would come into court when they See fit."

This exchange set in motion a definition of rank and authority that had to be moved forward with great delicacy. One of the sitting justices, George Lee, demanded that the recalcitrants be forced to give up their law books, copies of which were sent to each county for the use of the

---

18. The use of alcohol and tobacco in the courtroom was forbidden. Drunkenness, even on the part of sitting justices, had marred many seventeenth-century proceedings. A Statute of 1676–77 warned that drunken magistrates would be fined and, upon a third offense, removed from office (Hening, 2:384). No instances of drunken behavior, grand jury presentments, or reprimands by the council against justices for the period 1700–1750 have been found in the counties studied. Examples of contempt and apology cited are found in Essex Orders, Nov. 21, 22, 1727; Westmoreland Orders, May 29, 1739, Jan. 29, 1744/45, Mar. 26, 1746.

19. Westmoreland Orders, June 28, 1738; Henrico Orders, June 6, 1720. The few instances of contempt by an attorney before 1750 in these counties (eight) resulted from a lawyer's questioning the justices' legal expertise. See below, chapter 4.

court. The men who had issued such a peremptory challenge to their equals on the bench were summoned and threatened with a fine. Perhaps to prove their magisterial rank they kept the court waiting for eighteen months, then surrendered the books, whereupon the fines were discontinued.[20]

Apparently some of the lesser planters misread this symbolic exchange and sometime later also failed to appear in court when summoned for jury duty. The justices irately noted that even after the court "was So Indulgent to Send the Sheriff out to Call them who it Seems were in the ordinary," they ignored this officer's summons and "informed the Court that they . . . would Come when they had done dinner." Standing upon its collective dignity, the magisterial gentry noted that "for [this] Contempt this Court do hereby Inflict the fine of Twenty Shillings upon Each of them." Moreover, the fines were not remanded.[21]

In each instance the particular action involving authority and the deference due it moved in predictable patterns and in varying degrees of importance as demanded by the nature of the exchanges involved. The various presentations and definitions of self were publicly acted out, with no intermediaries between bench and community. Once authority's rightful place had been defined, another action—another dramatic exchange of a different sort—could proceed.

Act 2. Law and Mutual Obligations: Debt Cases

Law acts as a form of social control, and its application by officials shows how the rules of society work. Eighteenth-century definitions of law described it as the "rule of justice" or "giving to every man what is his due."[22] To insure that every person received his due the law defined obligations and set the boundaries by which people could tell what to expect from one another in public intercourse. For Virginians, living in a plantation economy dominated by the staple crop, tobacco, that meant that the law had to deal with indebtedness. So chronic was debt that one observer noted that "great number of Litigious suits" and concluded that "to be arrested for debt is no scandal here."[23] The reason this was so was

20. Westmoreland Orders, Feb. 22, 1736/37.
21. Ibid., Apr. 1, 1741, Mar. 1, Aug. 31, Oct. 31, 1738.
22. Samuel Johnson, *Dictionary of the English Language*, under "Law" and "Justice." A useful definition of law as a "rule-making" process in which "primary rules" are elaborated in action, or at a "secondary" level by officials, is Hart, *Concept of Law*, pp. 77–96, at 92. Lon Fuller protests this functional definition, insisting that moral questions are not so easily separated from functional, positive aspects of law. See the exchange in Olafson, *Society, Law, and Morality*, pp. 439–505; Fuller, *Morality of Law*.
23. Journal of Nicholas Cresswell, Dec. 12, 1774, Leesburg, Loudon County, Va.

that the law recognized social and economic reality: in a society with no circulating specie, where everyone paid debts in tobacco, the condition of everyone from planter magnate to yeoman was at least modestly leveled by dependence on the market. Hence, the law ensured social order and guaranteed that every man would receive his due—the money owed him—when it provided the forum for face-to-face meetings where the propertied majority settled obligations before the justices.

The personal quality of such encounters was aided by the fact that lawyers were forbidden to involve themselves in small debt cases. Usually, the defendant-debtor had already given the creditor-plaintiff a power of attorney to confess judgment on the debtor's behalf if the debt was not paid according to an agreed-upon schedule. This power of attorney was bestowed when the money or credit had been extended to the debtor. The parties then filed this agreement in court as a public record of the debt at the time of its creation. Confession of judgment did not regularly occur unless the debtor defaulted. Yet such defaults did happen, and at that point the rituals of court day provided a way for creditor and debtor to resolve their differences.

When a debtor had defaulted, the plaintiff stood and presented his claim and moved for judgment by petition. The defendant had the right to contest this, and now stood, protesting the justice of the confessed judgment. The debtor thus intervened before the court could declare a judgment against the recalcitrant. Declaring that he protested the plaintiff's bill and "saved to himself" all exceptions to it, the debtor pleaded for time "to imparl," a request which since the seventeenth century was routinely granted for preparing his defense, if he had one. By imparling, the debtor hoped to come to an agreement with the plaintiff out of court, or if that failed, to hire one of the few professional attorneys in Virginia. Judging from the frequency with which these cases are later inscribed with the words "dismissed, the parties being agreed," one can conclude that mutual obligations were upheld and public honor maintained for the most part by private agreements.[24]

Even justices of the peace had to submit to these procedures. In Henrico County, Peter Randolph, a planter, sued justice John Ellis, who admitted that the action "against him is Just for Ten pounds Current money." Ellis was ordered by his fellows on the bench to honor the debt

---

24. The law forbade an attorney to take a fee in any cause brought by petition for a small debt, and for detinue and trover by petition for any sum under five pounds (Hening, 4:426–28); an exception was made in 1736 for collecting debts on behalf of a client in another county when the plaintiff could not be present (ibid., pp. 486–87). Imparling was in common use from the 1730s onward; see any county order book. I am indebted to W. H. Bryson for discussing procedural details regarding this issue of debt with me.

and to pay costs. If a planter grew impatient for payment of a sum after judgment had been made in his favor, the law specified that he wait a year and a day before seeking a writ of *scire facias* to recover the debt. The reluctance of members in this participatory act to become harsh about payment reveals itself in one planter's regretful decision to proceed "against John Ward on a Judgment obtained by the said Bolling of a longer Date than ten Years."[25]

This on-going ritual of suing and being sued kept planters and farmers coming to court every month to see who was recovering against whom and what their own roles might be at any given moment. That state of affairs kept Ralph Wormeley of Middlesex County constantly attuned to what was happening at court day. For months Wormeley dunned his neighbors, especially John Turberville of Hickory Hill, for their debts, asking that they "not oblige me, contrary to my wish, to adopt another mode of applying, which necessity only shall urge me upon." Wormeley's preference for an amicable settlement was heightened by his need to hold *his* creditor, Thomas Reid, at bay. Finally obtaining an execution against Turberville, which was served at court, Wormeley quickly scribbled to the sheriff of Westmoreland County: "Sir: Please pay to the order of M. Tho. Reid of Northumberland the sum of £100 (the first paid into yr. hands) out of the money made by virtue of the Exec. levied on ye estate of J.T. Esq. of Hiccory Hill—& for so doing this shall be your warrant."[26]

In those rare instances in which a case of debt was genuinely contested, a defendant still invoked the community's awareness of mutual obligation by "praying oyer" of his cause and "putting himself upon the country," demanding that a jury hear his case. The assembled county then heard the clerk demand of the plaintiff, "A.B. come forth and prosecute the action against C.D. or else thou will be nonsuit," and then of the defendant, after the plaintiff (who rarely failed to appear) had entered his declaration, "C.D. come forth and save thee and thy bales or else thou wilt forfeit thy recognizance." Though the jury's participation helped to insure that communal custom and experience were part of the decision, the law and the final declaration rested with authority—the justices before whom the case was argued. Except where the jurors delivered a verdict in these disputes, debts—at all times the single most numerous civil cause before the county courts—were settled between the two

---

25. For the *scire facias* action brought by John Bolling, Jr., see Henrico Orders, June 3, 1753; and ibid., *Randolph v. Ellis*, Mar. 1, 1762.

26. Dec. 20, 1783, May 17, July 2, 1784, Aug. 23, 1788, Mar. 1792, Jan. 23, 1795, Letterbook of Ralph Wormeley, 1783–1802, Wormeley Family Papers. The time involved here was extraordinarily long; nonetheless, it was quite common for debt causes to grind on for several years, especially if an actual trial of the issue took place.

parties alone, in face-to-face definitions of mutual obligation, in a public forum.[27]

Act 3. The Legal Authority of Communal Sanction: The Grand Jury

A third kind of action cast the spotlight of public attention further from the bench, into circles broader than that of the propertied planters and farmers. The biannual convening of the grand jury was a familiar ritual in which twenty-four "grave and substantial freeholders" gathered after being notified two months in advance by the sheriff to be at the May or November court. From the twenty-four, fifteen at least were impaneled. As the court came to order, the clerk stood and called out: "You good men that be returned to enquire for our Sovereign Lord the King, and the body of this county . . . answer to your names, every man at the first call, and save your fines." Though the justices were clearly the head of the "body of the county," the grand jurors also functioned with authority, swearing, three at a time, to uphold the oath their foreman took with his hand on the gospels. Jurymen were bound to "present no man for hatred, envy, or malice, neither [to] leave any man unpresented for love, fear, favour, or affection, or hope of reward; but [to] present things truly, as they come to . . . knowledge, according to the best of your understanding. So help you God."[28]

Though freeholders of the county, as grand jurymen, shared in the authority of the court, they did not thereby earn the right of rising from jury box to magistrates' bench. Grand jurymen did not become justices. Faithful servants of the court, these freeholders often continued to appear

27. The clerk's words were prescribed by statute (Hening, 2:59–60). For examples, see any county order book. Jury trial of debt causes before 1750 was rare—usually not more than three to seven per year. On the increase of jury trial after 1750, see below, chapter 4.

28. Grand juries met in April and December in the late seventeenth century (Hening, 2:74), and the courts were admonished to hold at least one session a year (ibid., pp. 407–8). Juries were to meet in May and November after 1705. Courts were warned that failure to call the grand inquest would result in a fine of four hundred pounds of tobacco against each justice (ibid., 3:368). Surveying the county records between 1720 and 1750, one finds that no grand jury ever presented its justices for failure on this matter, nor were fines levied against the justices by the General Court, as far as the records show. Nevertheless, though most counties always called at least one jury in a calendar year, in small counties where population was scattered (e.g., Northumberland) the courts did not always see fit to call two juries a year. The best record was York's, which missed only one grand jury—in November 1726. Middlesex and King George, on the other hand, were quite remiss, neglecting at least a dozen times to call the juries; in Middlesex entire years were skipped—in 1734, 1737, 1745. Gaps in county records make an average estimate nearly impossible, but for counties with fairly complete runs of order books, the generalization seems valid that courts held the grand inquest regularly.

for jury duty time after time, in addition to holding other county offices. The Rust family of Westmoreland may be fairly representative of their counterparts in neighboring Tidewater communities. Peter Rust served as grand juryman and foreman during the 1740s and 1750s. A man of modest means but excellent parts, he was forced to ask the court to bind out to various masters three orphans left by Samuel Eskridge because their estate could not sufficiently recompense Rust, who had been entrusted with their welfare. Rust also served as road surveyor, a duty he shared with George and Vincent Rust. Vincent, also a grand juryman, was given the lucrative post of tobacco inspector. He let his rank go to his head, and was fined for insolence, but four months later he was back in good grace and received a license to keep tavern. Jeremiah Rust served the court with his relatives, though in humbler fashion: he was paid 540 pounds of tobacco for cleaning the courthouse. Despite long years of service in various capacities the Rusts never did become justices.[29]

Once sworn to their duty, farmers and planters like the Rusts rose to the clerk's bidding to "stand together and hear your charge," as the county at large was admonished to keep silent "under paine of imprisonment" while the charge was being given. A formulaic summary of general moral principles as well as of types of offenses to be investigated, the charge was delivered by the senior justice or the deputy king's attorney. Modeled on such English examples as those contained in Chamberlain's *Complete Justice*, the Virginia charge reminded listeners that religion and morality were "the only Foundations whereon Society and civil government subsist." Man's laws should reflect God's and were sadly necessary, since conscience alone would never suffice to restrain "Fashionable Vices" in the "depraved state" of human existence. It was the purpose of law to deter men from evil, promote the general good, and ensure that the "particular Rights of every individual may be preserved & maintained."[30]

---

29. On the Rusts, see Westmoreland Orders, Jan. 29, 1754, Nov. 28, 1753, May 27, 1755, Mar. 29, July 25, Nov. 28, 1758. In Caroline, Campbell found that out of 343 jurors only 28 ever attained magisterial rank (*Colonial Caroline*, pp. 351–56). Williams found the same absence of former jurors on the benches of Middlesex and Surry ("Political Alignments," pp. 91–101); see also Williams, "Small Farmer." The differentiation between magisterial and grand jury planters seems to have been emerging in the late seventeenth century. See Kelly, "Economic and Social Development." Most grand jurymen owned about five hundred acres during their time of service in the first half of the eighteenth century.

30. *Complete Justice*, pp. 470–85. See also "Charge to a Grand Jury," (n.d.), Latané Family Papers, 1667–1800. Chamberlain's work contains the model "A Compendious Charge to be given at the Quarter Sessions," which follows a discussion of the law divided into its two parts: "First the Laws Ecclesiastic for the peace of the Church, and Laws Civil, or Temporal, for the peace of the Land" (*Complete Justice*, p. 470).

It was for this dual reason—to sustain the common weal and to protect individuals—that the jurymen were to present offenders who violated God's laws or were guilty of civil nuisances. The grand jury was exhorted to name all whom they found to have violated the Sabbath, missed church, scoffed at the sacraments or scripture, blasphemed, or got drunk. In second order of importance were offenders who sold drink without a license, failed to keep up roads, let their mill dams fall into disrepair, or "conceale[d] Tithable persons to the great Griefe and Damage of the Inhabitants of this County." The court further delegated its power to use "wit and cunning" to the jurors by reminding them that they were to present "all those who you know are guilty of any hanious Crime Either against almighty God, the King & Queens Maj[es]ties, or Wronge done to your Neighbour—although the said Cryme be not Expresly nominated or Sett downe." Having withdrawn to consider this weighty charge, the jury drew up the list of persons to be presented according to their own knowledge or to information given by the churchwardens or by two witnesses, carefully noting the names of the informants under each specific presentment. When the jury reentered the courtroom, the foreman stood to read out the presentments, which were then entered on the record. The court thanked the jury, and it was dismissed, the clerk crying out to the undersheriffs, "Make way for the gentlemen of the grand inquest."[31]

Having played their mediatory role between authority and community, the grand jurymen resumed their seats in the courtroom, and the action shifted back to the principals—the justices of the peace—who ordered the culprits to appear at next court. There the court artfully combined "cunning, wit, and power" in a manner guaranteed to uphold authority, and involve communal custom, by putting offenders to shame on the public stage of court day. That Virginians recognized the impact of shame on their public personalities is revealed in the vast numbers of nonappearances to answer presentments. Such "nonaction" was a presumptive admission of guilt, and was so considered by the court, which ordered the appropriate fine levied against all persons "being thrice solemnly called but appearing not." Nonappearance enabled the court to exact monies for the relief of the county's poor, a practice that had the additional advantage of relieving the tax burden on propertied gentry and yeomen. The occasional outright confession of guilt confirmed the utility of the

---

31. The county charge quoted here is also divided, with moral offenses first and civil nuisances second. See "Some helps for the Grand Jury of Middlesex, 1693/4," Middlesex County, Virginia Deeds, etc., 1679–94, no. 2 [1a], VSL. I wish to thank Anita Rutman for this reference.

courts' practices. When John Stuard was presented for profanity, he failed to appear and bade the sheriff tell the court that he "confessed himself to be guilty and was ashamed to appear before the Court, but would Willingly Submitt to the Courts Judgement."[32]

Formal authority itself was not immune to this sort of corrective pressure. Indeed, being a holder of public office and an exemplar of propertied personality made a justice even more subject to psychological and social sanctions. A great wagging of tongues, therefore, assailed the sensitive justice Landon Carter when he had to step down from the bench and confess the rightness of a presentment for swearing, pay the fine, and resume his place. The mortification of Robert Wormeley Carter on his own presentment was eloquent, though privately confessed. To his diary, Carter confided, "I take shame to myself it being for swearing; I recollect the matter; an insolent fellow accused me of usury; which provoked me & put me off guard. May God pardon me." Perhaps this awareness that even formal authority could be subjected to customary sanctions through the law tempered the severity of judgments. When John Forrister was presented for operating "a tip'ling house" without a license, the court discovered that he could not pay his fine. Declaring that they knew him "to be very poor and that he hath a Wife and Several Children," the justices accepted his earnest promise never again to sell liquor illegally. In view of their familiarity with this case, the justices "in Compassion beg leave to Recommend him to the Governor as an object of Charity."[33]

In all such instances arising from the grand jury's sitting, formal authority mingled with familiar custom. Authority itself was shared with the grand jurors, and the communal nature of acts involving ritual confession and expiation of sin was heightened. Since shaming affected the great as well as the simple, such acts touched all free members of the county. (For the most part, slaves and servants were dealt with by their masters on the plantations.) Freeholders guilty of missing church, failing to keep up their roads, having illegitimate children, swearing, or getting drunk were publicly identified and reproved.[34]

Beneath them in the social order, and usually restricted to the porch at court day, were the unpropertied. Yet even to them, whose lives only occasionally were touched by the justices on the bench, the public stage of court day was accessible, and they, too, played a part in the drama that displayed qualities both formal and familiar.

32. Henrico Orders, July 6, 1741.
33. Richmond Orders, July 4, 1745; Robert Wormeley Carter Diary, entry of Aug. 9, 1791, Carter Papers; Henrico Orders, Aug. 4, 1746.
34. Tabulation of presentments reveals that missing church was the most common of-

Act 4. Authority and Its Obligations before the Law: Slaves and Servants

So far, we have observed exchanges between the formal and familiar spheres of Virginia life that involved those propertied actors whose public personalities and identities received definition and affirmation at court day. Beyond the circles of the great and the middling ranks of the society, however—at the periphery of these exchanges—stood men and women in varying degrees of unpropertied servitude. If law was something more than a coercive tool employed solely to the advantage of the propertied gentry, court day had to reveal that additional quality. The recognition of the significance of slaves and servants by the court was signaled both in its treatment of such persons and in the props and appurtenances deemed appropriate for their rank.[35]

The presence of the lowest members of Virginia society on the courthouse porch was recognized in August 1750 when the Richmond County Court ordered its sheriff to "employ some person to rail in a Yard with good saw'd Whiteoak Rails and Locust posts Twenty foot in Wedth from each Corner of the Courthouse five foot high, The rails to be within three inches of one another, And to sett up four Benches in each of the Piazzas and one under each of the Windows in the body of the Courthouse of a

---

fense in Middlesex, Essex, Lancaster, and Northumberland and second most common in York, Caroline, King George, Richmond, and Westmoreland. Women presented for bastardy represent the second most numerous group of offenders. Prosecution of them and of those who missed church was vigorous. The presentments are not an index of bastardy in Virginia. To these figures one would have to add informations and complaints of churchwardens and masters against servant women. No county attempted to prosecute putative fathers with any rigor before 1750. A new law of 1769 encouraged free white women (neither servants nor slaves) to come into court and accuse the reputed father, provided he was not a servant (Hening, 8:374–77). The new law abolished whipping as the punishment for those unable to pay the twenty-shilling fine. A man could be jailed if he failed to pay a recognizance bond of ten pounds; if found guilty, he was liable for child support at a rate determined by the court. Tabulation of presentments for 1750–70 reveals a marked drop in bastardy presentments. Since bastard children had to be bound out at the parish's expense and constituted a public charge on property, one can only wonder why sanctions against property in the form of fines were not more regularly imposed and why fathers were not more vigorously pursued for child support. Whether the reluctance to shame a planter or farmer by bringing him into court on this charge outweighed the monetary burdens imposed by supporting illegitimate children at the public's expense is a tantalizing but unresolvable question. On grand jury tabulations, see below, chapter 4.

35. Property, of course, embraced everything that was "held" or "pertained" to the person, no matter how humble. Thus, religion, social obligations and rights, vesture, and diet all fall under this heading. The upholding of gentry rights to property in land especially not only signaled their control of the social order but allowed lower orders to expect *their* property to be upheld. On the symbolic and public nature of private property and its ties to "fundamental rights," see Gooch, *Political Thought*; Little, *Religion, Order, and Law*, pp. 176–89; Nenner, *By Colour of Law*, pp. 36–39.

Convenient hight and Breadth for people to set on."³⁶ Though not directed exclusively for the benefit of servants and not at all for that of slaves, such an order nonetheless testifies to the court's awareness of the lower orders of society whose standing and due were confirmed by the court's actions in their behalf.

The formal authority of the justices was invoked by servants as a reminder of obligations owed these denizens of the piazza, who were themselves a species of property and possessors of very little. Occasionally, a servant's plea was brought by an intermediary but more often by the servant himself. The "wit and cunning" of the court, as well as social standards of rank based on race, were in full play as servant Thomas Cox complained against his master, William Woodson. The justices listened, agreed "that the said Cox hath not been kept as a white servant ought to be," and ordered that in future his master should provide him with "Sufficient diet, lodging, and cloathing, and . . . not immoderately Correct him."³⁷

White servants had rights above those of black servants or slaves, as the above instance demonstrates. Yet obligations incumbent on authority to give black Virginians their due were occasionally, if infrequently, invoked with success by Afro-Americans. Beaten and imprisoned by Elias Newman, a black woman named Sarah argued that she was over twenty-one and free, contrary to Newman's claim that she was his wife's slave. In this instance, an attorney-at-law, John Martin, acted as Sarah's representative, though whether appointed by the court for her *in forma pauperis*, as was sometimes the case, we do not know. Newman's protests to Sarah's bill were ruled insufficient, and he was forced to carry his case on appeal to Williamsburg, where we lose sight of it.³⁸

Servants, black and white alike, usually came into court of their own volition. Like the rest of society, they stood, unrepresented by attorneys, in face-to-face meeting with authority. In fact, it was precisely the justices' jealous sense of that authority that worked for the lesser ranks of the social order. Certainly that is the reason why the court ordered a planter publicly whipped for beating the slave of another without the sanction of the law. Cruel or arbitrary punishment was not opposed for

---

36. Richmond Orders, Aug. 6, 1750.
37. Henrico Orders, Mar. 5, 1722–23.
38. Essex Orders, Nov. 20, 1745. For examples of courts providing an attorney *in forma pauperis* (usually the deputy king's attorney), see King George Orders, Apr. 1, 1737; Middlesex Orders, June 2, 1747, for freedom dues for Mulatto Frank (Frank won the case July 7); Richmond Orders, Apr. 2, 1739. The King George justices provided the king's attorney to a poor widow who wished to sue the sheriff for maladministration of her deceased husband's estate.

its own sake but rather because of the threat it posed to constituted authority—its own—which the court protected. Yet here again, the interplay of authority and custom, formal and familiar, is obvious, and both types of actors in the drama got something out of the situation. That same quality of the law—that it protected the public, propertied personality of authority while intervening for dependents as well—moved the farmer Job Shadrick to complain to his patron, Augustine Washington, a gentleman justice. Abused by John Bayes, the captain of a troop of soldiers, Shadrick insisted that Bayes "suffered them to beat him in a Barbarous manner." Washington had written to Bayes for an explanation, "but instead of Complying he flung the Letter in the fire and said Col. Washington might kiss his backside." For his insult, Bayes was arrested, brought into the public forum, and forced to give security for his good behavior.[39]

In some degree those qualities that we have seen in the other acts—shame, intercession by the "gentle" members of society for inferiors, jealous protection of authority—seem to have coalesced in the act that revealed the rank and rights of the lower orders. Thus one indentured servant's canny use of the court provides a fitting climax to the dramatic play we have been observing. Captured and brought into court after attempting to run away, Alexander Stewart loudly demanded protection, since he was "inhumanely rased as well In his Diett and Great Severity" by his master John Livingston, Jr. Sensing the spectacular potential of his position, Stewart maneuvered the court into ordering that he be "stript in Court and it appearing to the said Court that the said Alexander has bin severely whipped by ye many Stripes on his Naked Skin Contrary to any authority by Law for so doeing," the justices issued a public reprimand. Though Stewart was to return to Livingston's service, the court admonished the master to treat his servant "in a more Christian and Human Manner than he before has and that he doe Not suffer him to be used any otherwise," lest upon "further Complaint and Just Occation & Cause" he be dealt with severely by the court.[40]

Though the justices of the counties did not regularly interfere with the private law administered on the plantations to servants—and never, as far as we can tell, with regard to slaves—it is nevertheless true that law held meaning and consequence for the lesser ranks of society. The trials

---

39. York Orders, June 17, 1728; Westmoreland Orders, Apr. 21, 1757. The Westmoreland court drove home its patronage powers by locking up the unfortunate Bayes until "two good Securitys" could be found to guarantee his behavior. The justices then offered two of their most eminent fellows in Virginia, Thomas Ludwell Lee and Richard Henry Lee, as securities.

40. Essex Orders, May 19, 1752.

of slaves for felony in oyer and terminer sessions were a kind of spectacle that deserves separate treatment. Yet even there one finds that the formal letter of the law was regularly moderated by familiar custom. The king's law also functioned in those instances where Afro-Americans stood on trial for their lives before the justices. Yet it is perhaps significant that those sessions were separate from the regular meetings of court day, and we should not try to force a total unity of action upon a culture whose prevailing views were ambiguous and tortured at best, in that slaves were regarded simultaneously as human beings and as chattel property.[41]

Planters and farmers, free blacks and mulattoes, servants and tenants —all left the stage of court day in Tidewater Virginia secure in the sense that they had shaped and ratified communal affairs, that the rhythm of public life continued, and that the authority of the gentry firmly guided customary institutions. That authority, expressed through the application of law, upheld the defense of property and, through that, the public identities, the well-being, and the security of most of society. The law could only give every man his due if it was replete with suasive images and commonly accepted values. Where it failed, it did so because the Virginia society failed to grapple with the contradictions inherent in chattel slavery based upon race. Besides being a mode of social control whereby authority was sanctioned and norms of behavior were enforced, the law regularly and predictably appeared as a sentinel guarding the boundaries and defining the relationships between the worlds of formal authority and customary, familiar county life.

Contemporary English opinion, so highly valued in eighteenth-century Virginia, wisely held (though it failed to put into practice) the conviction that law should rarely enforce through the mere fear of punishment. Rather, it should promote acquiescence among a people persuaded of its value. "We find by experience," wrote Chamberlain in 1681, "that it is not frequent punishment that prevents offences.... It is better prevent-

---

41. Philip J. Schwarz of Virginia Commonwealth University has kindly shared with me his preliminary conclusions on slave trials ("Slave Crimes in Eighteenth-Century Virginia," work in progress). He contends that by the 1770s, 60 percent to 80 percent of the slaves tried were pardoned, their sentences commuted, or the goods they stole devalued. Like the whites accused of felony, the overwhelming majority of slaves tried were not executed for felony. Like whites also, their most common offense was breaking and entering and theft of goods. My own conclusions on the paternalist nature of Virginia's ruling-class attitudes have been strengthened by work in the local records, but were informed by Mullin's excellent *Flight and Rebellion*. Morgan, on the other hand, sees slavery in eighteenth-century Virginia as a "competitive" rather than a "paternalist" system. It seems to me that it was quite possible for planters to be exploitative and still reveal, in their public and private conduct, the basic attributes of paternalism. See E. S. Morgan, *American Slavery*, pp. 325–26 (fn. 33).

ing, than redressing offences."[42] As long as the routine, the rituals, the repetition of the acts we have observed continued—as long as shared perceptions were publicly expressed and communication between various ranks of society was guaranteed—court day flourished. In their deft handling of the occasional displays of violence, hauteur, vulgarity, and the ills attendant on chattel slavery, Virginia's justices promoted the interplay between formality and familiarity in county life.

Whether the existence of court day with its attendant controls of public opinion and censure had a beneficial effect upon private law on the plantations, we can only speculate. Certainly, one senses that in its formal architecture, its dramaturgy, and its visual and aural symbolism the courthouse was a sort of "everyman's plantation." To a degree everyone in the county "belonged" there and rightly expected to receive what was due him as he defined himself, his rank, and his relationships to others. Authority, in the persons of the justices, managed to give various ranks of Virginians what was theirs, as the law was supposed to do, by a judicious mixture of "cunning, wit, and power." At its best court day was the arena in which authority, law, and custom mingled in ritual exchanges. Deference to authority was expected all down the line, and in exchange for that deference superiors accepted the obligations of their offices. Mutual obligations had to be acted out as well, as both business and self-image were advanced in the settlement of debt. Communal sanction ratified and mediated authority by means of the grand jury. Over all, the public law, the public authority of the king's court, loomed large in everyone's mind.

Coke would have been pleased at the commingling of formality and familiarity wrought by the gentlemen justices of the peace in Virginia. Of the Commission of the Peace he had once said that it was "such a forme of subordinate government for the tranquility and quiet of the Realm, as no part of the Christian world hath the like, if the same be duly executed."[43] The due execution of the office by Virginia's justices kept court

42. *Complete Justice*, p. 485.
43. Coke, *Fourth Part of the Institutes*, p. 170. Rhys Isaac has suggested that during the 1760s the Baptist conventicles provided a novel sense of communal order and social sobriety in a formerly chaotic society. Isaac sees those qualities as very potent in the Tidewater, "where no cultural tradition existed as preconditioning for the communal confession, remorse, and expiation that characterized the spread of the Baptist movement" (Isaac, "Evangelical Revolt," p. 359). On the contrary, I suggest that precisely because religion, order, and law were vital elements of gentry culture as expressed in the ritual of court day, Isaac's Baptists were (correctly) perceived as direct threats to an already existing liturgical and dramatic occasion—a small but significant difference in our interpretations. The description of court day as the "principal meeting" of Virginia life was made by an English traveler. See "Observations in Several Voyages and Travels in America in the Year 1746. (From the *London Magazine*, July 1746)," *WMQ*, 1st ser., 15 (1907): 147.

day alive as the stage upon which the dynamic between authority and custom, formalism and familiarity, guided vigorous evolution of a culture intensely proud of English law "from antiquity not to be traced."

Critics of the Law in the Country

Appropriately, the lawyers of Virginia celebrated the coming of age of their profession with an ode to a very different world and to a distinctly elite mode of communication. In 1730 the Maryland printer William Parks established a printing press in Williamsburg. After printing the laws of the Assembly passed that year and Governor Gooch's grand jury charge already mentioned, Parks published John Markland's *TYPO-GRAPHIA: An Ode, On Printing*.[44] Markland, a county lawyer from Blissland Parish, New Kent County, composed this patriotic panegyric while practicing law and running the ordinary at "Bonnchees" at the courthouse in Hanover with fellow attorney Thomas Prosser.[45] Markland first celebrated Gooch's arrival, which finally put an end to the squabbles between governor and Council, or governor and House. Gooch's arrival augured a day when Virginia would be ever more like England, and,

> Ev'n Party-Rancour dy'd away,
> And private Spleen

would be dismissed under Gooch's influence.

Significantly, Markland's ode especially hailed the rise of printing, which would now reveal:

> VIRGINIA's Laws, that lay
> In blotted *Manuscripts* obscur'd,
> By vulgar Eyes unread. . . .

Now that Parks could command his hoard of type to arrange itself to make sense in print,

> Whether an antient Law that dormant lies,
> The *sage judicious* FIVE revise. . . .

Proudly, Markland pointed here to the five burgesses who had been appointed to compile a revision of the statutes of Virginia during the recent session of the House. The author did not need to remind fellow attorneys

---

44. Williamsburg, 1730; on Parks, see Wroth, *William Parks*, pp. 15–18.
45. On Markland, see York County Orders, June 16, 1735; WMQ, 1st ser., 20–21 (1911–13): 61; Lemay, ed., *Poem by John Markland*. On Thomas Prosser, see VMHB 13–14 (1905–7): 213–14.

that the "*sage judicious* FIVE" were John Holloway, the England-trained attorney and speaker of the House; the attorney general, barrister John Clayton; barrister Sir John Randolph, who soon succeeded Holloway as speaker; William Robertson, England-trained attorney and clerk of the Council; and Archibald Blair, brother to the commissary of Virginia and the only nonlawyer member of the committee.[46] The acknowledged, public service that the legal profession was performing in revising the laws was not allowed to pass unhailed by Markland. Casting his peroration in traditional Country images of virtuous behavior, he concluded:

> Happy the *Act*, by which we learn
> The Gloss of Errors to detect,
> The Vice of Habits to correct,
> And sacred Truths, from Falsehood to discern!
> By which we take a far-stretch'd View,
> And learn our Fathers Vertues to pursue,
> Their Follies to eschew.[47]

Clearly, in Markland's mind the joining of printing and the legal profession heralded a day when the cosmopolitan "far-stretch'd" perspective would advance the welfare of Virginia. What gave his writing added timeliness was the conflict between the Country justices and the Virginia bar headed by the Williamsburg Court attorneys of the day. Markland's ode had hardly been published before the small but brilliant band of barristers and attorneys in the capital found ample opportunity to essay a sharp but temporarily ineffective sortie upon the extensive powers and the outlook of the Country justices.

Not surprisingly, the issue on which Williamsburg lawyers assaulted the justices was the same one that had dragged local officials into the limelight in 1713—tobacco. In 1730 the House of Burgesses enacted a new law which provided for the inspection of all tobacco and the destruction of that which did not pass the scrutiny of appointed inspectors at designated public warehouses, and included a prohibition against paying public debts in trash tobacco. By these measures the government hoped to ensure quality controls, which would raise the price of Virginia's staple in a market that had been ailing since 1712. Governor Gooch and his allies anxiously guided the bill through the House.

When it passed into law, an uproar immediately ensued. The loudest protests came from poorer planters, who felt that their tobacco would

---

46. On this, the third revisal and compilation of the laws, following those of 1661–62 and the published compilation done in London between 1684 and 1687, see *JVHB* for the session 1727–34, pp. xvii–xix, 36–40.

47. Lemay, ed., *Poem by John Markland*, pp. 10, 11, 14.

more often fail inspection. Unable to afford carts and slips to take their crop to market, the smaller farmers had to roll the tobacco along muddy roads, and the weed became contaminated with dirt. Moreover, since the poorer planters cultivated less luxurious crops on inferior land, they were certain that their harvests were doomed. The inspectors, appointed from Williamsburg, were men of substance; to further counteract opposition to the plan, it was pointed out that the notes given at inspection could be used for payment of all debts, public and private within the county, thus providing a needed medium of exchange in the colony.

But opposition did not come solely from the lesser ranks of society. Large planters feared that the establishment of public warehouses and inspection would destroy the patron-to-client relationship so carefully nurtured since the late seventeenth century. Those planters grumbled, but they could not countenance the violence that broke out in the Northern Neck in 1731. Burnings of warehouses by mobs expressed a discontent with the law which many wealthier patrons shared. But that disruption of the social order was intolerable, and laws were passed to punish the arsonists.[48]

The governor himself pleaded in an anonymous pamphlet for the restoration of order and acceptance of the bill. Styling himself "Justice Lovecountry," Gooch thereby allied himself with the Country, dismissed charges that the law was intended to help the rich and hurt the poor, and managed a tutorial on the nature of law in Virginia, in the bargain. It made only good sense, Gooch argued, to avoid shipping the tobacco with stems, inferior leaves, even "seconds," the smaller growth of leaves that grew up on the stalks after first trimming. Bulk shipping had been the order of the day, with each hogshead sold individually, since hogsheads varied considerably in weight and amount of tobacco they held. In his *DIALOGUE Between Thomas SWEET-SCENTED, WILLIAM ORONOCO, Planters, both Men of good Understanding, and Justice LOVE COUNTRY, who can speak for himself....*, Gooch exploded "the Roguery of some that shall be nameless" who "confidently buzzed about . . . [that] by Law, the Rich intended to ruin the Poor." Not only did the law help the poorer planters by providing a medium of exchange, Gooch argued, but the burgesses had striven to be as selfless as possible in safeguarding the rights of the powerless. In the pamphlet, at least, Will and Tom are convinced. Gooch also suggested that the peace of the Tidewater lay with the justices whose guise he had put on for the sake of his homily. The duty of magistrates, he said, lay in faithfully executing the laws, "the Peoples Direction in moral Actions."

48. For an excellent survey of the events surrounding the passage of the law and reactions to it, see Horne, "Opposition to the Virginia Tobacco Inspection Act."

Justices were "to give them all the Light they can, into the Interest and Meaning of them." As for the planters themselves, Gooch urged them to "live as become honest Men, minding only your own Business; Fear God, honour the King, and meddle not with those that are Given to Noise and Violence." Gooch censured especially racegrounds, "those Schools of Gaming and Drunkenness," and warned planters never to "go near the County-Courts, unless Business calls you thither." Yet in concluding, the governor softened a bit, realizing the need for community socializing: Will concluded to his friend Tom, "Adieu: the Justice is a good Man; he gave us very good Advice: But I must go to see a Race sometimes, for all that."[49]

Gooch needed all the support he could muster for his new law, for protests and petitions continued to pour into Williamsburg. For example, planters complained about vicious inspectors like Joseph Carter of Northumberland, who "spightfully burnt James Pollards Tobacco, ... threatened to split Peter Rivers' head, and offer'd to turn him out of Doors."[50] Hanover justices regretted their choice of Thomas Anderson for the post of inspector, now saying "the Court was Surprised into that Recommendation, without considering the Inconveniencys that would attend it."[51] Anderson, already heavily in debt, could be swayed too easily as inspector, and was replaced. Petitioners demanded that the inspectors be elected, or at least appointed by the justices of the peace. This last demand dramatically underscores the degree of trust Virginians placed in their justices.

Opposition still smoldered years later when the 1730 law was renewed. Park's *Virginia Gazette* garnered an even more attentive audience than usual when it carried in the summer months of 1738 an exchange of letters between TIMOTHY TOUCH-TRUTH and MORFOREO on the tobacco laws. TOUCH-TRUTH was implacable in his opposition to the law, the inspectors, and even the justices of the peace. The House had recently approved of justices' recommending candidates for inspectors, but TOUCH-TRUTH contended that the inspectors were "Arbitrary Judges" of little capacity and less sensitivity, precisely because they were appointed by the governor "who cannot be acquainted with their Abilities." To those who proudly pointed to the justices and their recommendations, Timothy scornfully retorted that the honesty of the inspectors hinged entirely on the "Direction of a few persons [the justices] who perhaps

---

49. Williamsburg, 1732, pp. 14, 15–17, 19. See also R. L. Morton, *Colonial Virginia*, 2:516–17.
50. *VCSP*, Oct. 9, 1732, 1:218–19.
51. Ibid., Feb. 20, 1739–40, pp. 233–34.

may not vallue the general good of all men but may be byasst by Interest to themselves or perticular friends or a mixture of both."[52]

TOUCH-TRUTH overstepped himself badly by this last remark. It was one thing to complain of inspectors, but quite another to suggest that the magistrates were partial or looked to their own private Interests. Had Timothy openly accused them of being "rogues," he could hardly have aroused the ire of the county gentry more thoroughly. Reaction to the statements of TOUCH-TRUTH was so negative that his erstwhile opponent offered a weak defense for the indiscreet remarks.

MORFOREO commented that the sentiments of Virginians in the ordinaries and courthouses across the Tidewater were against Timothy and his opinions: "I understand Exception has been taken, to what Mr. *Touchtruth* has wrote towards the Close of his Letter; which I cannot but Acknowledge at first Sight, seems to reflect upon some Persons in Power. . . . I shall not pretend to justify Mr. *Touchtruth* in this Observation; but this I think I may venture to affirm, that no Body can tax him with saying that those Gentlemen *are led by the* N O S E."[53] But the disarming concession of MORFOREO to the independent judgment of the magistrates did nothing to settle the issue that TOUCH-TRUTH had raised—that perhaps magistrates were not the selfless paternal guardians of the community they were thought to be. Two weeks later a blunt, forthright interpretation of the implications hidden in the TOUCH-TRUTH letter was presented by PHILANTROPOS.

While some Virginians huddled over their summer tumblers of sangaree or grog, discussing the latest controversy surrounding the inspectors, PHILANTROPOS kept a clear head. In this planter's opinion there was seditious sentiment lurking behind the recent letter of TOUCH-TRUTH: "I believe many Inspectors have not done their Duty: And perhaps some Magistrates have not done theirs. But I never heard any wise Man cry out against Magistracy, because some Magistrates were faulty. *Wat Tyler*, and *Ket* the Tanner, were indeed of that Opinion; and as they made Use of *Club Law* to support it, were effectually confuted by *Ratio Ultima Regum*."[54]

Here was plain talk, and no mistake. Men still lived in Virginia who remembered their fathers' talk of Bacon's Rebellion. The literate gentry, and even those who could not read but listened to tales of English history, knew of the leveling principles espoused by Tyler in 1581 and the lower-class forces in the Civil War, and the gentry well understood that the

52. *Virginia Gazette*, July 28–Aug. 4, 1738.
53. Ibid., Oct. 13–20, 1738.
54. Ibid., Oct. 27–Nov. 3, 1738.

Clubmen represented an attack on men of property. Even if the old radicals had possessed a certain Country virtue in attacking Court corruption, Virginians knew what PHILANTROPOS was saying. Attack the magistracy and you undermine all our liberties, our fortunes, perhaps our lives—what other conclusion was there?[55]

No further letters on the TOUCH-TRUTH essay were forthcoming. By December the controversy was largely forgotten, and the governor himself had reenforced the magistrates' rank in his public plea for support of the renewed tobacco law. After seven years of trial, Gooch contended, "by a Concession due to the Support of so wholesome an Establishment, the Justices, in the several Counties, have the Nomination, I might almost say the Appointment, of the Inspectors, committed to them." The governor had no intention of overruling local patrons and possibly endangering his pet project. He did, however, encourage the justices to support the inspectors and watch them carefully. As a result, he thought, "their mistaken Neighbours will the sooner be convinced, how much an indulgent Restraint, on which their own, and the Public Welfare depend, is to be preferred to Liberty, so destructive to Both."[56]

The controversy over tobacco was apparently resolved with public peace secured and the patronage power over inspectors lodged firmly with the justices of the counties. Yet this victory for the Country was not uncontested, and the lawyers of Williamsburg continued to lobby for a curtailment of Country power in the name of better procedure and in favor of a less paternal, moralistic social order, as well. Ably led by a coterie of eminent barristers and attorneys, especially John Clayton, John Randolph, Edward Barradall, and John Holloway, the lawyers who had come to Virginia between 1700 and 1732 or managed to get some variety of legal training as natives boasted a lustrous bar in the capital (see table 3).

Country partisans had every reason to continue to identify lawyers with the Court interest when they reflected on the recent violent debates over the 1730 tobacco law. That bill had passed the House only with the intervention of the speaker, who broke the tie. Since the speaker's landings near the capital were the site for the projected public warehouse, the public was sure that lawyer Holloway's decisive vote was not altruistic. That same man had earlier "turned Projector and nearly ruin'd himself," as Randolph recalled.[57]

---

55. The term "Club Law" refers to any lower-class movement, and its use antedates the appearance in 1645 of the conservative Clubmen, who fit so awkwardly into Hill's treatment of radical popular movements. See *World Turned Upside Down*.

56. *Virginia Gazette*, Dec. 15-22, 1738.

57. Holloway had been the leading member of the House committee that reported a favorable opinion of the 1713 tobacco act. For his activities there, and his role in 1730, see

Court Day and Its Critics, 1720–1750   101

TABLE 3 *Some Members of the Williamsburg Bar, 1700–1750*

BARRISTERS:[a]

John Clayton, Inns, 1682, Attorney General, Justice, James City County
Stevens Thomson, Inns, 1688, Attorney General
John Carter, Inns, 1714, Councillor, Judge of General Court
John Randolph, Inns, 1715, Attorney General, Justice, Gloucester County
Wilson Cary, Inns, 1721, Councillor, Judge of General Court, Justice, Elizabeth City County
Lewis Burwell, Inns, 1733, Justice, Gloucester County, 1737, James City, 1736
Thomas Nelson, Inns, 1733, Justice, York County
Peyton Randolph, Inns, 1739, Justice, York County, Attorney General
Richard Francis, Inns, (?), Clerk of Council, 1741

ATTORNEYS:[b]

Henry Holdcraft, 1703, England born and trained
John Holloway, 1705, England born and trained
William Robertson, 1705 (?), England born and trained
Richard Hickman, 1710 (?), England born and trained
Simon Jeffrys, 1712, Virginian (?)
Godfrey Pole, 1715, England born and trained
Charles Aderson, 1716, Virginian (?)
William Hopkins, 1722, England born and trained
James Nimmo, 1723, born in Scotland, England trained (?)
Edward Barradall, 1726 (?), Virginia born (?), barrister
William Bowden, 1730 (?), England born and trained
Benjamin Waller, 1738, Virginia born and trained
Dudley Digges, 1738, Virginia born and trained
Benjamin Needler, 1739, England born and trained
St. Lawrence Berford, 1739, England born and trained
Stephen Dewey, 1739, Virginian (?)
John Palmer, 1740, England born and trained
James Power, 1742, England born and trained
William Nimmo, 1743, Virginian (son of James)
George Wythe, 1747, Virginia born and trained

Source: Swem, *Virginia Historical Index*; Hayden, *Virginia Genealogies*; L. G. Tyler, *Encyclopedia of Virginia Biography*, vol. 1; Jones and Hamilton lists of American members of the Inns of Court; county records. Note the British emigré character of the bar around Williamsburg.

a. Barrister here indicates not only membership at one of the Inns but a practitioner of law as well. There were other Virginians who are listed as holding membership in the Inns. Only men who were actively involved with the courts of law during this era are listed here.

b. Attorneys are listed by approximate date when they began practice in the General Court in Williamsburg or in the hustings court or those of York and James City counties. Many more lawyers pleaded before the General court; these men are those living in Williamsburg or in the adjoining counties.

Lawyers tended to argue in favor of "projectors" and mercantile ventures and to oppose old-fashioned attitudes and homegrown legal abilities in the Country. A 1739 case in the General Court made this point unmistakably clear. It began simply enough, with county complaints against Inspector Samuel Oldham of Westmoreland. On May 31, 1737, the county court investigated him, but reappointed him on September 27, even fining and reprimanding another planter who accosted Oldham and poured out a torrent of abuse and oaths (Oldham counted five) on the inspector's head, "misbehaving Very much." The court itself, however, did not trust Oldham. Three weeks later, at the behest of Daniel McCarty, gentleman justice of Westmoreland, the Council removed Oldham for "divers Evil practices and Misdemeanours" in the performance of his duty as inspector. Stung by the reprimand and angry at his fellow justices for their part in his downfall, Oldham brought suit against Isaac Allerton and his constable, Pope. The case, which otherwise might have passed as an insignificant personal quarrel between local worthies, made history instead, of sufficient importance to appear as one of the cases outlined by the prominent Williamsburg attorney and law reporter Barradall.[58]

The case of *Oldum á Allerton and Pope* laid bare differences of opinion that had been germinating for years between lawyers bent on procedural reforms and the justices of the Country. Although the case was decided in favor of Justice Allerton, Barradall's arguments neatly summarized the different ideas he and Randolph (with others) had been developing for years about the nature of law in Virginia. Argued in the spring of 1739, the case was one of trespass for taking away a slave in order to make up the costs levied against Oldham, the inspector. Justice Allerton had sent Constable Pope to bring Oldham before him for breaking open and removing some samples out of hogsheads of tobacco at Wicomico warehouse. The justice claimed that the law demanded that such samples be put back after inspection, and Oldham had not done so. Thus, according to Allerton, the planter Joseph Gardner was right to bring suit against Oldham, and to pay the costs of damages, the slave was seized. But the jury returned a special verdict recounting these complicated facts, and the cause went up to the General Court.[59]

Barradall argued the cause of the plaintiff Oldham against Justice

---

Horne, "Opposition," pp. 26 ff.; also *VMHB* 25 (1917): 384 (fn. 7). The text of the 1713 law is not in Hening; see *VMHB* 26 (1918): 49–52. See also Winfree, ed., *Laws of Virginia*, pp. 75–90.

58. Westmoreland Orders, May 31, 1737, Sept. 27, 1737; *EJCV* 4:401, 405.

59. Barton, ed., *Virginia Colonial Decisions*, 2:B 331–43.

Allerton. He also saw an opportunity for promoting a lawyer's understanding of what a justice ought to do in Virginia's county courts and what he could not do. The lawyer argued that a judge who usurped a jurisdiction not his or exceeded his powers was liable for suit by an aggrieved party. This was commonly held to be true at law, and no one could contest such an argument. But the question here revolved around whether the law required the inspector to return the samples of tobacco to the hogsheads. Quoting the tobacco act, Barradall showed that the law prohibited an inspector from taking or converting "to his own Use" samples from the tobacco. The lawyer also showed that Justice Allerton had indicted the inspector only for not returning them, not for converting the samples to his own use. Thus the prosecution of Oldham and the taking of his slave were not lawful. The justice and Constable Pope, said Barradall, "are both Trespassors."

Barradall got to this point very quickly, and the cause seems simple enough. But by far the better part of this thirteen-page argument was devoted to remarks on the nature of Virginia's county magistracy, what was wrong with the institution, and what ought to be done to change the attitudes of the men holding the office of justice of the peace. The plaintiff's attorney observed "that all inferior Courts & Judges are in their nature & Constitution limited & circumscribed Some to Place as Courts of Corporation & Justices of Peace. . . . To w'ch I may add Justices of Peace in Cases where they have not an ordinary & gen' Jurisd. but only a particular Power or Authority given to them by some Act of Parliament Everyone of these limited Jurisd. must take Care to keep within their own Bounds."[60]

Coming closer to lived experience, the lawyer asserted, "We have common Experience of Actions a[gainst] Justices for whipping putting in Stocks &c. where he exceeds his Jurisd." This point was purely rhetorical hyperbole; such instances were rare, and Barradall knew it. But for the sake of his argument it was necessary to paint the justices in lurid colors as arbitrary ogres who only infrequently suffered for their insolences. The lawyer admitted that a justice might suffer if anyone could bring an action against him for a mistake in judgment. But that never happened, he asserted. Only when a magistrate exceeded the bounds plainly laid out in statutory language were actions against him available to a complainant. A peculiar inconvenience against a justice could not be argued [in law] against a general inconvenience to all aggrieved parties if they could never bring suit against a justice. "And surely there cannot be a

60. Ibid., B 334.

greater Inconv. than to suffer a Country Justice where his Power & Authority are plainly mark'd out & bounded to deviate from or exceed the Power given to him." Besides, the lawyer said, juries were notoriously easy on justices if only a small error in judgment was involved. "On the contrary where there are any Marks of Violence or Oppression of Partiality or Passion they make them smart for it in Dam's as indeed they ought."[61]

The real point of the lawyer's argument, however, came when he begged his auditors to consider "so dangerous it must be to the Liberty & Fortunes of the Subject to vest a single Just[ice] with so much Power as must be the Conseq[uence] of the Doctrine on the other Side." It was not safe to argue that a justice could convict not only for an offense stated in a statute but also for one that he simply felt had occurred—such as failing to return tobacco to an aggrieved planter's hogsheads. "This would be transferring the legislative Power to him & open a Door to all the Violence & Oppression imaginable. Justices may be governed & blinded by their Passions. I wish there was not something of that in this Case. But however that be it must be allowed to be too dangerous a Power to be lodged in a single Hand. And therefore the Laws have very wisely provided this Fence of an Action where the Just[ice] goes beyond the Power & Authority given him."[62]

Here was the real issue. Were county magistrates in Virginia to be carefully circumscribed with statutory, positive law, or were they free to mix administrative, judicial, legislative, and executive prerogatives together as they had been doing? The placing of the tobacco inspectors under the patronage of the justices may have been a mistake, so Barradall hinted. "Human Nature is too depraved to depend altog'r upon the Virtue & Integrity of the Judge. Power is apt to intoxicate & spoil the best Tempers. . . . I dare say it was never the Intention of the Law makers when they inflicted this Penalty to put it in the Power of a single Justice to ruin any Insp'r he pleased." Besides, the warrant ordering the inspector to appear was irregular—it demanded that the inspector appear only before that particular justice and "not any other Justice as the Usual Form is." Moreover, Oldham had refused to come and the judgment against him had been given in his absence, although the justice knew that he was an inspector and could not be absent from the warehouse without risking a penalty for that offense. Finally, the lawyer cited precedents that demanded that a summary conviction had to show the facts of the offense as set forth in the statute under which conviction was stated. This was

---

61. Ibid., B 335, 336, 337, 341–42.
62. Ibid., B 339.

particularly necessary in cases in which the defendant had been deprived of a jury trial.[63]

All of these points made such eminent sense and the need to rein in the power of independent-minded justices was so obvious that the lawyer could only express astonishment at the verdict. "Judgment was given for the Deft. [Justice Allerton] October 1739 by a great Majority of the Court."[64] The governor and Council had struggled too long to gain acceptance of the tobacco bill to jeopardize it now by alienating the justices under whose patronage the unpopular tobacco inspectors had been placed. The legal arguments of the lawyers may have been clear, well-reasoned, and judicious, but that made no difference. The power of the local magistrates was so entrenched by that point that nothing seemed able to dislodge it; no number of irregularities in procedure or practice was sufficient to warrant interference with the judgments of the local magistracy.

Barradall's disappointment at the verdict in 1739 was not a new experience. Both he and John Randolph had been complaining for years of the General Court's reluctance to overturn county decisions. Randolph's outspoken opinions at least lived up to the family motto *"Fari quae sentiat"* ("Say what you think"). So persuasive was he that on two occasions he managed to get the court to hear further arguments the following morning after they had decided to uphold county decisions. Randolph railed at the poor training of Virginia clerks and justices, noting in one case that a plaintiff's suit deserved to have been barred by the county court's erroneous entrance of a dismissal when it should have entered that the plaintiff took nothing by his bill. Randolph managed to get the General Court clerk, at least, not to make such errors "by my advice." But, he noted, the judges refused to make the counties hew to the line on such matters, for the mode of entering judgments in the Country was done that way, and "if it is not right all Judgment must be void." Randolph concluded in disgust, "In the Country Courts there is no such Entrey yet."[65]

The eminent barrister also argued against county justices' claims that their allowance of gates across roads did not constitute a nuisance, since Virginia conditions were hardly similar to those in England. But most

63. Ibid., B 343, citing *Rex v. Chandler* 1 Sal. 378.

64. Ibid. Unfortunately one cannot tell which General Court judges voted which way since the vote is, in this instance, not recorded. However, during the same October term, sitting judges included Gooch, Commissary Blair, William Byrd II, John Custis, and John Carter. Moreover, other barristers and attorneys were present who knew well enough the point Barradall was making. (See B 331 for a list of sitting judges in October 1739.)

65. Ibid., 1:R 22.

of the time county decisions were upheld by a General Court reluctant to be too severe with the proudly independent gentlemen justices of the Country.[66]

Barradall shared Randolph's annoyance. County decisions were upheld against his learned arguments as well, and the attorney moaned in despair after a lengthy discourse that his treatment on the law of descent "seemed to be little understood. It was new to the Court, as it seemeth." Barradall also cared little for the Country rhetoric piously invoked by some who continued to insist that religion and natural justice were the bases of sound legal interpretation. Even more dramatically than he had in his arguments in *Oldum*, Barradall set himself against the old-fashioned legal moralism of the Country tradition in two arguments, one in 1738 (*Anderson qui tam* against *Winston*) and the other in 1735 (*Waddill* against *Chamberlayne*).

In the *qui tam* action, the parties finally agreed, and no judgment emerged from the arguments. In that case, Barradall wanted the court to uphold the legality of charging 6 percent interest on money loaned, as the 1730 law on contracts allowed. He argued, "With Deference to the learned Gentleman's Opinion, I think some Men under some Circumstances may as lawfully take 10 per Cent as others may 5. I mean *foro concientiae* & abstracted from positive Laws. And this most of the Writers of the Law of Nature agree. I own that Usury seems to have been condemned by the ancient Laws of England." Nevertheless, he concluded, let the impartial observer look to Puffendorf, Grotius, and Roman Law. Those cosmopolitan sources agreed that usury was universally allowed, and only ecclesiastical superstition had forbidden it. Perhaps aware of how unpopular his defense might make him in certain quarters, the lawyer finished by saying, "I should be sorry to be thought an Advocate for excessive Usury as it is certainly introductory of great Oppression & I am heartily glad it is settled by Law." Whether the court was swayed by his argument, Barradall could only guess.[67]

In the 1735 case, however, he had just as strongly scorned the pious sentiments of those who believed that some semblance should exist between the laws of God and those of men. Governor Gooch, at least, could not have been well pleased with Barradall's remarks, for the governor had already revealed his predilection for viewing law as a monitor of moral behavior and a reflection of virtuous intent. Undaunted by the presence of Virginia's popular Country governor, Barradall argued for a

---

66. Ibid., 2:B 33, 39–40; B 43, 66. For an example of the practice of erecting gates across a public highway, see the Richmond County example cited above (fn. 4).

67. Ibid., 2:B 201–7 at 204–5 and 207.

view of law that was prophetic in its dimensions but wholly at odds with the ancient Country notions of Virginia justices.[68]

In *Waddill* the Williamsburg barrister found that his knowledge of the law of warranties was unappreciated. The defendant was charged with knowingly selling a terminally ill slave. The court gave in a verdict for the plaintiff, but Barradall moved for an arrest of judgment on the grounds that no warranty had been entered in the sale. "The Charge here," he contended, "is no more than selling a Thing of Small Value for a great Price and not discovering the Defects. And however inconsistent this may be with natural Justice It is tolerated by the universal Consent of Mankind where buying and selling is used." Barradall knew that his eloquence in defense of the maxim *caveat emptor* would be attacked. He observed, "I expect to be told that this is arguing in Favour of Fraud; that this makes Buying and Selling a mere cheat; and learned Lessons we shall hear no doubt concerning the Immorality of the Thing." Scarcely concealing his disdain for such unsophisticated ideas, he scornfully went on, "But however such kind of reasoning may serve to gain popular applause and raise a High Idea of the Orator's Integrity it will never I am sure prevail with discerning Judges." If the General Court could not see the opening he had just made through which they could escape Country notions unworthy of eminent magistrates, Barradall opened it still further. "The Laws of Society and Civil Government," he concluded, "are not founded upon the strict Rules of natural Justice. Public Convenience oft requires they sho'd be dispensed with. . . . To make specious harangues concerning the Morality or Immorality of an Action that is to be determined by the Laws of a particular Society is arguing neither like a Lawyer or [sic] a Politician."[69]

In that last sentence, Barradall made quite clear the differences that lay between professional lawyers in Virginia and the lay traditions of law in the Country. In the minds of lawyers the purpose of the law was to facilitate the speedy and expeditious completion of business. If the court

---

68. Horwitz, *Transformation of American Law*, argues that colonial lawyers might have conceded a different basis for statutory law from the customary, ancient sources of common law, which were held to be somehow rooted in the law of nature. Horwitz (pp. 6–7) even cites the *Anderson v. Winston* case regarding usury. He fails to consider, however, the striking attack on the prevalent doctrine of common law issued by Barradall in *Waddill*. See below.

69. Barton, ed., *Virginia Colonial Decisions*, 2:B 48–49. Notice that Barradall seems to draw back from the implications of his argument by suggesting that he is speaking strictly of civil laws only (and thus exempts common law from his attack). His rhetoric betrays him when he includes the "Laws of Society" in his attack in addition to mere "Civil Government."

upheld old-fashioned ideas of the natural law that could be construed to prohibit sharp business practices, he concluded, "there could be no such Thing as buying and selling." Nevertheless, as in the *Oldum* case, the judges were not moved. The plaintiff's case was upheld in April 1735, and another blow was given to the hopes of lawyers who desired a more up-to-date notion of what law was supposed to be about in Virginia.[70]

Despite such frustrating setbacks in the General Court, the lawyers of Virginia could take comfort in 1732 that their profession was finally receiving public recognition and standing. In that year the Virginia House passed a law that specified that prospective attorneys would henceforth be examined by a board of General Court attorneys appointed by the governor and Council. Several years earlier the House had voted a special word of thanks to Attorney General John Clayton because Clayton had written the 1727 law that made it easier to collect small debts and relieved attorneys of having to give security before representing clients who were out of the country. In 1732, Clayton was no longer head of the House Committee for Courts of Justice, but could rely on the goodwill of the House and the judicious work of the committee's clerk, England-trained attorney Benjamin Needler, to guide the new bill for licensing attorneys through the House. No serious opposition was encountered in 1732.

The law exempted all barristers and those attorneys already practicing in the General Court from having to submit to an examination and licensing. Since those same gentlemen were the pool from which the examining board was to be drawn by the Council, whose members were the General Court judges, an interlocking elite of judges and lawyers was formed through which access to the legal profession would henceforth be controlled from the capital. Although the power of local justices over their own courts' proceedings was still intact, access to the bar was determined by the Court, not the Country.[71]

For ten years the 1732 licensing law provided the means by which aspiring young lawyers entered the profession of law in Virginia. As the number of licensed attorneys increased across the colony, the traditional alarm in the Country about the power, designs, and character of lawyers surfaced once again. By 1742 the generation of barristers and attorneys that had fought for a licensing act and argued against the informality of Country legal procedures was passing from the scene. Between 1732 and

---

70. Ibid., p. 50.

71. The 1727 statute is in Hening, 4:182–97; the 1732 statute is in ibid., pp. 357–62. The latter act was brought in for consideration after the 1727 act was continued. See *JVHB*, May–July, 1732, pp. 127, 132, 165, and the introduction to the session concerning Clayton's work and the listings of the House committees and their clerks.

1743 General Court barristers and attorneys Clayton, Randolph, Holloway, John Hopkins, Needler, Samuel Eskridge, Barradall, and the General Court judge who favored a Virginia-born, paid judiciary, William Byrd II, all died. On the morning of June 14, 1742, an aged and infirm Henry Fitzhugh, of Stafford County, struggled to his feet in the House and asked leave to present a bill repealing the 1732 licensing act. A grandson of the famous seventeenth-century lawyer, Fitzhugh was a graduate of Christ Church, Oxford, and first and foremost a landed gentleman, not an attorney. The House was clearly on the side of Fitzhugh, as they had roundly rejected a proposal from Joseph Ball and Thomas Edwards to allow a set salary for the deputy crown attorneys in the county courts. Fitzhugh easily secured the repeal of the 1732 law and immediately moved that a bill be brought in to require lawyers already practicing to take an oath that they would not exact fees in excess of limits set by law. This bill also passed easily. Within six months, Fitzhugh and his aged colleague from Goochland, William Randolph, who had aided him in repealing the licensing law, were both dead.[72]

The passing of an older generation of burgesses and attorneys, however, did not settle the issue of whether Virginia's legal profession should be formally licensed, controlled by General Court practitioners, and allowed to increase in numbers as it had during the previous decade. By 1745 the burgesses were being urged to reconsider their repeal of the 1732 law. In 1744, after an acrimonious debate, the House had permanently killed a motion to extend the 1742 law that prohibited the taking of excessive fees. The chairman of the Committee for the Courts of Justice was thirty-seven-year-old Charles Carter, who enlisted the support of twenty-eight-year-old Philip Ludwell, the brilliant attorney thirty-four-year-old Benjamin Waller, and Gawin Corbin, scion of one of the most eminent Middlesex County families and, like Ludwell and Carter, connected to the Council. Those men had reported to the House the difficulties involved with the 1742 exorbitant fee bill, and the termination of that act cleared the way for a revival of the 1732 law. After introduction, debate, and readings during the 1745 session, the act was signed into law in March 1746.[73]

---

72. *JVHB*, May 17, 1742, p. 23, on the crown attorney salary proposal; ibid., June 14–19, 1742, for the repeal of the 1732 law, pp. 62, 64, 65, 66, 67, and 69, and on the exorbitant fee act (given in Hening, 5:171, 181–82).

73. *JVHB*, Sept. 11–Oct. 25, 1744, pp. 86, 87, 88, 109, 113, 115, 136, 148, on the controversy over renewing the 1742 law. For the new act of 1746, see ibid., Feb. 28, 1745–46, pp. 165, 206, in which the committee recommended against renewing the 1742 act. For the engrossment of the bill after amendments and the April signature into law, see ibid., p. 220. The act is in Hening, 5:345–50.

Two years later, in 1748, a general revisal of the laws of Virginia was undertaken, and the 1746 act was renewed, with one significant addition. The 1746 law had demanded that a prospective lawyer first get a recommendation from county justices who knew him that he was a man of probity and good reputation. Barristers and those attorneys already practicing in the General Court at the time the 1746 law was passed were once again exempted from taking out a new license. However, they, as well as new attorneys, had to swear the oaths of allegiance and the oath of an attorney before the lower courts in which they wished to practice. The 1748 law repeated this provision, but added that to prevent "trifling and vexatious appeals from the county courts" no attorney practicing in the General Court was from henceforth to practice in the counties. Barristers were again exempt, and General Court attorneys were allowed to continue working in the counties within a day's ride of Williamsburg, where many of them had extensive practices already, namely, York, James City, Warwick, Elizabeth City, and Gloucester. The clear implication of the law went beyond its stated intent and reserved the area right around the capital for attorneys of the supreme court. To a very large degree, the bar of Virginia, like the court system itself, had become a two-tiered affair, with the better members of the guild naturally gravitating toward the more exciting cases, larger fees, and professional camaraderie of the Lower Peninsula.[74]

Though this distinction between General and county bars was repealed briefly in 1757, it was reinstated in 1761, renewed in 1766, and ratified again for seven years in 1769. From 1748–49 until the closing of the courts in 1774, then, no significant legislation altered the nature or standards of the bar in Virginia. The legislation of the 1740s, and its reconfirmation later, demonstrated that public awareness of lawyers as a distinct "profession" had finally emerged in colonial Virginia.[75]

Yet a far more persuasive confirmation of this notion can be made and an estimate given concerning the impact of the profession on Virginia life by leaving the rather tedious details of legislative history behind,

---

74. On the 1748 revisal, see the superb master's thesis by G. Morgan, "Virginia Law Revision." For the text of the 1748 law, see Hening, 6:140–43.

75. Hening, 7:124–25, 397–401. The law of 1761 altered the 1748 law slightly. Only barristers could practice in the counties and the General Court after 1761. In other words, not even the General Court attorneys who had been allowed to continue practices in the counties right around Williamsburg according to the 1748 law were thereafter permitted that indulgence. The law of 1761 further strengthened the separation between General Court and county bars. Men like George Wythe, Robert Carter Nicholas, and other eminent, Virginia-trained attorneys were confined to the General Court from 1761. See also Hening, 8:198, 385–86.

and looking once again at the law in action. By 1750 social, economic, political, and cultural stirrings were signaling the dawn of a new era. As the legal profession of Virginia burgeoned in numbers, power, and importance, complaints and suspicions rose proportionately. But for the first time an alarming number of attacks were issued also against the gentlemen justices of the peace. Between 1750 and 1774 the traditional confrontation between Court lawyers and Country justices took on new and startling dimensions that permanently reshaped the legal culture of Virginia.

Chapter 4
Country Justice Besieged, 1750–1774

This absurd Pride, so frequent here for a Justice of Peace
—GEORGE FISHER, "Narrative"

On March 4, 1771, the Worshipful Court of Richmond County, headed by the formidable Colonel Landon Carter, gathered to deal with the county business. To their shock, they discovered eloquent evidence of the low regard some citizens had for the gentlemen justices of the peace. The court orders for the day take indignant note of "an Insult of the most Extravagant Nature having been Maliciously offered upon the Bench in which the Justices set to hold Court by daub'g it with Tar and Dung in many places." The irate justices offered a reward of ten pounds current money "for the Discovery of such Atrocious Offenders" who presumed to denigrate the dignity of the county bench.[1] As far as we know, the offenders were never caught. But this scene and the activity that caused it speak to the latter-day observer, as they did to the gentry, in unmistakable language: discontent with the county justices was widespread and alarming in its proportions by 1771.

What had happened between 1750 and 1771 to bring about such a startling demonstration of public disrespect for Country justices? Although one has to trace several important developments that established the context within which a crisis of confidence about the justices' performance erupted, those developments themselves do not supply the answer to the question. The answer was, in fact, both quite simple and yet so complex that the local justices never managed to respond to their critics. Briefly put, in the years from 1750 to 1774 the performance of, and the public's attitude toward, the local justices was affected by two opposing demands. The religious upheavals of the 1760s spoke eloquently of the anxieties afflicting many Virginians concerning the moral tenor of their colony's life. Not only Baptists, but also prominent members of the gentry, the Anglican clergy, and the governors urged a moral reformation upon a society that was increasingly caught up in racing, gaming, cockfighting, and indebtedness on a scale heretofore unimaginable. For some people at the county level the justices were perceived to be

---

1. Richmond Orders, Mar. 4, 1771.

failing in their duty to uphold the old notion that legal principles and action ought to be rooted in moral precepts and ideas.

Yet, not everyone felt this way. Indeed, some, Edward Barradall, for example, had long since rejected such pious notions. The justices were criticized from that quarter by a growing legal profession, whose main concern was not to equate law with principles of moral behavior or community sanction but to ensure that it was procedurally and substantively correct and, above all, efficient. Precisely because of their need to do their clients' burgeoning business quickly and with some hope of getting paid for their labors, Virginia attorneys and merchants increasingly clamored for a better legal system, more able judges, and, above all, for an acceptance of the idea that law was "scientific."

Caught between two urgent agendas and unable to satisfy either group of critics in every particular, the local justices struggled to keep up with demands, but by the 1770s they were clearly dispirited and their adherence to an ideal of public duty and service was perceptibly in decline. Proposals for reform were advanced which were actually friendly to the idea of local justices who were not "professionals" but laymen, but these were opposed by the Country gentlemen, who feared that they would merely advance the cause of unscrupulous lawyers to the detriment of their own and their counties' interests. Surprisingly, the lawyers were able to appropriate the language of the Country tradition to advance their own arguments in favor of an independent and professional judiciary.

Comparing the activities of court day in the period from 1750 to 1774 with those of a court day during the preceding thirty years, one immediately understands that the procedures and the length of time it took to bring a case to trial both seemed to argue (with the lawyers) in favor of a professional judiciary. The ideas of the lawyers for the Country courts can only be appreciated by placing the rise of the profession within the context of county procedures and activity after 1750. Many humbler Virginians wanted their courts, and especially the gentry officers, to return to simpler, more virtuous days, when court day was a meeting place for people of all ranks instead of an increasingly acrimonious and alien forum filled with the mysterious language of professional law. The criticism of gentry culture in general underlay those demands. In the short run Virginia's justices moved to meet the lawyers; in the long run they sealed their doom by satisfying no one. In the popular mind a rapacious merchant-creditor class, a dissolute gentry culture, and an unscrupulous legal profession were all parts of the same general malaise.

The Decline of Court Day and Rising Social Tensions

The attention of the county magistrates between 1750 and 1774 focused increasingly on the spiraling number of civil debt cases and the burdens that the disposition of those cases placed upon the justices. Complaints against the slowness of county justice found their way into the legislature, into the pages of the *Gazette*, and even into the courtrooms themselves in the form of accusations of partiality and prejudice. Regardless of the source or the form of such protests, however, the justices insisted on addressing the problems in their own way and on a piecemeal basis. In 1752 the Council ordered the county clerks to send in a list of justices who sat and of those who never qualified in court and failed to sit. The county lists were then purged, and a presumably more dutiful list of commissions was drawn up shortly thereafter.[2] Such an intervention on the part of the Council stemmed from protests against the slowness of county proceedings, a slowness that county regulations had done little to alleviate.

For example, in King George County the court adopted a bylaw that declared that justices were to meet by noon between March and September. This 1739 declaration was followed by another a year later warning attorneys that the court would not be delayed by their absences from court, a warning repeated again in 1743. Westmoreland justices also declared in 1739 that their court would sit before noon. Northumberland County magistrates appointed a deputy clerk in 1750 because the chief clerk was often ill and failed to appear at court. In 1725 and again in 1731 Westmoreland regulated its procedures by specifying that in order to be paid witnesses had to be summoned by the clerk. That practice was instituted to eliminate volunteer witnesses who wished to make some money by offering their services. To avoid delays the court further decided that after a conditional order had been issued in a suit, no time to imparl would be allowed afterwards; instead the order would change from an "order nisi" (conditional) to a final order.[3]

---

2. *EJCV*, 5:378–79. On March 23, the crown was sent the "Representation of the Council of State and Judges of the General Court" asking for an increase in salary due to the "great Increase of the Business in the Supreme Court," much of the increase because of appeals from the counties and the colony's expanding population and volume of trade. Ibid., pp. 379–80.

3. Northumberland Orders, Aug. 13, 1750; Westmoreland Orders, July 29, 1725, Feb. 25, 1731, Feb. 27, 1738–39; King George Orders, Mar. 2, 1738–39, Jan. 4, 1739–40, Sept. 2, 1743; Henrico Orders, Oct. 7, 1745. Since 1727 (Hening, 4:195) the English law regarding jeofails had been in effect in Virginia, as well as statutes regulating amendments of pleadings before judgment. See Hening, 4:195, 233. Pleadings and procedures to amend pleadings were loosely construed in Virginia's colonial courts, as both practice and the

Attempts at procedural reform initiated by the burgesses themselves ran into opposition from another quarter. During the 1748 revisal of the laws the burgesses tried to take some of the burden off the General Court by passing the "Act concerning Juries," giving full power to county grand juries over "all offences made penal by the laws of this colony," thus attempting to decrease the criminal docket the supreme court had to deal with and to allow more time for actions at law and in chancery. The king's attorney general, Mathew Lamb, objected to the power this lodged in the local courts. Although this act was eventually allowed to pass, the companion bill to the jury act was disallowed. "The Act for establishing the General Court" failed because of the lack of a suspending clause; but perhaps more importantly, because the act raised the amount for an original process in the General Court from ten pounds to twenty pounds current money and forbade appeals from the county courts to causes that involved less than ten pounds. Intended to impede appeals from the counties, these provisions were opposed by British merchants, who were fearful that they could never collect debts from county juries and justices, fears shared by their professional attorneys.[4]

In the counties themselves the magistrates were becoming discouraged with the formidable dockets that faced them. By the 1760s those dockets were so crowded that the court "day" of the 1720s, which took two to three days in the 1740s, was often a four- or five-day session. Justices began showing up for court the first day but failed to return for the subsequent sessions. That practice was more serious than it may first appear, for by the 1750s courts had begun to docket their business and arrange various duties so that administrative details were dealt with first. Jury trials and complicated legal matters were not begun until the second or third day. So notorious was the habit of justices' slinking away after the first day that Essex County in 1764 petitioned the governor for relief. The justices recommended John Corrie for the bench, saying, "The Sitting members beg leave to represent to his Honor that this Gentleman resides near the Courthouse and that on the Third and fourth Days of the Courts sitting their are Seldom more than four members to Dispatch the Business of the County." On May 2, 1764, Corrie took his oath.[5]

---

wording of these statutes indicate. See also Marshall, *Papers of John Marshall*, 1:148 (fn. 7), 196 (fn. 3), 222 (fn. 3).

4. G. Morgan, "Virginia Law Revision," argues persuasively that the lawyers who worked on this revisal, such as Wythe, Benjamin Waller, and others, became frustrated at the disallowance of key pieces of legislation. Whether these frustrations actually increased the profession's disaffection from crown policies is debatable. For the provision for suspending clauses, see Labaree, ed., *Royal Instructions*, 1:128–29.

5. Essex Orders, Mar. 21, May 2, 1764.

In 1770 the Council, with some annoyance, denied the petition of Elizabeth City's court for a new Commission of the Peace, deeming the old one sufficient and adding that multiplying justices would only exempt men from militia service, "which is the sole End for which some People seem desirous of becoming Magistrates." The Council also censured Justice John Bowyer in another county for partiality in determining suits brought by clients who employed his brother, the lawyer Luke Bowyer.[6]

The declension in public-spirited service was a matter of general comment. Landon Carter confided bitterly to his diary in 1772 that "the Public duty hardly seems to be anybody's concern. However the 6, 7, 8 I made a shift to get Justices enough to hold court, where except the Second day a good deal of business was done; but on that day it seemed as if everybody strove to be quite indolent which kept me continually calling out upon them; and at last I was obliged to assure the whole court that as I now saw they wanted to shake off their Spur I was determined to leave them."[7] Part of the difficulty, however, lay with just such imperious men as Carter himself. If his own son Robert Wormeley Carter and some of his fellow junior justices resented Landon's high-handed comments and behavior in Richmond County, they were not alone. Other counties registered similar complaints against the haughty nature of the senior justices.

In 1720 Henrico justices had petitioned the Council to appoint William Randolph to their bench, even though "there are already Commissioned a Sufficient number of Justices." The court wanted William to sit alongside Thomas Randolph, Henry Randolph, Jr., and Richard Randolph because "the business of the County wou'd be dispatched with greater Expedition, and a more regular manner, if such a person were Judge who more perfectly understands the matters of Law now arising." The Council granted this request on November 11, 1720, "but forasmuch as there are already two of his Brothers Justices in the said County, it is the Opinion of the Board that a Letter be Writt to the said Court directing that care be taken the said three Brothers do not Set together on the Tryal of any Cause that shall come before that Court."[8] By the late 1740s, the dominance of the Randolphs had become so absolute that many sessions were kept running by them alone; that occasioned confrontation and acrimony which undermined both the public image of the bench and the willingness of other gentlemen to serve.

6. *EJCV*, 6:378, 540. The Council also rejected a petition for a new commission for Northumberland. Ibid., p. 427.
7. Greene, ed., *Diary*, April 14, 1772, 2:668–69.
8. Henrico Orders, July 4, 1720; *EJCV*, 3:533.

Whereas cases of contempt of court had usually revolved around public definitions of self by half-drunken planters, a more caustic and bitter tone in those confrontations became noticeable after mid-century. In Henrico in August 1744, Field Jefferson, the uncle of the author of the Declaration of Independence and later presiding justice in Lunenberg, insulted Richard Randolph "in a Bold and Contemptible manner." Responding to a remark made by Randolph during questioning, Jefferson retorted "that he (the said Jefferson meaning himself) got his money as honestly as he did (meaning the said Randolph)." Though Jefferson later apologized and was briefly a member of Henrico's commission, his resentment of the Randolphs was real, and it was not unique. By the 1750s, the Duval family, of Huguenot merchant stock, was rapidly rising in Henrico, so much so that by 1769, Samuel Duval headed the Commission of the Peace, Benjamin was sheriff, and William Duval represented the family interests as a county attorney. Incensed at some slight offered him by the upstart Duvals, Richard Randolph on June 1, 1770, complained to the Council of Samuel's arrogant behavior toward him. Little disposed to become involved in local squabbles, the Council on June 15 dismissed Randolph's complaint as "trifling."[9]

Similar fractious and unsettling acrimony pitted Thomas Pinckard against Edwin Conway in Lancaster. In Westmoreland an infuriated plaintiff incurred a jail sentence and was bound to good behavior for "saying in the face of the Court that Col. Fitzhugh had such a Sway in this Court that he could not have Justice done him."[10] Exasperation with the county courts' procedures prompted one writer to Rind's *Gazette* to claim that, though a justice himself in New Kent, he had sat as a witness in Charles City County's court in a case in which he was retained for forty-four days; when he left, the case was still not settled.[11] In 1773, Justice Meriwether Smith and A TRAVELLER exchanged opinions and insults about the unlearned procedures and burdens of office among justices in Essex County.[12] Clearly, both court records and *Gazette* pieces reflect a growing dissatisfaction with the justices' performance in office, a performance lamented even among the gentlemen justices themselves.

The explanation of why the courts seemed to be faltering and why the older presiding justices were perceived as being inadequate appears to

9. *EJCV*, 6:346; ibid., June 15, 1770, p. 353. On Jefferson, see ibid., 5:275; Henrico Orders, Aug. 6, 1744, Mar. 4, 1744–45.
10. On the Conway-Pinckard dispute, see Lancaster Orders, Apr. 12, 1745, July 12, 1745. On the Conway-Pinckard family connection, see Hayden, "Conway, Edwin," *Virginia Genealogies*; Westmoreland Orders, Feb. 24, 1747–48.
11. *Virginia Gazette* (Rind), Feb. 22, 1770.
12. On the TRAVELLER essays, see below.

be connected with the nature of legal learning in the colony. Justices traditionally relied on Dalton's *Countrey Justice*, Swinburne's *Wills and Testaments*, and the statutes of England and Virginia for their legal education. Theirs was not unlearned law, but the justices had not been accustomed to public scrutiny or challenge before 1750. With the arrival of a printing press in Williamsburg and more treatises on law read by an aggressive and rapidly rising legal profession, however, the hegemony of the justices over legal culture began to come apart. As population and trade increased apace, the inadequacies of traditional, Country justice were deplored by lawyers.

The impact on local courts that the rise of the profession occasioned was slow to arrive but inexorable and physically real to a county observer. The appearance of the courtroom and the dramatic confrontations that occurred informed him of the change. Contemporary descriptions of county courtrooms before 1750 almost never mention a lawyers' bench inside the bar. That is hardly to be considered an oversight, for the same descriptions *do* specify a place for the deputy crown attorney inside the bar, and one cannot suppose lawyers' benches would have been overlooked had they been deemed important. The bench of the justices, elevated above the courtroom one to three feet, looked directly upon the assembled county through the 1730s. In 1737, however, Essex justices ordered "Robert Spilsbee Coleman [to] make a new barr for the attorneys at this Court within the barr yt is now built with a place for them to write upon with Six drawers thereto." Lancaster's new courthouse, built in 1740, specified nothing with regard to a lawyers' bench. Yet by the 1750s evidence in other counties indicates that bookcases, more elaborate benches, and special privileges were allowed lawyers in the county courts. Moreover, when an attorneys' bench was constructed, it sat facing the justices, with the lawyers' backs to the county. The interposition of the lawyers' bench architecturally represented what the rise of a profession meant in cultural terms, since the courtroom had formerly been dominated by face-to-face proceedings.[13]

As the stature of lawyers grew with the addition of special furniture to the courtrooms, the unquestioned authority of the justices diminished somewhat. Whenever a lawyer was reprimanded for contempt in the county courts, the cause was invariably one that involved criticism by the lawyer of the legal abilities and wisdom of the county bench. Justices bridled at those attacks, barred the offenders from practicing until they

---

13. Essex Orders, Nov. 21, 1737; Westmoreland Orders, July 27, 1757; Middlesex Orders, Apr. 2, 1765; Northumberland Orders, Sept. 10, 1750. On Lancaster's new courthouse, see Orders, Aug. 8, 1740.

publicly humbled themselves, and then usually forgave the penitent attornies. Lawyers Richard Parker, John Mercer, William Kennan, Cawan Dulaney, Moseley Battaley, Thomas Prosser, and David Boyd were all reprimanded at one time or another for their criticism of the courts.[14]

Whether the lawyers could actually boast a superior brand of legal learning is arguable. Justices, for example, usually got their training through experience, starting as young men in the Commission of the Peace and learning through reading and observation what their fathers, uncles, and other relatives and acquaintances of mature years did in particular cases. The contrast between the legal knowledge of justices and that of lawyers was the subject of pointed contemporary comment and served to underscore the distinct quality of being a lawyer, a quality somehow different from that commonly associated with a justice.

In 1736, barely four years after the first statute licensing lawyers was put into effect, Justice George Webb of New Kent County published his manual *The Office and Authority of a Justice of Peace*. Intended for the justice who wanted guidance when deciding a matter out of sessions, this publication made no reference to lawyers. Rather, Webb wrote: "I have avoided all References to Laws and Law Books, but have collected and recited out of them so much as I found necessary to my Subject: The far greatest Part of our Inhabitants are unfurnish'd with those Books, or diverted from Reading them, by the necessary Affairs of their Plantations, and by the innocent Pleasures of a Country Life."[15]

One senses the same reluctance to endorse fully the formalism of print culture in the eulogium offered upon the death of Anthony Walke. Published three days before Christmas, 1768, in the *Virginia Gazette*, his obituary advertised with regret the passing of a former justice, county lieutenant, and burgess, whose greatness was all the more admirable because "from a slender education, such as a little reading and writing as the times could then afford, he made a wonderful proficiency in true and solid knowledge greatly preferable to a knowledge of words and language." As his tombstone said, Walke "behaved himself with an uniform regard to Justice tempered with Mercy, and in all respects consulted the best interests of the county over which he presided."[16]

---

14. These attorneys were charged with contempt, threatened with disbarment, and, after humbling themselves publicly before the justices, allowed to return to practice. Mercer was particularly and repeatedly belligerent; on his career, see below. For the others, see Northumberland Orders, Nov. 10, 1740, Mar. 9, 1741; Westmoreland Orders, June 28, 1738; King George Orders, Dec. 7, 1752; Lancaster Orders, Dec. 12, 1746, Sept. 10, 1737, Dec. 12, 1746, Jan. 20, 1758; VMHB 14 (1907): 213–14.
15. Webb, *Office and Authority*, p. ix.
16. VMHB 5 (1898): 142; *Virginia Gazette* (P and D), Dec. 22, 1768.

The contrast between that species of Country wisdom and the (perhaps) more formal but suspect learning of lawyers was commonly acknowledged. The feisty justice of Richmond County, Landon Carter, put it best. Sneering at an attorney who had challenged his wisdom, Carter retorted with crushing contempt: "I replied that it pleased me to find a Gentleman Pique himself on a little Mechanical knowledge, which to be sure all forms of Pleadings must be allowed to be on; [that] we could not imagine they were so eazy to be in the Spare hours that some people had behind Counters; That Attorneys were always lookt upon as so many Copyers and their Knowledge only lay in knowing from whom to Copy Properly."[17]

Nevertheless, by the 1770s the rise of these "copyers" had been felt in Virginia. One of them, Richard Starke of New Kent County, attorney and clerk to the various committees of the House of Burgesses, determined to reissue Webb's manual. Starke died before completing his task, and his publisher's explanation reveals an awareness of the importance of the profession whose abilities Carter disdained to respect. Upon Starke's death "his Friends prevailed on some benevolent Gentlemen of the Law to continue the Work, for the Benefit of a numerous and distressed Family." The publishers Purdie and Dixon confidently explained: "The Learning and Abilities of these Gentlemen cannot be doubted; but as they wrote without having any Communication with each other, and could not well spare the Time from the necessary Business of their Profession, it is to be feared that some few Errours may be found, which . . . the Publick will make all due Allowances for."[18]

If these sentiments seemed to point to some kind of perceptible cultural distinctiveness, some real public identity and function of lawyers, in what exactly did it consist? Fortunately, by tracing the licensing of lawyers between 1732 and 1774, by examining the training of 151 of them in the Tidewater of Virginia during those years, and by noting the function of the General Court bar, we can at least tell what some of the differences were. Moreover, tensions within Virginia society in the 1750s and 1760s tended to put lawyers on the defensive, since their profession was linked (not unjustly) in the public mind with straitened credit, badgering plaintiffs, increased litigiousness, and longer court sessions. The response of the lawyers was to demand an overhaul of the court system and to claim that far from being the enemies of virtue, they were in fact its stanchest defenders. By 1772, to an amazing degree, many Virginians apparently agreed with them.

17. Greene, ed., *Diary*, 1:92–93 (Journal of House).
18. Starke, *Office and Authority*, preface.

To be a lawyer in Virginia after 1732, one obviously had to obtain training of some sort in order to pass the oral examination before the General Court barristers and attorneys appointed by the governor and Council to see to the task of upholding standards. One could either train in England, at the Inns or in the chambers of an English barrister, or one could study with a clerk-attorney in the counties. By far the largest number of Virginia lawyers were trained by the latter method. Hence, on the basis of education or training, one can hardly suggest a radically different experience for county lawyers from that pursued by the sons and nephews of the gentry who became justices of the peace. Fewer than twelve Virginians actually attended the Inns, received a call to the bar, and returned to active legal practice before 1776. Fewer still of these twelve practiced in the counties, tending instead to gravitate toward the General Court bar. That elite capital bar was dominated by England-trained gentlemen and by English immigrants, who regarded their country cousins with disdain.

After 1748 the bar of Virginia was formally divided, and attorneys had to choose whether they would practice in the counties or in Williamsburg, but they could not do both. Barristers were exempted, but there were so few of them that this made little difference, and few were inclined to practice in the counties. However, the law also exempted General Court attorneys having practices in a roughly forty-mile radius around Williamsburg. The long-term effect of this exemption was to give the courts around the capital a panache and reputation for efficiency and sympathetic handling of lawyers' and merchants' concerns that was envied by practitioners who were doomed to endure the slower proceedings in the Country courts.[19]

There is no convincing evidence, then, that Virginia lawyers actually boasted superior training that naturally set them off from justices and incurred the wrath of the benches. Nor were lawyers drawn from the vulgar herd. Most of them came from families that were engaged in planting, merchandising, preaching the gospel, or practicing physic or the law. If native-born Virginians were not distinctive either in education or class background, however, their function tended to separate them from the local justices of the peace.

By law no justice could practice as a lawyer in the county where he sat. Moreover, justices were never paid a salary. If a lawyer actually was put

19. The dominant pattern of lawyer education in Virginia was a few years' study and copying with a practicing attorney. See details below, also A. M. Smith, "Virginia Lawyers," pp. 59–205. The 151 attorneys studied for these counties were documented as having been in active practice according to surviving court records, private papers, and obituary notices in the *Gazette*.

onto the Commission of the Peace, he would lose his practice in the county where he sat. The pattern of licensing reveals that most Virginia attorneys followed the court days in several counties, licensing themselves, for example, in four or five contiguous counties in the Northern Neck. The peregrinations of the lawyer naturally discouraged the idea that he could be counted on to sit as a justice for between one and three days every month in one county.

Beyond such practical impediments, however, lay the function of a lawyer in the courtroom, and that quality set him apart from the majority of Virginians, and even somewhat from the county bench. Justices naturally prided themselves on their ability to read the statutes, interpret them, and apply them for men and women whose world was oriented not toward sight, toward printed and permanent symbols, but toward hearing, and face-to-face communication. The public discourse and role of a lawyer was largely directed *toward* the already "print-literate" bench or toward an argument with another attorney. Highly recondite phrases and references naturally filled the air of a county courtroom as the number of lawyers increased; what was heard must have seemed increasingly alien, and not surprisingly, such sounds gave real substance to accusations that the courts were filled with "lawyers' gibberish."[20]

Many counties knew that their justices were not practicing lawyers. Those counties where an occasional General Court attorney or a gentleman who had been at the Inns for perhaps a year but was not a practitioner was supposed to sit also knew that those individuals were not the men who faithfully attended court each month (see table 4). The barristers and attorneys responsible for examining prospective lawyers at Williamsburg were, of course, initially all England trained. Only gradually did that group begin to include native-born and native-trained members (see table 5). Yet the growing numbers of natives entering the legal profession could not wholly allay the suspicions among Virginians that more lawyers meant more complicated procedures, longer court sessions,

---

20. The lampooning of legal argot began in the *Gazette* in 1736 (Dec. 3–10) with the publication of a British piece, "A Rapsody, occasioned by a Review of the Common Misery of Human Kind, especially in that Part of the World called Great Britain." The complaint couples "Book-sellers, the Devil," with "Gangs of Attorneys, Wreathocks of the law." The unintelligible sounds of legal "book-learning" were summarized:

Bonds, Writs, First Days of Terms, and *Scire Facias*,
 Scapes, *Affadavits*, Precedents, and Capias;
Actions, Arrests, *Mandamuses*, and Pleas,
 Stamps, Executions, Errors, Trials, Fees;
The *Habeas Corpus*, and the *Certiorari*
 Hard Words, and Harder Deeds, that only vary.

TABLE 4 *Barristers, General and County Court Attorneys, and Inns of Court Members on County Benches in the Tidewater, 1750–1770*

B Barrister (attended Inns and called to English bar)
I Inns (invited to join or attended)
A General Court Attorney
a County Court attorney

York: Peyton Randolph, B, A, a; John Blair, Jr., B, A

Charles City: William Byrd III,[a] I

Elizabeth City: George Wythe,[b] A, a; Wilson Cary, I

Gloucester: Beverley Whiting, I; Lewis Burwell, I

Henrico: Ryland Randolph,[a] I

James City: John Blair, Jr., B, A; John Randolph, B, A; Robert Carter Nicholas, A, a

New Kent: James Power, A, a

Warwick: none

Middlesex: Christopher Robinson,[b] I; Gawan Corbin,[b] I, Henry Churchill,[c] B, a

Essex: Robert Beverley,[b] I

Caroline: Edmund Pendleton, A, a

Lancaster: none.

Northumberland: none.

King George: Alexander Rose,[b] a, A (?)

Richmond: John Tarpley, a, A; Travers Tarpley,[c] a

Westmoreland: Philip Ludwell Lee,[b] I; Robert Vaulx,[c] a; Robert Carter,[b] I; William Bernard,[b] a

Stafford: John Mercer, A, a; Thomson Mason, B, A, a; Thomas Ludwell Lee,[b] I

Source: County order books; *EJCV*, 5:388–95; Jones and Hamilton lists of Americans at the Inns of Court (see note 21).
Note: Insufficient records and lists of justices prohibit definitive statements about Hanover, King William, King and Queen, Prince William, and Fairfax counties.
[a] Never sat in the commission to which appointed.
[b] Sat rarely.
[c] Lawyer who gave up practice to sit, or appointed but served as clerk or attorney and declined to sit as justice.

TABLE 5 *General Court Examiners of Prospective Lawyers, 1732–1772*

V = Virginia born
E = England born

1732–42:

John Clayton, barrister, E

Sir John Randolph, barrister, V

Edward Barradall, barrister, E

Benjamin Needler, attorney, E (trained in England)

Richard Francis, barrister, E

James Power, attorney, E (trained in England)

1748–58:

Peyton Randolph, barrister, V

St. Lawrence Berford, attorney, E (trained in England)

Stephen Dewey, attorney, V

William Nimmo, attorney, E (trained in England)

1758–72:

George Wythe, attorney, V

John Randolph, barrister, V

Robert Carter Nicholas, attorney, V

Source: Compiled from *EJCV*, 1734–41; names appearing on licenses of lawyers in county court records, 1732–70.

more delays, and more money for attorneys, but very little relief for the ordinary yeoman or planter.

No doubt Virginians only vaguely sensed what we know: after 1750 the bar grew rapidly, far more rapidly than the population of the Tidewater. By surveying the careers of 151 barristers and attorneys practicing between 1716 and 1770, we can see that 108 were native born, and most of these studied with clerk-attorneys. A few attended William and Mary for a year or so.[21] England-born and England-trained practitioners who immigrated to Virginia totaled 27 in the area studied; of those, 21 came before 1750, only 6 thereafter. The remaining 16 licensed attorneys have so far eluded absolute identification, but fragmentary evidence strongly indicates that they, too, ought to be included in the group of native-born and native-trained attorneys. At least 20 of the known lawyers were second, third, or fourth sons of planters, merchants, or clerics, and 11 of them were lawyers' sons.[22]

Despite the fact that by the 1750s lawyers had become an increasingly familiar aspect of Virginia life during the course of a quarter of a century, public sentiment displayed a growing antagonism toward the profession. One example is the sudden change that occurred after 1755 in literary references about lawyers. To what extent Virginians had access to the *Virginia Gazette* is not clear. Signature rates indicate that literacy was a skill marginally possessed by two-thirds of able-bodied white males, and that rate may have started to stagnate after 1750. Even in the Tidewater general access to printed information was limited. Thus, in 1775, Robert Carter complained to John Pinckey that his paper was not reaching Northern Neck residents, causing "several Subscribers to Said Papers ... to murmur, Saying that a NewsPaper was a very uncommon thing among them."[23] Yet one supposes that many Virginia planters and

21. Smith, "Virginia Lawyers," pp. 360–62, attempts a listing of Virginia attorneys who attended William and Mary. This cannot be an accurate list of practitioners, as indicated by Smith's incautious use of the Jones and Hamilton lists of men invited to attend or join the Inns of Court. Both the Inns and the college played a very minor role in legal education before 1779.

22. Wills, inventories, and genealogical information were compiled for prosopography of over 250 lawyers. Of these, 151 can be demonstrated to have been in active practice in the Tidewater counties under study here. Paternal occupation of English immigrants has often been impossible to trace; rank of native-born attorneys is known for all but the sixteen obscure men indicated above. The designation "planter" or "merchant" is often used interchangably in records, reflecting the fact that many merchants, attorneys, physicians, and clergymen were planters of sorts. There is little evidence for concluding that the emerging "profession" comprised "new men," outside the ranks of the lesser gentry. Patrick Henry and Edmund Pendleton seem to have been exceptions, Jefferson, Waller, the Randolphs, and the Tarpleys, the rule.

23. Lockridge, *Literacy*, pp. 77–78, 90, 93. Robert Carter's remark is in Robert Carter Daybook Letters, 1775–79, July 19, 1775, from the Library of Congress (typescript used courtesy of the American Antiquarian Society Manuscripts Department, Folder 3). Almanac distribution is difficult to document. As early as the 1750s the almanac was being used, at least among justices in western counties. See the almanac collection at the American Antiquarian Society, containing one of Colonel William Preston's Augusta County almanacs, which he used at court day to make notes in while on the bench. On the rise of the book trade and the spread of print culture, see Molnar, "Publication and Retail Book Advertisements."

farmers probably had access to that bosom companion of rural life, the *Virginia Almanac*. Between 1729 and the Revolution that source of advice, whimsy, and observation regularly provided information on crops, weather, astrological signs, and, in particular, court day. A table of court days was always prominently displayed, and reader demands insured that the table was printed on several pages and in readable type.

Between 1729 and 1755 the almanac had nothing to say about lawyers. Yet between 1755 and the Revolution antilawyer doggerel and epigrams, moral tales, and pithy observations about the designing, rapacious nature of the legal profession were a feature in every issue, usually attached to the headings of the months of April and October, when the General Court met. Lest anyone think that only the superior court lawyers were heinous, the almanac always published a cautionary word or two against the profession immediately below the table of county court days also. Often, the antilawyer lines for April and October were juxtaposed against a moral tale vilifying gaming, playing at cards, heavy drinking, or some other social vice. The epigrams under the county court tales were entitled, variously, "Of Courts," "The Lawyer and his Client," "The Law-Suit," "On Lawsuits," "Two Lawyers," and "A Word of Advice." Taken as a body of literature, the tales are a barometer of rising anxiety about the way in which the legal profession appeared to accompany indebtedness, strife, unwarranted decadence in social mores, and general devolution of the virtues commonly associated with the Country, such as sobriety, attention to duty, and responsible and direct relationships with social superiors and inferiors.

One of the almanac's cautionary tales drove the point home. Upon being sworn before a judge, a "grave old Country Blade" was warned not to perjure himself "lest he went to the Devil." The honest Briton retorted that he did not fear Satan, "for I have given him my eldest Son, and he ought to be content with one out of the Family." Asked to explain his remark, he told the Judge, "*Why, truly, I have made him a* Lawyer, *and you know the* Devil *was a* Lawyer *from the Beginning*. A Lyar you mean, says the other. I know not, replied he, what Distinction there may be made in *London*; but I am sure, by sad Experience, *we in the Country know no difference between* a Lawyer *and a Lyar*."[24]

---

24. *Virginia Almanac*, 1762. Compiled by the Philadelphian Theophilus Grew, the almanac was hailed among Virginia county readers for expressing their sentiments. The censure of lawyers was maintained as a yearly feature of the almanac through 1774. Often these sentiments were juxtaposed with verses reprimanding gentry vices such as gaming. For examples of complaints against the rapaciousness of lawyers and their incomprehensible language, see the almanac for 1759, which quips: "Habeas Corpus, Latitat, And Words the Client knows not what; But to the Lawyers they are plain, Because they bring

The belief among Virginians that lawyers were somehow connected to the vast cultural and social changes that afflicted Virginia during the 1750s and 1760s was articulated by the lawyer John Wayles. A representative of the tobacco firm of Farrell and Jones, Bristol, Wayles wrote to his employers in 1766. In 1740, he said, a planter's debt of one thousand pounds to a merchant would have appeared outlandish. Yet twenty-six years later, "ten times that sum is now spoke of with Indifference." Whereas before, "I don't remember to have seen such a thing as a turkey carpet in the Country," now, "nothing are so common as Turkey or Wilton Carpetts, the whole furniture, Roomes, Elegant and every appearance of opulence."[25]

The contrast Wayles saw appears to have been based on solid knowledge and not mere impression. One scholar calculates that the value of Virginia's coastal trade alone increased sharply at a rate of 4.6 percent over twenty-five years. Comparing export and import values of 1737–42 with those of 1760–69, David Klingaman concludes that a great deal of money was being made by those gentlemen involved in this trade. Klingaman suggested that the coastal trade was increasing 44 percent faster than the total population of Virginia, which grew at about 3.2 percent per year.[26] Obviously, exports from the Tidewater grew steadily during the 1750s and 1760s.

Far more startling, however, are conclusions that one can advance by comparing Klingaman's statistics on trade to the population increase measured in tithables in the Tidewater area alone, excluding the Piedmont, Southside, Eastern Shore, and Valley areas. By recording the figures given each year in ten Tidewater counties whose records are complete between 1720 and 1770 and interpolating where necessary, one finds that as wealth increased in the Tidewater, which was the source of the exports, population in the same area scarcely grew at all. The benefit of the coastal trade, therefore, was confined to the wealthier gentry. Though Virginia as a colony grew at an annual rate of 3.2 percent, population growth in the Tidewater was a far more modest 1.48 percent for 1740–50; 0.57 percent for 1750–60; and 0.46 percent for 1760–70. The opulence and indulgence of the gentry elite during the 1750s and 1760s naturally sprang from their conviction that they were in fact in-

---

him Store of Gain." Purdie's almanac for 1766 warned: "Contentions which in some do lurk / Now set the lawyers tongues to work / But he in quiet sound doth sleep / Who doth from law and physick keep."

25. Hemphill, ed., "John Wayles," p. 305. On gentry concerns over declining standards of virtue, see Isaac, "Evangelical Revolt"; Wood, "Rhetoric and Reality," pp. 27–31; Greene, "Search for Identity"; Evans, "Rise and Decline of the Virginia Aristocracy."

26. Klingaman, "Development of the Coastwise Trade."

creasing their actual wealth. Not surprisingly, the growth of the legal profession attended the need for expert and expeditious handling of trade affairs.[27]

By confining one's study to eight counties whose records are in optimum condition and comparing the rate of licensing of lawyers to population growth in those counties, one can arrive at a species of "base estimate" for the growth of the profession between 1740 and 1770. The results of such a comparison reveal why Virginians correctly felt that lawyers, indebtedness, opulence, and litigiousness all went together. While population lagged far behind, lawyers and elite wealth both increased significantly from 1750 to 1770 (see table 6). Records from each of the three peninsulas—Lower, Middle, and Northern Neck—show the same pattern. Debt remained the major issue in the courts. Most of those causes in the 1730s and 1740s were settled by summary judgment or by planters asking leave to "imparl" in hopes of arriving at an understanding with one another outside of court. Jury trial before mid-century rarely amounted to more than 3 or 4 juries per year per county. But between 1740 and 1770 all this changed. In Richmond County in the Northern Neck, jury trials increased from 4 to 5 per year in 1740 to between 11 and 20 by the 1760s, and to almost 30 by 1770. To the south in Essex, 30 juries per year was normal by the 1750s. Between 1758 and 1763, 170 juries settled 80 actions on the case, 31 actions brought under the heading "debt," and 29 cases of assault and battery. Between 1763 and 1770, 215 trials settled debt and case (which was almost always concerned with debt), and a few assault, detinue, and trover and conversion causes. In Charles City on the Lower Peninsula, the pattern was similar. In 1737 the county managed its affairs with only 3 jury trials. By 1745 the number had jumped to 17; by 1760 to nearly 20 a year, though the tithable population rose only modestly—from 1,310 in 1737 to 1,708 in 1762.[28]

---

27. Obviously, legal culture in Virginia was inextricably bound to the general planter culture of the colony. As that culture became more complex and the old hegemony began to fragment, the expectations that various interests had of the law were accentuated. Greene seems to concur in the judgment that the 1740s are a critical decade. He suggests that planters, merchants, and lawyers composed perhaps 2 to 5 percent of the total white population, but offers no estimate of the number of lawyers in practice. See "Society, Ideology, and Politics."

28. Statistics for jury trials compiled from county order books, 1730–70, with a sample county taken from each of the three areas in the Tidewater. Jury trial was allowed for any common law action except one in which a statute forbade its use (e.g., for settlement of small debts by petition and summary judgment). Since 1699 (Hening, 3:175–76) jurors had had to be holders of £50 sterling real and personal estate in the counties, £100 sterling in the General Court.

TABLE 6 *Ratio of Numbers of Lawyers to Population in Eight Tidewater Virginia Counties, 1740 to 1770*

Years	Average Number of Lawyers	Average Size of Population	Ratio
1740–50	33.39	16759.5	1 to 501
1750–60	44.87	18428.0	1 to 412
1760–70	57.44	19393.0	1 to 338

Note: Figures assume an annual death rate of .025 (25 per 1000). Optimum conditions would produce a rate of 20 per 1000; no colonial area known exceeded this rate. Certain areas of the Chesapeake apparently suffered from particularly bad malarial swamps. Thus, Daniel Blake Smith finds mortality in one parish of York County to have been shockingly high even well into the eighteenth century. See his essay "Mortality and Family." Smith's figures on adult males, however, are calculated only for the period 1665–99. To date there is no available work by historians or demographers by which a life table for the eighteenth-century Chesapeake can be reconstructed. Smith's 18th century figures, from 1700 to 1734, apply only to children ages one to fourteen. In the absence of cohorts within which to place known lawyers, even their longevity cannot form the basis for any conclusive proof of an improved death rate. Still, though inconclusive, the presence of grandparents and the ages of men reported in wills and inventories seem to me basis enough for making the educated guess at a death rate of 25 per 1000 for this period, 1740–70.

The table is biased toward the Northern Neck, where full runs of county order books survive. Given the mercantile activity along the James, the closer proximity of the General Court, and more population per county in the Lower Peninsula, the rate of lawyers to population there may have been even higher than these figures indicate. The counties from which the table was constructed, using tithable population figures and record of licensing, are: Westmoreland, Lancaster, Northumberland, Richmond, and King George in the Northern Neck; Middlesex, Caroline, and Essex in the Middle Peninsula. My special thanks to Gloria Main for aid in constructing the table and for discussing the results of research.

When Virginians looked at the business conducted in these lengthier sessions and concluded that merchants and lawyers always seemed to travel together, they were justified in so thinking. The prominent lawyer John Mercer had long been recognized as a merchant-speculator who had turned to the practice of law by 1730 and amassed a fortune. John and Travers Tarpley on the Neck took care of the legal concerns of the family business while brother James ran a thriving store in Williamsburg with William Prentis. Alexander Rose represented merchant John Orr in Westmoreland County; John Hamilton pursued debtors in King George on behalf of Whitehaven merchant John Lawthwaite. In Northumberland, John Park represented the interests of Messrs. Hunter and Company. John Wayles in Charles City represented Farrell and Jones, and in Henrico, the Huguenot Duval family moved successfully from merchant affairs into public life, placing two brothers on the county bench and a younger son in the bar to carry on its legal affairs. Middlesex County residents knew David Kerr as the scion of the merchant firm of George and Edward Kerr and the protégé of the Honorable Richard Corbin, Esq., whose affairs Kerr sometimes handled.[29]

Lawyers and merchants were themselves frustrated by the long delays, despite the impression held by some Virginians that it was the fault of the attorneys that business was suffering as cases ground through the courts. In 1746, Fairfax County petitioners proposed that formal quarter sessions be established in which justices would be obliged to clear their dockets of cases or suffer a penalty. This notion was rejected by the House, as was a similar 1764 plea by merchants that a circuit court system be established that would conduct civil business separate from purely administrative affairs. In 1749 the House had set the exchange rate at which a debt could be collected in Virginia currency in lieu of sterling at 25 percent advance. British creditors howled that they were being robbed, since the rate of exchange in 1751 was more than 30 percent and rose steadily thereafter. Although the burgesses settled the legal status of bills of exchange and established promissory notes as binding contracts, they refused to repeal the 1749 law. Instead, in 1755 they allowed local courts to decide what the proper rate of exchange was on any cause that came before the bench. Though appearing to be a concession to merchant demands, the new law merely guaranteed lengthy litigation and appeals since county court justices were no more inclined to be sympathetic to debt collection than any other group of Virginia planters.[30]

---

29. Examples cited are taken from surveys of cases in the county order books and from wills and inventories naming attorneys who did business for eminent families and firms. Most attorneys could earn a minimum of £500 per year by 1750 in county practice. The more eminent and aggressive ones earned considerably more and left substantial estates. Mays, *Edmund Pendleton*, 1:25–41, believed that three or four attorneys could carve up the business of a given county. Usually whoever got the appointment as deputy king's attorney was one of the successful coterie. Nothing I have seen in my own work contradicts Mays's conclusions. He and Smith, "Virginia Lawyers," pp. 25–31, concur in the estimate of a minimum figure of £500 per annum for a county practice in 1750. County levies in the order books indicate that the deputy crown attorneys were paid between 1,000 and 1,400 pounds of tobacco per year for services, depending on the county where they worked.

30. Hening, 5:526–40, for the 1749 act; 6:478–83, giving additional powers to the local courts. The Fairfax petition was rejected. See *JVHB*, Mar. 17, 1745–46, p. 190. The 1764

In desperation, merchants and lawyers schemed to avoid dilatory proceedings in the counties. A partial remedy could apparently be had in the courts around Williamsburg. No doubt the mercantile business in Yorktown and the superior battery of lawyers and justices who were advised by General Court attorneys had something to do with this. As early as 1746 an English traveler remarked about Yorktown's courts that "as much idle Wrangling is on Foot, as in any Court in Westminster-Hall." Of the lawyers the Briton remarked that they had "an excellent Time here, and if a Man is a clever Fellow, that Way, 'tis a sure Step to an Estate. 'Tis Necessity that has driven the Practitioners of the Law hither, from Europe, and other Parts of America, and I remember few that had not made it very well worth their While."[31]

Though the England-trained lawyer was probably not as much in evidence by the 1760s around the courts of the capital and York as formerly, the region still seemed a better forum in which to get business done. In 1765, William Allason, Virginia agent for the Glasgow firm of Baird and Walker wrote his brother Robert about a debt owed the firm by one of the Lees for seventy pounds. While Lee was sitting in the House, Allason was frustrated in his attempts to force payment. Even worse, if he brought suit against Lee "either in the county he lives in or the Generall Court Judgment wou'd not be obtained in less than three years." Instead, Allason concluded, "I propose Suing him for it in the Borough Court of Williamsburge where it would come to triall in a few months."[32] The hustings court could be relied on for somewhat more sympathetic and expeditious handling of merchant concerns, since the

---

petition of the merchants is in ibid., Nov. 2, 1764, pp. 233–35. The House rejected most parts of it on November 8 (p. 245), especially the part praying for the establishment of courts of assize, the censuring of justices, and the pressing of demands that debtors be forced to swear an oath when pleading payment on a protested bill of exchange. The representation of the merchants noted the dilatory proceedings in the county courts and bemoaned the increase in case load, which increasingly prohibited their pursuit of debtors in the General Court, where they were wont to appeal for redress (p. 234). See also Gipson, *British Empire*, 2:58–63; Ernst, "Genesis of the Currency Act of 1764" and "The Robinson Scandal Redivivus." Delays in the courts were encouraged by peculiar disabilities of English law. A common law court could not issue an injunction to force disclosure of a document, nor could a court of equity award damages on a bill. Thus dual suits in law and bills in chancery were necessitated. Often, suitors pressed for various parts of a debt in the counties and at the same time pursued the entire sum in the General Court, a practice that, if the justices caught it, was a bar to action on the petition for settlement. For a Halifax County example, see *Irby v. Read*, Aug. 18, 1769, copy in Tazewell Papers, Correspondence, 1650–1793.

31. *WMQ*, 1st ser. 15 (1907): 147.
32. William to Robert Allason, May 21, 1765, Allason Letter Book, 1757–70.

bench was headed by John Holt, the mayor and himself a merchant. His associates were John Blair, Jr., barrister and clerk of the Council; William Prentis, merchant and partner in business with Blair, Wilson Cary, and James Tarpley; and Benjamin Waller, a prominent attorney and the clerk of the General Court.[33]

The agent for the firm of James Buchanon and Company wrote his masters concerning a debt suit that county courts could not be trusted because of justices and jurymen. "It would be dangerous to trust Your Claim to the Decision of a Jury, and therefore it is brought in Chancery: which I fear will be tedious and at last doubtful." To the firm of Hyndman and Lancaster, after another caution against county juries and the length of chancery suits, went this advice: "What I would propose to do with the ... account ... when I get it, is to dismiss the suit in Chancery here, & bring a fresh suit at Common Law in York County Court for the Balance ... and so shall be able to get the Money in a few Months."[34] So anxious was one man to use the courts around Williamsburg that he brought the censure of the House of Burgesses on himself for serving a process on a witness appearing before a committee. When hauled before them for contempt, Roger Gregory assured the burgesses that his "sole Motive for requesting Suits to be brought ... in the Court of *York*, was the Certainty of a more speedy Determination there, than he could expect [elsewhere]."[35]

By the late 1760s it appears from Allason's estimate that the backlog of cases would have necessitated three years of sustained work in the General Court to clear the docket. Robert Carter Nicholas wrote to Landon Carter regarding a General Court suit that he had won in Carter's behalf, "I never was so much fatigued with the Business of any Court, as the last; & tho' it has been over a Day or Two, I have not yet recover'd my Spirits. I must take a Trip up the Country in hopes of getting a fresh Stock of them."[36] Actually, when one studies local court records, one discovers that only two or three cases a year were being appealed to the General Court from each county. Yet by 1774 Virginia contained some 500,000 people, sprawled over sixty-one counties. In combination with original processes at law and in equity and the criminal

---

33. On the Hustings Court judges, see *WMQ*, 1st ser., 16 (1907–8): 147–49.
34. Nov. 24, 1767, Jan. 9, 1769, William Nelson Letter Book, 1766–75.
35. *JVHB*, March 6, 1772, p. 218. See also letter of Gregory to lawyer John Tazewell, Feb. 29, 1772, ibid., p. 207. Gregory was an eminent justice and planter in King William County.
36. Nicholas to Carter, May 9, 1764, accession no. 1959, Landon Carter Papers.

trials, the appellate docket made up a staggering burden, which demanded the attention of the government.[37]

The response of lawyers to criticisms leveled against their profession and the remedies proposed by them to reform the inadequate court structures of Virginia reveal a paradox in the colony's legal history. Lawyers essentially argued in favor of more professionalism, more training, salaried judges, and a more "anglicized" court structure. Even though the membership of the bar became more American between 1740 and 1770, the propositions of reformers largely amounted to making the legal system more English than before. Moreover, it is by no means clear that a consensus existed throughout Virginia that it was the court system that was at fault. Some people clearly believed that the very profession of law itself was part of the problem. For their part, however, the lawyers maintained a consistent attitude of constructive criticism in favor of their profession.

As early as October 1745 readers of the *Virginia Gazette* and those accustomed to listening to the reading of the paper in the courthouse taverns were exposed to the proposals of COMMON SENSE, put forward after the author "perused some occasional Lawyers Debates in your Paper, with regard to County Courts, and Lawyers." No issues of the *Gazette* for the years 1741–45 exist; yet the comments of COMMON SENSE indirectly reveal the content of the debates. Due to the repeal of the 1732 licensing act in 1742 and the arguments going on in the House of Burgesses about lawyers, the *Gazette* pieces probably dealt with the profession of law, its necessity, and its relationship to the legal culture of Virginia. COMMON SENSE argued for a rigorous training of both justices and lawyers. The blessings of English law, he said, had been conferred upon Virginia "by the joint Care of Judges, and Lawyers, adhering to known Rules; which are founded on the Perfection of human Reason; but not within the Reach of every common Capacity." Lifted directly

---

37. Greene and Harrington, *American Population*, pp. 140–41; numbers of appeals judged from survey of county order books. The absence of complete runs of county records makes impossible a definitive statement of the ratio of lawyers to population in the Tidewater as a whole. For the entire colony, if one assumes fewer lawyers in less densely populated western counties and more in the Tidewater, especially on the Lower Peninsula, and a rough (conservative) average of between 3 and 5 lawyers practicing per county, the bar probably numbered between 183 and 305 persons by 1774. I am indebted to John Murrin for his calculations of approximately 180 clergymen for all denominations in Virginia at 1774. If both our estimates are correct, lawyers were outnumbering clergymen in Virginia sooner and and in greater number than in Massachusetts. On the Bay Colony, see Murrin, "Legal Transformation."

from Coke's *Institutes*, this sentiment reiterated sentiments put forth by eminent Virginia lawyers from William Fitzhugh to Edward Barradall. Unlike those doughty fighters, however, COMMON SENSE did not wish to alienate the Country. In the struggle against tyranny and corruption, he argued, professionally trained "Lawyers only can make the Defence, urging the known Rules of Law." The liberties of Virginia would not be secure "'til we have skilful Judges to preserve [the law's] Purity; who will soon confront ignorant Pratlers, and force them to become Lawyers, or fail of Employment." The remedy for bad law was clear: "Our own University might teach the Law . . . and admit none to practice who had not taken their Degrees therein. . . . From thence we might hope for a new Set of competent Judges."

These proposals were daring in their departure from Virginia's Country traditions. COMMON SENSE firmly believed that until professional judges were available, justices of the peace "should in Conscience, study the Trust reposed in them, or else chuse known Lawyers for their Associates, to explain the Law in all difficult Cases." Moreover, each county should choose a justice of exceptional ability and pay him a salary, and three or more such justices should sit jointly over a district of counties for the hearing of causes. "By this or some such Method, whereby skilful Judges may be imployed, it is only possible, that the Happiness of our Constitution can be preserved, and diffused, to all the Branches of this Dominion."

Besides hinting at a more powerful, and implicitly more independent, judiciary separated from the Council, which now composed the supreme court of Virginia, these remarks are the earliest recorded proposals for a district court system, professional legal education, and implicit censure of lay justices in eighteenth-century Virginia. Yet COMMON SENSE proved that he deserved his pseudonym. The fault lay as much with ignorant pettifoggers, whose smattering of legal knowledge threatened to impose "false Law," as with the "Justices, who would otherwise act honestly, to the best of their Judgments."[38] Force poor lawyers to be better ones, choose judges from the ranks of lawyers, and construct a more elite district court system to sit between county and General Court levels—those were the proposals.

Those ideas changed very little between 1745 and 1774. They were essentially the same arguments Court lawyers had been making since the late seventeenth century. In advancing them, however, the lawyers of Virginia were acutely sensitive to the public displeasure that had ac-

---

38. *Virginia Gazette*, Oct. 3–10, 1745.

companied the rise of their profession, a displeasure which was becoming more vocal and pronounced by the 1760s.

The lawyers' response was a somewhat nervous one, for they recognized that they were perceived as responsible for Virginia's ills. Yet they also bravely maintained (along with their merchant clients) that ignorant juries and justices were to blame, too. Letters to the *Gazette* in the 1760s and 1770s revealed a growing hostility among Virginians toward merchant creditors, Scottish factors, and the lawyers who pursued debtors in the courts. The danger for the legal profession was that they would become permanently identified with an elite, foreign creditor faction in the public mind. The censures by lawyers of county proceedings tended to promote that identification.

In 1771, PHILO-PATRIAE wrote to the editor complaining that county juries were "composed mostly of Knaves, Villains, and Blockheads, by whom honest Mens Properties and Estates were frequently forced from them, without Redress." The ignorant and easily duped jurors, he claimed, were no protection at all for the plaintiff. "This," he exclaimed, "is stiled, in Law, being tried by our Peers." The writer suggested that the courts appoint juries for one-, two-, or three-year terms, and be composed of the most intelligent freeholders—in other words, that a special jury system be implemented and that the first day of trial at the county courts be set apart for causes to save witnesses the trouble of being brought back to court.[39]

The plea for special juries was reiterated in 1774 by *Virginia Gazette* editors Purdie and Dixon under the heading "Proposals for the House of Burgesses." Those suggestions stated that special juries should be paid salaries and that, when vacancies arose in the Commission of the Peace, faithful jurymen should be put on the commissions, "and in Time our Benches will be filled with abler Magistrates."[40]

The issue of jury trial and the behavior or partiality of juries in favor of debtors was obviously tied to the larger socioeconomic problems of the colony. It was by no means clear that everyone thought that the central problem lay with jurymen, or even with the justices, though criticism of the bench was intense. Rather, public sentiment was decidedly antimerchant and unsympathetic to the 1766 proposal of BENEVOLUS, who

---

39. Ibid., (P and D), Dec. 12, 1771. On the growing antagonism toward the Scottish factors and merchant-creditors who railed at county juries and the rhetorical defense of debtors by lawyers such as Thompson Mason, see Dabney, "Letters from Norfolk." See also, Price, "Rise of Glasgow"; Roger Atkinson's comments in L. B. Morton, *Robert Carter*, p. 196.

40. *Virginia Gazette* (P and D), May 19, 1774.

wrote a promerchant, antijustice letter accusing the magistrates of not sitting regularly because they were "men of small Fortunes" who needed to attend their own business affairs. By paying the justices a salary, the writer concluded, as Maryland did, better justice would result from better attention to duty on the part of the magistrates.[41]

Far more indicative of the plight of many small farmers and planters, however, was the letter of another BENEVOLUS writing in 1771 against book debt. Planters of Virginia, he believed, were being ruined and should band together in support of a Northern Neck plan to sell goods at the cost of import and storage plus 10 percent, instead of the usual 30 percent cost imposed by merchants, who met every spring and fall at the General Court sessions to set the prices they would charge for goods. Another writer, signing himself A POOR PLANTER, pointed out the iniquity of the old 1732 law that allowed a merchant to bring in his ledger and swear his oath as to the sum a planter owed him. Most farmers and planters had no way to disprove this in an action on the case, and roguish merchants could make a tidy estate in this manner.[42] This letter seems to indicate that wager of law was not used in colonial Virginia. So too does the enormous number of county court entries grouped under "action on the case," which guaranteed recovery by relying on argument and reserved the possibility of jury trial and removal to the General Court. That effectively avoided wager of law, which could be used in an action or debt or detinue.[43]

---

41. Ibid. (Rind), Dec. 11, 1766. On Maryland, see Carr, "County Government," p. 199. Maryland by 1696 boasted a Supreme Appeals Court composed of governor and Council and a Provincial Court at Annapolis, which exercised jurisdiction over criminal and civil matters and received appeals from the county courts. Maryland justices never exercised jurisdiction in chancery matters, nor could they make bylaws or set procedural rules in their courts (ibid., pp. 245–62). Rather, procedures were copied from rules sent down from the Provincial Court (pp. 285–311). Maryland tried its slaves with a jury and attorney until 1717, when it copied Virginia's oyer and terminer proceedings (p. 270). On the bar, see Kershaw, "Development of the Maryland Bar."

42. On the 1732 law, see above, chapter 2 (fn. 15). The letters of POOR PLANTER, Virginia Gazette (Rind), Feb. 25, 1773, and BENEVOLUS, ibid., Feb. 7, 1771, contrast sharply with the protests of merchants against ledger debt. The merchants insisted that the practice favored debtors and pleaded with the burgesses to be allowed more time in which to press their suits. See JVHB, May 2, 1765, p. 316.

43. I have found no evidence to suggest that wager of law was ever used in Virginia. This practice, by which a defendant gave sureties to appear in court and then took an oath, to be upheld by eleven neighbors, that he was telling the truth and owed no debt, had disappeared in England. Action on the case could be used to recover damages for torts not committed by force, actual or implied. Where there was a contract, express or implied, the nonobservance of duties constituted the tortious breach of the contract; hence, a debt could be recovered under this action, and this was routinely done in Virginia.

Given the developments of the previous twenty years, it is all the more remarkable that Virginia's bar came to be identified with the patriot cause, with the party of virtue, and against the merchant-creditor minority in the colony by 1774. To understand how the lawyers managed to escape being tarred with the brush of Court corruption, one must examine the second type of demands and criticism being leveled against justices, courts, and lawyers. The call for moral rearmament and a return to a more virtuous public and private life was not heeded by the gentlemen justices at large. The lawyers, on the other hand, quickly learned how to manipulate Country rhetoric, and they followed the example of a rising young group of politician-lawyers in 1766 in censuring corruption in the General Court and placing the profession on the side of Country patriots.

Law and Morality

By the time Anglican divine Devereux Jarratt came into his pastorate at Bath Parish in Dinwiddie County, he had already decided that the time had come for a thoroughgoing reformation in Virginia. Like Presbyterian minister Samuel Davies, Jarratt regarded as "heathenish" the more moderate call issued by his predecessor to the congregation that they *"walk in the primrose paths of a decided, sublime, and elevated virtue."* By the 1760s alienation from opulent gentry culture, from private as well as public gentry behavior, and from gentry attitudes about the social order was spreading throughout Virginia, especially among Baptists and Presbyterians no longer content with the formerly familiar, but now tedious and formal, rituals of court day. As early as 1751 an irate Anglican clergyman had censured a justice for social conformity and reluctance to enforce the laws against vice. Such men were fearful lest they be considered "much out of the Fashion, as if they sho'd conform in their Dress to the starch'd Simplicity of our Forefathers."[44] Correspondent "B. M." launched a savage attack on the scandalous behavior of justices who countenanced vice. If a visitor to Virginia stopped at a county courthouse, he asked, "might he not see a *free* People swearing and reeling, cursing and gaming, in Presence of the M———te, to whom the Execution of the Law is intrusted? and the good-natur'd J———ce assuring them of Exemption, by doing the same Things himself?—You also know, Sir, that your living, above the Restraints of these Acts, has never occasion'd you

44. Jarratt, *Life of Devereux Jarratt*, p. 89; *Virginia Gazette* (Hunter), Mar. 28, 1751.

the Loss of one Vote at an *Election*, nor prevented your ascending *the Bench* in Court, under the character of Worshipful."[45]

This indictment of the lax justices was followed by another letter which excoriated county courts for continuing to grant tavern licenses. Another clergyman begged a county's deputy king's attorney to use his influence against further licensing. Far from serving their original purpose of providing shelter for weary travelers, he said, the taverns had come to be "the common Receptacle, the Rendezvous of the very Dreggs of the People."[46]

The clergyman's letter was sent to publisher William Hunter by the same "A. B." who had written to the *Gazette* in March. That critic of the courts scored the entire system of patronage and paternalism, which the local gentry gloried in, by pointing out that justices could not afford virtuous conduct, because "it wou'd be out of your Power to ingratiate yourself with your Neighbours, and lay them under such Obligations to you." It was ever the delight of great men, he went on, to show their magnanimity, and so "our great spirited Gentlemen are fond of shewing their Courage, in encountering the Authority of the Legislature, and breaking 'thro the Cob-Webb of Law, to demonstrate that such noble Minds will stoop to no Restraints." Virginians who wrote letters were of course themselves probably members of the gentle class of people, but they seem to have genuinely yearned for the virtuous justices of the past, "with whom it seems to have been the Custom to enumerate *good Sense, Morality,* and *Reverence to the Deity,* among the Ornaments or Constituents of a Gentleman."[47]

What these writers wanted, however, was precisely a return to the "sublime, and elevated virtue" of the golden age of the gentry, so scorned by Jarratt. The conduct of many gentlemen in the courts readily belied their claims on the deference of the many, according to contemporary descriptions left by travelers of the time. One such account, colored by especially negative experiences with the justices of the hustings court in Williamsburg, applauded the "plain honest Countenances" that the author encountered in the country folk. Even there, however, George Fisher found many "base and unworthy actions" among the gentry, actions against which "the most generous and candid minds can hardly forbear writing their inward disdain in severe censures."[48]

45. Ibid.
46. Ibid., Apr. 11, 1751.
47. Ibid., Mar. 28, 1751. See also Jan. 2, 1753, censuring cockfighting. On the rise of social criticism by Presbyterians, see Pilcher, *Samuel Davies*; Isaac, "Religion and Authority," pp. 3–36.
48. "Narrative of George Fisher," WMQ, 1st ser., 16 (1907–8): 100–139, 147–76, 121–23.

Formerly clerk to the county court of York, Fisher returned to Virginia during the 1750s after many years in England. He was not impressed by the changes that had stolen over the court personnel in Virginia during his absence. Upon meeting William and Thomas Nelson on a business matter, Fisher was dismayed. "I had in early Days lived in York, and been acquainted with Old Mr. Nelson the Father of these Gentlemen," he reported. Unlike old "Scotch Tom," the younger Nelsons "received me with a concious Dignity ... blamed my enterprise ... wondering that any one could be so weak as to prefer living in Virginia to Brittain."[49]

Like so many of their fellow justices, the Nelsons affected "an arrogant, hauty carriage, which in the opinion of most men is a necessary or insepparable accomplishment in what they call a Person of Note ... [to] indicate to you that in his own thoughts he was a Person of no mean Rank or Dignity." Unlike their predecessors, however, the present generation of gentlemen justices, in Fisher's opinion, deserved neither deference nor emulation, because of their dishonest, corrupt practices. By the 1750s it was common practice for a justice to obtain an ordinary license: "The Person of influence in these Parts ... obtains a Lysence at the County Court whereof he is himself a Member, and puts into it some Lazy Person or other, at a Salary, or so much per. cent, as is likely to pint off the greatest quantities of Liquors for him ... by which means, tho' the Proprietor (by the Courtesy) avoids the Reproach of being deemed an Ordinary keeper, and the scandal of what is then transacted; yet he reaps the greatest share of the Profits." Highly censorious, Fisher echoed the clergy's plea that no more ordinaries be authorized to corrupt the populace. The root cause of a decline in public and private virtue, however, was "this absurd Pride, so frequent here for a Justice of Peace or other person of rank, putting a loose Lazy fellow into his Ordinary, with the view of avoiding the reproach of his being himself the Keeper, which in Fact he is. ... In my humble sense of the matter, the disorders and irregularities committed at such houses, are often time the Consequences of very needy circumstances in the Deputy of which the real Landlord takes a base advantage." The greedy attachment to money, Fisher thought, belied the public image of a virtuous justice who "betrays herein his real principles."[50]

Writers to the *Gazette* confirmed Fisher's opinions, censuring the absence of prayers at the meetings of the courts, drunkenness on the part of justices, vile and obscene language, and the general spirit of extravagance, luxury, and dissipation that attended ruinous lawsuits and liti-

49. Ibid., pp. 103, 120, 135.
50. Ibid., pp. 167, 168.

giousness. Singling out Hanover County, BENEVOLENCE accused clerks, attorneys, sheriffs, and justices there of being "void of gratitude and humanity" and demanded that Virginians "suppress the unnecessary and vile practice of going to law . . . [or] be totally ruined" by lawyers' fees and court costs.[51]

County residents who served on the grand juries fell back on their presentments to make the same point about their society. In 1744 the burgesses had reformed the 1705 law that "hath been found insufficient to restrain and discourage wickedness and vice." The new law cited "different opinions [which] have . . . prevailed touching the meaning thereof" and omitted former offenses such as heresy, blasphemy, witchcraft, and scoffing at the sacraments and scripture from the penal code. Nonattendance at church and swearing of oaths were retained but with an important and novel proviso. Justices were hereafter enjoined from prosecuting a guilty gentleman for more than four oaths, no matter how many he swore. Such a change seems trifling, until one compares grand jury presentments for the period 1720 to 1750 with those of 1750 to 1770 (see tables 7, 8, and 9). Moreover, the courts neglected to call grand juries in many counties during the latter period, and in 1752, when Hanover residents petitioned the House of Burgesses for more stringent enforcement of vice laws, their plea was rejected. In 1727 a similar request from Surry County had been honored by an act passed during the 1730 session.[52]

Grand jurymen discovered that their presentments against gentlemen for swearing, gaming, and letting their dogs run free after game were routinely dismissed by the justices. Seeking a way to express their displeasure with such arrogant behavior, the jurymen discovered a statute passed in November 1762, which urged them to present Virginians who failed to list their lands, tithable dependents, and wheeled carriages for tax purposes. Part of the response was an attempt on the part of the juries to provide "for the support of the present war," as the wording of the act explained. But more than disinterested patriotism was involved in the extraordinary number of presentments under this heading.[53]

---

51. *Virginia Gazette* (P and D), May 28, 1767, June 11, July 16, Aug. 11, 1768, (Rind) June 10, 1769.

52. The 1705 statute is in Hening, 3:358–62; the new act is in ibid., 5:225–26. For the petitions, see *JVHB*, Feb. 8, 1727, p. 13; ibid., Mar. 6, 1752, p. 20.

53. For examples of gaming presentments and dismissals and for letting dogs run (1738 statute against this is in Hening, 5:60–63), see Essex Orders, May 16, 1749, Aug. 15, 1749, May 16, 1750, Aug. 21, 1750; York Orders, May 15, 1749; Richmond Orders, May 5, 1755, May 5, 1760; Lancaster Orders, July 10, 1747. See also *Virginia Gazette* (Hunter), April 24, 1751, for the governor's request that the burgesses do something to restrain the

TABLE 7 *Grand Jury Presentments, 1720–1750*
(most numerous offenses)

York:	1. Not listing tithables 2. Missing church 3. Having bastard child 4. Swearing
Charles City: (1737–50)	1. Missing church 2. Having bastard child 3. Failing to keep up roads 4. Swearing
Henrico: (1721–24; 1739–46)	1. Failing to keep up roads 2. Swearing 3. Missing church
Middlesex: (1725–26; 1732–37; 1740–50)	1. Missing church 2. Swearing 3. Having bastard child
Essex: (1725–43; 1745–50)	1. Missing church 2. Swearing 3. Being drunk
Caroline: (1733–50)	1. Failing to keep up roads 2. Missing church 3. Having bastard child 4. Swearing
Lancaster: (1729–43)	1. Missing church 2. Swearing 3. Having bastard child
Northumberland:	1. Missing church 2. Swearing 3. Having bastard child
Richmond:	1. Swearing 2. Missing church 3. Being drunk
Westmoreland:	1. Having bastard child 2. Missing church 3. Swearing 4. Committing adultery/fornication
King George:	1. Having bastard child 2. Missing church 3. Retailing liquors without license 4. Swearing

142 *Faithful Magistrates and Republican Lawyers*

TABLE 8 *Grand Jury Presentments, 1750–1770 (most numerous offenses)*

County	Offenses
York: (1750–54; 1759–70)	1. Missing church 2. Not listing tithables 3. Having bastard child
Warwick: (1749–62)	1. Missing church 2. Not listing tithables 3. Having bastard child
Henrico: (1752–69)	1. Swearing 2. Missing church 3. Failing to keep up roads 4. Having bastard child
Middlesex:	1. Not listing tithables (1768–70) 2. Having bastard child 3. Swearing 4. Failing to keep up roads
Essex:	1. Missing church 2. Failing to keep up roads 3. Having bastard child 4. Not listing tithables (post 1762) 5. Gaming (1760–63)
Caroline:	1. Not listing tithables (post 1762) 2. Failing to keep up roads 3. Missing church 4. Having bastard child
Lancaster:	1. Missing church 2. Swearing 3. Having bastard child 4. Not listing tithables (post 1762)
Northumberland:	1. Missing church 2. Swearing 3. Having bastard child 4. Not listing tithables (post 1762)
Richmond:	1. Missing church 2. Not listing tithables (post 1762) 3. Swearing 4. Failing to keep up roads
Westmoreland:	1. Failing to keep up roads 2. Having bastard child 3. Missing church 4. Not listing tithables (post 1762)
King George:	1. Having bastard child 2. Missing church 3. Committing adultery/fornication 4. Failing to keep up roads 5. Gaming (1760–61)

TABLE 9 *Courts and Grand Juries Missed, 1750–1770*

	Grand Juries Missed	May and November Courts Missed
York	3	0
Warwick	20	11
Henrico	12	4
Middlesex	26	16
Essex	6	0
Caroline	9	0
Lancaster	2	2
Northumberland	3	1
Richmond	14	2
Westmoreland	11	3
King George	26	11

Note: If two grand juries were called every year, as required by statute, between 1750 and 1770, 38 juries would have sat for each county. Some courts followed Westmoreland's example in the Stamp Act Crisis of late 1765 and closed. Figures given here are sessions missed over and above the number in that (roughly) eight-month period. Note that the number of May and November courts missed is exceeded by twice as many grand juries that were not called. In other words, courts, when sitting in May and November, were neglecting to call the grand inquest.

Compilation of exact numbers of presentments and judgment as to significance of the failure to call the grand juries are rendered difficult. Several counties (e.g., Lancaster, Henrico, Caroline) begin during this period to neglect listing the presentments, noting merely that the grand jury had been called. Whatever the nature of the presentments not listed, in most cases they were all ordered dismissed immediately by the court, another indication that the justices were not interested in judging proper penalties for these offenses when a formidable administrative and case docket awaited their attention.

As early as 1753, Francis Jerdone wrote from Yorktown to a friend in London about a secondhand "chariot" the Englishman had sent. Jerdone advised William Hamilton that "I have sold the chariot you sent me by Capt. Paterson for forty pistoles, being £43 curt. to Col. Folke Moseley, which was the most that I could make of it . . . second-hand goods being no way saleable here; for our Gentry have such proud spirits that nothing will go down, but equipages of the nicest and newest fashions. You'll hardly believe it when I tell you that there are sundry chariots now in the country which cost 200 guineas, and one that cost 260."[54]

Given such extravagance and the gentry's attempts to evade taxes, the grand juries' presentments seem to have been especially aimed at the quality of Virginia. Like the presentments against swearing, gaming, and hounds, however, presentments for avoiding taxes were usually dismissed, and no fine was imposed when the guilty party paid his back taxes.[55]

Given such censures on the private habits and public performance of the courts and justices of Virginia, it is quite remarkable that the lawyers, who were deemed just as corrupt by many critics, managed to emerge by the late 1760s on the side of virtue. Allied by family, aspiration, and function with the gentry, the lawyers were not likely comrades for Presbyterian, Baptist, or evangelical Anglican reformers of Virginia's mores. Yet because of a series of events between 1766 and 1774 lawyer complainants against inefficient courts and justices were able to ally them-

---

gaming spirit in Virginia. In 1736, George Webb had argued in his manual *Justice of Peace* (p. 165) that statutes against gaming were only intended to prevent vagabonds and the lesser orders of men from "unlawful, crafty, and deceitful Gaming," since common law did not prohibit gaming as such. By the 1750s, it would appear that the grand juries were not impressed with this version of "anglicization" and began to demand the same standard of conduct from the gentry that they demanded from the lesser orders of society. The 1762 statute on tithable evasion is in Hening, 7:539–43.

54. Jerdone to Hamilton, Sept. 20, 1753, *WMQ*, 1st ser., 8 (1899–1900): 37–42. On the economics of the 1760s, see Land, "Economic Behavior"; Herndon, *Tobacco in Colonial Virginia*, pp. 44–52. The tables constructed by Herndon indicate that prices rose after the 1730 tobacco law from 12s. 6d. per hundredweight to 20s. by the 1750s. Exports rose from 34 million pounds per annum in 1731 to between 38 and 53 million pounds per annum in the 1750s. On the credit situation and the planters' response, see Egnal and Ernst, "An Economic Interpretation"; Egnal, "Economic Development"; Hanson and Egnal, "Economic Development . . . a Critique." The increased wealth coming from the expanding grain production in the Tidewater, and the degree to which this was aggrandized by the few, greater planters on large farms, rather than by smallholders, deserves careful study.

55. The burgesses clearly intended the law to be used to generate support for the war since the counties would be reluctant to open their purses. The straitened credit situation and the lack of ready money were subjects of comment in 1754 in a letter of George Hume to Jonathan Hume in Scotland. Writing from Culpeper County, George declared: "Money is so scarce it is a rare thing to see a dollar, and at publick places where great monied men will bet on cock fights, horse races, etc., ye noise is not now as it used to be—one pistol to 2 or 3 pistoles to one—it is now common cry 2 cows and calves to one or 2 to one or sometimes 4 hogsheads tobo. to one and yt gives no price, so I do not know how we shall maintain a war" (*WMQ*, 1st ser., 8 (1899): 89). Opulent and profligate display by the few in the 1760s would obviously give rise to resentment if hard economic conditions continued to afflict the many in Virginia counties.

selves with the religious censurers of gentry behavior. In a dazzling display of rhetorical displacement, articulate lawyer-politicians reached back into Virginia's Country past and drew from it the means by which the corruption of mores, declension of court day, increased litigiousness, and merchant-creditor rapaciousness could all be blamed on the Court at Williamsburg. The crises that emerged from the Robinson and Chiswell scandals provided the opportunity and means. The 1772 bill for reforming the courts of justice demonstrated how effectively the lawyers managed to cut their ties with merchants and join forces with patriotic justices in a chorus of Country outrage at threats posed by Court practices. For the moment, and indeed for many years thereafter, the underlying cultural and socioeconomic changes that had given rise to disenchantment with Virginia's legal culture and its officers were obscured by a bitter constitutional struggle.

Patriot Lawyers and the Reform of the Courts

Lawyers in Virginia were inevitably involved in the politics of the colony by the 1760s because the rise of their profession in society was mirrored in corresponding seats in the House of Burgesses. Whereas Massachusetts lawyers composed only 3.5 to 8.8 percent of the members (1760 to 1770) in that colony's house, 39 lawyers sat as important committee leaders in Virginia's 630-member House of Burgesses between 1720 and 1776. Of the 39, 28 sat after 1745, and those 39 attorneys made up 6 percent of the total membership. In addition, various Williamsburg lawyers served as clerks to important committees of the House; lawyers' skills had been important in drafting the 1748 revisal of the laws; and even critics of the profession like Landon Carter had been forced to admit that the lawyers of the House were distinguished as "the Admirers of Reason and Liberty of Conscience" for their long-standing opposition to the dominant Robinson clique in the House and for Peyton Randolph's courageous opposition to Governor Dinwiddie in the Pistole Fee Controversy.[56]

56. A careful survey of House members reveals no further important lawyers for the counties under study than those Greene found in "Foundations of Political Power." There were other lawyers sitting for counties to the west, but these men seem not to have been important committee heads. Lawyers seem to have entered politics slightly sooner and in slightly larger numbers in Virginia than in Massachusetts. For that colony and the statistics cited, see Gawalt, *Promise of Power*, table 8, p. 67. On the two professions of law and divinity in Massachusetts, see D. M. Scott, *From Office to Profession*. Like Virginia, Massachusetts experienced a gradual but steady devolution of local court power from

From the opening decades of the eighteenth century everyone recognized the potentially awesome power of a lawyer who could manipulate book print, advise the government, or alternately harangue the multitudes. The urgent need for regulation had inspired Spotswood's furious accusation against the burgesses in 1715 that they listened too readily through the medium of upstart lawyers to "the Giddy Resolves of the illiterate Vulgar in their Drunken Conventions."[57] Only the widely acknowledged abilities of John Mercer saved him, time and again in his various confrontations with county justices, from being permanently disbarred. The Council itself noted his formidable legal and political value, but made it clear that "it is expected he will alter such Parts of his Behavior as have drawn upon him [the] Censure" of the courts.[58]

So confident of their abilities and power did the clerk-attorneys of Virginia become that they could afford to trade insults with justices, and with one another. In 1766, Marmaduke Beckwith, clerk of Richmond County, threatened Thomas Jones, clerk of Northumberland, that he, Beckwith, would print in the newspaper the fact that Jones had refused Beckwith an execution sworn out against Colonel Presley Thornton. Jones replied, "As to your putting it in the Gazette, (as you express yourself) you are extremely welcome; the Clerk of Northumberland's Action, dares stand the Scrutiny of the ill natured ignorant Vulgar."[59]

Despite the bravado and the very real abilities that lawyers knew they

---

1774 to 1805. See Hartog, "Public Law of a County Court"; Gawalt, *Promise of Power*, pp. 95–168. See also Carter's remark on lawyers in Greene, ed. *Diary* (Journal of the House), 1:116–17. On the long-standing split in the House between Robinson's clique and the emerging profession, see Griffith, *Virginia House*, pp. 149–51. By 1774 other colonies recognized the formidable legal talent of Virginia. See Wills, *Inventing America*, pp. 3–18, on the Virginia delegation to the First Continental Congress.

57. Spotswood's remarks cited in Dodson, *Alexander Spotswood*, pp. 128–31, during the debates over the licensing of lawyers. See above, chapter 2. On the genteel nature of print culture and the ability of lawyers and pamphleteers to write and speak convincingly to the lesser orders of society, see Isaac, "Preachers and Patriots" and "Dramatizing the Ideology of Revolution"; Wood, "Democratization of Mind."

58. Mercer, like his friend and fellow attorney Moseley Battaley, was reprimanded in several courts. Both men were removed from their respective commissions of the peace later in life for continuing to practice as lawyers at the same time. Both were eloquent pleaders and sarcastic critics of fellow justices. See *EJCV*, 4:318, 328, 348, 432, 1738; Oct. 28, 1739, p. 443; 5:311, April 11, 1750, Battaley for "giving abusive Language" to Benjamin Grymes, presiding justice of Spotsylvania and for acting as justice and lawyer, pp. 311, 312. Mercer was reprimanded again in 1753 (ibid., 5:419, 434) and left out of the commission in 1757 (ibid., 6:42–43). See also Essex Orders, Mar. 1738; *VMHB* 23 (1915): 72–78.

59. *WMQ*, 1st ser., 23–24 (1915–16): 259–60. On the law books used by attorneys, see Bryson, *Census of Law Books*; *VMHB* 9–10 (1901–3): 394–403; ibid., 7–8 (1899–1900): 300–302; A. M. Smith, "Virginia Lawyers," pp. 246–58. Against the abuses book-learned men might generate, the *Virginia Gazette* offered its own printed safeguard. Under the heading "The Benefits of the Press to the People," it warned, "Magistrates may be deceived;

possessed in a semiliterate culture, many sensed that their profession fitted into Virginia's Country past rather awkwardly. The young James Madison was openly skeptical of his friend William Bradford's attempt to put a good face on a decision to enter law. Bradford compared law to mercantile activity and conceded, "It must be owned, that the conduct of the generality of lawyers is very reproachable but . . . that ought not to make their profession . . . the necessary consequence of it. . . . As gain is the sole pursuit of the merchant he is much more likely to contract an inordinate desire of wealth than the lawyers, whose pursuit is as much after fame as Wealth." Madison could only offer the laconic reply that the profession of law demanded a use of "many parts of knowledge you have acquired. . . . It is a sort of General Lover that wooes all the Muses and Graces." The image of the profession as seducer was not quite what Bradford probably hoped to encounter as a justification for taking up the law.[60]

There is nothing remarkable about the gradual growth of a body of men claiming special abilities and talents which they were able to employ on behalf of others. The evolution of a culture into a more complex one and the accompanying specialization of knowledge is a familiar story.[61] Yet the earlier censures against lawyers had not merely been that they were poorly trained or ignorant or that the court system within which they operated was defective. Rather, the very nature of what a lawyer was had been debated in Virginia since the 1680s; these debates pitted the patronage, corruption, and power of Court lawyers against the independence, virtue, and liberty of the Country. The attacks upon gentry power, opulence, and bad example in the 1750s and 1760s had done nothing to alleviate the traditional English Countryman's suspicion that lawyers were inherently corrupt and greedy and that they were engaged in an artificial, unnatural practice of stirring up trouble among neighbors and artfully concealing their designs in bewildering language.

However, the lawyers of Virginia were gradually able during the 1760s to shed this sinister reputation. The Parsons' Cause, the Chiswell Affair, and the Robinson Scandal all contributed to the rehabilitation of the legal profession's reputation in the public eye.

Courts may be awed, and Men in what Station soever, are always fallible. But the Press will ever afford injured Innocence an Opportunity of carrying its Cause before the awful Tribunal of the Public; which, in a free Country, is ever to be feared" (Mar. 14, 1755).

60. *Papers of James Madison*, Aug. 12, 1773, 1:90–92, Sept. 25, 1773, 1:95–97.

61. The working definition of a "profession" used here is that of a group claiming an ability to utilize a special skill in the affairs of others. Moreover, they are identified as such in society and are perceived by their contemporaries as being "professionals." The comments in the *Gazette*, the *Virginia Almanac*, private papers, and court records indicate that the bar in Virginia was perceived as such a group by 1750.

The Parsons' Cause began with the passage of the twopenny acts of 1755 and 1758 under whose provisions the ministers of the established church were to be paid the total of sixteen thousand pounds of tobacco at the fixed rate of two pence per pound. By the late 1750s the price of tobacco exceeded that two-pence-per-pound rate, and the clergy felt that their livings, and hence, social status and independence from anticlerical vestries were threatened. Charges and countercharges were hurled by gentry and clerical elites within the church, culminating in three actions in the county courts of Virginia. The twopenny act of 1758, though disallowed by the Board of Trade by 1760, was used as the basis for the ministers' suits in which they sought to recover the amounts owed them and lost under the now disallowed act.

In August 1762 the Reverend Alexander White brought suit in King William County. The Reverend Thomas Warrington brought suit in Elizabeth City County in January and March 1763; the most famous of the three causes was initiated by the Reverend James Maury in Hanover County in November 1763, and the cause was decided by December. It was in this last cause that a young member of the rising legal profession named Patrick Henry used the occasion to place his profession on the patriot side of what was now a hot political controversy. He thus pitted the planters—both justices and lawyers—against a rapacious clergy, vile courtiers at home, and even (probably) a king who hypothetically would disallow emergency measures and demand that such disallowances be interpreted retroactively.[62]

The gentlemen justices on the three county benches did, as Rhys Isaac concludes, act with "uncertainty, ambiguity, and even a measure of deviousness," in their handling of the causes. Moreover, the disinclination of the better sort to sit on the juries did guarantee a more anticlerical cast among the jurors, who listened with rapt attention to the declamations of the young Henry.[63] What one must recall is that the county courts were by this time already being attacked on both fronts—by professional lawyers, and by the common people—but for different reasons. The uncertainty of the justices in these causes must be seen within the broader context of the crisis that gripped the local courts from the late 1750s on.[64]

---

62. See R. L. Morton, *Colonial Virginia* 2:751–819; Isaac, "Religion and Authority," pp. 11–21. Unfortunately, Hanover, King William, and most of Elizabeth City County court records were destroyed during the Civil War. Henry's speech was not recorded at the time; the only version of it is James Maury's bowdlerized version. See Isaac, "Religion and Authority," p. 20 (fns. 69–70).

63. Isaac, "Religion and Authority," p. 19.

64. Undoubtedly, the empanelling of juries from among the lesser ranks of yeoman and

The issue of Court corruption versus Country virtue, so expertly exploited by Patrick Henry in late 1763, was brought into prominence again in 1765 and 1766. The Stamp Act Crisis, of course, seemed to vindicate those who saw a corrupt, rapacious Court ministry at work at home in England. But far more disturbing for Virginians were the twin spectacles of the Robinson Scandal and the Chiswell Affair, which both erupted in 1766.

The speaker of the house, who also held the office of colony treasurer, John Robinson, had the bad taste to be carried off by "Torments of the Stone" before covering his embezzlement of funds on behalf of his Court gentry friends. His aristocratic allies in the House and on the Council were left to face a furious series of denunciations. Younger members of the House demanded and received inclusion in the councils of power in return for helping to contain the extent of the damage and scandal. The offices of treasurer and speaker were separated at this point to prevent too large a grant of power from residing in the hands of one man, and as Joseph Ernst argues, the power of the most aristocratic Court gentry declined from that moment on.[65] Equally important, however, the rise in power and importance of several lawyer-politicians began at that time as well. The aristocratic barrister Peyton Randolph had hoped to succeed Robinson in the joint offices of speaker and treasurer, normally the preserve of the Courtly "Council" families. Randolph was not happy at the histrionics of members of the bar like Henry who made bids for popularity in their orations rather than direct their arguments to sober judgments among gentlemen. Still, he joined with his brother John in agreeing to share political power with lesser lawyer-politicians like Henry, Benjamin Waller, Robert Carter Nicholas, and the formidable lawyer-pamphleteer Richard Bland.[66]

Far from being a trivial event, the bailment of Colonel John Chiswell by General Court judges after his examination and confinement by

---

planters which occurred in the Parsons' Cause were part of the demands on the part of lawyers and other reformers for special juries in Virginia, a demand which republican lawyers after the war continued to press. See below, p. 213.

65. Clearly, the legal profession, like the gentry class as a whole, was composed of greater and lesser persons of varying degrees of wealth and rank. Despite the growing sense of a professional identity, differences between "new men" like Henry and aristocratic members of the bar like Randolph continued to persist. Nonetheless, as Landon Carter's diary and other contemporary accounts indicate, the bar was becoming readily identifiable by the 1760s. For example, see the special supplement issue of October 18, 1770, of Purdie and Dixon's *Virginia Gazette* detailing the order of the late governor Botetourt's funeral procession in which "Gentlemen of the Law" were assigned a place.

66. Ernst, "Robinson Scandal."

county justices on a charge of murder exploded across Virginia's counties, into private letters, onto the pages of the *Gazette* as news of the greatest import. The tavern brawl that ended in the death of Robert Routledge was a fitting setting in which to redeem the reputation of local justices and Virginia's lawyers by pointing to the actions of the General Court judges. Only George Wythe thought it permissible for three of the judges to bail Chiswell, and he gave as his reason the conviction that the General Court was like that of king's bench, where all high offenses of a criminal nature lay and from which there was no appeal. Other lawyers attacked this notion in the *Gazette*, with DIKEPHOLOS insisting that Virginia's courts derived their authority from its own statutes, from British statutes, and from the customs of the British courts. MARCUS FABIUS and MARCUS CURTIUS denied the analogy altogether. All authority vested in the General Court stemmed from acts of the Assembly, they argued, thus reviving the pre-1684 notion that the Assembly itself was the court of dernier resort in Virginia. An earlier letter had explicitly stated that both county and General courts were the creation of the House and that no statute existed that empowered the higher court to alter or set aside a decision of a called or examining court. If a particular judge could alter the justices' commission of a man for a probable felony, "the relation between the County and General Courts [is] altered, and the constitution . . . unhinged."[67]

Privately, attorney John Tazewell raged to Thomas Burke when William Byrd III decided to prosecute Robert Bolling for a vicious satire criticizing the bailment. Tazewell wrote, "If the censures, the proceedings of ignorant, ill designing or partial Magistrates, be liable to prosecutions, pains & penalties, our boasted freedom becomes a shadow, and our Lives and properties at the discretion of particulars. . . ." Damning the General Court judges' attempts to cover their actions, Tazewell railed, "What? Shall they dare *act* what others shall not dare to *speak of*? 'tis necessary indeed for them to have recourse to some scheme by which their actions may not come to light . . . had they been conscious they had done right, they would trusted to the Justice of their proceedings, & not by their threatenings, prosecutions & endeavours to h[inder] any person from an I[nquiry] into their conduct."[68]

Ironically, the outcome of the Chiswell Affair was a temporary cessation of criticism leveled against local justices. Though one writer suggested that all "magistrates . . . are originally, if not immediately, ap-

67. Bridenbaugh, "Violence and Virtue"; Lemay, "Robert Bolling"; *Virginia Gazette* (P and D), Apr. 18, June 20, July 6, July 25, 1766. See also Wythe's letter, Aug. 1; DIKEPHOLOS, Aug. 29; FABIUS and CURTIUS, Sept. 12, Oct. 3, 1766.
68. Tazewell to Burke, Sept. 28, 1766, Thomas Burke Papers.

pointed by [the] people" and that "a strict scrutiny into the behavior of magistrates would tend very much to promote the impartial administration of justice," more positive letters also appeared. ALGERNON SYDNEY wrote to reprimand the censures against "honest county magistrates," who served without pay and had bravely refused to officiate during the Stamp Act Crisis. Far more insidious was the "union in one person of the discordant and heterogeneous dignities of Privy Councellor, Judge of the G.C. and Member of the intermediate body of the Legislature." For two more years letters appeared at various intervals, reflecting on the nature of courts, judges, and the constitutional issues that the Chiswell Affair had raised. The real threat to Virginians' liberties, wrote MONITOR, came from British courtiers and those who thought like them, who denied the importance of actual representation. He especially affirmed that the "*British* constitution is not to be newmodelled by every *court* lawyer any more than the liberties of *America* are to be reasoned down, or wafted away from us, by the silver tongue, or venal breath of a *court* judge." That attack on Blackstone and Mansfield was followed by the letter of FABRICIUS affirming that men of "*birth and fortune*, in every government that is free" should be honored among the people, provided they administered the law with cool deliberation. Such patriotic magistrates "will not carry on the war of honour against conscience... nor will they be governed by the honour of a *Courtier*; and execute all the ill purposes of a court against their country."[69] Not since Beverley's *Essay upon the Government of the English Plantations* had the Country spirit been so aroused against the pretensions of the Court in Virginia.

The lingering taint of the Chiswell Affair and the continued attacks on the inadequacies of local courts and justices continued to stir up bitterness and fears in Virginia in the late 1760s. The consensus of outrage against the General Court forged in the Chiswell scandal was insufficient to soothe old hostilities or quiet the clamor for more efficient courtroom proceedings. Richmond County's deputy king's attorney Richard Parker grew impatient with Landon Carter and insulted his ability; whereupon Carter answered, "I set and would set to keep such impudent lawyers as himself in order. He boldly replied that I was an impudent Judge, and that he would not be Browbeaten by any man. I told him I would shew him that I would not and that by and by." Another member of the Richmond bar, David Boyd, proposed a novel method of stopping proceedings at law with a kind of chancery bill that was not called an injunction. Carter lost his patience. To Boyd and two fellow magistrates

---

69. *Virginia Gazette* (P and D), Apr. 18, May 30, 1766; ibid. (Rind), Mar. 17, June 19, 1768.

who had sided with the lawyer, the presiding justice argued that "give his bill what name he pleased it must have the nature of an injunction." Carter refused to entertain Boyd's idea because upon the slightest pretext someone could move to stop a case at law and proceed in chancery even when a clear remedy at law existed. Under a genuine bill of injunction an oath had to be sworn after a remedy at law for the cause was shown to be lacking. Carter's greatest objection, however, was expressed in his defense of the ancient traditions of the law, which he and all Country justices were sworn to uphold. Despite the magistrate's great discretionary powers, Carter believed that common law procedure was superior to equity. Move toward equity, he argued, and "every thing in time [will] be thrown into a Court of Conscience, which I beg leave to say would be a Court of the greatest latitude in the world whenever the Judges shall be allowed then to throw aside the evident rules and doctrines of the Common law."[70]

The idea of judge-made law, in excess of that already made under regular common law procedure, did not set well with Carter, and for good reason. He remembered the Chiswell scandal, and in 1774 was shocked at the fate that befell Lancaster justice Thomas Pinckard. Pinckard, a descendant of John Pinckard who had been a justice in 1688, had, despite occasional friction, been counted an ally of the Conway family of Lancaster. Appearing as a witness in a suit, Pinckard was accused by Carter's old *bête noire*, lawyer Richard Parker, of having perjured himself. Furious at such a suggestion, Pinckard sued Parker, who in turn informed the General Court grand jury that Justice Pinckard was a perjurer. Tried by "his country," a jury of resident freeholders, Pinckard was acquitted, but when the General Court judges ordered both parties to pay costs and cease litigation, Pinckard haughtily replied he would do so only if Parker promised to comply. The General Court responded by suspending Pinckard from his office as justice.

Carter was outraged. Noting in his diary that Pinckard had "had hard luck," he stormed: "I have heard Patriotism roaring aginst the handle made of Wilkes' Private Character to overset the Constitution; and in what does this differ from that? Suppose a man thus arraigned of felony and not found guilty by his Country; and a higher power than his Country, a mere Aristocratic power excommunicates him for that which his country would not find him guilty of. Is not this overturning the Present Constitution, and introducing a mode of Procedure bordering on an Arbitrary and Oppressive mode?" Reflecting darkly on his own experiences with lawyers, the potential allies of the Court, he concluded,

70. Greene, ed., *Diary*, 2:406–7, 726, 727.

"Happy am I that I was so sensible of an insult, as to leave a court that any —— Lawyer might go and arraign [me] of some atrocious crime, and though my country should refuse to find me guilty, this Power must and would have turned me out."[71]

Despite Carter's continued hostility, public debate on the issue of court reform gradually reached another consensus. Various writers to the *Gazette*, signing themselves PHILO-VIRGINIAE, PHILO-PATRIAE, and PHILO-JUSTITIAE, suggested the remedies that lawyers had been promoting since the 1740s: pay the justices a salary; construct a circuit or assize court from the more able justices; and cut down the fees taken by the clerks and the colonial secretary for legal work. On March 26, editor William Rind noted that the burgesses were about to take up the Bill for the More Easy and Speedy Administration of Justice. Over the past years, Rind asserted, "the Causes of Delay, in the County Courts, have been variously endeavored to be investigated in the public Papers, not without some illiberal Reflections on the Justices." The root cause, he believed, was simply the increase in business, which required several days' attendance "joined to an Expence which many worthy Justices are not able to sustain." Certainly the wealthier members of the gentry seem not to have been appearing regularly on the bench. Landon Carter's observations about Richmond County seem to reflect the general dismay in Virginia over gentry laziness: "Let what ever will be advanced in the public Gazettes to spirit Gentlemen up to a diligent discharge of their duty to the public."[72]

Led by lawyer Richard Bland, in March 1772 the House of Burgesses finally turned its attention to a remedy for forcing gentlemen to their duties in the courts. The provisions of the Bill for the More Easy and Speedy Administration of Justice summarized the demands of lawyers and merchants for a more efficient and recognizably English court structure. The justice-burgesses made little opposition to the bill, and the measure very nearly became law. The bill stated that hereafter the General Court would hear only civil causes. Original process therein was to begin at ten pounds sterling, twelve pounds current money, or two thousand pounds of tobacco. Judges had to be native residents of Virginia, a provision that reflected the colony's long-standing hostility to placemen. Newly created courts of assize would meet twice yearly at assigned places to hear causes of general gaol delivery, assizes, and oyer and terminer.

---

71. Ibid., 2:808. On Wilkes, see Rudé, *Wilkes and Liberty*, pp. 162–69, 203–4, on support in Virginia for the exiled radical; Wood, *Creation*, pp. 14–18.

72. *Virginia Gazette* (P and D), Oct. 24, Dec. 12, 1771; ibid. (Rind), Nov. 21, 1771, March 26, 1772; Greene, ed., *Diary*, 2:405.

Each judge of the General Court, who would also sit in assizes, would be paid three hundred pounds per annum and was to pick two assistant judges from the justices in the district where he sat, the assistants to receive a per diem allowance of thirty shillings.

County courts were restructured, with five justices sitting exclusively in quarter sessions in February, May, August, and November. All chancery bills and cases concerning demurrers, special verdicts, cases agreed, and writs of enquiry of damages to be executed were to be heard and a judgment given. Clerks were to write up a special docket for these cases, and those not cleared within twelve months from the commencement of the act would be used as evidence to fine the justices fifty pounds apiece. The office of sheriff could hereafter be held only by those justices who remained to deal with administrative matters and lesser causes. Quarter sessions justices would receive a per diem of five pounds current money to be divided among them according to how many days they sat. Salaries were to be derived from assessments against plaintiffs for cases brought and lost. To prevent interminable pleadings and in recognition of the growth of the legal profession and the charges against pettifoggers, the bill stated that only two lawyers were allowed to plead on any cause before sessions.[73]

73. On Bland, see Colbourn, *Lamp of Experience*, pp. 142–49; *DAB*, 2:354–55. Bland (1710–76) argued in his pamphlet *The Colonel Dismounted* that Virginians held the same rights under English law as native Britons, a proposition denied by Blackstone and other English jurists. See also R. L. Morton, *Colonial Virginia*, 2:784–819, on Bland, the two penny act, and the resulting pamphlet literature. The proposed assize bill of 1772 was introduced by Edmund Pendleton, who read it March 23. Debate on the bill continued through March 26, the bill was ordered printed on the March 28, and it then died. See *JVHB*, pp. 266–77. The bill was enclosed in Dunmore's letter to the Earl of Hillsborough, May 20, 1772. Debt causes were singled out in the bill as a matter of great concern. Cases agreed as referred to in the bill are those in which the facts were written up, their correctness and thoroughness attested to by the parties, and a decision requested without trial, a common means of debt settlement in Virginia. Demurrers, objections to facts or forms of the indictments, often arose in causes in which the indebtedness was of long duration or the details unclear or contestable, often the case in Virginia local courts. Special verdicts rendered by a jury decided matters of fact and left matters of legal interpretation to the justices. They were useful for obtaining straightforward accounts of past facts in cases of debt. Yet justices were sometimes annoyed by lawyers who demanded that juries be told to find a special verdict. See the April 4, 1759, Charles City Orders, in which an attorney for the defense was "suggesting That there was a Point of Law arising upon the Facts in this Case [and] Motion[ing] That the Court would direct the Jury to find a Special Verdict and the Court was of opinion That in Case the Jury Thought That there was a point of Law arising left it at large for the Jury to find as they Pleased." Such episodes merely highlighted the tensions between lay justices and jurymen and the frustrated professional bar. Writs of inquiry were sworn by the plaintiff against a defendant admitting liability for damages by default. In England, the sheriff usually tried such a cause by giving an interlocutory (tempo-

Although Governor Dunmore gave the bill his personal blessing, it failed because the House could not decide on a satisfactory method of raising the monies for the judges' salaries. Dunmore informed his superiors of the bill's demise. By the spring of 1774 more causes were being tried in the General Court than had been tried in any session in any administration in the history of Virginia. No relief was to be forthcoming for colonists who read the grim humor of Purdie and Dixon's *Almanac* for October: "Now the General Court begins, when the lawyers gibberish, which though it be not so sacred as the Hebrew, nor so learned as the Greek, nor so fluent as the Latin, nor so amorous as the Italian, nor so covetous as the Spanish, nor so courtlike as the French, yet it is a speech by which they can get more money than by any of the others."[74]

Many justices of Virginia continued to agree that the real reasons for the delays, the inadequacies, and the ever-increasing volume of business lay not with the court structures but with lawyers. Landon Carter sneered at the proposed law, which he described as the scheme of lazy lawyers "to indulge themselves, and get the same and more money by travelling from Court to court with the same causes and of Course less business to themselves, though more fees to the Perishing client. But as to the dispatch of Justice I will be hanged if it can move quicker in that mode than it may in the present if these Gentlemen could be made to suffer for their own real delays."[75] Carter complained to his diary later in the year, "All 3 days before this spent at Court, chiefly in obliging the Lawyers to say anything out of the causes that they are engaged in, and making the most absurd motions imaginable."[76]

To the *Gazette*, "C. R." protested in classic Country terms against paying justices a salary, "for the day that we come to work for hire, we shall lay a foundation for that corruption, which is, from experience, so justly to be dreaded by every state." Few courts were meeting before noon any longer, he complained, and since lawyers, sheriffs, and clerks, who already were paid for their labors, were also dilatory, what

---

rary) judgment after a jury assessed damages. The court then gave final judgment. In Virginia such writs were commonly issued in which debtors confessed indebtedness to a creditor and by the writs were commanded to pay according to an appointed schedule. The text of the law and Dunmore's letter are in PRO: CO 5/1350, fols. 77–79. All references throughout are from copies of crown-copyright records in the Public Record Office, used at Williamsburg, Virginia, Virginia Colonial Records Project. Citations appear by permission of the controller of H.M. Stationery Office.

74. Dunmore to Dartmouth, Mar. 18, 1774, PRO: CO 5/1352, fols. 5–15; *Virginia Almanac* for 1770 (P and D), heading for October.
75. Greene, ed., *Diary*, 2:709–10.
76. Ibid., p. 585.

would be the practical value of paying justices, anyway? Upon reflection, "C. R." had to admit that lawyers had borne a large share of the blame in the public mind for dilatory proceedings. They should offer no excuses, he thought, but he was unable to work up a genuine rage against lawyers.[77] Indeed, between 1771 and 1774 public observations about the profession seemed to improve, and attorneys were admitted to be both potentially patriotic and interested in genuine reform of the courts.

In 1772, as the burgesses were considering the proposed reform of the court structure, defenses of the legal profession began to surface in the *Gazette*. From Edenton, North Carolina, PHOCION reproved the popular prejudice against lawyers in general that he found rampant in Virginia and North Carolina. Admittedly, some unscrupulous lawyers charged exorbitant fees, he said. But honest planters and merchants knew honest lawyers, respected their abilities, and resented general and careless charges against the profession. PHOCION knew he would be ridiculed, but "notwithstanding any Sneer at my Presumption," still asked, "are the Lawyers more deserving of Reproach than any other Set of Men?" Coming to the aid of lawyers was difficult, he admitted, for "a Defence against *any* Charge, which may be clouded in obscure Insinuations, is attended with much Difficulty. A defence against *popular* Accusation appears to particular Disadvantage."[78]

Yet others rose to the defense as well. In December, Rind's *Gazette* published an essay entitled "Character of a good Lawyer" on the front page. The good lawyer, of course, was "a man of virtue," public spirited, who made a noble practice of the law, not reducing it to "a grovelling, mercenary trade." By placing lawyers under the protection of the party of virtue and disassociating them from the "mercenary trade" the author clearly signaled to his readers that lawyers belonged to the Country, not to the corrupt Court, which worked for British merchant-creditors. Most lawyers were honest, he insisted, and those who were not will "not have it in their power to do much mischief, as they certainly will be treated, not only by their brethren, but likewise by the Judges, with the contempt and abhorrence that they deserve."[79]

77. *Virginia Gazette* (Rind), April 26, 1770.
78. PHOCION, *Virginia Gazette*, Feb. 13, 1772.
79. Ibid., Dec. 24, 1772. Despite the genuine success of the lawyers in cutting their perceived ties to the creditor-merchant interest before the Revolution, the connection emerged again in the 1780s. An important symbolic step in the severing of those ties in the early 1770s had been the signing of the Nonimportation Agreement, June 22, 1770, by sixteen of the most eminent attorneys in Virginia. See *JVHB*, pp. xxvii–xxi. The lawyers were Peyton Randolph, Robert Carter Nicholas, Richard Bland, Edmund Pendleton, Henry Lee, Thomas Jefferson, Severn Eyre, Paul Carrington, James Mercer, John Wayles, John Bannister, Bolling Starke, William Roane, John Blair, Jerman Baker, and John Tazewell. On the

Satire and antilawyer anecdotes still appeared in the *Gazette*, of course, accusing them of un-Christian behavior or under the title "The glorious Uncertainties of the Law," lumping them together with Divinity and Physick as members of the "three genteel Professions," among whom the lawyers were guilty of more "petit Larceny" than the other two. Yet obituaries of Virginia lawyers were almost uniformly respectful and laudatory of these "professors" of the law; far more severe censures were entered against factors and merchants.[80]

In April 1773 the paper published a remarkable poetic piece entitled, "A Lawyer's Prayer: A Fragment." Unlike the satirical doggerel that was more characteristic of the paper ("A Lawyer's Bill," for example), this piece was soberly presented as an evocation of virtues proper to a lawyer. The self-reflections of the virtuous lawyer enjoined upon himself an upright life and a public-spirited disdain of lucre:

> Mine be the conscience void of blame,
> The upright heart, the spotless name;
> The tribute of the widow's prayer,
> The righted orphan's grateful tear;
> To virtue and her friends, a friend,
> Still may my voice the weak defend.[81]

This April sonnet was followed in May by the essay of TIMOLEON against casuistry in the law, which never once suggested that lawyers were to blame. Rather, from February through June three essays of A TRAVELLER censured county court justices and scorned Essex Justice Meriwether Smith's attempt to vindicate local magistrates. In an incident similar to the Chiswell Affair, Justice Griffing Boughan of Essex County

---

emergence of a "lawyer" or "court" party in the 1780s, see below, chapter v; Risjord, *Chesapeake Politics*. For some reason Risjord is reluctant to label the legal reformers in Virginia a "lawyer party" similar to that in North Carolina and Kentucky. Yet the similarities that bind these factions in the Upper South states into a common interest seem to me obvious. See Risjord on debts, court reform, and the significance of the 1784 port bill, pp. 84–85, 109–16, 132–38, 148–56. He argues persuasively that lawyers and many planters upheld British demands for debt collection after 1783 as a matter of honor in a truly republican society, even at the risk of their own fortunes.

80. *Virginia Gazette*, (P and D), Jan. 10, 1774. For lawyer obituaries, see ibid., Sept. 19, 1766 (P and D), Aug. 13, 1772, Jan. 21, 1773 (Rind); antimerchant and antifactor letters (P and D), Oct. 21, Nov. 4, 1773.

81. For "A Lawyer's Bill," see *Virginia Gazette* (Rind), Jan. 14, 1773. "A Lawyer's Prayer" appears ibid., April 1, 1773. Between 1773 and 1790 antilawyer doggerel disappeared from the almanacs and from the *Gazette*; criticism of the justices did not. "A Lawyer's Prayer" was reprinted once (though not subsequently, it seems) in Benjamin Workman's 1790 Richmond, Virginia, *Almanac*.

illegally took away his convicted slave, and from fear that Boughan might one day hang one of their own slaves when he sat as an oyer and terminer justice, the court allowed manifestly guilty slaves to go free.[82] Smith himself had to agree that much of the fault lay with the senior or presiding justice of the courts for not behaving with gravity in session as well as out. But TRAVELLER rejected both Smith's excuses and his warnings about seditious talk. The pillars of society would not be shaken if magistrates were criticized, he asserted, and the only real question was "whether ignorance or injustice is most culpable in a public officer."[83]

The tenor of the remarks of TRAVELLER in his closing essay reveals a fondness for the lawyers' point of view that ignorant attorneys should be disbarred and only an elite should administer law. That was an old suggestion, of course, and had been at the heart of Williamsburg barristers' censures of county justices and lawyers for most of the eighteenth century. "*Laws* speak the *deliberate* and *impartial reason* of the *whole society*," TRAVELLER argued, "and uninterested [sic] Magistrates are likely to execute them with fairness." But ignorant and designing lawyers and justices were the norm in Virginia. Modestly, he concluded: "I do not pretend to be deeply read in the law." But he recommended that Smith follow his own example, since "I sometimes, at a leisure moment, *amuse* myself in perusing the laws of a country, under whose happy establishment I live in such a free and perfect enjoyment of civil liberty."[84]

As the year 1773 drew to a close, more ominous events elsewhere drew the attention of Virginians away from the debate about their legal culture and their courts, lawyers, and judges. Yet the initiative for reform of the court structure of Virginia had merely faltered; after that date it would be taken up by the legal profession, regardless of opposition from the justices. For the moment, Meriwether Smith and his colleagues on the county court in Essex and elsewhere were safe. Events were to prove, however, that he had already lost the support and the traditional respect of Virginia's planters and smallholders. The lawyers of Virginia had struggled mightily to achieve reform of the courts, both to recover their own fees and to expedite clients' business. They had suffered obloquy in the press, insults and reprimands in the county courts, and genuine embarrassment at the ignorant and vile pettifoggers who admittedly made up the lower echelons of the profession. Yet, as Virginia faced a confrontation with Great Britain, its lawyers moved to defend the patriot

---

82. Ibid., May 6, 1773, April 15, May 13, June 3, 1773.
83. Ibid., May 13.
84. Ibid., June 3. On Smith's later career as leader of opposition to court reform in the House of Delegates, see below, chapter 5.

cause. Freed from association with merchant-creditors and the unpopular General Court bench, the profession would very soon be established on even firmer foundations by some of its most articulate spokesmen and political pamphleteers. Reform of the courts had not been forgotten, however. When the issue arose again, the cause would be moved forward as part of the quest for Country virtue in a new republic. And the movers would be republican lawyers.

Chapter 5
Republican Lawyers, 1774–1790

To virtue and her friends, a friend
—ANONYMOUS, "A Lawyer's Prayer"

On April 12, 1774, the fee act, under whose provisions Virginians paid their court clerks and other officials, expired. That act had been routinely renewed since its passage in 1745. Now the General Court sought the opinions of lawyers as to whether the court might not continue to operate in the interim before the May session of the House of Burgesses convened to renew the act. Conservative lawyer and former county justice Edmund Pendleton agreed that the General Court could proceed with its business until May. But another lawyer, Thomas Jefferson, proclaimed that he saw grave constitutional questions in the General Court's presuming to act in perpetuating a law that owed its life to legislative, not judicial, fiat. The House would probably have renewed the act in May had it not in the meantime heard of the closing of the port of Boston. In the ensuing uproar, Lord Dunmore dissolved the House. By so doing, the governor failed to get the fee act renewed, and because of the popular clamor against letting British creditors press for debts in Virginia courts, both county and General Court actions abruptly halted.[1]

The casual observer of the role that justices of the peace played in this drama might conclude that the local squires were at one with their neighbors. Dunmore thought so. He wrote home complaining bitterly of the refusal of Virginia justices and lawyers to hear and argue civil causes. To Lord Dartmouth, the governor sourly observed: "There is not a Justice of Peace in Virginia that acts except as a Committee Man. The abolishing

---

1. The first version of the fee act is in Hening, 5:326–44. County courts remained open for probate of wills and prosecution of petty crimes, and administrative details were attended to, but no civil causes were heard. See Curtis, "Role of the Courts" and "Virginia Courts During the Revolution"; Shepard, "Administration of Justice in Revolutionary Virginia" and "Courts in Conflict." Curtis does comment on the opposition of justices to the provisions of the 1772 assize bill ("Role of the Courts," p. 130), but the issue has to be seen within the context of the long-standing debates between advocates of reform and tradition-minded defenders of local justice. The data in this chapter refer to the following ten counties: Richmond, York, Middlesex, Caroline, Henrico, Essex, Westmoreland, Northumberland, King George, and Lancaster.

the Courts of Justice was the first Step taken, in which the men of fortune and preemince [sic] joined equally with the lowest and meanest. The General Court ... is in much the same predicament; for, though ... a Majority ... with myself ... would steadily perform their duty, yet the Lawyers have absolutely refused to attend, nor indeed would the People allow them to attend or evidence to appear."[2]

Dunmore here revealed a great deal more about the reputations of judges and lawyers in Virginia respective to the impending constitutional crisis than he realized. Just as Virginia Whigs had suspected since the 1760s, the central judiciary of Virginia was hopelessly corrupted by Court attitudes. Since the men who sat as General Court judges were also the "aristocratic" members of the Council, it is no surprise that tyranny and corruption marked the judges of Williamsburg. Furthermore, lawyers, who traditionally had not been thought of very highly by the Country, and justices, who had recently been under attack for their dereliction and lack of public spirit, nonetheless joined the patriot cause against the easily identified menace of the royal governor and his councillors. As early as 1765 Westmoreland justices signaled who local squires (for the most part) would support in a crisis. Citing "the very great Impropriety of Acting in an Office which at once requires the Discharge of Duties, utterly Inconsistent with each other," the justices closed their court to protest the Stamp Act. As traditional guardians of the rights and liberties of the people, the justices believed they could not both fulfill their morally obligatory role and faithfully execute their office under the oath sworn as the king's justices of the peace.[3] That maneuver temporarily dampened much of the growing criticism of county justices, and during the crisis with Britain, county lawyers and justices presented a fairly united front against the corruption, tyranny, and arbitrariness that they felt characterized the persons sitting in the Governor's Palace, Council, and General Court.

Writing as the "British American" in the *Virginia Gazette*, barrister Thomson Mason traced the constitutional crisis to the despotic precedents set down by the Stuarts. At no time during the crisis had anyone yet

2. Dunmore to Dartmouth, Dec. 24, 1774, Earl of Dunmore Correspondence, PRO: CO 5/1353, fols. 7–39, no. 23.
3. *Pennsylvania Gazette*, Oct. 31, 1765, in Van Schreeven and Scribner, *Revolutionary Virginia*, 1:19–21. Westmoreland was joined by Northampton magistrates, who declared the act null and void and unconstitutional. *Virginia Gazette* (P and D), March 21, 1766. The animus of planters against merchants was voiced in the House in 1774 when justices testified that support for court closure was conceived to be an excellent way of vexing "the Merchantile part of the British Nation ... to interest them in favour of the Colony." *JVHB*, 1775, pp. 234–37. One should note, however, that stopping debt collection also removed an enormous burden from the shoulders of much-criticized and listless magistrates.

suggested that local justices of the peace constituted self-perpetuating oligarchies in the counties and might be inconsistent with a virtuous, free society. Like most of the lawyers who wrote during the debates, Mason echoed the already ancient complaint of the Country of Virginia, following the same lines that Robert Beverley and COMMON SENSE had pursued. Mason attacked corruption and tyranny and warned the great gentry of Virginia of the folly of Rome's aristocracy, who had failed to support the sober judgment of the equestrian class, "the middling ranks, who are always the most wise and virtuous people of a state." Like those ancient Roman nobles, Virginia's aristocratic families could not expect that by trying to remain neutral "their houses, their fish ponds, their parks, their villas, and their gardens, would remain untouched, when the laws of their country were abolished." Mason concluded in his letter 9 on July 28 that "if the laws of your country can be duly enforced," the potential tyranny of corrupt judges could be restrained.[4] Just as the lawyers of 1688–89 had labored to secure the tenure of judges during good behavior and to abolish the corruption of the bench and its dependence on a despotic monarchy, so now Virginians were to begin securing one of the long-standing demands of the Country, which had been raised by Robert Beverley, hinted at by COMMON SENSE, and demanded after the Chiswell scandal in 1766.

The successful resolution of the constitutional question of an independent judiciary in 1776 was Virginia's guarantee against corruption of the law by despotic power. For the sake of both private and public virtue, judges would never be councillors, either of the king or of the state, in the new republic. Settlement of this important point, however, inevitably led Virginians to reexamine other questions about the law, the courts, and the justices of the peace that had lain dormant after 1774. The revisal of the laws in which Thomas Jefferson, George Wythe, and Edmund Pendleton were engaged between 1776 and 1779 set the agenda under whose provisions the issues of the 1760s would be reargued. War, the reluctance of the new legislature to act precipitously during the late 1770s, and local resistance postponed action on the agenda. But the reconstruction of Virginia's court system and the assault on the time-honored prerogatives of justices of the peace was at hand.

4. On the Stuarts, letter 6, July 7, reprinted in Van Schreeven and Scribner, *Revolutionary Virginia*, 1:177–82; on Rome and corruption, letter 7, July 14, ibid., p. 185; on judges and the law, letter 9, July 28, ibid., p. 199.

The Sources of Republican Law

The coming of the Revolution in Virginia obscured whatever differences had lain between justices and lawyers regarding their roles and importance in the Old Dominion. Even as hostilities began, however, leading thinkers and actors in Virginia politics made clear their determination to have done with the remnants of English tradition. From his view of both ancient and recent history, Jefferson identified the county oligarchies ensconced on the court benches as his opponents in the quest for a virtuous, republican society. According to Jefferson, the county courts were harbors which protected corrupt monarchical practices and were not, as the Country justices had long maintained, the guarantors of the best traditions of ancient and customary law. Looking to New England, Jefferson saw that the towns there were filled with elected selectmen, who dominated the less significant counties. He could not help but be struck by the contrast with Virginia where the nonrepresentative justices controlled everything in their localities. "Those wards, called townships in New England," Jefferson maintained, "are the vital principle of their governments, and have proved themselves the wisest invention ever devised by the wit of man for the perfect exercise of self-government, and for its preservation." From 1776 until the end of his life, Jefferson continued to demand an end to the customary institution of local Virginia. In a virtual declaration of war he said: "As Cato, then, concluded every speech with the words *Carthago delenda est*, so do I every opinion with the injunction: 'Divide the counties into wards!'"[5]

Like many of his contemporaries who had come of age during the 1760s, Jefferson had been influenced by Country opposition literature, which warned of corruption of virtue and liberty through the use of power and favoritism. That aspect of Country thought that had censured lawyers as partners of Court corruption was either lost on him or ignored as inapplicable to Virginia's patriotic bar. He found a virtuous prehistory of Virginia, like the pre-Norman past of England, by which to judge what had happened to his state.

---

5. Jefferson to Samuel Kerchival, July 12, 1816, *Writings of Jefferson* (Washington, ed.,), 7:13; Jefferson to Joseph C. Cabell, February 2, 1816, ibid., 6:544. By this point in his life, Jefferson regretted somewhat the principle he so stoutly defended in 1776—the independence of the judiciary from political control—partly because of conflicts with the federal Supreme Court, partly because of disillusionment with the political process, which should have directed, through republican wisdom, the framing of laws that the judges could then merely execute. He continued to feel that judges at the local level ought to be elected and fretted about his failure to place Virginia's county courts on an elective basis. See below. When Jefferson conceived of the idea of an independent judiciary has been the subject of some debate. See Curtis, "A Communication."

One of his contemporaries, Edmund Randolph, wrote what their generation's view of that past had been in his *History of Virginia*. Randolph traced the sources of the political ideology that inspired Virginians to revolution as far back as Bacon's Rebellion in 1676. Whether he was merely attempting to show that Virginians had always loved liberty or whether he really believed that Bacon and his followers were true Whigs we shall probably never know. But his comments are instructive if we wish to know where the group of new lawyers coming of age in Virginia between 1750 and 1780 found the explanation they needed to understand what was wrong with Virginia's laws and court system. Randolph suggested that Virginians of the late seventeenth century "were ... brought to reflect upon principles which from their intercourse with the mother country, they had in a manner, although imperfectly and superficially, caught from Locke, Sidney, Harrington, and Hooker, and which served as stations from whence to begin a career of political thought."[6]

In and of themselves, the political writings of a few Whig pamphleteers could never have generated a revolution, whether such an event was a political separation or a new way of thinking about law and society. But Randolph was probably right in suggesting that the reading of such pamphleteers helped to encourage young lawyers like Jefferson in identifying what a just society was like, how laws were to be framed, and what the proper role of a judge was in such a culture.

The proposals that Jefferson advanced for setting Virginia's legal culture in a thoroughly republican mode grew out of his Whig reading of history. As Trevor Colbourn has shown, that historical understanding allowed Jefferson the luxury of positing a "golden age" of the law, just as Country apologists had posited a golden age of simplicity in English life. For the Country apologists the golden age had been thought to have prevailed until at least the time of Elizabeth I. Building upon his reading of Lord Kames, Coke's *Institutes*, and even Blackstone's *Commentaries*, however, Jefferson concluded that customary law had long ago been traduced by foreign innovations and artificial distinctions introduced by a landed, Norman aristocracy. The purity of Saxon law could only be restored, Jefferson thought, by rooting out the corruptions of Christianity, educating people in all walks of life, and abolishing hereditary aristocracy by redistributing land through gavelkind instead of primogeniture or borough English. Jefferson clearly believed that Virginia suffered from having been led by an ignoble, landed, Christian aristocracy. Of the more conservative Pendleton, who was skeptical of Jefferson's interpretation of the past, the Albemarle sage rhetorically asked, "Are we

---

6. Randolph, *History of Virginia*, p. 157.

not the better for what we have hitherto abolished of the feudal system? Has not every restitution of the antient Saxon laws had happy effects? Is it not better now that we return at once into that happy system of our ancestors, the wisest and most perfect ever yet devised by the wit of man, as it stood before the 8th century?"[7]

In his lengthy essay "Whether Christianity is a part of the Common Law?" Jefferson answered the title query in the negative and the rhetorical question put to Pendleton in the affirmative. A devout Anglican and proponent of a plan to limit suffrage in Virginia to the holders of permanent property, Pendleton highly valued stability in institutions and virtue in the people. Jefferson, too, believed that virtue was important, yet disagreed with the conservative Pendleton about its nature and how to guarantee it. He blamed the machinations of popish monks for the chicanery of land law in England and believed that the Anglo-Saxons originally never even wrote down their laws. In any event, after Magna Charta common law in its pure form disappeared, to be replaced by written and statutory law. Christianity was introduced in England between 598 and 686, Jefferson said, and by the eighth century, falsifications by monks were well on their way toward completely obscuring the true nature of law, a process that was completed by the time of Charles II in the seventeenth century. One commentator during that benighted monarch's reign had cited "Houard, in his Coutumes Anglo-Normandes, I. 87," remarking that the laws of Alfred had chapters 20–23 of Exodus attached to them. "These he calls Hors d'oeuvre of some pious copyist. This awkward monkish fabrication makes the preface to Alfred's genuine laws stand in the body of the work." As example, Jefferson pointed out that whereas Jewish law required death as the punishment for murder, Alfred's laws fixed fines and wergilds in proportion to the condition of the deceased.[8]

7. On the American Whigs' use of the past, see Colbourn, *Lamp of Experience*. On the "enlightened" use of history and the philosophes' view of the Christian past, see Gay, *Enlightenment*, 1:207–419. On Jefferson's reading of Kames, Coke, and Dalrymple on feudal property, see Chinard, ed., *Commonplace Book*, pp. 16–65. On the ties between Whig concerns about virtue and Christianity, see McLoughlin, "Role of Religion." On the American use of Coke, see Mullett, "Coke and the American Revolution." Waterman, "Thomas Jefferson and Blackstone's Commentaries," surveys Jefferson's admiration for and fear of the Vinerian Professor's ideas. Primogeniture, of course, refers to the laws by which nonpartible inheritance passed to the eldest son; borough English reverses the process —the youngest son inherits in favor his older brothers; gavelkind was a species of tenure common in Kent in which property descended to all sons. Jefferson to Pendleton, Aug. 13, 1776, *Papers of Thomas Jefferson*, 1:491–94.

8. Pendleton to Jefferson, *Papers of Thomas Jefferson*, 1:488–91, reveals Pendleton's conservative opinions. Jefferson's essay on Christianity and the common law appears as appendix 1, in *Virginia Reports*, 1:137–42.

The conspiracy on the part of the landed aristocracy and church hierarchy to subvert Saxon customary law, Jefferson continued, had been given voice in the preaching that demanded the giving of tithes to the clergy. But a modern scholar, Jefferson wrote, could tell that laws regarding murder, retaliation, usury, bailment, and other topics were "never the laws of England, not even in Alfred's time; and of course, that it [the additions to Alfred's law] is a forgery. Yet, palpable as it must be to a lawyer, our judges have piously avoided lifting the veil under which it was shrouded . . . the alliance between church and state . . . has ever made . . . judges accomplices in the frauds of the clergy . . . and [they have] declared at once that the whole Bible and Testament, in a lump, make a part of the common law of the land, . . . thus identifying Christianity with the ecclesiastical law of England."[9]

Echoing the theme sounded years earlier by COMMON SENSE, Jefferson maintained that only lawyers could be on guard against threats to the virtue of the Country. The clergy, the aristocracy, the judges—all those Court figures conspired against the law, but the lawyer who pursued the law as a science could ally himself with the Country. Pendleton was wrong if he expected the family oligarchies that dominated the county courts to be on the side of scientific law and popular, republican virtue.[10]

Phillip Mazzei, Jefferson's friend during many of the debates over the law, scorned the conservative Pendleton as well, describing the revisers as a group of "prominent lawyers, four of whom were also philosophers." Going to some pains to isolate Pendleton and reduce his learning to the status of mere pedantry, Mazzei claimed that the four "shared the same view on all subjects, but Mr. Edmund Pendleton, who was fonder of the court items in newspapers than of philosophy, often disagreed, and, above all, on matters of religion and property held in trust or by a limited owner." Jefferson himself never belittled Pendleton's learning, and indeed remained friends with him. George Wythe, of course, shared Jefferson's point of view, and George Mason seemed to, although he soon revealed himself to be as conservative as Pendleton.[11]

Jefferson and Wythe had observed the debates over the assize scheme

9. Jefferson, *Virginia Reports*, 1:142. How Jefferson's abolition of entail and primogeniture was connected in his mind with the notion that corrupt land holdings and corrupt Christianity were linked is not entirely clear. See Keim, "Primogeniture and Entail"; Berthoff and Murrin, "Feudalism, Communalism, and the Yeoman Farmer," p. 283.

10. "Editorial Note on the Revisal of the Laws," *Papers of Thomas Jefferson*, 2:314–15.

11. Contrary to Mazzei's description of them as lawyer-philosophers, both Mason and Thomas Ludwell Lee resigned their posts on the grounds that they were not lawyers. Mazzei's attempt at characterization is revealing, for it represents the notion of legal rationalism so dear to republican reformers. See Marraro, trans. *Memoirs of the Life of Philip Mazzei*, pp. 214–15.

of 1772 and were also aware of the educational reforms that had been promoted at the college before the Revolution. As governor, Jefferson moved to guarantee republican virtue for Virginia by revising the curriculum at William and Mary, advancing both liberal education, and practical science. Of the various professoriates he created, only that of law and police flourished, under the brilliant care of his mentor, Wythe. There can be no doubt that Jefferson and Wythe believed that to secure a republican legal culture the commonwealth would have to rely on an elite cadre of professionally trained lawyers and judges, who were not only technically skilled but also broadly educated in republican letters. The reform of the legal system of Virginia was tied inextricably to Jefferson's proposals for educational reform. With these improvements and the disestablishment of the Anglican church he planned to destroy the remnants of monarchism in Virginia. Jefferson was no egalitarian concerning the legal profession. He did not share the optimism that had been voiced in 1773 by a writer who had signed his missive to the *Virginia Gazette* COUNTY JUSTICE. That correspondent, probably reflecting on the defeat of the assize bill, pleaded for a professorship of law at William and Mary, a notion that Jefferson endorsed. But COUNTY JUSTICE observed that as a justice of the peace he had long observed "great confusion, want of argument, of reasoning, and, I conceived, of law, too, in the pleadings of some of our lawyers." To remedy this, COUNTY JUSTICE suggested that the 1748 provision that had separated county from General Court lawyers now be removed in order that the diffusion of law "as a science" be promoted throughout Virginia.[12]

Jefferson was not sure that he liked this idea. Although the 1748 provision was, in fact, removed after the ties with Britain were cut, Jefferson worried that swarms of petty lawyers would corrupt the grand designs for republican law that he had in mind for Virginia.[13] In various bills included in the revisal of the laws of 1776–79, he left little doubt that he laid the hopes for a republican future of legal culture squarely on the shoulders of a professional bench and bar. His Bill for Establishing a

---

12. *Virginia Gazette* (Rind), Dec. 30, 1773. On the college, see Thomson, "Reform of the College."

13. Jefferson expressed his alarm at the hordes of pettifoggers in Virginia to Wythe. See Jefferson to Wythe, March 1, 1779, *Papers of Thomas Jefferson*, 2:235. Jefferson feared for the General Court's role as "an excellent nursery for future judges," due to the "inundation of insects . . . from the county courts." He also believed that judges should be chosen only from the members of the General Court and High Court of Chancery bars. In 1792 a new law did pass in Virginia restoring restrictions on lower court attorneys that prohibited lawyers from taking the same cause from the county on appeal to the new district courts. See below.

General Court attempted to revive the old assize scheme and would have sent the judges of the General Court on circuit throughout Virginia to try cases that were pending on appeal. That provision was stricken from the bill that became law. At the same time, in December of 1776, Jefferson put forward his Bill for Better Regulating the Proceedings in the County Courts. Justices were to levy the sum of ten pounds every year to purchase law books for their use and were to accept public grievances and claims against the counties at any session, instead of once yearly. Such directions, highly reminiscent of the old 1714 directives from the House of Burgesses to the justices about grievances, were predictably not popular with the justices of the peace. Even so, these measures were mild and merely indicated Jefferson's attempt to promote better law among the lay judiciary.[14]

His conviction that the local courts were fundamentally unrepublican, however, finally found expression in Bill Number 95 of the proposed revisal, submitted to the Assembly in 1779. The Bill for Constituting Justices of the Peace and County Courts abolished the customarily hereditary office of justice of the peace. Every county would henceforth elect a number of aldermen, who in their turn would be considered as nominees, ex officio, for the posts on the county court. Anyone chosen who did not swear into the Commission of the Peace would automatically be barred from the next commission.

Clearly, Jefferson was thinking of his New England "wards" when he proposed aldermen and elective office as means of circumventing the old family oligarchies. But there was an additional reason why he felt this had to be done. Tied to the bill on the county courts was Jefferson's Bill for the More General Diffusion of Knowledge. Each county's three aldermen were to divide the county into hundreds and apportion the children therein, who would attend a public school erected by the county courts. There was no substitute, Jefferson believed, for the proper education of county residents, who would then be able to choose the aldermen who would be their judges in the local courts. Even at this stage, Jefferson did not suggest that local judges should be lawyers. He had even praised the early settlers of America in his *Summary View of the Rights of British America* in 1774 for being "farmers, not lawyers."[15]

14. Even the conservative lawyer Pendleton firmly defended the necessity of a circuit court system. To William Woodford he wrote that the assize scheme "passed the Delegates by a Majority of 8, and was rejected in the Senate by a majority of one, so that tho' dropped, a small number of the whole were in it's favor, it will be adopted 'ere long, as our Judiciary System is lame without it" (Jan. 31, 1778, *Letters and Papers of Edmund Pendleton*, 1:247). The General Court bill is in *Papers of Thomas Jefferson* 1:621–44; the bill regulating proceedings is in ibid., 650–52.

15. Bill for Constituting Justices of the Peace, *Papers of Thomas Jefferson*, 2:578–82;

The impact of the Country tradition on Jefferson was as profound as it had been on Virginia as a whole. A virtuous people, in his mind, had to be educated to enable them to live morally upright lives and be wise enough to choose their leaders. County education and an elective lay bench fit well into that scheme. Unfortunately, in June 1779 when the revisers submitted their report, the Assembly tabled the entire affair. When the battle over the legal structure of Virginia was taken up again in 1784 by Jefferson's lieutenant James Madison, far more drastic measures were advanced by republican lawyers.

Between 1776 and 1783, the actual workings of the local courts were not a pressing issue, since all debt causes were suspended and the commonwealth as a whole had more important things to worry about than the performance of local justices of the peace. However, the moral tenor of Virginia life, an issue raised by the Baptists in the 1760s against the laxness of the gentlemen of the counties, was an issue in the republican debates about virtue in Virginia culture. No one suggested that the local courts return to the prosecution of moral offenses, a task they had performed (rather indifferently) before the Revolution. But in fact, the various county committees, often composed of justices, did do just such a job during the Revolution. Ferreting out suspected Tories was a part of the duty to maintain the virtue of communities during the war. In Princess Anne, for example, local justices found William and Sarah Axtead brought before them for expressing views revealing them to be "inimically disposed to the United States of America" and for saying "that the present Dispute would never be settled unless by Mobbs." Between 1779 and 1782 various men were arraigned for treason in Princess Anne and in other county courts throughout Virginia. To a certain degree, then, the old obligation of the courts to act as the moral guarantors of the county persisted throughout the war. Grand juries' presentments still dealt with petty crime, and justices like Colonel Will Roane of Essex delighted their counties by the ferocity of their antiloyalist baiting.[16]

Jefferson's education bill, ibid., 526–35. See the extended footnote to this bill, ibid., pp. 534–35, and Jefferson's later remarks about the defeat of his education schemes by wealthy justices who foiled his attempt to replace the hereditary nature of power in the county with one of "merit" or talent based on education and legal expertise in Koch and Peden, eds., *Life and Selected Writings*, p. 50. In Jefferson's original draft of the *Summary View* the phrase read "laborers, not lawyers." See *Papers of Thomas Jefferson* 1:133, 137 (fn. 35). Much of the 1776–79 revisal was tabled. On its later fate, see Cullen, "Completing the Revisal of the Laws."

16. A Court of Commissioners, made up of the justices and other prominent citizens, was established in each county. Of these five judges an observer wrote that upon their recommendation by the committees of the counties, the Virginia Committee of Safety approved them, and "an appeal lies from them to the Committee of Safety." See diary of Robert

Yet such an interim state of affairs enabled the county courts to survive a bit longer precisely because the Revolution disrupted civil business, by far the largest burden the local courts had had to shoulder. The unsettled state of affairs so depressed Amherst County Justice William Cabell, Sr., that he recorded in his diary on February 19, 1774, "My Docket as a Majistrate, from the Confusion of the times, becoming unnecessary for preservation, I have this day destroyed the same as being in the way, & answering no good purpose to preserve them." Prominent justices like Ralph Wormeley of Middlesex, his relatives the Tayloes and the Corbins, and Robert Beverley of Essex were all driven from the ranks of the Commission of the Peace either for being overtly loyalist or for being too cool about the patriot cause. Wormeley later explained to an English correspondent that he could never stand for office in an independent Virginia—he was too unpopular due to his lack of enthusiasm.[17]

When the crisis came, another great family also passed from the ranks of Virginia justices and judges: William Byrd III vacillated over what position to take and agonized to Wormeley about "the horrid Disposition of the Times & the frantick Patriotism of those who have taken the Lead." Siding at the last minute with the patriots from fear that Dunmore's proclamation to black slaves would promote race war, Byrd nonetheless moved too late. In his own hand at the bottom of Byrd's letter, Wormeley penned the epitaph for the scion of the great Westover family: "He was not trusted. He lost everything." On January 1, 1777, William Byrd III committed suicide in his mansion, Belvidere, outside Richmond.[18]

Honeyman, Jan. 2, 1776–Mar. 11, 1782, p. 15, Robert Honeyman Papers. See also Curtis, "Virginia Courts," pp. 137–38; Hening, 9:103–6 (1775) for the statute establishing five commissioners or judges to enforce county committees' actions in favor of the new commonwealth. On the Princess Anne events, see Creecy, ed., *Virginia Antiquary*, Sept. 12, 1780, 1:103–4; ibid., Sept. 9, 1779, May 25, 1782, 1:115–16. On the Tory-baiting antics of John and William Roane, see *WMQ*, 1st ser., 18 (1908–10): 270–78.

17. Diary of William Cabell, Sr., Feb. 19, 1776, VSL. Cabell's disgust with the new politics of Virginia reflected the disenchantment of many old families. He made his February entry in huge, scrawling letters, and prior to this, on January 25, recorded, "I left the new Committee of safety after having set 7 daies inclusive which I have not rec. ? for ——." On the Tory sentiments of the local leaders in the Tappahannock area I am much indebted to my student Dirk J. Giseburt; see his "Life of Loyalty." Wormeley's letter is in Ralph Wormeley Letterbook, 1783–1802, July 30, 1796 (partially torn, apparently to an English correspondent), Accession No. 1939, Wormeley Family Papers.

18. On Byrd, see Ralph Wormeley Letters, Byrd to Wormeley, Oct. 4, 1775, Wormeley Family Papers. On Byrd's life, see *Correspondence*, 2:604–14. On the disruption of old social patterns in the 1780s in the Tidewater, see Main, "One Hundred." See also demographic statistics on selected Tidewater counties in Gee and Gorson, *Rural Depopulation*, pp. 11–13; Main, "Distribution of Property."

The question of who could be trusted to guarantee the security and the virtue of the people was bound to come up again as soon as the conflict was over. Republican lawyers like George Mason, Jefferson, and St. George Tucker had one solution. Other Virginians trusted less in a cerebral republican elite than in their own local, common sense attitudes. Yet between 1784 and 1787, the republican lawyers were able to erect an entirely new court system on the ruins of the old county courts.

Beginning in 1783 a flood of resumed debt causes inundated the county courts, and county residents were far more interested in getting their business done than in discussing the importance or significance of guaranteeing Country, republican, or any other kind of virtue—whether that term was taken to mean civic duty or adherence to certain moral codes. The inefficiency of the courts had already been attacked by critics before the Revolution, but reform had thus far failed to affect the performance of the local benches. The climate of opinion that prevailed between 1783 and 1787, however, provided the republican lawyers with precisely the leverage they needed to force their professional prescriptions for a republican legal culture in Virginia through the legislature.

The Country Justices and the Failure of Republican Virtue

By a law of 1777 no debts were to be collected in the courts of Virginia in cases in which a British subject was the plaintiff, nor were debts to be collected by Virginians unless due to the commonwealth. It was felt that during the war no effective means could be had to execute debts when the very life of the state depended on citizens contributing what little they had to the commonwealth and not to a private creditor.

In 1782, to aid Virginians ravaged by the war and in recognition of the shortage of specie, the Assembly allowed for payment of debts in hemp, tobacco, and flour, with the county courts fixing the value of those items. Virginia merchants who were partners with British subjects could now proceed with attachments. Later the same year and again in 1783 laws provided that titles of land and slaves could be used to make payment, since a drought in Virginia had made the allowance for payment in crops worthless.[19]

Merchant Charles Yates of Fredericksburg was not pleased with the Assembly's actions. In 1782 he wrote to a correspondent, "Our Courts are said to be open now—however the last Assembly have put a lock Chain on the Wheels of Madam Justice—No Executions are to Issue til

19. Hening, 9:377–80, 471, 474; ibid., 11:75–76, 176–80, 349.

March 1783, and then the Debtors have it in their Option to pay persons Receipts for Tob[acco] Flower [sic] or Hemp in Lieu of Specie, at such prices as the Courts shall fix when the Executions are taken out—for my part I think it hard to be paid what one does not want especially as it is probable the Justices will rate the Articles too high to turn the penny with them." To William Vernon, Yates wrote in a resigned manner, "Our Courts of Justice were shut up, and although within these 12 Months they have been opened to Suitors, it has been with such restrictions that I have not judged it worth while to commence any action."[20]

By late 1783, however, Yates and the rest of Virginia had commenced actions with a vengeance, pressing for debts in several courts at once. Although the pressure to absolve British debts may have been part of the volume, it is clear that most of the debt cases in the county courts were among Virginians attempting to settle their affairs in the midst of economic turmoil. The floodgates now opened. It had been usual for county court in the 1740s to sit for two days a month to finish the county business. During the early 1750s most courts had been able to sit only two days during the regular months, adding an additional day or two in May and November when the grand jury was called. By the 1760s, however, four- and five-day sessions were common. In Richmond County that pattern quickly reemerged after the war; the court sat for three days in August 1783. In November 1786 the justices had a caseload which did not permit them to rise for five days. Hearing twenty cases a day, the justices also received petitions for summary judgments of debts, listened to grand jury presentments, made county officers' appointments, and labored under obligations to certify letters of administration to executors of estates to prove wills, deeds of land, and indentures.[21]

While Northern Neck counties such as Westmoreland or Northumberland could still sit for only three days in May or November and hear or postpone hearing between 40 and 75 cases per session, further south the situation was worse. Essex and Middlesex counties sat from four to six days, and Henrico could not deal with its load of 50 cases a day in less than four days. Caroline County justices heard 130 cases in an August session of 1783 but, like most magistrates, did not actually hear arguments on them, postponing to a future date the arguments and decision.[22]

20. Charles Yates Letterbook, 1773–1783, Aug. 19, 1782, Nov. 25, 1782, Mar. 31, 1783, Accession No. 3807. He commenced suits in York, Culpeper, and Fairfax counties after his March letter to William Vernon.

21. Richmond Orders, Aug. 2, 3, 4, 1783, Nov. 6–10, 1786.

22. Westmoreland Orders, May 25–27, 1784; Northumberland Orders, May 1784; Essex Orders, Aug. 1786; Middlesex Orders, May 24–26, 1784; Henrico Orders, Apr. 4–8, 1785; Caroline Orders, Aug. 1783.

Republican Lawyers, 1774–1790   173

An increase of debt cases and court days might have been endured had the court merely postponed hearings. Much worse, however, was the number of courts canceled for lack of justices attending. When that occurred, witnesses, lawyers, and suitors of all kinds simply had to wait until the next month before attempting to obtain justice. If Virginians had reason to complain in the 1780s over missed courts, the situation worsened in the 1790s.[23]

What explains the continued absence of justices from their duties on the county bench? First, it appears that this problem affected both those courts presided over by members of the traditional ruling families and those run by "new men." Many justices began to refuse the commissions sent or resigned their offices during the 1780s. When the governors of Virginia began sending circular letters to the clerks of the courts during that decade, they wished to know who was actually sitting on the Commission of the Peace. From the reports of the clerks who responded to these letters, one can conclude that some changes were taking place in the personnel of the counties. In Westmoreland County, the clerk reported in 1790 that the 1770 commission had been awarded to fifteen men, of whom ten acted while five did not. Commissions of 1783 and 1789 were awarded to six men each time, of which only three men acted altogether. While many of Henrico's justices had ties to prerevolutionary antecedents, Richmond County's clerk reported in 1812 that six of the twelve justices who had received their commissions during the 1790s were not acting.[24]

It is difficult to say whether the same men continued to sit on the county benches as had sat before the Revolution. Richmond County had been served by justices from the Carter, Beale, Belfield, and Barber families since the 1720s. When the clerk made his report in 1812, however, no Carters or Belfields were sitting on the bench, and Richard Beale was listed as one who "never sits in court." Although a Sydnor and a Glascock can be found with pre-Revolution ties, the rest were new arrivals.[25] Recent studies of Norfolk and Albermarle counties have confirmed the

---

23. Of some thirty instances of canceled courts, twenty-four occurred between 1790 and 1800, in every county except Westmoreland. Obviously, more days were missed than these; because of gaps in order books precise figures are unobtainable. The increase in cases would be more easily studied if docket books had survived the period. Some may still exist in county clerks' offices; if so, they have not been identified as yet.

24. Westmoreland Orders, Nov. 1790; Register of Virginia Justices and County Officers, VSL. Henrico's Seldens, Cockes, and Adamses continued to sit up to the 1790s; the Randolphs, prominent until 1774, did not sit after the Revolution.

25. Register of Virginia Justices, VSL; Richmond Orders, Apr. 7, 1725, Sept. 6, 1732, Aug. 5, 1734, Jan. 7, 1740, Jan. 3, 1743, July 4, 1748, Aug. 6, 1750.

appearance of some new men on the commissions there. In sum, no general pattern is discernible.[26]

A far more important issue is the declension in the status of being a justice. The question revolves around the office itself and whether it was a defensible position, whether held by new men or by old. The decline in deference shown to justices was indicated in several ways, and the evidence was fairly unmistakable. Before 1776 the justices had been almost too successful in punishing various "contempts" of the court, so that by mid-century the records reveal almost no instances of Virginians "offering Sawcey Remarks" to a justice. Yet contempt could be offered in several ways, and the postrevolutionary period had more than its share of examples. Rare though it might have been for a Virginian to openly affront a justice, Tidewater residents began showing a nonchalant attitude toward their duties as jurymen and witnesses. Those episodes, which occurred regularly between 1780 and 1800, undoubtedly brought to mind the desultory state of affairs that had prevailed from the 1760s to 1774. If, as also happened, the justices themselves failed to show up for a Quarterly Court on the first day appointed, the grand jury was disbanded and no presentments were made that session.

For example, in Essex County six grand juries were canceled in ten years because of a lack of justices. In addition eleven men were fined during that period for nonattendance as jurors and witnesses. In March 1788, Northumberland justices were forced to cancel the presentments of their grand jury from November, "it appearing to the Court that the grand jury was illegally summoned."[27]

As if the nonattendance of justices and jurymen alike were not enough to sully the court's reputation, other incidents contributed to the decline. After the abolition of the office of colonial secretary, the county courts were left to their own devices for obtaining clerks. The clerk was there-

---

26. On Norfolk, see Shepard, "Administration of Justice"; on Albemarle County, see Smith, "Changing Patterns of Local Leadership." In King George County, Peter Jett and Townshend Dade were the most assiduous attending justices, not more prominent "old family" men like Charles Ashton or John Skinker, named to the commission as late as June 1, 1797, but rarely sitting. Jett resigned his commission after ten years' faithful service. He was almost never attended on the bench by Strothers or Thorntons, the families who dominated the pre-Revolution courts. See King George Orders, Mar. 7, 1793, Oct. 6, 1803, May 7, 1789, Jan. 1, 1725–26, Feb. 4, 1736–37, Nov. 2, 1750.

27. Essex Orders, Mar. 17, 1788, Aug. 18, 1789, Aug. 16, 1790, May 20, 1791, Mar. 18, 1793, Nov. 18, Mar. 23, 1796, May 17, 1797, Mar. 20, Aug. 15, 1797, May 15, July 16, 1798; Lancaster Orders, Aug., 1786; Northumberland Orders, Mar. 9, 1789. Brent's offense was never specified. He was either not a freeholder or may have been a tavern owner, overseer of a road, or other officer that automatically made him ineligible to serve as grand juryman.

after one of the justices, elected by the bench. In Westmoreland County the court elected James Bland in January 1785. Two months later, however, the court decided:

> It appearing to the Court that a former Court held in January last when James Bland was elected Clerk of the Court, there was not a legal Court; that Joseph Land Gentleman sat as a Magistrate altho his Resignation prior to that Court was recorded at his own request and it appearing to this Court that the said James Bland and Samuel Templeman had made an agreement that the said Templeman should have half the profits of the Clerkship if he would vote for the said Bland as Clerk which he did so on that day. It is the Opinion of this Court that the appointment was illegal and void and that the Office is vacant.[28]

The Westmoreland justices proceeded with their business throughout the next few months until August 29, when Bland walked into court and stunned them with an order from Richmond. "A Mandamus was offered in Court by James Bland from the Hon'ble the General Court to restore the said Bland to his Office of Clerk which being read and considered by the Court, it is their opinion that he be reinstated in his Office agreeable to the Order of the said Mandamus."[29] Why the General Court overruled the county justices is not clear. In any event the overturning of the decision was surely distasteful to the justices, accustomed as they were to conducting their courts without outside interference.

Two years later in King George County the court proceeded to elect a new clerk only to find itself deadlocked five to five between Charles Ashton and Lawrence Berry. The justices adjourned the December court and repeated the poll in January, but to no effect. Finally, in February, Berry was elected, although the county had gone for three months without a court session. The justices had finally written to the Assembly, and the Committee on the Courts of Justice had brought in an order bill in January that directed that in the future, when a tie occurred, the sheriff or senior magistrate was to break it, and that the same should be done immediately in King George. It had been rare indeed in former days for the courts to ask the aid or opinion of anyone outside their own body. This episode demonstrates the growing awareness of justices that they were merely extensions of a central authority, which they had to reckon with.[30]

28. Westmoreland Orders, Mar. 29, 1785.
29. Ibid., Aug. 29, 1785.
30. King George Orders, Dec. 6, 1787, Jan. 3, 1788, Feb. 7, 1788; *JVHD*, Jan. 3, 1788, p. 101; ibid., Jan. 7, p. 108; ibid., Jan. 9, p. 109.

In an attempt to stave off increasing criticism of their performance and strident demands for reform, the justices began instituting various procedural rules hoping to rescue the courts' reputation. Though noble in intent the rules were no more effective than they had been before the Revolution. In Lancaster the clerk was ordered to bring the records into the county instead of keeping them in his house in Richmond County, as the court had formerly allowed. In July 1787 the court ordered that "the Clerk give publick notice that for the future Petitions for Debt will be tried at the Monthly Courts." By guaranteeing access to records and keeping petitioners who wanted a summary decision on debt cases out of quarter sessions, the justices hoped to cut down the interminable delays of the courts.[31]

Essex County ruled in November 1792 that all grand jury presentments over five pounds would be heard only at quarter sessions, and all others at the monthly courts. The grand jury of that county was always careful to add to its presentments the peculiar ending that "if any thing therein should be defective in point of form, it might be amended." Obviously, the grand jury was not about to allow the guilty to escape on a technicality of form alone.[32]

York County had attempted from the beginning to speed the process of adjudication. In 1783 the court gave notice that it would "preemptorily proceed on the Docket at the ensuing April Court when all causes wherein the Plaintiff shall fail to appear and prosecute his suit will be signified and where the Defendant shall make fault, Judgement will be given against him unless such cases where good cause shall be shown by the suitors or their attornies for further continuance."[33]

Nothing seemed to help. The cases dragged on, the courts were sitting irregularly, and angry Virginians were protesting. Years later, in his work on Blackstone, St. George Tucker remembered the pressing need for circuit or district courts. "The backwardness of the county courts in doing business soon occasioned a vast accumulation of suits in the general court. In the year 1787 it was computed that the suits then depending therein could not be tried in less than five years, and they still continued to accumulate." The only mechanism left at the county level that might have brought the justices into line was the grand jury itself, and Virginians did not scruple to use it. No more graphic evidence exists of the decline in the status of county justice than the number of times grand juries presented the county magistrates themselves. Such a practice

---

31. Lancaster Orders, Sept. 18, 1783, July 16, 1787.
32. Essex Orders, Nov. 18, 1792, grand jury presentment, Aug. 21, 1786.
33. York Orders, Mar. 18, 1783.

was unheard of before the Revolution except in rare instances. Yet in twenty years' time, between 1785 and 1805, grand juries in the Tidewater brought in presentments against their justices at least twenty times, all to no effect. Richmond County presented its court "for neglecting their duty in regulating ordinary licenses, according to Law." Essex cited its magistrates for not rating the price of liquor. Henrico chided its justices for failing to fix tavern rates, but when a long list of tavern keepers were presented for overcharging, the court prosecuted the keepers and dismissed the presentments against itself.[34]

Not all presentments against justices were for failure to attend to administrative duties. A Lancaster grand jury presented its justices "for not attending their Duty in Court & thereby impeding Justice." Two justices in Henrico were presented for failing to return lists of taxable property that they had been ordered to take down. That last offense was more serious than it appears. In 1785 a law had passed the Virginia Assembly which reflected a growing concern on the part of many Virginians that the Revolution had loosed the bonds on the social order and allowed the rise of unsavory political newcomers to the seats of power. Many members of the old county families viewed the rise of such men with undisguised contempt. Ralph Wormeley described the state of politics in Virginia to Richard Corbin's son, then in England, in the most Cassandra-like terms. "The crude state of politics in this country is what one would have expected from a Government so crudely formed. ... We are to use Mr. Burke's expression, grubbing up trade to plant taxes ... and what every enlightened politician in Europe has discovered to be an erroneous system, we are establishing with all the vigor of legal coercion."[35]

The worries of Wormeley were reflected best in the action taken by George Mason. Ever since his resignation from the revisers' committee in

---

34. Presentments also included justices for not appointing road surveyors. See below. Richmond Orders, Nov. 3, 1788; Essex Orders, May 21, 1787; Henrico Orders, Mar. 7, 1787. Tucker's assessment of the backlog of cases is in his edition of *Blackstone's Commentaries*, 4:11.

35. Lancaster Orders, May 10, 1795; Henrico Orders, May 3, 1784. The voting law discussed below, originally part of the revisal of 1779, was included in the chancellor's revisal of 1785 and appears as such in Hening, 12:120–29. Ralph Wormeley Letterbook, June 13, 1786. Two years before, Wormeley had observed the economic confusion of Virginia following the cessation of hostilities. As the collection of outstanding debts became more onerous, Wormeley wrote to his exiled brother James, "In short ruin has overtaken our country and will overtake us: we have not the consolation to have panem et circases [sic], not even the miserable consolation of the dissipated; we have only panem and the Sheriffs" (Wormeley to James Wormeley, Feb. 22, 1784, Ralph Wormeley Letterbook, Wormeley Family Papers).

1776, Mason had watched with alarm the course of the Revolution in his country. By 1779 he was convinced that unless immediate steps were taken, Virginia would soon fall into the hands of the worst sort of demagogues. Mason believed that the wrong kind of men were being elected to the House of Delegates. Men of property and civic responsibility, men of public virtue, men whose property-owning interests made them sober repositories and guardians of private virtue in Virginia were not being elected. Yet it was simply not admissible to suggest that the people were not intelligent or virtuous enough to elect the proper men to positions of power. To raise that thought was to damage fatally the integrity of a republican theory of government. Mason believed that he could supply the solution to the puzzle.

He observed in early 1780:

> The Members of the late Assemblys have been the nominal, rather than the real Representatives of the people; many of them have been the Choice of a Handful, a Neighborhood, or a Junto. An ignorant or obscure Man may have considerable Influence within a narrow Circle . . . unfortunately Elections are now so little attended to, that a factious, bawling Fellow, who will make a noise four or five miles around him, and prevail upon his party to attend, may carry an Election against a man of ten times his weight and Influence in the County, and men of modesty and merit are discouraged from offering themselves; this is the true Cause why we have seen our late Assemblies filled with men so unequal to the Office.[36]

Mason may have had James Madison in mind when he lamented the defeat of "men of modesty and merit." In any event it is certain that Mason believed that the corruption of republicanism was already at work in Virginia. Originally, according to the wishes of the revisers, tax commissioners were to be elected in each county. Mason expressed the fear that because of the weariness of people over continual elections, the county courts were appointing the commissioners and setting a dangerous precedent which guaranteed that the county bench would have patronage power over those important officials. Yet Mason did not suggest a return to the status quo. He was no Wormeley, and his worries over the county court's appointment of tax commissioners indicate that reform was still important to him.[37]

---

36. *Papers of George Mason*, ca. June 1, 1780, 2:630.

37. The statute that provided for the election of tax commissioners is in Hening, 12:243–55 (1786), revised to recognize Virginians' lack of interest in electing those officials. Between 1776 and 1786 the county courts had come to appoint the commissioners, since they could not interest the county in an election. The original statute for

According to Mason's plan, a county wherein a majority of freeholders eligible to vote had failed to turn out for the election would be denied its seat in the General Assembly. By that means, Mason believed that the truly virtuous man could stand for office, and if a majority of the good people of Virginia actually did vote, he, the representative of virtue and probity, would be elected every time. Mason's proposal was included as part of the revisal in 1779, tabled, and brought forth again as part of the so-called Chancellor's Revisal in 1785, which was a compilation of the revised statutes of the commonwealth, starting from the 1769 revisal and including those that had been suggested in 1776–79. In fact, the Assembly considered Mason's proposition too extreme and struck out his demand that a county lose its seat if its freeholders failed to vote. Instead, offenders were to be fined a portion of their normal yearly tax, which was then to be added to what they owed the county.[38]

By 1786, Mason's proposal for securing virtuous leadership in the House of Delegates had become law. Since that statute was so obviously aimed at securing virtue in public by encouraging men of impeccable private morals to run for office, one needs to ask what characterized the concerns of Virginians about public and private virtue. The colonial era in the Tidewater had been dominated by paternal justices who functioned as guardians of public and private mores through the workings of the county court and grand jury system. But by the 1760s apathy and lack of rigor began to vitiate that system, and Baptists criticized the justices in their traditional role as community leaders. What then was the relationship between law and virtue in the postrevoluntary period in the Tidewater counties?

The records of the grand jury presentments for the period 1780–1805 reveal in a striking way how the nature of law and virtue had changed in the Tidewater. The period between 1720 and 1750 had been dominated by a concern for nonattendance at church, swearing, bastardy, public

---

electing commissioners is in Hening, 9:349–68 (1779); the purpose of the law was to establish commissioners to assess the value of lands put up for sale against paper money issued by Virginia or the Continental Congress. By a new statute of 1780 (Hening, 10:358–61) justices were fined five thousand pounds of tobacco for failing to appoint the commissioners—already an admission that election had failed as a means of securing those officials in their duties.

38. The statute on elections is in Hening, 12:120–29. See Mason, *Papers of George Mason*, 2:631–32, and notes. For details on the arduous task of overcoming difficulties involved in finishing the revisal, see Cullen, "Completing the Revisal of the Laws." Cullen observes that Jefferson's drive for simplicity, especially in language and in the composition of the law on descents, did not allow for future judicial interpretation, a problem Edmund Randolph had to confront as chairman of the new Committee of Revisers (p. 86).

drunkenness, and other moral misdemeanors. Between 1750 and 1770 failure to keep up roads and to list tithables had characterized the counties' sense of what constituted reprehensible behavior. Immediately after the Revolution one still finds occasional presentments for nonattendance at church, fornication and adultery, swearing, and profaning the Sabbath by buying and selling goods or "fishing and oystering" on the Lord's Day.[39] In fact, occasional references can be found to such offenses right through the period, such as Westmoreland's 1802 presentment of July 26 against "George Washington, Reubin Sanford & Spencer Garner for Stacking Wheat on the Sabbath Day." The largest number of presentments, however, were for offenses of a different kind.

Between 1780 and 1787 the grand juries of every county presented large numbers of people for not listing themselves, their slaves or dependents, or their property for the county tax lists. The concealment of tithables ranks in the top four offenses in all the counties studied, although the offense disappeared from the records after 1787. The most persistent charge throughout the entire period, ranking first in number of people presented in seven of the ten counties, was against people for not keeping up their roads. Those presentments were issued against surveyors and overseers, who were also often justices, and against people for felling trees, putting up fences across the roads, turning the road after it had been surveyed, or digging canals or ditches across county highways.[40]

Perhaps the most interesting presentment of the grand juries for this period was that against nonvoters. That presentment had none of the routine character of the road presentment. Neither was it confined to a few short years, as was the presentment for concealing tithables. Nonvoting remained among the three most often committed offenses well into the nineteenth century, and further indicated a decay of the sense of duty among the justices of the Tidewater. When the names of the men presented for this offense are examined, one finds that many of the counties' justices and leading figures were themselves neither voting nor attending the court. The presentments were not directed solely against prominent souls, for wealthy and middling freeholders alike were numbered among the guilty.

Most counties began presenting nonvoters in 1787, two years after the passage of the new law and immediately after the elections of 1786. By

39. Most of these occur in the Northern Neck counties; the more populous and relatively more urban counties, such as York, Essex, and Henrico, had none. See King George Orders, Aug. 6, 1795; Westmoreland, May 25, 1784; Northumberland, May 12, 1783; Richmond, Nov. 5, 1781; Westmoreland, Nov. 28, 1780.

40. The three exceptions were York, Middlesex, and Caroline, where concealment of tithables and not voting were the most often committed offenses.

law the clerk and sheriff were required to give the grand jury a copy of the names of property-owning voters in the county and the poll of the election. By comparing the two lists it was obvious who had absented himself from the elections for assemblymen and congressmen. Although the law did not explicitly extend to nonattendance at presidential elections, that did not deter the grand jury in Henrico. In 1789 it named twenty-seven of its citizens on that charge. Even with the loss of some county records and the work of badly trained justice-clerks who often failed to indicate what presentments were for, the offense can be traced and identified as regular, serious, and widespread. In ten counties in eighteen years at least 670 freeholders were presented for this offense.[41]

Virginia's grand juries had no more luck presenting nonvoting freeholders than they had with offenders against private virtue. As often as men were presented, the justices dismissed the presentments "for reasons appearing to the Court," as they always rather archly phrased it. The grand jury of Westmoreland grew impatient with this attitude when its presentments of May 1793 were again dismissed the following March. After presenting the court itself for failure to district the county and appoint road surveyors, the jury acidly remarked: "It's a public Grievance to the good People of this Commonwealth that whereas the Many and Considerable fines heretofore imposed by this Worshipful Court upon the presentments of former Grand Juries have not been appropriated to the purposes intended by Law; Whereas if such appropriations had taken place the County Levy consequently would be much lessened, the people in some measure eased of Taxes, and public offenders made to contribute to the support of Civil Government."[42] The justices bowed to public pressure—temporarily. They fined four men and dismissed the rest. Although grand juries continued to present nonvoters, the magistrates reverted to their old ways, dismissing the offenders or remitting the fines imposed.

Both new and old members of the courts were presented for not voting, and just as regularly both kinds of magistrates threw out the presentments. That lack of devotion to enforcing public virtue represented a continuing lack of attention to the issue which had begun in the 1750s. If it now made no difference what kind of magistrate one found on the bench; if new men as well as old were not voting themselves; if grand jury admonitions to benches containing old and new men were in vain, only one conclusion was possible. It availed the governor and reformers

---

41. Henrico Orders, Mar. 2, 1789; Essex Orders, Nov. 17, 1800; and a survey of grand jury presentments, 1787–1805, in the counties studied.
42. Westmoreland Orders, May 28, 1793, Mar. 25, 1794, May 27, 1794.

nothing at all to battle with the courts over the kind of men put on the Commission of the Peace because being a justice simply did not generate a sense of duty, nor did the office automatically elicit deference.

At first glance one might suspect that the grand juries were attempting to hold the old families to their Country sense of duty by insisting that they sit on the bench, that they vote in elections, and that they perform in the public sphere with good example and principled action as they were supposed to. Certainly some of the men presented were members of the old Virginia elite. The new faces replacing them, however, did not escape presentment either. In York County, for example, the grand jury presented justices like Augustine Tabb, William Waller, Stanley Robinson, and Abraham Archer for not voting. While grand jurymen Augustine Denos, Allen Chapman, or Charles Lavis might not have been as wealthy as some justices in their county, it would be wrong to conclude that the more middling or poorer freeholder was here vexing only the wealthy by presenting them for not voting.[43]

The reason for such a cautionary statement is that very ordinary freeholders shared the questionable honor of being presented along with such local magnates. In the York presentment naming these old family justices fifty-two other men were presented, most of them totally obscure. Furthermore, the freeholders on the grand jury were hardly lower-class representatives. Besides Robert Armistead, the jury included William Moody, whose personal property holdings of ten slaves, eight horses and two "chairs" marked him for as eminent a gentleman as Justice Starkey Robinson.[44]

If no clear differences between presenters and presented can be drawn from York examples, the difference one might expect to find between the devotion to duty among old families and that among new men is also slight if one views additional counties. Before the Revolution Lancaster's court was usually convened by a combination of Carters, Balls, Conways, and Seldens. By 1781, James Selden had refused to qualify as a justice, and commissions reported in the years 1786, 1795, and 1797 revealed no Carters save Thomas, who never qualified and was never sworn. There were no Conways or Seldens, and only James Ball continued to sit regularly. The grand jury presented Ball for not voting in 1795 on August 17. The next morning, before the court continued on the docket of cases, the presentment against Ball was ordered dismissed, "Present, James Ball,

---

43. York Orders, May 16, 1791; Archer, Robinson, and Waller had prerevolutionary connections to the court, as did Tabb.

44. York County personal property tax lists, 1782–1809, for 1791. Robinson was assessed for eight slaves, seven horses, and two chairs.

Gentleman." In 1803, Ball was again presented with perpetually absent Thomas Carter.[45]

In Essex County, Roanes, Warings, Daingerfields, Garnetts, and Brockenbroughs figured prominently on the court. While Robert Payne Waring, William Roane, and John Daingerfield sat occasionally in the 1780s, the more regular justices were Mace Clements, Joseph Bohannon, or Thomas Pitts. The grand jury presented justices Newman Brockenbrough, who sat very rarely, and James Upshaw, who succeeded his father John in 1788 on the bench. New justices like Lewis Dix and John Bougham were presented, as well as nonjustices of the old families like Muscoe and Henry Garnett.[46]

The same example could be drawn from King George and Richmond counties. Both continued to have some of the prerevolutionary figures on the bench and a number of men who had no antecedents there. The grand juries presented each type for not voting, reprimanded the justices as a whole for not attending to duty, and received satisfaction neither in increased attendance nor in enthusiasm for enforcing presentments against nonvoters and other malefactors.[47]

Despite the obvious grounds for interference by the commonwealth the justices were still fiercely protective of their independence. In July 1792 a letter was read in York court from the governor raising certain questions about men proposed for a new commission. Evidently, the governor had himself suggested that he thought there might be men more appropriate than those the court had listed. The court directed its answer to inform the governor that "the County Court of York in answer to the Letter from the Governor on the subject of Recommendations of Magistrates, observe, that it is their opinion that under the Constitution the Court alone have a right to judge of the necessity of an Increase of Magistrates and of persons proper to fill up vacancies. They further conceive that it would be shrinking from a Duty to the Constitution and their own Oath imposed on them to do any thing but to require the appointment conformable to their recommendation." Middlesex justices were also annoyed with the governor, who had attempted to interfere

---

45. Lancaster Orders, Aug. 17–18, 1795, Dec. 20, 1781; Register of Virginia Justices, VSL, May 16, 1803.

46. Essex Orders, Feb. 16, 1784, Aug. 16, 1790, May 16, 1791, Apr. 16, 1793, Aug. 23, 1799, Feb. 17, 1787, May 19, 1800, Nov. 17, 1800, May 21, 1805.

47. King George Orders, March 2, June 1, 1797, Mar. 4, 1805, for presentments against justice John Pollard, John Skinker, John Taliaferro, Charles Stuart, and Michael Wallace and nonjustices Landon Carter, Jr. (who did not succeed his father, Robert Wormeley Carter, on the bench), several Fitzhughs, and Ashtons. Richmond Orders, Feb. 7, 1780, May 7, 1787, Aug. 4, 1795.

with their recommendations in 1784. In response the court testily observed: "This Court thinking themselves under the Constitution competent to the recommendation of persons proper to act as Justices of the Peace in the said County, Do again recommend to His Excellency Benjamin Harrison Esquire, Governor of this State Ralph Wormely Carter, Jr., Philip Ludwell Grymes, Robert Spratt, and William Steptoe as proper persons to serve as Justices of the Peace for this County."[48]

The stubborn refusal to acknowledge that a thorough reform of the county system was in order was coupled with a refusal to prosecute fellow justices and other freeholders for not voting. Furthermore, the courts were sending forth signals to their counties which were hopelessly confused. On the one hand they continued to demand the deference that they conceived to be their due, persisting in the practice of appointing a commonwealth attorney to charge the grand jury to prosecute citizens for misdemeanors. On the other they did nothing to enforce the presentments when made. It was no great surprise then that the courts were the objects of attack by Virginians, who derided them as self-perpetuating oligarchies unsymptheic to republican ways, and not particularly concerned with republican virtue, either.

Virtue, after all, was clearly a part of the purpose of having a republican, and not a monarchical, system. How could one guarantee the virtue and hence the freedom of a people if violations of the law went unpunished? Yet there was an obvious inconsistency in the charge to the grand jury given in a county after the Revolution and the performance of the justices in Virginia's Tidewater.

For example, the deputy commonwealth attorney in King George County rose and delivered this charge to the grand jury in 1792:

> Gentlemen of [the] Grand Jury. It will be unnecessary for me to observe to you, that your duty as good Citizens requires that you should be particular and impartial in your Presentments as I suppose no arguments drawn from considerations of this kind will have greater weight with you than that Solemn and Sacred Oath which hath been administered to you, and which fully points out your duty—My task will only be to observe that you are to present all blasphemous, wicked, & dissolute persons such as are guilty of profane cursing and Swearing—Offences and Breaches of Penal law

---

48. York Orders, July 16, 1792; Middlesex Orders, Apr. 26, 1784. Why the governor should have questioned these names is unclear. Carter, Grymes, and Steptoe had eminent connections and qualifications for the bench; Spratt did not. There seems to be no reason for supposing that Harrison, himself of a conservative bent, would have been one to place new men on a county bench contrary to the wishes of the justices.

within Twelve months and no longer unless otherwise directed by Law—as Overseers of highways, owners of Mill-dams, retailers of Liquor without license, Etc.[49]

While the grand jury did present offenders who sold liquors above rated prices or forgot to obtain license for ordinaries, the charge must have sounded strange to them. Presentments for liquor offenses were usually the fourth most numerous category in all counties after concealment of tithables, roads, and nonvoters. The justices were agreeable to prosecuting liquor violators, for collection of penalties decreased the county levy on freeholders considerably. The prosecution of "blasphemous, wicked, & dissolute persons" or "Breaches of Penal Law" was another matter.

The most obvious breach of penal law was that occurring among nonvoting freeholders and nonprosecuting justices. Not only did justices not prosecute but justices who served as sheriffs and clerks obstructed the will of the grand jury. In nearly every county court, records indicate that had the grand juries been successful in obtaining lists of freeholders and copies of the polls for each election, nonvoting presentments would have been much higher.[50]

While it was fairly common for a constable, sheriff, or deputy to be presented for a breach of office before the Revolution, the courts now presented sheriffs and clerks for failing to furnish them with a copy of the poll. In Middlesex, King George, Northumberland, Essex, and Westmoreland sheriffs and clerks were presented—and just as regularly absolved by the justices. Sheriffs were also presented for not calling a grand jury or for summoning a few bystanders to make up the number needed if those called did not show up for duty. When those facts are added to the presentments that have survived (keeping in mind that there are large gaps in county records) it is clear that the courts were seriously derelict in performance of their duties.[51]

---

49. King George Orders, May 3, 1792.

50. Grand juries also presented the executive of Virginia for not furnishing the counties with copies of the laws, as statute law required. Such presentments were never acted on, and almost certainly such violations were not cognizable by county grand juries. Nonetheless, the incidents seem to be interesting examples of republican zeal on the local level expressing criticism of Virginia's ruling leaders. See Henrico Orders, Aug. 8, 1786; Westmoreland Orders, Oct. 28, 1799; Lancaster Orders, May 29, 1794.

51. Orders are missing for Richmond County for the years 1795–1809; Westmoreland, 1795–97; King George, 1770–86; Northumberland, 1798–1807; Caroline, 1789–99; Middlesex, 1797–99. Sheriffs were permitted by statute to fill the requisite number needed for a grand jury from bystanders after 1796; see Shepherd, vol. 1, c. 10, p. 363.

Grand juries in the city of Richmond joined their county brethren in expressing concern that the courts were ineffective. The grand jury presentments for Richmond were almost exclusively concerned with offenders of the liquor laws and keepers of "disorderly houses." Occasionally, gambling houses were presented, especially after 1800 as the city grew and men were charged with offenses such as "building a Necessary in the Yard of the Eagle Tavern, which has become a nuisance to the Neighborhood." The grand jury was most concerned, however, with the rowdy element of the city, which appeared to be connected with the liquor trade, and the disorderly houses (a euphemism for houses of prostitution). Most disorderly house charges were brought against women. In presenting Sarah Vaughn and her two daughters the grand jury cited "unlawful abuse of Josiah Clarke and his wife as calling him a rogue, a damned rogue, a damned villain, and her a damned whore, and for frequent fighting at their House late at night and swearing they would flog the said Clarke, and also for harbouring sundry Apprentices, vizt. those of Mr. Voss, Mr. Minor & Mr. Stephenson."[52]

The disturbances in Richmond continued despite the presentments and prosecution of liquor law violations. In 1797 the grand jury pleaded with the court to do more. "We of the Grand Jury deeply impressed with the necessity of putting a stop to many nuisances which as present exist in the City, which requires an ordinance should be made to regulate the great number of tipling Shops which are at present in this City; and also present their being kept open later than a certain Hour in the Night; which would in some measure prevent the corruption of our servants, and put a stop to the frequent robberies which are committed in the City."[53]

The court responded by attempting to prosecute the disorderly houses and gambling parlors to such an extent that in November 1803 grand juryman Richard Young complained that after he was sworn and had done his duty on the jury, one William Rowlett cornered him. Questioning him "respecting the discharge of his duty as a Grand Juror . . . he proceeded to threaten the said Richard Young by saying 'he had better mind his own business.'"[54]

If Richmond was symbolic of the future of law and morals in the commonwealth, a concern for private virtue on the part of Virginia

52. Richmond City Hustings Orders, Aug. 13, 1792. After complaining of the "necessaries" on Aug. 8, the grand jury repeated the complaint a year later on Aug. 13, 1792, this time for two of the noxious buildings on the capital grounds.
53. Ibid., May 8, 1797.
54. Ibid., Nov. 14, 1803.

justices was not particularly noteworthy. In March 1805 the grand jury had another complaint:

> The Grand Jury beg leave to present as a grievance the great disrespect shewn by the Shopkeepers of this City, to the law now in force directing the various shops, etc. to be shut up on the sabbath day; the continual riots and disorder which are the consequence of this violation they conceive to be no less derogatory to the laws of the state, than to the respect due to the sacredness of the day.... They beg leave to recommend to the court to direct the Constables to attend to this evil; to reprehend the apparent inattention, and to insist that they shall make this a duty, not to be in any degree dispensed with.[55]

It is clear from such sentiments that some members of the community heartily wished the court to proceed in minding the business of the citizens, as it had before the Revolution. There is not much evidence to suggest that the courts, in county or town, were especially inclined to do so, or that they could have succeeded. The plain fact was that public officials were disinclined to mind people's private virtue and were even quite lax when private misbehavior spilled over into the public arena. When one searches the records for presentments of a moral nature, it becomes obvious that as their colonial past receded in time, Virginians could count less and less on their officials to oversee such violations.

That does not mean that no one in Virginia cared about such matters, for the various grand jury statements clearly show that some cared very much. A survey of the ten counties and their presentments between 1780 and 1805 indicates that presentments for adultery and fornication were nonexistent in York and Henrico, while they numbered as few as four in Middlesex or six in Lancaster and as many as fifty-one in Northumberland, fifty-six in King George, twelve in Richmond, and eleven in Westmoreland—in other words, high in the Northern Neck.[56] Those presentments occurred from the early 1780s through 1805 in some of the counties. But whereas Lancaster presented a few people throughout the entire period, Richmond's twelve cases all occurred before 1787.[57] In

55. Ibid., Mar. 12, 1805.
56. These numbers are obviously not exact; gaps in the records necessitate rather crude approximations. They are, however, indicative of the overall nature of the presentments.
57. Lancaster Orders, May 21, 1804, Aug. 20, 1804, for seven men disturbing worship and breaking the Sabbath; Richmond Orders, Nov. 5, 1781, Nov. 3, 1783, May 2, 1785. Richmond's presentments for swearing, like those in Westmoreland and Northumber-

1796 the first forty of fifty-six presentments in King George for such moral lapses were dropped, "the Attorney for the Commonwealth declining to prosecute the same."[58]

To contemporary Virginians the need for reform of the county courts was obvious. Clearly, there was a great hiatus between the need to preserve virtue in the public sphere by presenting nonvoters and dissolute persons, and the county justices' disinclination to live up to their sworn duty. Virginians who cared little about those matters could still bemoan the inefficiency of the court in expediting the resumed debt cases. Perhaps the most ominous conclusion that could be drawn from observing the actions of Virginia's justices in the early 1780s, however, was that they were overwhelmed by too much business and both unable and unwilling to devote any time to being their brothers' and sisters' keepers.

Virginians in the years following the surrender of Cornwallis had a sense that a great deal was wrong with the county court system and with the performance of the justices. Their discontent was registered in a series of petitions to the Virginia House of Delegates in language that was unequivocal in demanding reform. On June 8, 1782, the House of Delegates received a petition from Fairfax County "Protesting Certain Actions by the Justices of the Peace." Rural citizens of Fairfax were incensed by actions taken by certain justices living in Alexandria, who had assessed the county for building a new courthouse. Since the justices were not elected, the petitioners argued, they had no power to tax. The Fairfax citizens concluded that "the Justices of the County Courts are so far from being the Representatives of the People . . . that . . . they are a self-contained Body, with the Power of filling up their own Vacancies . . . whenever a Majority of the Members of any County Court shall happen to be leagued together in any sinister Views or Party-Interest." The sinister influence of the city of Alexandria should be removed, concluded the petitioners, by removing the county seat to a rural, centrally located spot.[59]

Some members of the Assembly heard that the petition had been drafted by none other than George Mason, member of the Fairfax court. If the delegates at Richmond wondered at Mason's role in the affair, they were not unaware that discontent over the county courts was widespread in Virginia. They waited to hear from the accused justices of Fairfax. The defense arrived in November. The town justices addressed themselves

---

land, exceeded fifty persons, again nearly all confined to the 1780s. Henrico presented ten before 1785; York, none.

58. King George Orders, June 2, 1796.

59. Virginia Legislative Petitions, Fairfax County, June 8, 1782, Box 1, VSL; see also Mason, *Papers of George Mason*, 2:733–36.

not only to the points in the petition but also to Mason's supposed authorship.

For their part the justices offered these observations. They admitted that they were not the representatives of the people. Nevertheless, they were certain that they were "amenable" to the people at large. The constitution of the commonwealth gave the governor veto power over their recommendations for filling vacancies, so they were hardly self-perpetuating. Perhaps, they suggested, the citizens had the vestries of the Episcopal church in mind when they were casting about for nonrepublican institutions, for those ecclesiastical bodies were self-perpetuating.

The justices were quick to assert that no suspicion ought to rest on the county magistrates, and in particular they objected to the tone of the petition. To them it seemed "to be pregnant with fears, suspicions, & jealousies of the Town Justices, & insinuates their being linked together in party interest, & sinester [sic] views." When the town magistrates had come to the bench, they had found the courthouse a leaking dilapidated mess. It still had no pillory, no stocks, and no ducking stool, and the prison was useless. Surely, providing for the well-being of the county in levying for such essential public objects was not conspiratorial.

As for Mason, the justices attacked him on his weakest flank. "If the suposed [sic] Writer (notorious for his non-attendance at Court) had a personal pique, or resentment against any one of the members, he ought not to have made his attack general; in which Case your Honours should not have heard from us."[60] Mason was hardly the man to don the robes of righteous indignation, for the common complaint of Virginians about the county bench was its deadly slowness, a slowness perpetuated by justices like Mason who were irregular in their attendance upon the business of the court.

Fairfax County was only the first of many to address the Assembly. Although the courts had functioned during the Revolution, their business had been confined to settling deeds, overseeing probate of wills, and taking care of other minor affairs of the county. With war's end, however, debt cases and actions of detinue, attachments, and executions of returns on delinquent debtors flooded into court. It was soon apparent that the county court system could not deal with the volume of business, which

60. Fairfax Petitions of Justices, Nov. 2, 1782, Box 1, VSL. Mason's attack on the justices of Alexandria is consistent with his opposition to the proposed port bill of 1784, a measure he regarded as an attempt to construct an artificial, regulated economy, which in turn would create a taste for luxury and promote wealthy men whose primary interests and means of influence were not rooted in agrarian society and whose presence on a county bench would be a source of corruption for all magistrates. On the port bill, see below, chapter 7.

threatened to bring to a standstill prosecutions of Virginians for badly needed money. As the citizenry began to think on the matter, some advanced remedies for the dilatory procedures of the court. If justices could not change the nature of the appointment or the efficiency of their courts, petitions to the Assembly might.

It was common knowledge, a petition from King and Queen County argued, that irregular sittings of the county courts were in large part to blame for the grinding pace at which justice was executed. All agreed that "in most Counties the business of the Courts is done by a few active magistrates, from whom it is unreasonable to expect more than a reasonable proportion of services." Since Jefferson's plan for electing the justices had failed in the proposed revisal of 1776–79, only one method remained by which trial of cases could be speeded. Few men in the modern age, the petitioners thought, could be expected to perform the duties of a justice gratis. Even though "the Community is much indebted to that respectable Class of Citizens called Justices for their gratuitious services,... Your petitioners believe that a new modification of the County and Corporation Courts allowing a certain number of Magistrates in each County a reasonable compensation for their services would remove those evils which they here complain of."[61]

Serving as paid lackeys of a central court or state had been unacceptable to the justices before the Revolution. The ancient, traditional Country independence prohibited a justice from being a kind of "placeman" or hireling. The fact that the idea of a paid justice was proposed by Virginia citizens, and not, as before the Revolution, by lawyers alone, indicated how much speedy resolution of business was valued in the new republic. The ideal of a disinterested, paternal Country justice was antiquated and, in any event, not being lived up to by the justices. The Fairfax petitions had scored justices in general for being unrepresentative of the people. The town justices had it in their power, "being always on the Spot, to avail themselves of the absence of the County Members, or by adjourning the laying of the County Levey, from Month to Month, until they find a Majority of their own cabal upon the Bench, to levey... exorbitant & unnecessary Sums upon the People."[62] As the petition indicates, there was still some residue of feeling that rural justices were more virtuous than townspeople and that the town justices represented a special interest, not a sober assembly of judges.

Residents of Norfolk County attempted to follow the Fairfax example.

---

61. Virginia Legislative Petitions, King and Queen County, Nov. 18, 1784, Box 1, VSL.

62. Fairfax County Petition, June 8, 1782, Box 1, VSL.

By 1792, Fairfax had succeeded in removing the court from Alexandria to a rural spot, leaving that town with its own Court of Hustings and excluding the justices on that bench from sitting as magistrates of the county. Norfolk citizens petitioned for the same privilege, protesting the promercantile sentiments of the borough justices and pointing to the unrepublican character of a common hall whose mayor, recorder, and alderman sat for life. Although unsuccessful in this petition, Norfolk had publicly voiced its dissatisfaction with magistrates and local government.[63]

Dissatisfaction was not confined to counties where town and country clashed. Deference to the position of the county justice eroded during the 1780s throughout the Tidewater, and efforts to arrest this erosion were hampered by actions involving justices. In 1780 a bizarre episode involving a justice shocked Virginians and furthered the deterioration of magisterial reputation. In that year New Kent County sent to the Virginia House of Delegates John Price Posey. A magistrate on the county bench, Posey became involved sometime during the next two years with the administration of the estate of John Parke Custis, late son of Martha Custis Washington. In 1783 Washington's wife and her brother Bartholomew Dandridge accused Posey of theft from the Custis estate. The scandal finally reached the desk of the governor, where it precipitated a minor constitutional debate.

Despite the connection of many delegates to their county benches a statute (Hening 9:478 [1778]) was passed by the Virginia Assembly that empowered the governor to remove a magistrate in the event of an accusation against him for malfeasance in office that the executive considered to be "proved." That summary justice involved no trial. Because the governor appeared to be exercising the function of judge as well as governor, reminiscent of his colonial predecessors, the Executive Council gave their opinion that the statute was unconstitutional. Posey could only be removed if found guilty in a court. The General Court thereupon began proceedings against Posey and found him guilty of a misdemeanor, for which he was fined two hundred pounds. Stripped of his office, Posey was convicted in 1786 of defrauding Dandridge, Custis's uncle. In 1787, Posey was jailed for assaulting the sheriff of New Kent. On the night of July 15, 1787, he broke out of jail with the help of confederates, and they set fire to the jail and the clerk's office. In the conflagration all of New Kent County's records were destroyed. Convicted of arson, the former

---

63. Norfolk lies outside the area under intensive study here, but the similarity of complaints is obvious. For details, see Shepard, "Administration of Justice" and "Courts in Conflict." Fairfax's court was altered by statute; see Hening, 13:79.

justice was hanged at Richmond on January 25, 1788. Newspapers followed the affair and broadcast the scandal far and wide.[64]

Advocates of reform and critics of the county courts did not need a cause célèbre such as Posey's to make their case against the traditional legal system of Virginia. The petitions from the various counties and the impossibility of getting business done in the courts were affecting the entire commonwealth. By 1784, James Madison, the young Orange County lawyer and Jefferson's trusted lieutenant in charge of fighting to a successful finish the battle for legal reforms in Virginia, decided to reopen the assault on the county benches. A carefully orchestrated plan of attack was put forth, and potential allies identified and sought out. Madison anticipated opposition to any proposition advocating reform of the county courts, but he was also aware that numerous petitions demanding action had been made and that even some justices, like Mason, had their own peculiar interests in seeing something done to reform a hopelessly overloaded, deadly slow, and increasingly unpopular county court system.

Virtue Ignored: Lawyers and Court Reform

At first, Madison believed that his plan would succeed. The bill was brought to the House in 1784 just after the complaints surrounding the county courts. Yet his proposal was to face a determined opposition for the next three years. To his father, Madison explained, "The difficulty of suiting it to every palate, & the many latent objections of a selfish & private nature which will shelter themselves under some plausible objections of a public nature to which every innovation is liable render the event extremely uncertain."[65]

Among other reforms the proposed bill would have provided a trial of issues of fact before one judge and a jury, speeding up processes that had heretofore been impeded for a lack of justices.[66] John Marshall

---

64. On the Posey affair, see Madison, *Papers of James Madison*, 6:346–48; Marshall, *Papers of John Marshall*, 1:96–97.

65. Madison to James Madison, Sr., Dec. 3, 1784, *Papers of James Madison*, 8:172.

66. Identical to a *nisi prius* reform instituted in England. See Madison to Monroe, Dec. 4, 1784, ibid., pp. 175–76. The bill would have taken many suits off the General Court docket for trial by circuit judges, who were to be the same judges as those sitting on the General Court. The bill would have made the assizes courts of dernier resort except for rare appeals to the Court of Appeals. The editors of the *Papers of James Madison* believe that Madison himself pushed the reforms in order to speed collection of British debts, and that opposition came from the county justices and lawyers, who feared they would lose control of the legal and economic affairs of the counties—points

believed that the plan would fail. Citing the opposition of the county justices, Marshall pointed out that magistrates "who are tenacious of authority will not assent to any thing which may diminish their ideal dignity & put into the hands of others a power which they will not exercise themselves."[67]

The assize bill passed the House in December 1784, but with a fatal proviso. Madison explained to Jefferson that the advocates of reform had at first rejoiced when Patrick Henry was elected governor and thus taken out of the House, where he had opposed the measure. Madison was pleased that the bill was almost a carbon copy of Edmund Pendleton and Jefferson's proposed reform of 1776. However, "in order to leave as few handles as possible for cavil the bill omitted all the little regulations which would follow of course, and will therefore need a supplement. To give time for this provision as well as by way of collecting the mind of the public, the commencement of the law is made posterior to the next Session of Assembly."[68] Here was the fatal error. By the time the reformers assembled again in December 1785 county court partisans had organized their opposition to Madison.

A Bill for Reforming the County Courts and for Other Purposes might have read "and for preventing assize courts."[69] Madison at first hoped that the county bill "if it can be put into any rational shape [would] be received by the other side as auxiliary to the Assize plan which may be resumed at another Session,"[70] but he was quickly disenchanted. The county court bill, he wrote, "proposes to select five Justices, who are to sit quarterly, be paid scantily, and to possess the Civil jurisdiction of the County Courts.... [It is] meant as a substitute for the Assize system... without possessing its advantages."[71] The proposal for stipendiary justices with cognizance over civil suits was quickly dropped from the bill. In the end the measure did nothing more than require the justices to clear their dockets quarterly, Madison complained to Monroe.[72]

---

to be discussed below. See the editorial notes in Madison, *Papers of James Madison*, 8:122, 164; text of the bill, ibid., pp. 165–72.

67. Marshall to Charles Simms, June 16, 1784, *Papers of John Marshall*, 1:124. Marshall also cited county court lawyers whom he described as too ignorant to stand before an able judge.

68. Madison to Jefferson, Jan. 9, 1785, *Papers of Thomas Jefferson*, 7:588.

69. Hening, 12:32–36.

70. Madison to Monroe, Dec. 17, 1785. *Papers of James Madison*, 8:445.

71. Dec. 24, 1785, ibid., pp. 455–56. The original proposal was to pay these justices fifteen shillings a day drawn from a levy on the suitors in the court. See ibid., pp. 466–67 (fn. 2).

72. Dec. 30, 1785, ibid., pp. 465–66.

In January 1786, Madison was forced to write to his mentor that to fend off proposals for outright repeal of the assizes plan, the advocates of reform had agreed to a suspension. The disheartened Madison wrote, "The various interests opposed to it will never be conquered without considerable difficulty."[73] The county court proposal, in Madison's mind, did very little to reform the justices, for it "requires them to clear their dockets quarterly. It amounts to nothing, and is chiefly the result of efforts to render Courts of Assize unnecessary."[74]

In fact, the county court measure did considerably more than Madison admitted. The act provided for a formal separation of the meetings of the county court into monthly and quarterly sessions. Quarter sessions met in March, May, August, and November, hearing grand jury presentments, petitions for debt, and criminal prosecutions. In an astounding concession to the inefficiency of the justices, the act allowed one justice to adjourn the court if not enough magistrates appeared. The stipulation was that the court had to be reconstituted in three days, but the practical result was that once adjourned the damage was done and the court would often not sit at all. As noted before, the grand jury would not meet at quarter session when the justices failed to show on the first day.

To speed up proceedings, the clerk was directed to preside over office judgments or "rules" where all pleadings were to be filed, imparlances taken, and proceedings in law and chancery entered into record before issue was joined. The justices were to review the rules and set them aside or to proceed on them as they saw fit.

Finally the clerk was to "proportion the causes upon the docket in the same manner as the clerk of the general court now does; from the first day of the court to the sixth, if in his opinion so many days will be expended in determining the causes ready for trial."[75] The monthly courts were to take care of all county cases except chancery decisions, jury trials, and disputes over points of law, demurrers, special verdicts, and the like.

By 1787 so much confusion seems to have arisen over the act and its unsatisfactory nature that it was amended, allowing both monthly and quarterly sessions jurisdiction over injunctions in chancery, as well as attachments, petitions, subpoenas for witnesses, special bail, and attachments against "absconding debtors." In other words the reforms of the

---

73. Madison to Jefferson, Jan. 22, 1786, ibid., p. 475.
74. Ibid.
75. Imparlances, as described above, chapters 3 and 4, were used by parties hoping thereby to come to an agreement before judgment was necessary in a court after issue was joined. The act is found in Hening, 12:32–36. The sheriff was to call the grand jury for each quarter session; formerly it had met twice a year, in May and November.

first act were largely negated, and the distinction between monthly courts and quarter sessions reduced to a fiction.[76]

Madison could have predicted the ephemeral nature of the soon-to-be gutted county court act. In December 1786 the assizes proponents made one last try for their project. The Senate had rejected the idea of stipendiary justices the previous January. Now in December the reformers launched their attack, without much moral support from their leader. On December 4, Madison wrote to Jefferson: "The delay in the administration of Justice from the accumulation of business in the General Court and despair of obtaining a reform according to the Assize plan have led me to give up this plan in favor of the district courts; which differ from the former in being cloathed with all the powers of the General Court within their respective districts. The bill on the latter plan will be reported in a few days and will probably tho' not certainly be adopted."[77]

If Madison had lost hope, the final vote on the assize bill did not reflect a lessening of partisanship. The final vote in the House on December 18, 1786, was 60 to 59 with Speaker Joseph Prentis, the Williamsburg lawyer, breaking the tie in favor of the bill. A protest was immediately registered that the clerk's tally of votes was at odds with the tellers' counts for the two sides. The clerk's count read 61 nays, enough to defeat the measure. The House decided to postpone action on the controversial measure until the following morning. Upon reconvening, the House heard a proposal to change the name of the measure to a bill for establishing district courts. That proposition, along with various amendments to the bill, lost 64–63. The entire proposal was now postponed until the next session of the legislature; but on January 1, 1787, the House indefinitely suspended the assize bill, and it never went into effect.[78]

The remains of the assize scheme were hardly interred before Madison and his allies Francis Corbin and Archibald Stuart rushed to the attack in favor of a district court plan. Although assizes had been defeated December 18, Madison's proposal to erect district courts at first was believed to have a better chance of success. To Washington, Madison confided that his proposal "accommodated more to the general opinion than the Assize plan, got as far as the third reading and was then lost by a single vote. The Senate would have passed it readily and would have even

---

76. Hening, 12:467–74 (1787).
77. Madison to Jefferson, Dec. 4, 1786, *Papers of Thomas Jefferson*, 10:576. A district plan had been discussed and postponed in October 1786; see *JVHD*, 1786, p. 107; *Papers of James Madison*, 9:192 (fn. 5).
78. *JVHD*, Dec. 18, 1787, pp. 106–7. The act was suspended Jan. 1, 1787, *JVHD*, p. 133.

added amendments of the right complexion. I fear it will be some time before this necessary Reform will again have so fair a chance."[79]

The opponents of assizes and district plans were now only too happy to cooperate when a bill was proposed to lengthen the term of the Genral Court. Here was a bill with something for everyone. An intermediary judiciary between county and General Court would be rendered unnecesary, and demands for reform would be satisfied as well. The bill passed the House easily, but as Madison explained to Pendleton, "The Senate have disappointed the majority infinitely in putting a Negative on it, as we learn that they have done, by a single vote."[80]

This elaborate charade fooled no one. An irate correspondent to the *Virginia Independent Chronicle* scored the Senate for failing to support even the less desirable reform of extending the term of the General Court. But the real villains were the "Delegates who are mostly Justices of the Peace," who "by a majority, reject[ed] the Circuit Court Bill, from an idea that a Superior Court sitting in each county twice a year, would lessen their importance and influence amongst the electors." The writer, who signed himself "A. W.," bitterly requested that the justices "pardon me for noticing that it is rather hard upon the suitors . . . to be put to a charge of fifteen or twenty pounds a year for transporting themselves, lawyers, witnesses, venire-men, Etc. to increase the consequence of some county Justices." What the county magistrates did not seem to realize was that since processes were cheaper to execute at the county level than in the proposed circuit courts, they really had nothing to fear from the establishment of the higher benches. The only reason for a circuit court to hear appeals would be where error had occurred, and errors could be easily remedied immediately at the county level if it were known that an appeal was likely to be heard quickly. Under the present system, argued "A. W.," "every cause of consequence is removed from the County to the General Court . . . when it is known that six or seven years delay may be obtained by this operation, [and] the County Courts [are] utterly neglected."[81]

Speedy resolution of debt causes was not, however, the only basis upon which "A. W." based his attack on the justices and the Assembly. Accustomed to the rhetoric of republican speech makers who appealed to Virginians to be virtuous citizens, "A. W." proceeded to turn such language against the opponents of reform. Only a few months before,

---

79. Madison to Washington, Dec. 24, 1786, *Papers of James Madison*, 9:225. See also *JVHD*, Dec. 19, 1786; editorial note, *Papers of James Madison*, 8:390. Corbin, though of Tappahanock Tory stock, was a Madison ally; see ibid.

80. Madison to Pendleton, Jan. 9, 1787, ibid., 9:243–45.

81. *Virginia Independent Chronicle* (Richmond), Mar. 28, 1787.

in December, a writer signing himself "A James River PLANTER" had pleaded with his countrymen to foreswear European fashions and manners. "So long as our manners, are thus incompatible with the principles of Republican government," he complained, "so long will that government depend on chance for its continuance." The remedy, according to that writer, lay in emulating "our brethren on our Northern frontier." The duty of Virginians in the capital city was to prove that "the lamp of patriotism burns with as fierce a flame upon the banks of James River, as upon those of the Potomack.... In union with them, we will bid defiance to all the allurements of luxury and dissipation ... and ... encourage and promote industry, frugality and economy."[82]

In April another correspondent recommended the policy set forth in the *Connecticut Magazine* for promoting virtuous frugality. The very first point was "fee no lawyers."[83] Yet the blame for bad law in Virginia did not rest with lawyers. "A. W." excoriated those justices who mouthed an empty rhetoric by demanding to know, "If virtue and integrity be the only supports of a Commonwealth, how can one subsist where knavery and falsehood are encouraged by law?"[84] If the Assembly and county officials really want to promote virtue, he continued, they should move immediately to establish a just and speedy system of courts in Virginia.

Despite an elaborate game of thrust and parry, however, the score between reformers and opponents was negligible on both sides. There were, in 1787, no assizes courts or district courts, and the 1787 act which applied to the recent county court act amended it into general debility. Why did Madison think his district plan was more amenable to "general opinion" than the assize bill? Both plans cut deeply into the discretionary prerogative of county justices. Both bills erected intermediary structures for appeal, with the attendant probability that writs of *supersedeas* or *certiorari* would overturn county decisions. Was Madison correct in identifying the opponents of a more professional court system? The letter to the *Independent Chronicle* seemed to confirm suspicions that justices and county lawyers sabotaged the scheme.

The critical vote occurred in December 1786. The original assize bill, which passed in 1784, had purposefully been arranged to take effect only after the Assembly of 1785. The county court act passed during this session, and the assize act was again postponed. In 1786, however, final

---

82. *Virginia Gazette or the Independent Chronicle* (Richmond: Dixon and Holt, publishers), Dec. 9, 1786.

83. *Virginia Independent Chronicle* (Augustine Davis, pub.), April 4, 1787.

84. March 28, 1787, ibid. On the general use of Country themes, such as virtue, by republicans, see Banning, "Republican Ideology" and *Jeffersonian Persuasion*, pp. 264–66, on Virginia.

amendments and discussion were offered, and in December came the 59 to 59 vote on the Madison proposal. Among Tidewater delegates the measure was supported by 9 delegates from the ten counties making up this study. Opponents from the same area numbered 6. Among the advocates and opponents were justices and lawyers. If one adds all Tidewater counties from Fairfax to Elizabeth City, excluding the Southside and Eastern Shore, the numbers are even more revealing. Delegates from sixteen Tidewater counties voted 22 in favor of the measure, and 8 Delegates from five counties opposed it. The real center of opposition was in the Piedmont and Southside counties. It may well have been that the justices and lawyers of those areas, who had only recently acceded to prestigious posts, were more jealous of independence or fearful of interference in local affairs. It also appears that tobacco-growing counties, where the population was relatively stable and homogeneous, saw no advantages in a new court system. Many counties in the old Tidewater, on the other hand, were heavily involved in growing grain; merchants flourished in Tappahannock, Alexandria, Norfolk, Yorktown, and Falmouth, and debt collection was essential if the counties were to recover from the ravages of war. Business simply could not be put off any longer, and the county courts had been tried and found wanting.[85]

The opponents of reform in the Tidewater came from Henrico, Hanover, Caroline, Middlesex, and Essex. Why Henrico's Nathaniel Wilkinson voted against the bill is not known; perhaps since he had sat as a justice since 1766, he felt personally threatened by the measure. Samuel Hawes and Anthony New of Caroline were both justices who had sat since the 1760s. New, born in Gloucester, owned 482 acres and eleven slaves in Caroline, served as a colonel in the Revolution, and thought of himself as a gentleman—so much so that he challenged Richard Corbin

---

85. *JVHD*, Dec. 18, pp. 106–7; Swem and Williams, *Register of General Assembly*, pp. 23–25. The Ayes, by county and occupation: *York*, Joseph Prentis, lawyer; *Charles City*, Henry Southall, planter, William Christian, justice-planter, a relative of Judge John B. Christian of the General Court; *Elizabeth City*, Miles King, justice-planter, George Booker, unknown; *Fairfax*, David Stuart, doctor, later Federalist partisan; *Gloucester*, Thomas Smith, planter, second president of Phi Beta Kappa at William and Mary, pro-federal Constitution delegate; *James City*, William Norvell, planter, William Walker, planter; *King and Queen*, John Lyne, justice-planter; *King George*, William Thornton, justice-planter, Daniel Fitzhugh, justice-planter; *King William*, Benjamin Temple, merchant son of merchant Joseph Temple, attorney of Bristol, England; *Lancaster*, John Gordon, justice-merchant, descendant of the merchant family begun by James and John Gordon; *Prince William*, Cuthbert Bullitt, lawyer, later judge of the General Court; *Richmond*, George Lee Turberville, lawyer; *Stafford*, Andrew Buchannon, occupation unknown but part of the Richmond merchant family of that name; *Westmoreland*, Daniel McCarty, lawyer, later justice; Richard Lee, justice-planter.

Republican Lawyers, 1774–1790   199

in the 1788 election for Congress in Essex County. Hawes had sat since 1767, was the scion of an old Caroline family, and was not known for his innovative character. Hanover County's John Garland remains obscure, as do his reasons for voting against the bill. But Parke Goodall of Hanover was a Caroline County resident, friend of Patrick Henry, and member of the group that had marched on Williamsburg to demand restitution for the powder Lord Dunmore had removed from the magazine. Like Meriwether Smith of Essex, he represented a localist mentality, which feared and shunned any increase of state power in Virginia. Smith and James Upshaw of Essex joined William Curtis of Middlesex as part of a Tappahannock group which was only lukewarm about the patriot dreams of the future. Middlesex and Essex counties had been notoriously infested with loyalists during the Revolution; the Tayloes, Corbins, Wormeleys, and Beverleys were all unrepentant Tories. Despite the trading interests in Tappahannock, which clamored for relief from the dilatory proceedings of the county courts, the Tappahannock block stubbornly refused to countenance establishing superior courts presided over by republican judges from Richmond.[86]

The prejudice of local leaders, who refused to see their "country" as anything bigger than the county where they sat as justices, clearly annoyed many lawyers. The barrister Joseph Jones complained to Madison in 1783, "Individual and local considerations appear to me to be too general and so fixed as to afford but small consolation to those who wish the policy of the State to be governed by more enlarged and liberal principles."[87] Bemoaning the lack of able men like Pendleton and Jefferson in the Assembly, Jones informed Madison in June of the failure of the delegates to pass a bill regulating county court proceedings. Jones labored along with other lawyers to get the circuit court bill passed and bitterly informed Jefferson in February 1786 that the "wretched combination of

---

The Nays: *Caroline*, Anthony New, justice-planter, Samuel Hawes, justice-planter; *Essex*, James Upshaw, Jr., justice-planter, Meriwether Smith, justice-planter; *Hanover*, Parke Goodall, justice-planter, John Garland, farmer; *Henrico*, Nathaniel Wilkinson, justice-planter; *Middlesex*, William Curtis, justice-planter. Supporters of reform were linked to more cosmopolitan views and demands of merchants, lawyers, and diversified planters than were opponents. Opposition to legal reform on this occasion is consistent with opposition to the federal constitution later. The vote on ratification reveals that Essex, Hanover, Henrico, and Caroline joined the Piedmont and Southside against ratification, although the Tidewater as a region supported the Constitution. See Ambler, *Sectionalism in Virginia*, p. 58; Main, *Political Parties*, pp. 244–67.

86. See also Main's appendix for Virginia, in *Political Parties*, pp. 442–48; Giseburt on the Tappahannock, "Life of Loyalty," pp. 62–88.

87. Jones to Madison, May 31, 1783, *Letters of Joseph Jones*, p. 109.

uninformed members, without an individual to utter their objections of the least pretensions to science except M–r–w——r S——th, proved too powerful for reason and eloquence in favor of the bill for establishing Circuit Courts."[88]

Personal reasons, fear of debt collection, even the need for money had been behind the opposition. Fearful that a new system might endanger the ranking of justices and prevent the senior man from collecting his salary as sheriff also had something to do with opposition. In December 1784, Richard Johnston wrote to Governor Henry complaining of his being left off of the commission in Caroline because he had been off the bench some time, thinking he lived over the line in Spotsylvania; he wanted his position as sheriff. John Page of Gloucester felt the same when justices of his county inadvertently left his name off of the recommendation for the position, "I have the vanity to think I can execute properly."[89] Spencer Roane's 1787 protest about the appointments of Tory Robert Beverley and Meriwether Smith ahead of other justices who had sat without interruption concluded, "It is needless to observe that the *office* of sheriff, *the only Reward* for Long Services as a magistrate, will be affected by a Reinstatement as the Recom,'n. w'd accomplish." A Prince George County justice grumbled about being passed over in 1789 in favor of a junior justice, convinced that "were I to remain in the Commission of the Peace for twenty years to come there would always be a Junior Justice between me and the Sherif'alty."[90]

---

88. Jones to Madison, June 14, 1783, ibid., p. 118; June 21, 1783, ibid., p. 120; Jones to Jefferson, February 21, 1786, ibid., pp. 146–47. Jones's sympathies were solidly with his profession. To Madison on May 30, 1786, he declared, "Something is indispensably necessary to be done respecting the Courts of Justice, or they will soon become grievances instead of giving relief.... The Court of Appeals ... [tries] one cause in a week ... owing it is said to the lawyers being worn down with laborious attendance on the preceding courts" (ibid., pp. 148–49).

89. Sheriffs were liable for failure to execute returns on insolvent debtors and were required to collect the taxes of the counties, even during the early 1780s when Virginians had little means of paying the levy. For petitions from sheriffs praying relief under these circumstances, see *VCSP*, 3:473; list of delinquents, ibid., pp. 591, 617; ibid., 4:9, 77–78, 174, 221–22, 275. By statute (Hening, 9:463 [1784]) sheriffs were absolved from liability for failure to collect taxes of 1783. By statute of 1793 (Shepherd, vol. 1, c. 18) sheriffs could proceed for summary justice against deputies whose failure to collect the appropriate sums had resulted in a fine against the sheriff. For comments of the sheriffs, see *VCSP* Dec. 1, 1784, 3:627; Oct. 8, 1783, ibid., p. 535. Local justices were concerned over the salary the sheriff's position brought with it. Henrico County levied on April 14, 1804, £7 10s.; Northumberland on February 12, 1787, levied $12.30 as sheriff salaries. Basic salaries were supplemented by fees; see York's April 7, 1789, levy of an additional forty pounds of tobacco to its sheriff "for summoning 3 Witnesses on behalf of the Commonwealth against Jos. Dunstan and whipping him."

90. Roane's complaint against Beverley and Smith (the latter of the two not a Tory

What county residents thought of all this is hard to say. Certainly the opposition to reform despite the need for speedy resolution of case loads did not sit well with many Virginians. And the worries of a justice over his rank or his sheriff's salary must have struck many people as selfish, conceited, and quite inconsistent with any Country or republican idea that a justice was a selfless public servant whose virtue deserved the deference of his county neighbors. If local opposition to reform had successfully blocked the circuit court bill of 1784, the partisans who defended the county courts had little reason to rejoice. Shortly thereafter, despite the circuit court bill's defeat and its suspension in January 1787, a district court bill passed the Assembly in December 1787.

The passage of the law that established district courts in Virginia actually marks the end of the period when justices of the peace had any political impact upon the legal future of Virginia. Originally, the republican lawyers had wanted to elect justices, in order to establish the office on a more republican basis. Frustrated by local opposition to this, the lawyers soon realized that more than mere elective officers would be needed to give relief to clamoring county residents. The General Court bill, which Jefferson had first proposed, included his own revisions of the defeated 1772 law that would have established assize courts and circuits in the colony. By insisting in his proposed regulation of the county courts that justices accept grievances year-round instead of once a year, Jefferson seemed to be reopening the controversy that had wracked relations between the House of Burgesses and the local courts in 1714. But even the conservative Pendleton articulated the implications behind the republican reforms: the defeated assize scheme, Pendleton wrote, had much to commend it for "the regular Subordination and uniformity of Judgments" that could have been rendered. But it was always difficult to get laymen to understand that county courts, like all others in Virginia, "are but branches of the same Court." The value of superior courts was clear—they would encourage "Industry & Oeconomy, and From thence resources adequate to every Public & private purpose."[91]

Even as late as 1788, Essex justices refused to accept the implications behind the passage and implementation of the district court bill of 1787. Protesting the insinuations made by Roane against William Ritchie when Roane attacked Beverley, the Essex justices hectored the governor and state government in general. Falling back upon its ancient dignity, the court noted that their "solemn recommendation" for people to sit as

but a justice absent during the Revolution) is in *VCSP*, 4:340. For further details of the (sometimes physical) confrontation between Beverley and the Roanes, see ibid., 5:228, 319–20. The complaint of Prince George Justice Edmund Ruffin is in ibid., 4:650–51.

91. Pendleton to Madison, Dec. 19, 1786, *Papers of James Madison*, 9:201.

justices ought to be affirmed, for "while we act as magistrates, [we] do not choose to be dictated to."⁹² Whether or not the justices chose, dictation was very soon to be the order of the day. Madison and his allies had begun the attack on the local courts in 1784 by trying to circumvent them in the assize bill debates. In December 1787, the district court bill passed the Assembly. When one views the impact that those new courts had on the administration of law in Virginia at both the county and state levels, one cannot help but conclude that the reforms proposed in 1745 by COMMON SENSE, expanded upon by other writers in the 1760s, and attempted by the proponents of the assize scheme of 1772 had finally made their mark on the legal culture of Virginia. The district courts were the accomplishment of republican lawyers.

92. *VCSP*, 4:417–19.

Chapter 6
The Impact of the District Courts on the Country, 1790–1805

They are but Branches of the Same Court
—JUDGE EDMUND PENDLETON, *Letters*

When Hugh Garland wrote his biography of John Randolph of Roanoke in the 1840s, he included some remarks by the querulous statesman that speak eloquently of the declension of local politics and institutions that Randolph had observed during his life. Randolph never retracted his acid remarks about the "chicane and low cunning" of county lawyers. As to the impact of such creatures on Virginia's legal and political culture, he was equally emphatic. "I should as soon expect," he concluded, "to see the Nelsons, and Pages, and Byrds, and Fairfaxes, living in their palaces and driving their coaches and sixes; or the good old Virginia gentlemen on [in?] the assembly . . . in lieu of a knot of deputy sheriffs and hack attorneys, each with a cruet of whiskey before him, and puddle of tobacco-spittle between his legs."[1] Of course, in his sarcasm, Randolph did not at all expect to see any such return to the gracious society and manners of the past. If Randolph's lament had any basis in fact, it must have stemmed from the devolution of the local courts, which began in earnest in the 1790s. When one examines the records of the district court and sees how the legal culture of Virginia after 1789 was shaped there and in Richmond, few if any doubts remain about the sweeping changes wrought on local court life by the new state courts.

The district records and private letters of the men who ran those institutions reveal the flight of lawyer-clerks from the boredom and tedium of county practice to the better salaries and more exciting cases heard in the district courts. The men who sat as judges on the district court benches gave fairly unmistakable signals that a new age was dawning in Virginia's legal history. First, a pattern emerged of district court correction of county court errors in procedure and judgments, eroding still further the prestige of local justices, already regarded as inefficient and perhaps even unrepublican by some Virginians. Lawyers dissatisfied with

1. Garland, *Life of John Randolph*, 2:225.

a county decision had only to wait upon the district judges and petition for admission to practice in the superior courts to escape the annoyance of seeing their clients' causes mangled by local justices. Besides suffering from a loss of status generated by superior court decisions overturning their own, local justices also witnessed the flight of better attorneys from their courts, and furthermore, no longer enjoyed exclusive jurisdiction over grand jury presentments and indictments. Serious crime was now dealt with by district court grand juries. Since the local justices had for some years prior to 1790 declined to prosecute petty offenses that might logically be deemed to be threats to private virtue and, hence, to public virtue as well, their scope of influence was steadily shrinking. The important figures and institutions were those operating at the district level.

The district court judges of Virginia were part of the old General Court judiciary of the state. The new court system was somewhat decentralized because the district courts sat in separate areas of the state. Functionally, however, the same judges sat on district cases as gathered together in Richmond as members of the General Court. Discussions about cases, procedures, and problems were filtered to a central judicial cadre, composed of some of the most eminent judges and lawyers of the nation. That judiciary operated to provide a central vision of law as an instrument facilitating the growth of a complex social order. Since Virginia lacked a strong executive under its constitution, many judges like St. George Tucker indicated their conviction that the judiciary would set correct policy and provide the legal machinery for a progressive political order, all of whose courts were, as Pendleton had remarked, but extensions of one court.

Virginia began its existence as an independent state with a General Court that merely continued many of its colonial characteristics. Restrictions on lawyers that had separated county from General Court practice were removed, and by a sheer lack of attention to detail, examination of lawyers passed from the supervision of General Court judges or their appointed board to the governor and Executive Council.[2] Just prior to the Revolution, a Massachusetts observer, Josiah Quincy, Jr., had written that Virginia's "Court of Justice is very ill-contrived." Quincy could not conceive "how such a constitution and form of judicial administration" as Virginia's was tolerable. He was amazed at the old court as it sat to hear a cause at law, "and the next hour, perhaps minute ... audit the same matter as a Court of Chancery and equity."[3] Separation of equity

2. On the nature of lawyers' examinations, see Cullen, "New Light on John Marshall's Legal Education."
3. "Journal of Josiah Quincy, Junior, 1773," *Proceedings of the Massachusetts Historical Society* 49 (1915–16): 465.

from law was a major reform effected after the Revolution when Virginia established a High Court of Chancery. That separation was jealously guarded by the professional judges who by 1788 would begin sitting as district court members.

Opposition to a proposed superior court system was, as the vote on the circuit court proposal indicated, strong but no longer as pervasive as before. Tidewater lawyers and justices in the Assembly voted for the new district court proposal, while the Piedmont-Southside area opposed reform.[4] The new measure garnered widespread support among Tidewater delegates, and passed 86 to 34. Fourteen members from ten Tidewater counties voted for the bill; only 2 delegates opposed it. Both James Upshaw and Meriwether Smith of Essex County now voted in favor of the new bill, whereas they had opposed the circuit court bill. On January 3, 1788, the assize bill was formally repealed, and the new court system was ready to be put into operation.[5]

The new measure had probably passed the Assembly on the heels of the defeated assize or circuit court bill because, upon reflection, the members knew that they could not simply let matters remain where they had been since the county courts reopened in 1783. The assize bill had been suspended because the vote in favor of it had been so close. Legislators were unwilling to cause more hard feelings among the opposition by pressing for adoption. Then, too, wise leaders correctly suspected that upon reflection and in facing angry constituents, many opponents would see the necessity of pressing forward on the issue of court reform. In April 1787 the *Virginia Independent Chronicle* carried the article of one ARISTIDES, which argued for reform. To those who pleaded that scarcity of money lay at the root of Virginia's current malaise, ARISTIDES could only answer, "When was it otherwise?" Old men like himself had never known a time when that was not a complaint, he said, but the real reason for Virginia's social and economic difficulties lay in the inability of her citizens to expedite business in the courts. As evidence, ARISTIDES pointed out: "There is not an article that we now buy, but what the

---

4. Main, *Political Parties*, pp. 244–67, and below, chapter 7. Agricultural and social historians have yet to clarify the correlation between voting patterns, ideological issues, and crops; we know, for example, that grain-growing areas in Virginia tended to vote differently from tobacco-growing areas but we do not know why. On the economy and population in Randolph's district, see D. P. Jordan, "John Randolph of Roanoke." Randolph's district included Buckingham, Cumberland, Charlotte, and Prince Edward Counties, a "rural area noted for the cultivation of tobacco. The population was homogeneous and virtually static; the number of white residents increased only about six hundred from 1800 to 1830" (p. 404).

5. *JVHD*, Dec. 18, 1787, pp. 81–82; ibid., Jan. 3, 1788, p. 102. The new courts did not, however, begin operating immediately.

merchant puts something on the price for the delay, expense, and trouble he may be put to in recovering his money; and it were easy to demonstrate that this alone is a heavier tax on us than all our other taxes together. Thank God we see the way of getting goods cheaper, and more money to buy them;—a ready administration of Justice will do both.[6]

In fact, Virginia's economic picture was brightening by the end of the 1780s, and one must look for additional reasons to explain the success of the district court bill in 1788.[7] One of the most cogent explanations lies in a letter that the young attorney Monroe wrote to Madison concerning the new court bill. Madison was no longer in Virginia, and leadership of the reform faction in the Assembly had fallen to younger men like Monroe. In December 1787, Monroe wrote that the measure for "district or circuit courts seems also to be dispair'd of by those who are desirous of amending this branch of our system." Opposition from men like Henry, Monroe believed, had killed the bill for good. In fact, the Assembly shortly thereafter passed the new measure. Monroe noted in an added paragraph to his letter that the reason for the change of heart sprang from the legislature's fear of an alternative proposal that would have again extended the term of the General Court in an effort to clear up the backlog of cases pending. So odious was that idea to the delegates that they fixed on the district court measure out of desperation.[8]

The following April, Monroe informed Jefferson that nothing was left of the old General Court "but the name, and in its stead [are] 18 district courts.... Each district court bears the same relation to the County Courts within it that the general court did."[9] The new measure provided that the Court of Appeals would comprise the judges of the General Court, admiralty, and chancery, which in turn would oversee the district courts. A fatal proviso of the new bill directed judges of the Court of Appeals also to sit in circuit in the district courts. Besides the impracticality of such a provision, which Monroe pointed out in his letter, such a practice might raise questions of the propriety of the judges sitting in the district courts and then hearing the same cases in their capacity as judges

6. *Virginia Independent Chronicle* (Richmond, Augustine Davis, pub.?), Apr. 4, 1787. John Marshall used this pseudonym in 1793; if this 1787 letter is Marshall's, it has not been identified as such. *Papers of John Marshall*, 2:201–7.

7. Alden, *The South in the Revolution*, pp. 367–75, discusses the economic improvement of the late 1780s.

8. Monroe to Madison, Dec. 6, 1787, *Writings of James Monroe*, 1:179. Extension of the General Court term had been the compromise proposed in January 1787 after the close vote on the assize bill. By December reformers had sufficient strength to oppose this second effort to lengthen the sitting of that court.

9. Monroe to Jefferson, Apr. 10, 1788, ibid., pp. 181–82; see also *Papers of Thomas Jefferson*, 13:49–50.

of the Court of Appeals. Monroe told Jefferson that "the plan is... unpopular with the former Judges, and is most probably highly defective. It is however not improbable the putting the matter in motion may produce some beneficial effects.... The reduction of the number of districts to 1/3 would perhaps be greatly for the better."[10] Monroe's supposition that the former judges of the General Court would find the new bill objectionable proved to be true. In July 1788 he wrote Jefferson again, telling him of the Judges' Remonstrance, wherein the magistrates objected to the provisions of the district court bill. In addition to the already sitting judges of the General Court, four more judges were elected by joint ballot of both legislative houses, and the General Court (which also comprised the High Court of Appeals) was ordered to divide among its members and the newly elected the duties of the districts. The judges objected, pointing out the questionable constitutionality of the legislature's orders that they perform new duties with no additional salary and with no real hope of being able to execute their new duties properly. The governor forwarded the remonstrance to the Assembly in June, but the delegates declined to take it up, instead passing a law suspending the district bill until January 1789.[11] Monroe viewed even the temporary defeat of the new law with foreboding, and told Jefferson, "I still reside here [in Fredericksburg] and perhaps shall continue to do so whilst I remain at the bar, especially if the district court law holds its ground."[12]

Finally, in 1789, a reformed version of the district court bill was put into effect. The five-judge Supreme Court of Appeals henceforth was composed of men who had been absolved of the onerous circuit duties of the district courts. Yet the number of districts was left at eighteen, and the fatiguing circuit on which the judges traveled to oversee cases of original process and those on appeal from the counties continued to be a demanding one. By 1789 it was clear that despite opposition from some local justices and lawyers in some parts of Virginia, a new era had at last dawned. In a companion act in the same year, the Assembly provided that county court judgments could be taken into the new district courts

---

10. Ibid.

11. The original law on the district courts is in Hening, 12:532–38; the act suspending that law, ibid., p. 644; the renewed law, ibid., pp. 730–63. On the Judges' Remonstrance, see Cullen, "St. George Tucker," pp. 100–108; *Letters and Papers of Edmund Pendleton*, 2:504–9. The judges objected to the interposition of the legislature in forcing admiralty and chancery judges to hear common law cases on circuit; the Assembly was, in the opinion of the judges, threatening the independence of the judiciary, thereby endangering one of the key points republicans had felt would guarantee public virtue—the insulation of the law from faction and intrigue.

12. Monroe to Jefferson, July 12, 1788, *Papers of Thomas Jefferson*, 13:353.

on a writ of error or a writ of *supersedeas* if the value of the matter in the cause was ten pounds or more.

That left a fair amount of civil litigation in the hands of the local justices, but in effect it meant that anyone doing a large business at law or engaged in sizable agricultural or mercantile concerns would naturally take his business to the district courts. The sense of drama that had once enlivened the proceedings of the local courts as eminent local squires settled their business in full view of the assembled county was diminished still further by the new statutory definitions of jurisdiction. Every month one or two district judges appeared at the designated location to hear cases that came from the surrounding counties. The value of the American dollar to the British pound in 1790 was about one to three; cases which could be removed from the counties on a writ of error or *supersedeas* therefore had to involve about thirty dollars—not a trifling sum, but not unusually high, either, especially in debt cases.

The recalcitrance and outright opposition of some county justices continued in the face of these new efforts to speed up judicial process in Virginia. The district courts had hardly been in operation a year before an angry assemblyman introduced a bill to punish delinquent justices of the peace, who shirked their duties in the local courts. The bill was defeated, and unfortunately there is no record of the votes cast for or against the measure.[13] Nevertheless, such a bill, introduced as it was so soon after the district court law became operative, clearly indicated the necessity of Virginia legislators' holding the justices of the local courts to their duty, diminished as those duties now were.

Virginia's professional judges such as St. George Tucker (a member of the General Court since 1785, on circuit as district judge after 1789, and judge of the Supreme Court of Appeals in 1804)[14] began receiving requests soon thereafter from men who desired the position of district court clerk, a position for which each judge had the power to cast a vote. One such request came from attorney James Shackelford of King and Queen County, who observed that he suspected that county and district practice might soon be separated. He also noted that he needed the money that would accrue to him from the clerkship and expressed fears that county and district practices might not be lucrative enough, given the number of Virginians entering the practice of law.[15] Most of the men who clamored for release from the duties of county court clerk were

---

13. *JVHD*, Dec. 15, 1790, p. 112.
14. On Tucker, see Cullen, "St. George Tucker"; Tyler, *Encyclopedia of Virginia Biography*, 2:34–35.
15. James Shackelford to Tucker, Jan. 20, 1788, Tucker-Coleman Collection.

lawyers anxious not to be left behind in the struggle for eminence at the bar, a struggle that clearly dictated that the ambitious lawyer try and attach himself to district practice. As those lawyer-clerks left county practice, local lay justices took over the clerkships, as they had been forced to do after 1776 when the abolition of the office of secretary of the colony had disrupted the colonial pattern of training lawyers and clerks.

Thomas Edwards wrote Tucker from Lancaster County, citing as evidence of his ability his training under his father, a former clerk of Lancaster. The younger Edwards had no desire to remain in that capacity when he could be clerk in the more exciting district court and earn a salary of four hundred dollars per year. Judge Henry Tazewell received similar requests from clerks and lawyers seeking a way out of county jobs. In addition to recommendations from Spencer Roane for one Catesby Jones to be district clerk in Northumberland District, Tazewell received a letter from Drury Stith of Brunswick asking for confirmation of his request to be clerk. In his letter, Stith revealed something of the continuing hostility that existed between young ambitious men and the old guard composed of county justices. Stith had made an enemy of one of the old county families and was all the more anxious for Tazewell to hire him as clerk "because should I now fail, he will be sure to attribute it to his influence with the judges." The "he" whose rancor Stith had earned was a Colonel Jones, one of the justices of Brunswick court.[16]

Certain clerks and lawyers wrote to the judges whom they knew, asking for preferment to district positions, but even those who did not take that step anxiously awaited the beginning of the new courts' term in order that they might begin practice in that jurisdiction and escape the drudgery and backwardness of county practice. Only two sets of district records have survived for the Tidewater area of Virginia, but even from such meager sources it is a simple matter to observe the growing number of lawyers who applied for admission to the district bar.

Such a development did not surprise judges like Tucker. When he began his law practice in Virginia in the early 1780s, he had complained to a fellow attorney, Robert Innes, of the drudgery of county practice. Innes wrote back, "It is true the fall from a gentleman of ease & pleasure to any laborious occupation is disagreeable." That twisting of the young lion's tail was only a friendly jibe at Tucker's genteel youth in Bermuda.

16. Thomas Edwards to Tucker, Jan. 24, 1788; Harrison Randolph to Tucker, Feb. 1, 1788; William Davies, a county lawyer, to Tucker, asking him to intercede for him regarding the clerkship, Feb. 5, 1788, Tucker-Coleman Collection. The request to Tazewell and the recommendation of Roane for Jones are in the Tazewell Papers, Feb. 5, 6, 1789. Tazewell received an identical letter from Harrison Randolph on Feb. 1, 1788, four days before a copy reached Tucker.

Innes sympathized with the young attorney's problems, but reminded him: "What in the name of wonder should give you more cause of complaint than most of yr. intimates—What think you of the Life I lead—a common drudge for a whole County—subject to the Caprice of any old Woman and Fool—badly paid—& with no prospect of even getting more than a bare competency." Undaunted, Tucker had continued to grumble, eliciting from James Innes, Robert's brother, a letter that poked fun at Tucker's mournful tale. "How like you the County Court practice?" wrote Innes. "Is it not grating to your feelings? I so cordially despise it that I have half a mind to turn itinerant preacher."[17]

With former county lawyers like Tucker on the new benches of the district courts, the pleas of younger attorneys for release from boring local practice received a sympathetic hearing. Thus, when the Fredericksburg District Court began its sessions in 1789, the judges and clerk were barraged with urgent requests from lawyers who were already licensed to practice in Virginia and now wanted access to district practice. The district clerk, however, objected when the men refused to pay the fifteen pounds required as a licensing fee, since they argued they were already licensed to practice in the other courts of the commonwealth. The district judges said that they realized that the same problem had arisen in the capital district of Richmond, and in that case, because of uncertainty as to procedure, the judges had referred the matter to the General Court, as the Fredericksburg judges now did as well. In the meantime the judges decided that in order that the lawyers' clients not be discomfited, the attorneys could temporarily be admitted to practice until a decision was reached.

The list of lawyers seeking admission to practice in the Fredericksburg District Court reads like a *Who's Who* of Virginia statesmen. Besides Deputy State's Attorney James Monroe, the list included John Marshall, John Taylor, Charles Simms, Bushrod Washington, and William Waller Hening. John and Robert Brooke, John Minor, Andrew Buchanon, Oliver Towles, John F. Mercer, Richard Brent, and James Moand filled out the balance. Within the year other prominent attorneys such as William Branch Giles, Charles Lee, and Edmund Berkeley came to practice in Fredericksburg. John Nicholas, a Spotsylvania county court lawyer, petitioned the court to be allowed to practice at the district level.[18]

---

17. Robert Innes to St. George Tucker, Mar. 25, 1783; James Innes to Tucker, Sept. 20, 1783, Tucker-Coleman Papers.

18. District records that included most of the Tidewater counties have not survived; these courts were located at Williamsburg and Richmond. Fredericksburg District Court Orders, 1789–1805, Apr. 20, 1789, Sept. 29, 1789, Apr. 9, 1790. The courts met twice a

In the Northumberland District the same pattern emerged as young attorneys sought to improve their forensic abilities before professional judges and to give a boost to their incomes as well. If one were to look for a representative example of what district courts did to the old family oligarchies of Virginia and what effect those new courts had on the county benches, we might consider Thomas Pinckard. The elder Pinckard had long been a justice, albeit a fractious one, of Lancaster County. In September 1794 the old justice's son Thomas was licensed as an attorney before Tucker in the Northumberland District. Unlike his father, he was never to sit as a justice in the county court, choosing instead the career of a professional attorney in the superior courts of the commonwealth.[19]

Another example pointing to the importance of the district courts and the declining importance of the county bench and bar was young Ellyson Currie who had studied assiduously Coke on Littleton and Wood's *Institutes* at Tucker's recommendation. He decided to obtain his license in 1799 before he was of age. In his correspondence with Tucker he never once mentioned county practice. Rather he had admiration only for the district and appellate courts, whose judges such as Tucker he unabashedly lionized. On April 1, 1800, Currie proudly took his place as an attorney in the Northumberland District, pleased that on that day Tucker had joined Joseph Prentis on the bench for the spring session.[20]

Two other elements lie hidden in the district orders which ratify the conclusion that the advent of these courts signaled a further devolution of the county benches. One is the nature of the cases themselves and the

---

year in April and September, sitting for about a week to ten days until most of the docket had been cleared. If the case load was not finished, the balance was explicitly carried over to the following term to prevent dismissals, a common complaint of litigants about county procedures. Fredericksburg District included Spotsylvania, Caroline, King George, Stafford, Orange, and Culpeper counties.

19. Northumberland District Court Orders, 1789–1805, Sept. 2, 1794. This district included Northumberland, Westmoreland, Lancaster, and Richmond counties.

20. Currie to Tucker, Dec. 12, 1796, Mar. [?], 1799, Tucker-Coleman Papers. Northumberland District Orders, Apr. 1, 1800. The district judges had to divide the responsibilities of sitting on the various circuits among themselves. Each of five circuits contained four district courts, and two judges were assigned to each circuit. Circuits examined here were the second and fourth. The second comprised the district courts held in Staunton, Charlottesville, Fredericksburg, and Dumfries; the fourth, the Tidewater district courts held for Northumberland, King and Queen, Williamsburg, and Accomac. For more details on the reorganization of the state courts, see Cullen, "St. George Tucker," pp. 106–19. Cullen argues that after the new statute (Hening, 12:497) which forbade a lawyer from taking a case on appeal from a lower to a higher court, young attorneys were even more determined to leave county practice. Older lawyers, who viewed traveling a circuit with distaste, stayed in Richmond to argue before the Court of Appeals (pp. 117–19).

extensive review given to county decisions by district judges. The second is contained in the nature of the grand jury presentments at the district level and the charge to a grand jury delivered by Judge Tucker. In these important respects, as well as in the attitudes of young attorneys and clerks, one can observe just how different law in the district court was from justice in the county.

The district courts had not been in operation very long when they began receiving a substantial number of cases from lower courts upon which they had to rule. For the period under examination—1789–1805—the districts of Fredericksburg and Northumberland dealt with approximately ten to twenty cases per day, sitting as a rule for a week or ten days per session twice a year. Causes that began as original processes in the district courts had to involve one hundred dollars, as did causes on appeal from the county courts. Causes that came before the district judges were largely debt causes, as well as ejectments, detinue, trespass on cases—in short, causes that one would heretofore have found in the county courts of Virginia. County benches continued to hear causes as before, but the presence of district courts more accessible than the old General Court and the superintendency of professional judges on the district benches attracted many suitors to the latter instead of to their county courts. A rough estimate of the original processes that the district courts were hearing can be drawn from the fact that only about one-third of the causes heard in the two district courts were on appeal from an inferior court. Most of the courts' time was taken up with suits that had actually begun in the district. Of the causes that were on appeal from the counties, approximately two-thirds of them were either overruled or sent back for retrial. Often the clerk was ordered to bring up the complete minutes from the county for the judges to examine more fully.[21]

At times there appeared subtle signs of the importance that the district

---

21. Some confusion on the amount of money involved in processes that came up to the district courts from the counties should be eliminated. The laws stated that original process in the district court had to involve £30 or $100, equal to three thousand pounds of tobacco. Cases that were on appeal also had to involve that amount. However, cases that were removed to the district courts on a writ of error or supersedeas could involve as little as £10, or $33.33, equal to one thousand pounds of tobacco (Hening, 12:730–63; ibid., 13:427–49). In a letter to Jefferson, Monroe wrote, "The County Courts, until lately, have had exclusive jurisdiction of sums under ten pounds only.... A late modification gives them original jurisdiction of sums under £30; but as well as I remember, subject as before to correction of the Superior Courts by Appeal or Supersedeas" (May 1, 1792, *Writings of James Monroe*, 1:228–29). Monroe is slightly inaccurate here. The distinction between the amount involved in an appeal and that involved in a writ of error must be kept in mind. The conclusions drawn above as to the proportion of cases on appeal come from a reading of the district orders for the years indicated.

courts were assuming in the eyes of Virginians. Justices in the local courts had traditionally been referred to as "Gent.," a term of considerable importance, but clearly distinguished from the more deferential "Esqr.," which was usually reserved for burgesses, councillors, and the like. From the outset the judges of the district courts acquired the appellation "Esquire." Perhaps more to the point, a jury in the Northumberland District Court in 1801 made the distinction between the two courts clear in its wording. In the trial of a case of detinue, the jury examining the county record decided, "We find that the . . . orders of the county court of Westmoreland quashing the . . . executions, etc. were finally reversed by the Honorable District Court of Northumberland." Failure to call the county court "honorable" or "worshipful" outside of the county itself may have only been an oversight, but even oversights sometimes say a great deal.[22]

Cooperation from the county courts was, as indicated above, not forthcoming sometimes without some stern prodding from the district court. In many cases it was necessary for the superior court to have full records of lower court proceedings before it could make a decision as to the validity of the appeal. Continued admonitions and orders to the counties to bring in such records were often ineffective. In April 1803, Judge John Tyler of Northumberland District Court granted a subpoena *duces tecum* against the clerk of Westmoreland County, ordering him to appear personally and bring with him the records of the cause pending before the court. In September 1804, the deputy state's attorney in the district court sought and received Tyler's permission for another subpoena against the clerk of Lancaster for the same reason. After the Revolution the clerk of the county court was one of the justices, elected to his post by his fellow magistrates.[23]

District decisions overturning county verdicts and judgments often contain a note of annoyance in them, and the district judges did not scruple to lecture the county justices and residents as to what they ought to have done. In the Northumberland District's fall term of 1803 the court overturned a Richmond County decision on a writ of *supersedeas* and completed its own judgment with the words "and this Court proceeding to give such judgment as the said county Court ought to have given, It is further considered that the verdict of the jury rendered in the said county court be overruled." In the minds of judges like Tucker, county juries were no better than county justices. He proposed setting a property qualification of one hundred pounds for district jurors, who would be chosen from a list sent up by each county. Jurors chosen from

---

22. Northumberland District Orders, Sept. 3, 1801.
23. Ibid., Apr. 4, 1803, Sept. 1, 1804.

such a list would sit on the causes that came up on appeal from the lower court of their counties. Despite Tucker's urging, nothing came of his proposal.[24]

The reason for district decisions that reversed lower court rulings was essentially simple. County courts were often sloppy in their attention to the law, even in cases in which it was perfectly clear what had to be done. In 1794 the Northumberland District Court reversed a decision from Richmond County. A man who wanted to build a grist mill on a creek in the county had approached his court for the usual process of swearing out a writ of *ad quod damnum*, under which the sheriff would call a panel of examiners and investigate what, if any, damages would occur to the county or to private property by the building of the mill. That procedure had been common practice in Virginia throughout the eighteenth century. The district court, however, felt constrained to overrule the county action that had granted the permission for building the mill because, for unexplained reasons, the investigation had proceeded without the presence of the high sheriff of the county. Since the law was quite explicit that the inquiry had to be conducted by this officer, the district court felt that the plaintiff's appeal from the county decision was justified.[25]

It was not merely the more efficient and more learned nature of the district judges' decisions that set the new courts apart from the old county benches. In the nature of the grand jury presentments that occurred at the district level and in a charge to one of these juries delivered by Judge Tucker one can see profound differences in the thinking of Virginians about what law was and what the law ought to concern itself with in the

24. Ibid., Sept. 6, 1803. For Tucker's proposal, see his edition of *Blackstone's Commentaries*, 3:64–71. Tucker's major complaint was that county juries were composed of idle bystanders who were not serious about seeing justice done. He also felt that the complexities of some causes, especially criminal causes, confused less-educated jurors and resulted in acquittals for dangerous felons. He had some real reasons to be concerned about this latter problem, as an examination of district grand jury presentments reveals.

25. Northumberland District Orders, Sept. 5, 1794. The impatience of the district judges with the stalling tactics of recalcitrant county officials is revealed in a rule adopted in the Northumberland District Court on Sept. 2, 1796, stating that when a *supersedeas* was issued to a county court judgment, the clerk of the district court was henceforth to issue a writ of *certiorari* as well, ordering the justices of the county "to certify a full record of such Judgment." Some idea of what the district judges were facing can be obtained by considering the Fredericksburg District's decisions on May 7, 1791. On that day, from a total of twenty-five causes heard, four county decisions were reversed, three were continued until next term, and, though seven were upheld, the district court had to issue six writs of *certiorari* to force clerks to bring up complete records in order to render a decision.

new republic. The first day of each term of the district court was reserved for the calling of the grand jury. Between 1789 and 1805 in the Northumberland District the grand juries brought in true bills against seventeen Virginians on charges of assault and battery, against five men for forcible entry and/or trespass, against five for "felony," against four for causing or participating in a riot, and against three men for murder. Clearly, as Judge Tucker pointed out in his indictment of Virginia juries, criminal activities were no laughing matter and demanded serious consideration on the part of district jurors.[26]

Between 1789 and 1798 in the Fredericksburg District the grand jury, led by foreman Mann Page, brought in indictments for grand larceny, murder, assault, and burglary. Page and his fellow jurors were alarmed as well about the state of the Fredericksburg prison, pointing out: that hardened criminals, debtors, runaway slaves, and others merely awaiting trial were jammed together "and their Situation highly uncomfortable & unwholesome."[27]

By comparison with the concerns of county grand juries, the district presentments seem to have been quite serious. The lack of concern on the part of district grand jurymen for presenting swearers, drunkards, and other petty moral offenders testifies to the changing attitudes about what the law ought and ought not be concerned with. For example, in April 1796 the grand jury in Northumberland District Court had ample opportunity to prosecute two men who opened their taverns for gaming while the district court was in session. Rather than indict these men for breaking the law, the grand jury contented itself with a recommendation to the state's attorney that he ask the county court of Northumberland to revoke the licenses of the offenders.[28]

Part of the reason for the lack of enthusiasm for enforcing public morality on the part of district grand jurors probably sprang from the notions they had about why they were on the grand jury in the first place. They were instructed in those ideas by Judge Tucker. To a grand jury sitting in April 1794, Tucker gave the following admonition: "A regular Inquiry, at stated, and those not distant, periods, into all offenses against the common happiness, and an impartial punishment, when they are discovered, without regard to the Circumstances or situation of the offender, promises to secure to the individual those Blessings, to attain which he became a member of a social Establishment. . . . You are to

---

26. Grand jury presentments taken from the first day of each session, Northumberland Orders. 1789–1805.
27. Fredericksburg District Orders, 1789–1805, Sept. 30, 1797.
28. Northumberland District Orders, Apr. 2, 1796.

consider yourselves therefore, as this day Constituted the Censors of the republic." Tucker finished his charge with the obligatory exhortation that not only felonies but lesser crimes as well, those which "corrupt the morals of our fellow citizens ought to be notified in your presentments." Tucker made a special note of informing the jurors that they should prosecute those people who tried to evade the federal duty on distilled liquors, the only federal offense cognizable in Virginia courts. As far as the record shows, however, no one was ever presented for that offense.[29]

It was not an accident that Tucker's charge on this occasion placed minor moral offenses down the list next to a federal statute whose violation Virginians would not have cared too much about anyway. Considering themselves the "Censors of the republic," meant for the men who sat in the districts of Northumberland and Fredericksburg that they should prosecute serious crimes. Tucker and the other judges on the district bench saw themselves as impartial jurists who came around twice a year to various courts and dispensed the law with as much reasonable decorum and efficient speed as possible. These men were not paternalists guarding the private mores of their counties. Without exception they had been lawyers, with little connection, if any, save negative recollections of boring practices, with the county courts and inferior magistrates of Virginia. The grand juries were neither exhorted nor do they appear to have been inclined to investigate the minor offenses of fellow Virginians. Neither did county grand juries continue to press home such charges, contenting themselves with presentments against road surveyors and those who failed to list their taxable property.

In short, because of a disinclination on the part of magistrates and county juries and structural changes in the Virginia court system, one basic function of law in the commonwealth had changed. Law, as opposed to antiquated notions of country justice, existed to enforce statutory prescriptions, to execute speedy and efficient decisions on debt causes, and to prosecute serious criminals. Temporarily, at least, practical concerns hid the idea that law ought to be concerned with investigating and enforcing the moral standards of a local community whose interests were homogeneous and whose overseers were the gentlemen justices of Virginia. Tidewater magistrates and lawyers who had sat in the Assembly between 1784 and 1788 had promoted both assize and district court bills out of a sense of desperation over the hopelessly choked backlog of

29. Grand jury charge, Apr. 1794, Tucker-Coleman Papers. Tucker had a special distaste for gambling, largely because he felt the vice was one of the root causes of violent crimes and degeneration in a purportedly republican society. See the "Charge to a Grand Jury," delivered to the Fredericksburg District Court, *Virginia Herald* (Fredericksburg), Oct. 5, 1802.

causes. Moreover, as the Tidewater declined in population and economic influence in Virginia, a speedy resolution of debt causes and administrative efficiency was essential if the older counties were to compete at all with the aggressive and fiercely localistic Southside and Piedmont counties, whose die-hard defender was the old patriot Patrick Henry.[30]

A good index exists of how much law was coming to be regarded by lawyers as the instrument of a complex and diversified social order. Consider the introduction to *The New Virginia Justice: Comprising the Office and Authority of a Justice of the Peace in the Commonwealth of Virginia, Etc.* written by the compiler, attorney William Waller Hening. First published in 1795, Hening's work began with a eulogium to the magistrate whose only compensation for his services is "a consciousness of having acted from patriotic motives." Hening judiciously omitted to mention that lawyers had for years proposed to pay justices and thereby improve the quality of their decisions by dangling the carrot of remuneration in front of them. After surveying the dubious quality of the Virginia magistrate, Hening graciously noted that he had "avoided the insertion of any Latin words in the body of the work: Conscious that to *be useful*, not to *appear learned*, has been his principal object."[31] Utility, then, not gentlemanly superiority, was to be the hallmark of the new Virginia justice. Hening was quite explicit in giving credit where it was due for the encouragement he had received for putting together the new handbook. The detailed instructions to the magistrates should not be complained of, said the lawyer, because "the author could not otherwise discharge his obligations to the gentlemen of the bar who have so generally promoted this publication."[32]

No sooner had Hening published his manual than the urge to abandon the county court in favor of a district position as clerk infected many justices as well as lawyers and county clerks. A law was passed in 1796 forbidding a justice from becoming a clerk of the district court unless he resigned his county office. Such a statute may have quieted the constitutional or legal qualms of district judges over having a county justice also

---

30. Henry, like Mason, had opposed legal reform and the promotion of commercial ports for Virginia. It seems likely that many of the "cosmopolitans" identified by Main supported reforms in the end out of fear of what might befall their region (the Tidewater) if Henry and his associates gained control of state government.

31. Hening's work was reissued in 1810 in a second edition. Both editions were published in Richmond. The above quotations are from the preface to the first edition, pp. v, vi, and see the glossary of legal terms for the justices (pp. 2–26), included, said Hening, that "they may draw their Mittimus less liable to exception than has usually been done" (pp. vi–vii).

32. Ibid., pp. vi, vii.

sitting in a district clerkship, but its effect was invariably to sift out the more able men from county practice and move them upward into district positions.³³

Virginia jurists such as Tucker were not content merely to instruct the counties on their failings or to encourage the publication of manuals such as Hening's. The Judges' Remonstrance against the district court bill of 1788 was not forgotten by jurists like Tucker, and in 1792 a case arose involving the district courts and their jurisdiction in which Tucker made quite explicit the judiciary's intent both to preserve its independence from legislative control and to ensure the utility and clarity of judicial procedure. In the case *Kamper v. Hawkins*, Tucker delivered his opinion on the question of whether the district courts had jurisdiction over chancery cases. A dispute on this matter had arisen in one of the western district courts and was sent to Richmond for decision in the Court of Appeals. Tucker's decision stated that the judiciary had the right to review and declare unconstitutional the laws passed by the Virginia legislature when such laws violated the spirit and intent of the 1776 Virginia Constitution. Since the statute separating law causes from chancery had been explicit in its directive, there could be no doubt that the new district courts, in succeeding the old General Court, were but extensions of that court of law and were in no ways courts of equity.³⁴

Some years later Tucker expressed some doubts about the wisdom of the constitution that he had so vigorously defended in *Kamper v. Hawkins*, but even those doubts were largely being put to rest by the actions of judges like Tucker. To the Reverend Mr. William Bentley of Salem, Massachusetts, Tucker admitted that the Virginia Constitution was badly balanced, since it stated that "all power of Government, legislative, executive, and Judiciary result to the Legislative Body." Yet, Tucker said, that was being remedied. So hesitant had the legislature come to be about interfering with judicial matters, Tucker asserted, that they "have very rarely (if in any case) taken upon them to decide upon any Question of a judicial nature." Tucker did not speculate for Bentley's benefit about the judges' own roles in fostering such caution in the legislature.

Concerning the district courts, Tucker laid out for the Salem minister the powers of those bodies, commenting on their "appellate Jurisdiction from the County Courts within their respective districts," and making clear that the districts functioned only in civil causes, their judgments

---

33. Shepherd, vol. 2, c. 16, p. 86.
34. Hening, 13:427–49. For a discussion of Tucker's opinions in *Kamper v. Hawkins* and the case's significance for the development of constitutional law, see Cullen, "St. George Tucker," pp. 120–27.

"liable to be reversed or affirmed in the Court of Appeals if the matter in controversy be of the value of one hundred Dollars, or be a free hold, or franchise."[35]

Constitutional independence of the judiciary, however, was not generally uppermost in Tucker's mind when he argued for the necessity of keeping equity and law separate at the district level. What impressed the judge was the need to minimize confusion and to expedite efficient procedure and speedy resolution of causes. Even before sitting as a judge, Tucker had observed cases being argued in the district courts and the General Court and Court of Appeals in Richmond. From reading some of Tucker's "Notes on Cases" and from observing some of the causes that were now appearing in district and county courts, one can begin to appreciate his conviction that professional judges were needed to oversee the law in Virginia.

Tucker made his notes while observing the higher courts between 1786 and 1811, even after his own accession to the bench in 1788. The young attorney soon came to appreciate the need for judicial oversight of procedural matters in Virginia's courts, especially on cases that came up on appeal from the counties. In the October term of 1786 the General Court received a bill of exception against the magistrates' decision in Halifax County in the case of *Gordon v. Bates*. The judges were unable to grant the validity of the objections lodged against the justices because the writ had been improperly drawn; the decision went in favor of the magistrates.[36]

Later in the same term Tucker observed a case in which the attorney for the defendant moved for a writ of *certiorari* to remove a cause from Rockbridge County Court "on affadavit that the plaintiff was Judge of the court & had great Influence therein & that Def[endant] conceived he could not get Justice there—The Court hesitated for some time, conceiving the allegation too general, but ... *Certiorari* awarded."[37]

The same day Tucker recorded the decision of the court in a case in which an order had been issued with a blank where the name of the county should have been. The process was executed "by the Deputy Sheriff of Caroline County who subscribed himself Deputy Sheriff, C[ounty] C[lerk]." Here, the state's attorney moved for a judgment against the sheriff, but the court noted that "the process being issued with a blank was void originally and can not be aided. Take nothing by the

---

35. Tucker to William Bentley, June 30, 1797, Ebeling Collection, by permission of Houghton Library, Harvard University.
36. Notes on Cases, Book 1 (General Court), Oct. 13, 1786, Tucker-Coleman Collection.
37. Ibid., *Bowyer v. McCampbell*, Oct. 27, 1786.

motion." The state's attorney then moved to quash the execution and requested permission to take out another which was granted.[38] From such instances as these, Tucker began to appreciate just how irregular the state of procedure was in the lower courts of Virginia, although he had a pretty good idea already from his own legal practice.

In the Court of Appeals the following spring, Tucker noted for personal reference that the court had decided to establish a rule in regard to county orders. In the future, if a county sheriff executed a writ and indicated that bail was taken by him but did not return a copy of the bail bond with the writ, suit could be brought against the sheriff. Tucker himself was soon to discover that writs of *certiorari* had to be issued constantly to lower courts to bring up a full record of causes for review by the district bench. He must have applauded the appeals court's decision above, just as he noted a lawyer's concern for procedure on another cause two weeks later. From Princess Anne County a cause had come to the Court of Appeals in which a defendant had fled the county to escape the ordinary process of law in a debt suit. An attachment against his person and property had been sworn out to deal with the matter, but the writ had omitted the words "privately" and "absconds." Nevertheless, the court ruled that the warrant and the attachment should stand. Tucker scribbled beneath his notes, "At which the Bar were astonished!"[39]

Tucker also observed the errors being committed by overburdened county magistrates from his place on the district bench and must have wondered if justice had always been so irregular in Virginia. In a relatively simple case before the Northumberland District Court, a motion for a writ of error against the Richmond County Court's judgment was awarded on the grounds that no issue was joined after the cause had been stated. Such an egregious departure from common procedure could only be explained by a combination of ignorance, apathy, and overwork on the part of the magistrates.[40] In fairness to the county justices one must concede that the causes over which they presided were becoming more complex, perhaps beyond the abilities of a lay magistrate to adjudicate.

The need to expedite debt causes, the growing professional expertise of attorneys, and the general fractiousness of Virginians bringing causes before the county benches were all clearly discernible realities in the postrevolutionary era. In Caroline County the magistrates tried to deal with a routine debt cause in which the defendant had defaulted on con-

38. Ibid., *Livingston* v. *Upshaw*.
39. Ibid., Book 2 (Court of Appeals), Apr. 9, 1787; *Newton* v. *Saunders*, Apr. 20, 1787.
40. Ibid., *William Lee* v. *Raleigh Downman*, Book 2 (Court of Appeals and District Court), Apr. 2, 1789. See also for this cause Northumberland District Orders, Apr. 2, 1789, *certiorari* ordered for a full record of the case.

fessing judgment and applying for a standard rate of payment. The magistrates awarded the plaintiff a rate of payment on the debt of £104 16s. at the rate of £52 8s. with interest at 5 percent until completed. The defendant then demanded a jury trial, claiming that he had paid the debt. He lost his nerve when the plaintiff accused him of defaulting, but he contested the court's decision. The cause was remanded to the General Court, since the justices were at a loss over what to do.[41]

Many Virginians were not satisfied even with the superior judgments rendered when the district courts started operating in 1789. In another case from Caroline County a jury trial had decided a cause for the plaintiffs who had entered a suit as executors of the will of a deceased relative. Despite the district court jury's decision the defense attorney immediately arose and objected that, as usual, the county court had not produced a full record but only a record of judgment for the *scire facias* action— there was no record of the original pleadings. His motion to dismiss the case was overruled, and he entered a bill of exception to the court decision. On his advice, the plaintiff appealed the case to the Court of Appeals in Richmond.[42] In the course of only three years—1787 to 1790— the record of Caroline County Land Causes and Appeals reveals that of twenty-four cases, fully a third were appealed to the highest court in Virginia. It was becoming evident that the county magistracy was no match for the technicalities of a more complex legal era.

So unpopular had the county courts become that within three years of the district courts' creation the Assembly was forced to take steps to prevent the new benches from being submerged in a flood of causes, both initiated there and appealed from the inferior courts. In 1792 the Assembly's Act Reducing into One, the Several Acts Concerning the County and Other Inferior Courts of This Commonwealth seemed to backtrack on reform efforts. In 1789 the Act Concerning Jeofails had stipulated that jury decisions were never to be reversed for lack of proper writs, language, or improper pleading; nor were judgments to be stayed or reversed in any inquiry of damages unless a substantive issue would have reversed or stayed the original judgment had there been a verdict. Moreover, demurrers were to be ignored unless a substantive matter of law was involved.[43] Sheriffs had been warned not to speak with jurors unless expressly ordered by the court, and persons wishing to be declared nonsuit in a cause had to say so before the jury retired to consider a verdict.

---

41. Caroline County Land Causes and Appeals, 1777–1807, *Buckner v. Stevens*, Aug. 9, 1787.
42. Ibid., *Mary and William Trigg v. John Burk*, Nov. 13, 1789.
43. Hening, 13:36–38, sections 1, 2, 8, 10.

No longer had plaintiffs been allowed to wait until they saw how a cause was going before entering such a plea. Those rules were clearly intended to speed up causes by urging justices not to quibble over technicalities but to do their duty as always, with an eye toward substantive justice.

However, in 1792 the new act recognized that appeals were coming into district courts so fast that exhortations to justices and rules governing procedure were insufficient to prevent the districts from being choked with causes. The new law stated that no writs of *certiorari* or *habeas corpus* were to be received by the justices after issue was joined or a demurrer entered. If such a writ did issue after cause was joined it was removed and then sent back by a writ of *procedendo*. The cause could never be removed again into the High Court of Chancery or district courts. Rather lamely, the act admonished justices to follow the example of district courts and the High Court of Chancery in matters of procedure.[44]

Perhaps the most vexed area of law over which the justices had always presided was that of equity. Unlike their English counterparts, Virginia justices had always had jurisdiction in this highly technical and confusing area of English law. As suitors pressed for remedies at law in postwar Virginia and, failing that, entered bills in equity before the justices, more and more confusion reigned. Partly as a result of the hopeless morass at the county level the legislature had suggested that the district courts exercise equity jurisdiction. Although in the Judges' Remonstrance the high court jurists had rejected that notion, they were nonetheless acutely aware that something had to be done to aid the processing of equity bills. In 1802 the legislature acted to create Superior Courts of Chancery in Virginia to aid suitors who had previously been forced to come to Richmond to appeal county equity decisions, which, of course, they frequently did. Recognizing the justices' inability to deal with the complexities of equity law, the legislature specified that in each county a master commissioner of equity be appointed. This resident of the county was to be allowed a "reasonable" salary, and to him alone were all accounts in equity cases to be referred for examination and report on behalf of the justices.[45]

---

44. Ibid., pp. 465–66. Writs of *procedendo* are those issued by a superior court when it appears that a cause has been removed on insufficient grounds. The writ orders the cause to be sent down "to be proceeded on" in the place it originated. Colonial reformers had tried to get this provision into the 1748 act on the General Court. When that act was disallowed (ibid., 5:506), the subsequent act in 1752 omitted this important procedural control of county appeals, although apparently it was not specifically objected to by English authorities.

45. Shepherd, vol. 2, c. 13, pp. 412–13 (1802).

More and more oversight and directions and more reprimands for noncompliance besieged the county magistrate by 1805. Not content merely to establish a commissioner in chancery, the legislature acted in that year to empower the commissioner to take oaths in cases referred to him by the county courts. Formerly only the justices could take such oaths. Now, in a further diminution of the status of the magistrate, the Assembly specifically prohibited a justice from being a commissioner.[46]

Although no one moved to eliminate completely the justices' powers in equity law, in fact they were quite circumscribed even prior to the establishment of a chancery commissioner in the counties and the erection of the Superior Courts of Chancery. The legislation of 1777 that established the High Court of Chancery in Virginia enabled any suitor to begin a bill in the high court or to appeal a county decision for as little as ten pounds.[47] By 1787 the Assembly acted to remedy the slowness of county equity proceedings and the inability of the High Court of Chancery to deal with bills. Much of the slowness stemmed from the archaic language and nature of the bills in equity, which could easily run on for as many as fifty pages in length. The new law of 1787 directed that in any equity proceedings brought to Richmond, after a subpoena had been executed, the plaintiff and defendant both had to file and respond within three months or the bill would be dismissed. The chancellors themselves were now empowered to issue executions on final decrees, instead of waiting for the General Court to do so. Any chancellor out of term, or the entire chancery court in session could hear an appeal or stop the proceedings of any inferior court within three years of a lower court decision.[48]

Although the formal structural power of a justice to preside in an equity case remained, the functioning judges for chancery decisions in Virginia by 1805 were the professional jurists of the superior courts. Such a development occurred because the new legislation diminished the formal power of a justice by making equity appeals easier. Perhaps equally important was the theoretical, jurisprudential reasoning about equity, which had to change to accommodate traditional Virginia institutions to new political and social realities. Historically, equity had evolved in England as a remedy to which the suitor could repair if no solution to his plea existed at law, or if the law was so rigorous as to be unjust. In theory, equity had depended on the conscience of the king. It was to the king, or to his chancellor acting in the king's name, that a suitor petitioned, to the fountainhead of justice tempered with mercy.

46. Ibid., vol. 3, c. 30, pp. 227–28.
47. Hening, 9:389–99.
48. Ibid., 12:464–67.

Virginia had never encountered the fractious controversies that convulsed other colonies, such as New York, over the establishment of equity courts. Virginia's colonial General Court appears to have operated as an equity court without any attempt on the part of the burgesses to dictate to that body what the nature of its decisions should be or to somehow give the consent of the House to equity rulings. Yet when the Revolution came, Virginia separated its General Court from a High Court of Chancery and, in good republican style, stated that decisions of equity, like any other legal decision, had to be based in "right reason." Right reason, it was argued, was rooted in natural law.[49]

There was nothing particularly novel about suggesting that equity was based in natural law, for the traditional explanations that English legal historians employed had already claimed that common law, equity, and even parliamentary statutes were expressions of the law of God and Nature. But Jefferson had expressed his disagreement with the notion of British jurists that that same law was integrally incorporated in the Christian faith. Like most of his educated contemporaries, Jefferson was no enemy to the concept of private virtue, and indeed believed that strict moral behavior in the private sphere was the foundation upon which public virtue rested, whether that public virtue was defined for the people at large as deference to a natural elite or defined for the leaders as a selfless passion for the public weal. In Jefferson's eyes, the history of Virginia law left little reason to put one's faith in the discretionary judgment of jurists. Equity, of course, had always been a suspect branch of law for the Puritans, Whigs, and the Country at large who held up as the proper remedy for tedious suits and lack of speedy justice the *nisi prius* session in which a judge and twelve jurors dispensed law with dispatch and in simple terms.[50]

Unfortunately, even though the republican principles of Virginia judges like Pendleton, Wythe, and Tucker were commonly acknowledged, the mere presence of a republican judiciary had not in fact solved the riddle of why Virginia society at large was not virtuous, in private or in public. Gradually, some Virginia judges, such as Tucker, began to doubt the ability of Virginians who sat on juries to arrive at just decisions. District court orders clearly indicate the willingness of judges to vacate the deci-

---

49. For an otherwise excellent survey of equity courts and the struggle that surrounded them, but which does not discuss Virginia, see Katz, "Politics of Law."

50. On Jefferson's views, see above, pp. 163–66; for example, Hale, *History of Common Law*, pp. 160–67; Locke, *Second Essay on Civil Government*; relevant selections in Olafson, ed., *Society, Law, and Morality*, pp. 117–48. The idea that equity is right reason and not personal discretion was one of many contributions of Lord Nottingham, the "father of equity." Maitland, *Constitutional History*, p. 466.

sions of county juries whenever they felt justified in doing so. What began as a suspicion of certain reformers like Jefferson—that lay judges and jurymen could not be trusted to see the purity of ancient and republican law as lawyers could—had grown in the minds of some judges to a conviction that laymen were not astute jurors.

Such a conviction did not mean that the judiciary urged equity decisions in preference to jury trial, especially not at the county level. Even the old county justice Landon Carter had excoriated the notion of putting more suits into equity jurisdiction when a perfectly sound remedy existed at law. Yet if judges did not encourage local decisions in equity, they had no doubt that that branch of law should be presided over by professionals. The establishment of the High Court of Chancery and the Superior Courts of Chancery by 1802 meant that equity was firmly in the hands of professional judges and lawyers and that juries and lay justices were to have little impact on cases removed into chancery in the commonwealth. What began in Tucker's decision in *Kamper* v. *Hawkins* as a warning to the legislature to keep hands off the judiciary ended as a virtual establishment of the Virginia judiciary as the elite body of professional judges presiding over courts filled with equally professional-minded lawyers whose ambitions had carried them out of county practice.

The county courts by 1800 tended merely to respond to the dicta of the upper courts, not to contest them as they had done formerly. Gone were the old remonstrances to the governor that a local court "conceived itself" able to oversee its own affairs. Instead, in 1804 the York County Court, "taking into their consideration an act pas'd at the last Session of Assembly entituled 'An Act concerning proceedings in Courts of Chancery & for other purposes,'" delivered an opinion with regard to the application of the said law as follows:

> (1) In all actions on the Case (Torts excepted) where the Jury render the Verdict for a gross sum in damages which is composed of principal and Interest six per cent Interest ought to be calculated on the principal damages recover'd and the Costs of suit from the day the Verdict was render'd til payment. (2) In actions of debt where the principal sum is found by the jury and the Interest asses'd in damages six per cent Interest is to be calculated only on the principal sum recover'd and Costs of suit from the day the Judgment was render'd til payment but not on the damages found. (3) That the said recited Act applies to Judgements render'd on Petitions on the foregoing principles as well as actions.[51]

51. York Orders, Aug. 21, 1804.

In the colonial era the minute details of legislative instructions to justices concerning rates of interest and how to distinguish petitions from debt actions on cases would have been considered unwarranted interference. Most colonial statutes concerning county proceedings had been drawn purposefully vague, allowing wide latitude in interpretation and even instructing the justices not to allow irregularities in form or pleading to interfere with their decisions. Those days had disappeared under the pressure for more speedy and efficient judgments and with the expansion of judicial horizons beyond the local county to the state court system and beyond. Technical matters of procedure were more important, and the cases were more difficult. Thus, such detailed instructions to inferior courts shorn of professionally trained clerks and the better class of lawyers only made sense.

By 1800 a striking incongruity confronted the Virginia suitor who came before a county court. Everyone recognized the broad powers of oversight and direction that were exercised by the superior courts over the justices and knew that the better lawyers and more important cases began at the district level. Yet the petitioner in chancery still began his bill before the justices as he had always done: "To the Worshipful justices of Essex County Court in Chancery Sitting, humbly complaining shew unto your worships your orator & oratrices."[52]

Old habits and linguistic forms survived into the early nineteenth century, but they were forms devoid of the vibrant meaning such oratund rhetoric once held when proclaimed in the tiny courthouses of the Tidewater in the colonial days. The antiquated language helped to validate the notion that the county court had survived enormous cultural and legal change in Virginia and that the same old gentlemen still presided undisturbed over their county neighbors. Perhaps there had been no genuine revolution at all in Virginia, merely a colonial rebellion for establishing the rights of liberty and property.

However, contemporary observers of the courts told a different tale. On a journey up the Tidewater toward the mountains one traveler came upon the Orange County courthouse where Madison had first seen his county's justices in action. In 1800, when this foreigner passed by, he found only "an old wooden building, which is used both as a court-house and a place of divine worship, a tavern, and half a dozen mean dwelling-houses." Journeying on to Madison County, the writer encountered "a jolly justice of the peace... a moral, upright man, whose advice often

---

52. Copy of a bill in chancery, June 17, 1799, Accession No. 6490, Latané Family Papers.

reclaimed the offender, when the enforcement of the law might have rendered him incorrigible." Clearly, the value of a local justice was still that he could apply his discretion to impart a sense of private virtue to the preservation of public peace. In the foreigner's view that kind of justice, which seemed so unprofessional and petty to lawyers and judges who were committed to seeing the law practiced in a scientific manner, seemed fine. The justice's main function in Madison County, however, was not confined to lecturing his white neighbors about obeying the law but extended to overseeing the slaves as well. Fear of rebellion from the black population had become one of the legacies of the Revolution; the contagion of rebellion was something that no one in Virginia could forget after 1800 in Richmond and in Virginia as a whole.[53]

Courthouses in the Tidewater declined visibly as the importance of what transpired inside them fell into desuetude. Writing during the Civil War, one northerner described Stafford County's courthouse as "a tumble-down and filthy building, and the jail, which stands in the middle of the road, is a miserable two-story affair, built of rough stone. The lower story is occupied by hogs, and the upper is reached by stairs from the outside." Even allowing for prejudiced reporting and the conditions of war, the scene described did not differ all that much from that given by an aged Virginian who recalled that the courts of his childhood served largely as occasions for political haranguing, athletic contests, buying of goods from "the ubiquitous Yankee pedlar, with his clocks, and showy goods spread out in gorgeous array on temporary counters in the courtyard."[54]

Judge Waller R. Staples recalled that lawyers continued to attend the county court because if any case was to be appealed, the suitors had to have a new set of attorneys, since county lawyers were barred from appellate practice. The judge probably thought he was offering the old courts and pettifoggers a compliment, but his recollections illustrate much of what both professional judges, like Tucker, and some ordinary laymen found obnoxious. Staples admitted that after the district courts were created, "most of the important litigation was carried on in those forums." But the judge still thought the spectacle of county lawyers to be an admirable one. "I do not hesitate to say," he added, "that some of the

---

53. Manson, *Stranger in America*, pp. 399, 402–6. On the fear of slave revolt, see Mullin, *Flight and Rebellion*, pp. 140–63; Miller, *Wolf by the Ears*, pp. 19–22, 126–29.

54. On the courthouses, see Happel, "Stafford and King George Courthouses," p. 192, citing Eddy, *History of the Sixtieth Regiment New York State Volunteers*, p. 209; Staples, "Address," p. 147.

finest displays ever made before any judicial tribunal in Virginia have been made in the County Courts. No rigid rules were enforced, or technicalities observed, and there were frequent opportunities afforded for the display of all the arts of the advocate, as well as the powers of the logician."[55]

Part of the mythological character of the antebellum South's collective self-image was created from such recollections. Indeed, local lawyers and justices received an overwhelmingly favorable report at the hands of southern literary and oratorical masters, many of whom, not accidentally, were lawyers. In Staples's remarks about the court officers, one notes the panegyric of the county court lawyer and the fact that the justice of the peace is hardly mentioned. The transformation of lawyers into something like folk heroes in a Country culture is nothing short of remarkable.

Indeed, when a young Baltimore author named John Pendleton Kennedy brought out his novel *Swallow Barn* in 1831, the mythology was already widely accepted. There is considerable reason to doubt whether Virginians of the early national period were quite as thrilled with the legal profession as these authors and speakers later recalled. But the literary genre that described the lawyer in glowing terms is too important to ignore. Kennedy, for example, sketched his impressions of court day as he had observed the occasion as a boy in Virginia in 1809. Kennedy had a firsthand opportunity to observe and later reproduce the events that surrounded the monthly meeting of the county court. Perhaps setting the genre in which Judge Staples followed, Kennedy gave most of his description to the performance of the county lawyer, to whom he gave in his novel the picturesque name of Philpot Wart.

Kennedy likewise contented himself with a cursory description of the county justice Frank Meriwether, painting the magistrate in nostalgic tints as a kind of romantic leftover of a bygone era. "It is pleasant to see him when he is going to ride to the Court House . . . in a coat of blue broadcloth, astonishingly glossy, and with an unusual amount of plaited ruffle strutting through the folds of a Marseilles waistcoat. A worshipful finish is given to this costume by a large straw hat, lined with green silk. There is a magisterial fulness in his garments which betokens conditions of the world, and a heavy bunch of seals, suspended by a chain of gold, jingles as he moves, pronouncing him a man of superfluities."[56]

55. Barton, ed., *Virginia Colonial Decisions*, 1:204 (fn. 1).
56. *Swallow Barn*, p. 31. Kennedy (1790–1870) spent his summer in Virginia in 1809 after his father's Baltimore business failed. For a sample of later nineteenth- and early twentieth-century literary evocations of revered homegrown lawyers, see Gwathmey, *Legends of Virginia Lawyers* and *Justice John*. The claim that Virginians loved their legal professionals is undercut somewhat by Gwathmey's lengthy explanation (*Legends of Vir-*

The courthouse itself Kennedy described as a dilapidated, unpainted building—of wood, not colonial brick. After the court was proclaimed, inside the upraised gallery the dozen or so justices "flung their feet upon the rail before them . . . lolling back upon their seats, ready to proceed to their judicial appointments." One can hardly imagine the spectacle of Landon Carter or Edwin Conway "lolling" with his boots upon the rail in front of the presiding magistrate's chair. One can only wonder whether Kennedy's next remark was intended in sarcasm or as a kind of romantic reverence when he suggested that this informality was "well calculated to inspire a wholesome respect for that inferior and useful magistracy which has always been so much a favorite of the people of Virginia."[57]

In fact, of course, the county courts had suffered an irrevocable defeat, both institutionally, because of the creation of the superior courts and, more importantly, symbolically, in the minds and affections of Virginians. The success of the republican lawyers in reforming the judicial system of Virginia is eloquent testimony to just how annoyed Virginians had become with the lower courts. By the time Kennedy wrote a kind of romantic nostalgia was permissible, even necessary, because the justices of Virginia had become so innocuous and because looking back in fondness always helps to face a future of uncertainty. Even in Kennedy's account it is not Justice Frank Meriwether, but lawyer Philly Wart who "has been elected to the Assembly for twenty years past, without opposition; and, indeed, the voters will not permit him to decline." Wart had never read anything but Coke on Littleton (also highly unlikely after the publication of Tucker's edition of *Blackstone's Commentaries*) and "practised in the times of old Chancellor Wythe and President Pendleton, and must necessarily have absorbed a great deal of that spirit of law—learning which was evaporated in the hands of the reporters."[58]

---

ginia Lawyers, pp. x–xi) of why the legal profession worked against the Readjuster Movement in Virginia between 1869 and 1883. On the movement, see the dated, but still valuable, book by Pearson, *Readjuster Movement*, pp. 148–50, on Readjuster hostility to the legal profession.

57. *Swallow Barn*, p. 171.

58. Ibid., pp. 184–85. Any notion suggesting unanimity of opinion between Wythe and Pendleton is totally romantic. They opposed one another at almost every turn during the 1790s, when Wythe's decisions as chancellor were time and again overturned by the conservative Pendleton as judge of the High Court of Appeals. The denouement came in 1802 when Wythe upheld a demurrer against a stay of injunction that would have prohibited a board of overseers of the poor to sell at auction the former Glebe Lands of the Episcopal Church according to the recently passed law which provided for this. Pendleton wrote a decision for the appeals court overturning Wythe's decision, but died before he could deliver it. Tucker had proposed a compromise but, upon election to the bench to succeed Pendleton, sided with Spencer Roane and those who upheld the confiscation. See Mays,

Thus, according to Kennedy, the golden age of Virginia law is not only colonial and local but early national, and presided over by the saints of the lawyer's pantheon, now long departed—Pendleton in 1802, Wythe in 1806. The "reporters" who copied out reports of cases for the use of professional lawyers are given short shrift because Kennedy, like many Virginians, suspected that professional lawyers were, on a day-to-day basis, not nearly as statesmanlike and profound as the fabled Wythe and Pendleton.

What is the legacy of such striking dissimilarities between the actual workings of the superior courts and professional lawyers and judges and these romantic literary images of a pastoral, bucolic county bench and bar in nineteenth-century Virginia? The most obvious conclusion is that mythos rapidly overtook social, intellectual, and legal reality in the minds—or, more accurately, the hearts—of Virginians. The myth of continuity with the colonial era's local legal culture played a significant role in shaping the subsequent history of Virginia's legal culture—as significant a role as the actual reforms and institutions that had modified the powers of local courts, justices, and lawyers. The dry bones of the county court, of local legal culture, rattled back into spectral life between 1800 and 1810 to haunt the dreams of republican lawyers and bestow a legacy of Country opposition sentiment upon Virginia and the South at large. What republican lawyers proposed, local Country thought would dispose in odd ways. There was to be a muted but undeniable challenge offered by the Country, as its ancient suspicion about lawyers awakened once again after a long sleep and Virginia entered its third century.

Pendleton, vol. 2, chapter 21, on the case *Turpin v. Locket*; Cullen, "St. George Tucker," pp. 243–63. On the religious alignments and preliminary skirmishes that led to this decision, see Buckley, *Church and State in Revolutionary Virginia*.

Chapter 7
The Legacy of Court and Country in Virginia Legal Culture

The god of thieves, lawyers, and merchants
—J. K. PAULDING, *Letters from the South*

In the summer of 1801, William Brockenbrough, a Virginia attorney linked by marriage and common business and family interests to the Ritchies and Roanes of Essex County, wrote a letter to Joseph Cabell. Reviewing the recent elections held in Virginia for the House of Delegates, Brockenbrough complained that "being a lawyer was with some a fatal objection, their taking it for granted that a lawyer was interested in multiplying laws and making them more complex." From the tenor of Brockenbrough's remarks and from other writings, one can clearly discern the revival of antilawyer sentiment in Virginia between 1800 and 1810. That revival seems all the more surprising when one recalls that the 1790s had come and gone with no perceptible revival of antilawyer feelings in the state. Indeed, the *Virginia Almanac*'s 1790 reprinting of "A Lawyer's Prayer" seems in its sentimental way to mark not only a changing taste in literary expression but also a willingness to indulge publicly the image of the lawyer as the friend of "Virtue and her friends."[1]

Yet the reform of the local courts, the successful implementation of the district court bill, the establishment of the principle of judicial independence by Wythe, Tucker, and other Virginia judges, though important accomplishments, did not lay to rest the old ghost of Country hostility toward lawyers. Between 1800 and 1810 the quarrel over judges, lawyers, and the place of the law in a virtuous, republican society reemerged and revealed serious divisions within the republican tradition, which found so much of its ancestry in the rhetoric and experience of the Country past. Ostensibly, the moderate republicans were bound to win

---

1. William Brockenbrough to Joseph Cabell, June 8, 1801, Accession No. 38-111, Cabell Papers. Richard Ellis, *Jeffersonian Crisis*, pp. 116, 121, cites the letter and argues that Virginia's legal profession was "one of the most respected and least criticized legal establishments in the country," an opinion which needs at least some qualification.

because they were in the seats of power, and the existence of a professional bench and the drive for a professionally trained bar were both established facts. Yet the dissenters, who sought a purer form of republicanism, should not be discounted as so many cranks. Romantic writers like Beverley Tucker, impassioned orators like John Randolph of Roanoke, essayists fond of convoluted style like John Taylor of Caroline—all are easily dismissed as irrelevant. But their nay-saying was heard, and received a sympathetic, if anxious, examination by the republican lawyers, the moderates who dominated Virginia legal culture in the new republic. For those men the task of reconciling the need for legal expertise, elite training, and technical prowess with republican simplicity, public service, and egalitarian law was a tortured and insoluble dilemma. Yet they were bound to seek a solution precisely because the rhetoric of the Country had been so much a part of Virginia's past that it was unthinkable not to try.

By 1800, Virginia as a whole was clearly identified with the Republican political cause and in opposition to the Federalist notions of the northeast. No one seriously entertained the idea of endorsing the Court notions of Alexander Hamilton after the events of 1798–99 and the election of 1800.[2] But within the Virginia republican tradition divisions did break out, divisions most generally recognized in the maverick break of Randolph and the "Tertium Quids" with the Jefferson administration. However significant on the national level, that controversy was in fact merely the most visible aspect of the anxiety shared by some Virginians who believed that something was fundamentally wrong with a republican society that seemed to be slipping more and more into a morass of luxury, avarice, and moral decay. Not surprisingly, that aspect of the Country tradition that had always identified lawyers as part of such declension now revived with an added timeliness.

When one reflects on the anxiety of the republican moderates, who saw the need for legal training, for internal economic improvements in Virginia, and for an agrarian banking system, and their hesitation to endorse those ideas publicly, a certain sense of déjà vu is inescapable. Such goals were difficult to reconcile with an egalitarian republican order. Richard Vamper, a cordwainer, pointed out the inconsistency of judges, lawyers, and merchants being addressed as "Esquire" while he rated only the title "Mr." Despite the Revolution, despite the republican rhetoric

2. Hamilton's identity within Court-Country positions is aptly described as "Walpolian Whig." Hamilton himself would have denied being a pure Court apologist; see Stourtz, *Alexander Hamilton*; McCoy, "Republican Revolution" and "Republicanism and American Foreign Policy." On the political ramifications of the more radical Country thought in Virginia, see Risjord, *Old Republicans*.

which built on the Country tradition, the need to reconcile the desire for a simple life with the goals of an expanding society was little different from the dilemma that confronted William Byrd II or Robert Carter.³ The mixture of Court and Country that had bedeviled the planters in the early 1700s must have appeared to lawyers to have been revived by 1810 in a perverse manner in their commonwealth. During the antebellum period that debate had serious consequences not merely for Virginia but for the entire nation of which it was, sometimes reluctantly, a part.

Reprise: Republican Lawyers and the Real Country

The debate did not arise suddenly in 1801 with William Brockenbrough's discovery that local voters did not trust lawyers. In 1793, John Taylor of Caroline County sent a short note with a packet of his most recent writings to Madison. The Virginia senator hoped that his literary effort would "produce in the Virga. Assembly a repeal of the bank laws, and an expulsion of bank papers, . . . and this will operate against the banking system in Congress."⁴ Taylor's pamphlet of 1794 attacked the idea of a national bank, but he clearly feared that Virginia had already been seduced by banking when the Assembly chartered the Bank of Alexandria in 1792.

The cautious endorsement of internal improvements by the Virginia House of Delegates actually started in 1784 in the abortive attempt to create several ports in Virginia. Theorizing that British merchants had resumed aggrandizing their interests even in spite of the recent Revolution, the House moved to specify certain towns which would have a monopoly on trade exports from the commonwealth. The need for an indigenous merchant class was perceived by Madison and received hearty

---

3. The complaint of "Richard Vamper" appears as a letter to the author in Wirt's *Old Bachelor*, originally appearing March 5, 1811, in the *Richmond Enquirer*. The essays were reprinted in 1814; for Vamper's letter, see Wirt, *Old Bachelor*, pp. 92–93.
4. Taylor to James Madison, Aug. 5, 1793, Branch, *Branch Historical Papers*, 1:258–59. On the Bank of Alexandria, see Hening, 13:592–98. Madison and Jefferson strongly opposed the branch of the U.S. Bank at Norfolk, Jefferson asking, "Could not a counterbank be set up to befriend the agricultural man . . . and would not such a bank enlist the legislature in its favor, and against the Treasury bank?" (*Writings of Thomas Jefferson* [Ford, ed.], 6:98). See also Starnes, *Sixty Years of Branch Banking*, pp. 21–23, on Jefferson's support for the Alexandria bank against the Bank of Maryland in Baltimore. Monroe's fears of the "banking spirit" were expressed in a letter to Madison, May 18, 1793, *Writings of James Monroe*, 1:254–55. Taylor's pamphlet *An Enquiry* was directed against the national bank, but he hoped Virginia would set an example by abolishing its banks (p. 80).

support, naturally, from areas around the proposed ports. Tappahannock, in Essex, was one of those areas in favor of the measure, and not surprisingly, the Ritchie, Roane, and Brockenbrough families of Essex County were enthusiastic about the idea. Predictably, the more conservative local leaders, like Meriwether Smith of Essex, George Mason of Fairfax, and their allies, opposed the measure as "unnatural" and unrepublican, just as they had opposed the reform of the local courts. On both points, the more moderate republicans carried the day, although the port bill was emasculated by opponents. The issue was rendered irrelevant with the creation of the federal union in 1789 but the episode was not forgotten. During the 1790s the need for a banking system of sorts and the encouragement of merchant activity in Virginia was argued by some of the same men who had led the fight for more efficient courts.[5]

Scholars have long known that the "Essex Junto," later known as the "Richmond Junto," which controlled Virginia state politics, had its origins in the Tappahannock families who were backers of various merchant and banking schemes. Moreover, historians have pointed out the links between the supporters of state banking, the backers of the James River and Potomac companies, the promoters of the Dismal Swamp Canal and the lawyers of the state. So closely identified in the public mind were these connections in 1816 that when George Fisher wanted to sue the Bank of Virginia, "he was unable to find an attorney willing to take the case, since . . . the banks were the most lucrative clients of lawyers."[6]

Private letters confirm the public perception that merchants, bankers, and lawyers were emerging as a coalition of talent, expertise, and shrewdness in the commonwealth during the early years of the nineteenth century. When Judge Francis T. Brooke recalled meeting the eminent John Marshall in Richmond, he did the Federalist judge a great honor by pointing out that "his house is small and more humble in appearance than those of the average successful lawyers or merchants." One wonders how many Virginians could identify with the lines from *Dr. Syntax's Tour in Search of Consolation*:

---

5. On the 1784 port bill, see McCoy, "Virginia Port Bill." Tidewater counties generally supported the idea; Piedmont and Southside opposed it. For George Mason's opposition, see Mason, *Papers of George Mason*, 2:859–63.

6. Harrison, "Oligarchs and Democrats," argues that banking and finance were the central mechanisms of the Junto's power. On Fisher's plight, see Starnes, *Branch Banking*, p. 53. On the investments of Tucker, Tazewell, and other lawyers in banking and internal improvement schemes, see Tucker to John Coalter, June 4, 1802, regarding investments in the James River Canal Company; instructions to his agent William Wilson to invest one thousand dollars in Alexandria bank stock immediately and another fifteen hundred dollars later, June 12, Dec. 1, 1800; and Tucker to Philip Barraud, concerning investments in Norfolk and the Bank of Virginia, April 15, 1804, Tucker-Coleman Collection.

A Lawyer now was to be found;
And where's the spot of British ground,
Where our experience doth not show
That such a spreading plant will grow,
And where his dwelling is not known
As the best house in any town?[7]

Far more significant than mere appearances were the plans being laid by Virginia's eminent state judges and lawyers to guarantee the perpetuation of republican legal culture in an elite of talent and eminence. The lawyers and judges of Virginia who feared that the republican experiment might falter unless guaranteed by institutional structures appropriated Jefferson's famous defense of an "aristocracy of talent." But that did not go unnoticed or uncontested. The replacement of familial oligarchies with cerebral and professional cabals struck many Virginians as thoroughly suspect.

John Taylor of Caroline probably first perceived the nature of the problem in 1801, the very same year that Brockenbrough discovered that local Virginians were beginning (again) to turn against lawyers. Writing to John Breckinridge, Taylor explicitly repudiated the notion that the judiciary ought to be independent. The labors of Wythe, Jefferson, Pendleton, and Tucker in the 1780s and 1790s to establish Virginia's judiciary on an independent footing could not be countenanced by Taylor. Much of his antagonism probably sprang from his fears about the federal judiciary. But as a principle, he instructed Breckinridge, "whether courts are erected by a regard to the administration of justice, or with the purpose of rewarding a meritorious faction, the legislature may certainly abolish them." Taylor's suspicions about the designs of the lawyers and judges in Richmond were soon proven to have ample basis. To another friend, Taylor confided, "I am fully convinced of the danger of the republican cause at this time. . . . I almost fear our administration are [sic] too good for human nature. . . . We mortals are either fools or knaves, generally speaking."[8]

Human nature was the very reason Tucker and some of his colleagues believed by 1801 that the bench and bar of Virginia had to move to

---

7. Brooke, "Narrative of My Life," p. 8. *Dr. Syntax's Tour*, published in 1820, is cited in Robson, *Attorney in Eighteenth Century England*, pp. 170–71. Compare the lines with Crevecoeur's that lawyers "are plants that will grow in any soil that is cultivated by the hands of others" (*Letters*, p. 135).

8. Taylor to Breckinridge, Dec. 22, 1801, Branch, *Branch Historical Papers*, 1:284–88; Taylor to Wilson Cary Nicholas, Sept. 16, 1802, Wilson Cary Nicholas Papers. Taylor was here reiterating Jefferson's original position in favor of a supreme legislature, the position Jefferson had taken when drafting the Virginia constitution in 1776.

institutionalize the gains made since the Revolution. Disturbed over the low quality of lawyers in Virginia, Tucker set about to adapt Blackstone's *Commentaries* for use in a republican society. His worries were shared by other lawyers and judges and by Virginians like the bard who penned a piece in 1798 lamenting:

> Since lawyers now so woefully increase,
> And many tongues divide the scanty fees."[9]

Some lawyers, like William Waller Hening, proposed to aid the project of setting legal culture in Virginia on a scientific basis by revising the manuals in use in the local courts. In *New Virginia Justice*, published in 1795, Hening had instructed local magistrates that they were supposed to consider their office to be one of routine execution of *statutes*, and that they were to be wary of hearing and determining matters of law out of session. Too often they relied only upon uncertain abridgments, Hening scolded, and they ought to remember Coke's dictum that abridgments were "of good and necessary use to serve as tables, but not to ground any opinion, much less to proceed judicially upon them."[10]

The most important aspect of setting the law in Virginia upon a sound basis, however, could not come merely from publishing manuals or the *Statutes at Large*. In his introduction to *Blackstone's Commentaries*, Tucker laid out for all to see exactly why Americans needed to study the law systematically under the tutelage of a republican theorist. Tucker had to concede that before Blackstone published his work, the aspiring lawyers in Virginia had been forced to read law "almost destitute of any scientific guide to conduct their studies." Unfortunately, when the *Commentaries* did appear, the wise Whig learning of Coke, so dear to Country apologists, was forgotten. "That rich mine of learning, his Commentary upon Littleton, was thought to be no longer worthy of the labour requisite for extracting it's [sic] precious ore." The Court sentiments of Blackstone were inappropriate for the vast, republican system of Virginia and the United States, wrote Tucker. Moreover, to understand the nature of law in society, the judge urged, the student should consider the dual sovereignty question and "consider how far the parts of a machine so immense, intricate, and complex, are likely to correspond, or interfere with the operations of each other." A nation that was advanced in scientific learning ought to be expected to promote an equally scientific approach to the study of law. Sensing the predilection in the Country past

---

9. The poetic effort is William Munford's in *Poems and Compositions*, p. 146.
10. Hening, *New Virginia Justice*, pp. 358–61.

for simple, hearty democracy, Tucker warned that the love of independence and democracy was no guarantee of their perpetuation. The Gauls, he pointed out, had enjoyed a sort of democracy, but their rude civilization perished, nonetheless. Comparing that simple society to the acorn, Tucker predicted the growth of a simple society—like Virginia's—into an enormous oak, complex and confusing. "In such a state," he firmly concluded, "in vain would the rude hand of the illiterate barbarian attempt to trace it's [sic] figure; science, only, is equal to the task."[11]

One cannot help but note that Tucker judiciously chose the Gauls, and not the Saxons, as the nation whose simple past could not survive in a modern, complex age. For Tucker, as for Pendleton, Jefferson's encomium to a Saxon past was not wholly convincing, though magnanimously, the judge did not point his example directly at the rather romanticized view of the English past defended by the Republican party's acknowledged head. Tucker explained that the study of the Constitution of the United States had to proceed hand in hand with the study of law as a science. Unfortunately, in a republican society men "of talents and virtue are not always the foremost in the course: persons of this description are generally more backward than those of inferior pretensions to the confidence of the people ... which ... they are infinitely more liable to abuse, than if their minds had been properly enlightened by study, application and science." That anxiety over the need for a properly educated legal elite drove Tucker to complete his Blackstone and to join in a conspiracy of sorts with Hening and Littleton Waller Tazewell which they hoped would secure the future of a republican legal culture in Virginia.[12]

Tucker had been appointed to the Court of Appeals in early 1804. Shortly thereafter, he began searching for a means of perpetuating the reforms of the revolutionary era. It was clear by that time that Mason's old attempt to force virtuous republicans to vote had not worked. Neither did the local courts seem to be particularly interested in vigorously stamping out vice and petty crime. The lawyers could not infuse virtue in local society. But by December 1804, Hening asked Judge Tucker to furnish particulars on a proposed bill for public education.[13] Tucker's plan for a

---

11. Tucker, *Blackstone's Commentaries*, pp. i, ii, viii, xxi–xxv, MS edition, Tucker-Coleman Collection.

12. Ibid., xxvi–xxvii. Not everyone shared Tucker's enthusiasm for law as a companion to liberal learning. Even some younger lawyers who studied with him wondered about the idea. See Joseph Watson to David Watson, Feb. 9, 1801: "Law, tho, called a liberal profession is surely one of the greatest enemies of general and liberal learning. The man who becomes a compleat [lawyer] will, I believe, be nothing else" (*VMHB* 29 [1921]: 138–39).

13. Hening to Tucker, Dec. 14, 1804, Tucker-Coleman Collection.

state university was quietly circulated among other lawyers and judges, and later in December, Tazewell wrote to Tucker congratulating him on the proposed plan, but warning him to keep their idea to himself:

> Under the most solemn injunction that nothing herein contained shall be mentioned, or even hinted at, until you hear further from me, I will communicate the *project* now contemplated, and of the success of which I entertain very little doubt. We design to obtain a donation from the State of all its interest in the Potomac James River Appomattox and Dismal Swamp Canals, together with 1000 of its Bank Shares. These will be vested in Trustees for the uses we spoke of. And to this fund will be added all Escheats forfeitures and other contingent interests which it is not now necessary to state. The profits of all which several funds to be applied in the first place to the establishment of one grand Seminary on the site we contemplated, and afterwards to be extended as circumstances may direct....
>
> Is it expedient at present to do more than merely obtain the grant, thereby protecting ourselves against future legislative caprice?
>
> I have the best of reasons for praying your strict regard to my injunction. The patient must frequently not see the healing medicine he is about to take less [sic] his sickly appetite reject that which alone can bring him health and life.[14]

By early 1805 the correspondents hoped that they could openly advertise their scheme. In February of that year the *Richmond Enquirer* published the "Sketch of A Plan for the Endowment and Establishment of a State University in Virginia." The concerns of Tucker and his confederates were placed squarely in the declaration of purpose: "To preserve a republican government in its full tone and vigour, and to prevent that degeneracy into which the best forms of government are too apt to fall, when not guarded equally by the vigilance of patriotism, and the lights of science."[15]

The plan proposed that the chancellor of the university be a man "learned in the law" and that, among his many duties, he preside over

---

14. Tazewell to Tucker, Dec. 24, 1804, ibid. See also the letter of Hening to Tucker, Jan. 8, 1805, ibid., on the mounting opposition to Junto control and its instructions, through the legislature, to the state treasurer about how to cast his vote for the directors of the Bank of Virginia. Public disfavor of the legislature's actions caused bank stocks to fall; many Virginians already worried about how the Junto's "bank would be made an engine of state." The state treasurer cast one vote for the fourteen directors, but his vote was equal to the largest number of votes cast by other shareholders. See Starnes, *Branch Banking*, pp. 30, 37–39.

15. *Richmond Enquirer*, Feb. 1, 1805.

the courts of the university in all matters of fact tried by a jury "as if the same were a county court." The continuing distrust felt by the legal reformers for the county magistracy was evident in Article 5, which erected university courts on the grounds of the institution over which the county bench would have no jurisdiction. Tucker suspected that many republicans would not be favorably disposed to what could be construed as the lawyers' elitist scheme. He referred to the revisal of the laws of 1776–79 and reminded those who asked how Virginians were to be prepared for a university course that Jefferson, Wythe, and Pendleton had advanced a perfectly sound scheme for general education. The county courts had not seen fit to allow that plan to proceed, but Tucker was convinced that, now more than ever, the idea was worthy of implementation.[16]

Even more discouraging to the legal reformers who perceived education as a key in establishing republican law and society was their knowledge that an education bill had finally passed in 1796. The duty to erect county schools, however, lay with the unreformed county courts, and predictably, nothing had been done. Even more depressing, not a single petition from county residents had been presented to their justices requesting that the plan be implemented.[17]

Some, like Jefferson himself, continued to think that the real threat to republican legal culture in Virginia lay in the perpetuation of family oligarchies on the county benches. John Taylor and Jefferson exchanged letters in 1816 on the nature of constitutional government, and in the course of the correspondence, Jefferson lashed out at "the vicious constitution of our county court . . . self-appointed, self-contained, holding their authorities for life, and with an impossibility of breaking in on the perpetual succession of any faction once possessed of the bench. They are in truth, the executive, the judiciary, and the military of their respective counties, and the sum of the counties makes the state."[18] Jefferson here summarized the old Country fears about corruption and the threat to virtue—military power, the corruption of justice by patronage and political favor, and the Federalist penchant for promoting banks and mercantile schemes. Together, they were the perfect embodiment of corrupt, Court policy. Yet, on this point, Jefferson was out of touch with contemporary opinion in Virginia. Taylor doubted that the county courts were really the threat to republicanism that Jefferson thought they were. Jefferson admitted that his concern sprang from personal knowledge of a

16. Ibid.
17. Maddox, "Free School Idea in Virginia," pp. 12–16.
18. Jefferson to Taylor, May 28, 1816, *Writings of Thomas Jefferson* (Ford, ed.), 11: 527–33.

nearby western county with a court "of 30 members of whom 20 are federalists (every third man of the sect).... No authority on earth... can break up this junto."[19]

Contemporary opinion in Virginia between 1800 and 1810 identified the dangers to republican virtue and law in the state. Scholars can now show what Virginians at the time sensed: in both Virginia and Kentucky in the state assemblies and in the Congress, the number of justices of the peace who were elected to office steadily declined and the number of lawyers rose. Public perception of the threats posed to a republican society fixed not on the old county court but rather on the rising elite of lawyers and judges. Tucker's proposals for establishing a university and the fracas that arose over the legislature's directing the state treasurer to vote for certain directors of the Bank of Virginia aroused many republicans—including Taylor of Caroline—to identify the causes of republican malaise. To Monroe he wrote, "The Virginia Assembly have wanted their wonted unanimity. Their divisions are yet trivial, and arise from the interest from banking—a system, spreading and forming a monied party."[20]

Taylor's own views on law he never made quite clear. In most respects, he favored laws that sprang naturally from the lived experience of the people, who would be virtuous because of their republican institutions. Taylor never worked out the difficulties involved in that scenario, but other Virginians had to, because the public's opinion of lawyers threatened to repudiate the credibility of the rhetoric that lawyers had invoked as early as 1745 when COMMON SENSE put lawyers forward as the friends of virtue—an image repeated in the *Virginia Almanac*'s "Lawyer's Prayer" of 1790.[21]

19. Jefferson to Taylor, July 21, 1816, ibid., 12:25–27.
20. Taylor to Monroe, Feb. 27, 1806, Branch, *Branch Historical Papers*, 1:291. See the Federalist accusation against the Junto in the *Norfolk Gazette and Public Ledger*, Nov. 16, 1804; on Taylor's gradual alienation from the moderate republican group, see Mudge, *Social Philosophy of John Taylor*; Simms, *Life of John Taylor*. On the decline of local institutions and justices of the peace, see D. B. Smith, "Changing Patterns of Local Leadership," pp. 20–25; Kuroda, "County Court System of Virginia"; D. P. Jordan, "Virginia Congressmen, 1801–1825"; Upton, "Road to Power." On the split between moderates and radicals in Kentucky over the role of the legal profession, see Ellis, *Jeffersonian Crisis*, pp. 123–70; Ireland, *County Courts in Antebellum Kentucky* and "Place of the Justice of the Peace." The proportion of justices in the legislature declined from 50 percent to less than 15 percent by 1850. See also Watlington, *Partisan Spirit*, pp. 79–84.
21. The definition of virtue in American culture after 1800 needs thorough investigation. The moral component of the term is clearly still alive, but takes on rather strange new guises. One of the more bizarre is the identification of republican virtue with the women of the republic, a notion articulated by Wirt in *Old Bachelor*, pp. 31–32, 59–60. On this issue, see Kerber, "Daughters of Columbia."

Between 1803 and 1814 many lawyers in Virginia took to the press, trying in every way possible to defend the need for an elite body of lawyers and judges to protect the people from ignorant and corrupt pettifoggers. Part of their task was to convince Virginians that the presence of a legal aristocracy was not inconsistent with a republican society. Their awkward, tortured rhetoric indicates just how aware the republican moderates were of the potency of the more radical brand of Country thought that had always regarded lawyers as a plague and a threat to virtue.

In the long run the reputation of lawyers was securely placed in the Country tradition by the mythologized image of Patrick Henry conjured up by the lawyer William Wirt. Wirt's *Life and Character of Patrick Henry* (1817) defended the rise of "new men" in Virginia's republican society. That use by the attorney general of the United States of populist arguments against elitism reveals just how nervous republican moderates were when confronted with the feistier aspects of the Country tradition. Far more so than Max Bloomfield concedes, the solution that Wirt arrived at eventually in his biography was the result of an intense struggle between 1803 and 1810 to rescue legal culture in Virginia in such a way as to preserve the importance of the elite judicial system that Tucker, Tazewell, and Wirt himself valued so highly.[22]

In his 1803 effort, *The British Spy*, Wirt first tried out the notion that lawyers were good republicans because they were not tied to the old oligarchic past but were, in fact, rising "new men." That idea did not convince many people in 1803. Between the first articulation of that idea and the appearance of the *Life and Character of Patrick Henry* in 1817, Wirt was joined by Tucker, Dabney and Frank Carr (all lawyers), and several other gentlemen in a series of essays entitled *The Old Bachelor*. Written between 1810 and 1813 those essays reveal the anxiety of the authors over the proliferation of "new men" in the courts of Virginia, explicitly denounce avarice, ambition, and greed among lawyers as the hallmarks of the new, untutored pettifoggers, and plead for a resolute defense of legal training and the concept of law as a science.

The tone of the essays that deal with the law in *The Old Bachelor* series is somewhat curious, until one considers them alongside a pamphlet published in Richmond in 1811 by Henry Banks entitled *Propositions Designed to Simplify and Expedite the Administration of Justice*. Banks probably wrote the piece in response to the creation in 1809 of fourteen superior courts, which replaced the old district court system. Fearful that the superior courts were concentrating more and more power

22. Bloomfield, *American Lawyers*, pp. 173–76, on the fictionalized account of Henry's life by Wirt.

in the hands of the judiciary and bar headquartered in Richmond, Banks demanded a return to a simpler past.[23]

At the same time that he leveled his guns against the legal elite of the state, Banks took aim as well at the Bank of Virginia, that arm of the Richmond Junto that had caused so much uproar in 1805 when Tucker, Tazewell, and Hening had sought to enlist its economic power in their attempt to found a republican university. The bank's unpopularity was forgotten temporarily in the general alarm and malaise caused by President Jefferson's embargo. But in early 1809 the hated embargo was lifted, and the controversies surrounding the rise of trade, the corruption that accompanied avarice, and the relationship of lawyers to merchants and banks were again topics of concern in Virginia. Banks published his *Observations Designed to shew the Propriety of establishing an Independent System of Banking* in January 1811. The belligerent author did not scruple to label the bank "the existing tyrannical monopoly," which its directors "wielded with partiality and terror." The consolidation of power and influence and the legislature's protection of the bank were anathema to the writer. The purpose of divesting the bank of so much power was clear—"political rights, moral justice, private interest and general expediency all unite" to point out the dangers to the state of such an institution. The measures Banks proposed would ensure that rampant speculation and avarice could be controlled by the establishment of rival, free banks, all controlled by a more impartial legislature. "My object," Banks concluded, "is to promote the general welfare of society, to assist Agriculture, Manufactures, Commerce, Arts and Science—to counteract the tyrannical influence of the Bank of Virginia."[24] Most people knew that the largest investors, stockholders, and directors of the bank were closely connected to the Ritchie-Brockenbrough-Roane coalition in the capital. Banks recognized the connection between eminent judges, lawyers, and the bank and made sure the public realized what was at stake.

In the *Propositions* about the judicial system, Banks advocated a return to simpler, locally administered justice. He proposed that jury trials

---

23. Banks, a wealthy Greenbriar merchant and practicing attorney, is a classic example of an eloquent, if odd, "official Country" spokesman using the rhetoric of the Country for his own ends. Banks tried for several years between 1789 and 1794 to collect monies owed him and the firm of Hunter, Banks, and Company, the tobacco merchants who outfitted a small flotilla for Virginia. The ships were all lost, and the partners demanded restitution for damages. See VCSP, 4:336–37, 371, 590, 638; ibid., 5:19–22, 161, 240, 306–310. Banks's pamphlet *Propositions* appeared in early 1811.

24. *Observations*, pp. 4, 24–25. Wirt's Old Bachelor response appeared in the *Enquirer*, starting February 1811.

be restored to a place of eminence and that the county courts' terms of sitting be greatly lengthened, "putting that important and truly republican system upon a more useful footing." Banks argued that simpler language and procedure ought to be instituted in the local courts to "check or overturn the vast unfathomable abyss of chicanery and iniquity, which has heretofore tended to promote the ruin of individuals; to degrade the general character of the country; to demoralize society, to give vice the pre-eminence over virtue, and to sew the fruitful seeds of dissention and distrust among all descriptions of people." He conceded that chancery causes were the most difficult and that local justices could hardly be expected to handle the complicated procedures of equity jurisdiction.

Furthermore, the author mused on the apparent paradox of Virginia's court dockets, which revealed "such a spirit of contention and litigation" but whose people generally exhibited "such general and honorable proof of moral and social habits and order." Warming to his subject, he identified the causes of Virginia's moral and social decline. The outside observer, he wrote, could only believe, on viewing this state of affairs, "that the social tie is on the eve of dissolution, and that the people are held together by a common necessity—or by the fear of jails."[25] The villains, of course, were lawyers and the banking monopoly. Want of a decent circulating medium, Banks argued, drove many to ruin, since the system of credit and barter made debts unsure. Given the avarice of attorneys, suits multiplied. The administration of estates by swarms of lawyers was equally ruinous and another example of the perfidy of attorneys. But Banks's stunning blow, by which he linked ruinous pettifoggers to the bank in Richmond *and* Virginia's legal elite, came when he concluded that his proposals would

> strip the Superior Courts of that inordinate and overwhelming power which seems to threaten a subversion of the true principles of republican government, and will induce thousands of young men, of the best talents to devote themselves to other pursuits than to rear their fortunes and fame upon the follies, vices and misfortunes of their fellow citizens!!
>
> Under the existing order of things, a young man can perceive no road open to honorable ambition, except in the profession of the law. It cannot therefore afford surprise, that none, or very few but of that profession, attain high stations in political power or popular favor.

25. *Propositions*, pp. 4, 8.

> This is certainly a public misfortune—because it must be evident, that the success of a lawyer depends upon the misfortunes of society.[26]

Here, at last, the gauntlet was thrown down, and the careful papering-over of the potential rift within the Country tradition between moderates and radicals torn open. The so-called "aristocracy of talent," in Banks's view, looked like nothing so much as an excuse for a few wealthy bankers, merchants, judges, and lawyers to aggrandize their own interests at the expense of other Virginians, all the while mouthing pious platitudes about republican virtue. Wirt, Tucker, the Carrs, and other eminent members of the bench and bar had no choice but to join issue; their forum was the Republican Thomas Ritchie's Junto press organ the *Richmond Enquirer*. Between late 1810 and 1813, Wirt and his friends judiciously and sympathetically admitted the faults of untrained lawyers and vigorously argued the absolute necessity of the very best training under an elite circle of judges and lawyers who would guarantee the republican quality of legal culture in Virginia. Wirt had briefly toyed with the romantic notion that simple, unprepossessing men could become eminent lawyers, since he himself had had little formal training. But Wirt's recollection of his fledgling legal practice was one which came down decidedly in favor of expertise in 1810, a position that he had described only tentatively in 1803 in his *British Spy*.

When one recalls the political factionalism in Virginia that later split various moderate republicans into national and sectional parties in the 1820s, it is easy to forget that those political squabbles were luxuries that could not be indulged in 1800. The domestic concerns of Virginians in the first decade of the nineteenth century revolved about the question of republican culture. No amount of interest in international affairs or even in the Republican party's control of national politics could equal the concern over Virginia's cultural attributes.

Wirt had sensed this and directed his third letter in the *British Spy* series to the subject of republican oratory as exhibited in the person of Patrick Henry, whose simple, rustic nature he would imaginatively manufacture fourteen years later. Henry was endowed with that quality Virginians admired—he was "an orator of nature.... His general appearance and manners were those of a plain farmer or planter of the back country." Wirt's *British Spy* concluded that oratory in defense of republican institutions ought to guarantee the speaker a place in American public life. That was about as far as Wirt was prepared to go in defending rustic simplicity in lawyers. His fourth letter, in which he described John

26. Ibid., p. 13.

Marshall, the chief justice (referred to only as the ***** *******), dismissed the accusations of Marshall's opponents that "he is a mere lawyer; that his mind has been so long trammelled by judicial precedent, so long habituated to the quart and tierce of forensic digladiation . . . as to be unequal to the discussion of a great question of state."27

Wirt concluded that superior intellect, assiduous study, and practice had made Marshall the eminent jurist he was. Finally, in the eighth letter, Wirt described the legal profession in Virginia as "the road to honor" and that profession where "persons of exalted intellect" were naturally to be found. Virginia boasted one of the most eminent bars in the United States, reported the Spy, "graced by the most shining geniuses on the continent." The only difficulty lay in the "melancholy groupe of young men who hang on the rear of the bar, like Goethe's sable clouds in the western horizon." Wirt pointedly employed that literary reference because uneducated Virginians from "the western horizon" and the more settled counties were to be the bane of the attorneys who argued for a select, elite bench and bar in republican Virginia.28

Wirt's description of the bar in the eighth letter turned to the subject of oratory and the abilities of lawyers not only to engage in broad, liberal study but to express the results of their labors in convincing argument. The best lawyers were those who were able to adopt a "behavior which steers between a low-spirited, cringing sycophancy and ostentatious condescension on the one hand, and a haughty self-importance and supercilious contempt of ones fellow creatures on the other." Virginia lawyers were wont to recoil so much from "the hollow, ceremonious professions and hypocritical grimace of courts," the Spy concluded, that their plain opinions perhaps did not sufficiently impress the hearer. Of course, as Wirt plainly guessed, his readers applauded such republican simplicity. But that simplicity was not such as could be obtained at the expense of legal learning, and Wirt never suggested such a notion in the *British Spy*.29

In late 1810, when Wirt began publishing the "Old Bachelor" letters in the *Richmond Enquirer*, he began the series with a description of his own legal career that left no doubt as to his opinion of the less-qualified

---

27. Wirt, *British Spy*, pp. 12, 22, reprinted from the *Virginia Argus*, where they appeared August and September 1802.

28. Ibid., pp. 28–29.

29. Bloomfield, *American Lawyers*, pp. 173 ff., reads the *British Spy* letters as a defense of homegrown simplicity; in fact, however, the section on the bar clearly indicates Wirt's contempt for ill-trained lawyers not versed in liberal learning and lacking a sense of their elite calling. Wirt's censures against the Court but in favor of oratory are in *British Spy*, pp. 30, 31.

members of the bar. To a certain degree, Wirt was echoing the complaints that Virginia's ablest lawyers had been making since the 1740s. In 1748, General Court lawyers had managed to bar county attorneys from practicing in Williamsburg; Jefferson had worried about the "swarms" of untutored lawyers in the 1780s; Tucker's *Blackstone's Commentaries* was intended to aid the cause of education; a system of republican instruction from county to university level had been a concern from 1776 to 1810. Wirt's own legal education was modest but good—he was apprenticed to an able lawyer in Maryland before beginning county practice in Culpeper County, Virginia. Recalling that incident, Wirt wrote, "Dissatisfied with the jejune course commonly pursued, and aspiring to something beyond mediocrity, I took the science from its basis, the law of nature; and raised upon it an unusual and most extensive superstructure of national and civil, as well as municipal law." Unfortunately, as Wirt discovered, when he came to the county bar, "I found that I was like a seventy-four-gun ship aground in a creek; while every pettifogger, with his canoe and paddle was able to glide around and get ahead of me." Deftly employing the literary device of preterition, Wirt related that he retired from practice "I will not say, in disgust" and described the "littleness, chicanery and sophistry" of a profession that he perceived as "an Augean stall which required cleansing," in need of "a fundamental reformation" to establish it in "all its appropriate dignity and attraction."[30]

Wirt and his associates had to respond to Banks's assertions that simpler law and a curtailing of the superior courts' powers would restore republican simplicity. In subsequent letters the Old Bachelor refuted the notion that the corruption of the Court was endemic in educated men. "Courtiers are not, generally, the most enlightened men of their nation," wrote the Old Bachelor. "But if they were, no reflecting man would ascribe their vices to their knowledge." Science and literature were the hallmarks of virtue, he went on, and only effete Europeans would indulge the senseless debate about whether learning increases the virtue of a nation. Returning to his notion of lawyers engaged in practical, oratorical defenses of republicanism, he explained, "I speak . . . of positive, active, discriminating, elective virtue; and not of a mere negative exemption from vice arising from climate and constitution, from relaxation, torpor, imbecility and inanity."[31]

Did Banks and the defenders of rural simplicity, the Old Bachelor

---

30. Wirt, *Old Bachelor*, p. 3.

31. Ibid., pp. 57, 59. Compare this with Jefferson's definition of vitue as *"utility to man,"* citing Lord Kames's *Principles of Natural Religion*, in Koch, *American Enlightenment*, p. 360.

asked, advocate ignorance or a return to the dominance of the courts by gentlemen of eminent family background? Warning of his experience with that breed of men, he told of a neighbor, "Mr. Martin," who was one of those gentlemen brought up in a life of ease and who engaged in no "pursuit of honest industry." Instead, "he learned to dress, to dance, to drink, to smoke, to swear, to game; contracted a violent passion for the very rational, elegant and humane pleasures of the turf and the cockpit, and was long distinguished for the best horses and game-cocks in the country." Was this what the advocates of rustic simplicity advocated? Citing the example of another friend who found Richmond a friendly and respectable town, the Old Bachelor admonished his readers that "*civility* & *politeness* were derived from words signifying towns." Law, the Old Bachelor firmly concluded, afforded the mind "many noble subjects of contemplation ... I speak of it in its proper and liberal, not confined and technical sense. If it has suffered in public estimation, it is not to be attributed to any cause inherent in the science itself, but to other extrinsic circumstances."[32]

Wirt had to concede that the critics of the legal profession had a point when they pointed to ignorant, avaricious, and designing attorneys in republican Virginia. The Old Bachelor essay proposed a system of public education as a remedy in the counties, echoing Jefferson's old ambition, which would finally begin to see fruition in Richmond when Thomas Ritchie pushed for the adoption of a Lancastrian system of education in the commonwealth. Wirt admitted that there were unscrupulous men, like the fictitious Lancelot Surrebutter. Not a good lawyer, he was "eminent in his profession in other respects," but a man "singularly skilled in that branch of legal learning which treats of the doctrines of fraud and usury." Under such a man innocent young Virginians like Wirt's fictitious "Henry Morton" failed "to ascend to the higher regions of the profession," and instead employed "their industry in its dirt." By cold, avaricious means and with a ruthless disregard for morality and virtue, the Old Bachelor continued, Morton degraded himself throughout a lifetime of chicanery and sly practices. Finally, when the Old Bachelor met Morton again, he "gazed upon him with amazement and with the most painful regret. Gone was the animated step that once seemed to tread on air.... On the contrary, he moved like a pestilence, and desolation was around his path, Virtue retired from the blasting spectacle, and poverty shrunk back with intuitive terror ... when they saw the merciless wolf upon his walk."[33]

32. Wirt, *Old Bachelor*, p. 102.
33. Ibid., p. 72. On the drive for public education by Junto members, see Griffin, "Thomas Ritchie and the Founding of the Richmond Lancastrian School." Wirt, *Old Batchelor*, pp. 80–81.

What could be done to eliminate such scenes in the profession of law? Shrewdly playing on the distaste with which many Virginians observed the bombast and self-seeking of politics, the Old Bachelor censured—not the lawyers—but a general lust and intrigue for office, which he had once hoped "was a remnant merely of the regal darkness . . . and which would gradually retreat and disappear as the day spring of liberty advanced. But as soon as I observed the decline of public virtue and intellectual power, which peace brought with it, I saw at once, that the hope which I had cherished on this head was fond and illusive."[34]

Again, the key theme for Wirt and his associates was the coupling of "public virtue and intellectual power." That "aristocracy of talent" in the legal profession and other walks of life was to guarantee the perpetuation of the republican experiment. In a burst of enthusiasm for legal learning that must have made Jefferson blanch, Wirt found paise even for Lord Mansfield, the Tory chief justice, whom Jefferson despised along with Blackstone and all other Court lawyers and judges. Admitting that "Lord Mansfield is no favorite with my countrymen," Wirt agreed as well that he may have been the tool of the Court, as republicans thought. But, he added, "I have lived long enough to know that it is possible, too, he may have received [that reputation] without deserving it." In the Wilkes outlawry trial, Wirt pointed out, Mansfield's legal learning had been eminently displayed on the side of fairness. Above all, Mansfield had declared that "I honor the king; and I respect the people. . . . I wish Popularity; But it is popularity which follows, not that which is run after. It is that popularity, which, sooner or later, never fails to do justice to the pursuit of *noble ends* by *noble means*!" Wirt exulted, "Let the vain and selfish hunter of popularity, the poor and low spirited intriguer for office, who calls himself a republican, read these sentiments of *a British Lord*, and blush."[35]

Actually, it might have been more appropriate for the contributors to the Old Bachelor essays to blush, for they had finessed, not answered, the criticisms of Banks. Moreover, their defense of an independent judiciary and their declarations in favor of a learned bench and bar who would defend republicanism simply did not convince many Virginians. The *Richmond Enquirer* was not the organ in which most critics chose to express

---

34. Wirt, *Old Bachelor*, pp. 84–85. Wirt attacked ambition for office on February 26 in the *Enquirer*, echoing Banks's criticism of the ulterior motives that inspired young Virginians to enter politics. Wirt's prescriptions were quite different from those proposed by Banks.

35. Ibid., pp. 86–87. This piece on Mansfield appeared February 26, 1811, in the *Enquirer*. On Jefferson's censures of Blackstone and the "honeyed Mansfieldism" of common law, see Waterman, "Thomas Jefferson and Blackstone's Commentaries," p. 459.

their discontent with the elite of Virginia, which looked suspiciously like a cabal of lawyers, merchants, judges, and bankers. Even so, the paper did publish a few controversial challenges to the establishment.

The district courts of 1787 had been replaced in 1809 by a new system of superior courts. Discussion in 1810 centered around a proposition to abolish the Superior Courts of Chancery and to replace those courts, which dated from 1802, with a simplified structure that combined chancery and law in one superior court. The actual proposition generated less debate than the fear in the minds of some men that the independence of the judiciary was being threatened. On January 24, 1811, a correspondent who signed himself "Wythe" pointed out that since the case of *Kamper* v. *Hawkins* the issue of whether courts were creatures of the legislature had been closed: that case had firmly established that they were not. On February 26, FRIEND OF THE PEOPLE responded, reviewing the complicated history of the *Kamper* case and the Judges' Remonstrance to the district courts erected in 1787. The only real reason for the remonstrance had come from Pendleton's suspicion that the new courts blended chancery and common law jurisdiction together in the persons of the judges who were to sit. If that blending could occur, said Pendleton, so could control of salaries, and judicial independence would be threatened. FRIEND OF THE PEOPLE pointed out that judges Tyler, Mercer, Henry, and Cary had said they would serve and leave the salary issue open—a proposition the *real* Wythe had urged on the entire court. But Wythe had been overruled, and when the next legislature met to set up the new court of appeals composed of five judges already sitting at law and in chancery in the other courts, the judges pointed out that one could not have two courts of appeal. Some judges went ahead and qualified under their new commissions, and that raised "much warmth and resentment . . . at a supposed dereliction of principle on the part of those who had accepted of the new office." The judges who had accepted the commissions could only sit in their new office, and a remonstrance was drawn up over the legislature's destruction of a constitutionally established court. That, said FRIEND OF THE PEOPLE, was all the fracas had amounted to. The legislature, being the voice of the people, still ought to have the final say in the structure and function of a republican judicial establishment in Virginia.[36]

Far to the west, in Jefferson County, the Charleston paper the *Farmer's Repository*, echoed some of those concerns over the unrepublican nature of a lawyer elite's control of courts and the legislature. In that town, on March 15, 1811, another partisan of the more radical Country tradition

---

36. *Richmond Enquirer*, Jan. 24, 1811, Feb. 26, 1811.

took to the press under the title ONE OF THE PEOPLE. In a recent bill which had passed the Assembly regarding militia duty an amendment had been added that continued the exemption of students at William and Mary from duty. The vote of Federalist Senator Lewis Wolfe was condemned as proof of "his partiality for the great and wealthy." Just how would Wolfe explain his vote? ONE OF THE PEOPLE knew: "Mr. Wolfe is a lawyer, versed in all the arts of sophistry and eloquence; and it may be, that he can assign substantial and unanswerable arguments in support of this vote." When Wolfe's friends tried to respond under the name ENEMY TO UNFAIR DEALING, the rebuttal of ONE OF THE PEOPLE revealed the depth of the animus directed by many Virginians against the legal culture of the commonwealth. "I am informed," ONE OF THE PEOPLE declared, "that seven or eight, out of the ten senators who voted against the repeal of the law, were practising lawyers; and it is more than probable, had enjoyed the sweets of this exemption, while they were at their several places of education. The inference, fellow citizens, you will draw for yourselves." Further inferences could be drawn, the writer pointed out, from the recent attempt made to raise judges' salaries. Furthermore, at the militia musters "these well born college bred gentlemen ... looking on as idle spectators" gloried in their aristocratic status.[37] ONE OF THE PEOPLE knew his Country tradition well. The duty to participate in militia service had always been one of the Country's sacred points, and exemption merely under the pretense of a "professional" occupation was no excuse in a republican society.

The censures of ONE OF THE PEOPLE obviously touched a nerve in Jefferson County, because on April 5, another writer, CANDIDUS, responded with a monitory to voters: "If you act with even common prudence your choice of legislators will light on men, who belong to your own classes, and whose interests of course are the same as yours—This cannot be said of either merchants, lawyers, or other professional men." There was the connection, again, which the Country had spotted in England in the seventeenth century, which Virginians before the Revolution had seen as the county bar expanded, and which all the protestations of republican lawyers about the need for an independent and educated legal establishment had clearly failed to answer. Jefferson's rhetoric in defense of the agrarian simplicity of Virginia had clearly gone awry, and he and members of the Richmond Junto were powerless to control the animosity of ordinary planters and farmers. The reason, of course, was simple: the Country rhetoric of the past had been replete with attacks on lawyers, merchants, the clergy, and anyone else who interfered with the

37. *Farmer's Repository*, Mar. 15, 1811.

natural place of independent men in society. Now, that strain of the Country was again haunting the republican lawyers of Virginia.[38]

On April 12, 1811, CANDIDUS laid out, step by step, the nature of a republican society. Agriculturalists and mechanics, he said, were the only productive members of a truly republican social order. Lawyers existed only to multiply laws and to advance their interests, "that laws be unnecessarily written; that controversies about property abound; that crimes and frauds be perpetrated!" The decline of Virginia was obvious to CANDIDUS, and it was the fault of the legislature, the elected voice of the people. The legislators of Virginia, of course, were lawyers. "The bar," CANDIDUS argued, "generates habits by no means auspicious to the deliberations of the senate. The species of employment in which the minds of judges and lawyers are engaged in expounding or ascertaining the meaning of laws already made, and in applying them to particular cases, is very different indeed from that which ought to occupy the mind of a legislator." Where Wirt defended oratory in lawyers, CANDIDUS attacked it, saying that legislators should be thinkers, not orators. "Nothing," he concluded, "can be more pernicious in a house of legislators than the garrulity of attornies. It seems only to disturb and perplex the really thoughtful man. It answers no purpose but that of consuming time, and wasting public money."[39]

There is no satisfactory way to judge the depth or gauge the pervasiveness of antilawyer sentiment among the vast majority of Virginians who did not write or leave documented evidence of their feelings about law in Virginia. But from the fragmentary evidence that has survived it appears certain that two very different interpretations of the meaning of legal culture in Virginia had emerged by 1810. That which was represented by the Republican party establishment in Richmond and which enjoyed the support of Jefferson clearly regarded the institutionalization of republican (Country) ideology under the direction of an aristocracy of legal talent to be the way of the future. Jefferson and many of his allies continued to believe that localism, ignorance, and the continued domination of the county courts by nonelected justices were the root causes of perceived threats to republicanism. On the other hand, a poorly organized, fragmented, and not highly articulate strain of radical Country thought persisted in political figures like Taylor of Caroline and Randolph of Roanoke and writers like Banks, CANDIDUS, and ONE OF THE PEOPLE. These men were not happy with the pseudoaristocratic pretensions of the Richmond establishment.

38. Ibid., Apr. 5, 1811.
39. Ibid., April 12, 1811.

In many respects not much had changed since the old days of the Court-Country battle, when county justices resented Williamsburg lawyers and General Court orders that interfered with the running of county life. Ostensibly, the Revolution had removed the Court from Virginia life, at least in political terms. No one in Virginia could genuinely be said to be of the Court persuasion. Nor could very many Virginians be labeled "Walpolian Whig," a term that best applied to Hamilton. But for some Virginians the success of republican lawyers in erecting a more efficient state court system was too high a price to pay for the bettering of decisions that were almost impossible to get from the county courts after 1783.

The republican lawyers of Virginia clearly believed that a certain deference to their talents had to be forthcoming and that there was nothing inconsistent with a republican society's habit of deference to superior intellect. As Pocock has indicated, that notion came very close to defining what "virtue" was all about. Virtue may not have *been* deference, but it was very closely allied to it. George Mason had tried to legislate it in 1780 and had failed. The education scheme of Jefferson, Tucker, and Tazewell and the belatedly successful one of Ritchie were both geared to promote the success of that notion. But the more typical partisans of Country thinking were never really convinced.[40]

Jefferson once said that he took his understanding of what history was from an aphorism that "history is philosophy teaching by examples." Jefferson's source for that phrase was Henry St. John, Viscount Bolingbroke.[41] The most eloquent exponent of the Country thought of the eighteenth century, he was a far greater Tory than Blackstone or Mansfield. Probably only Bolingbroke would really have gone along with a purely deferential society in which no favor was paid to "progress," internal improvements, legal learning, banks, or universities. Jefferson and his allies were not, in any existential way, pure Bolingbrokeians. Their moderate endorsement of modernity actually triumphed in Virginia, and the commonwealth joined with other states by the 1820s in promoting canals, railroads, schools, and, of course, the University of Virginia.

40. The terms "radical" or "conservative" can be used almost interchangeably for the antilawyer, antibanking, and, in most cases, anti-Federalist localists of Virginia. However one wishes to characterize them, they represent a direct link to the "real Country," as opposed to the "official Country," to use the distinctions advanced by Morrill. See his *Revolt of the Provinces*.

41. Bolingbroke, in his *On the Study and Use of History*, correctly attributes this idea to Dionysius of Halicarnassus, who quotes Thucydides as appearing to say that "the contact with manners then is education . . . when he says that history is philosophy learned from examples" (*Ars Rhetorica*, 11:2, in *Bartlett's Familiar Quotations*, p. 304 [fn. 3]).

At the university, Jefferson engaged the designated professor of law, Francis Walker Gilmer, in discussions about the purity of a republican legal culture. Gilmer, who accepted and then resigned the position because of ill health before his death in 1825, had studied law with Wirt, his brother-in-law, and exemplified the intellectual attributes that clearly set him and his fellow lawyers apart from the rustic simplicity that the mythmakers of Virginia agrarianism would later construct as their collective and definitive past. To his brother George, Gilmer wrote in 1816, "The prospect of making a fortune here by my profession is just as is every where else. Uncommon talents and asiduous industry cannot fail in the course of time to procure honor & wealth to their possessor." Reflecting the predilection of his mentor for oratory, he wrote to his nephew Thomas Walker Gilmer that "in the ancient Republics war & eloquence were the two departments which conferred the most glorious & lasting distinction." When young Thomas's tutor died, his uncle urged him, "Go to Cambridge or West Point. I should prefer the first. . . . Living at home or going to any village college is mere trifling. Take a great theatre, & urge your Father and Grd. Father to co-operate—500 $ now will be worth 5000 $ to you ten years hence."[42]

The pursuit of fame and distinction through law and eloquence became a hallmark of the Virginia jurists of the early nineteenth century, as Richard Beale Davis has demonstrated. Yet the legal profession of the Old Dominion never lost sight of the more radical critique of itself posed by the Country tradition. In many respects one could say that Virginia experienced very little in the way of a profound social revolution between 1776 and 1810, but necessarily had to contend with an intellectual and cultural upheaval that was nearly as unsettling.

The public villains of Virginia politics continued to be Federalists, especially those of the secessionist New England variety by 1810, and foreign depradations on the republic, the issue that drew the nation into war in 1812. But beneath the broad oratory and the emergence of the legal profession, considerable division within the Country tradition persisted. As Edmund Randolph wryly observed about the hodgepodge of factions that flocked to Jeffersonian republicanism in Virginia, "Parties in reli-

---

42. On Gilmer, see Davis, *Francis Walker Gilmer*, pp. 52–55, 71–72, on liberal learning as the key to greatness in the law and praise for Blackstone and Mansfield as the "architects" of the law. Gilmer to George Gilmer, Feb. 18, 1816, *Tyler's Quarterly Historical and Genealogical Magazine* 6 (1924): 17; letter to Walker Gilmer, April 8, 1817, ibid., p. 240; October 28, 1818, ibid., p. 242. Gilmer is apparently citing Edward Gibbon: "Arms, eloquence, and the study of the civil law, promoted a citizen to the honours of the Roman state; and the three professions were sometimes more conspicuous by their union in the same character" (*Decline and Fall*, 4:186).

gion and politics rarely scan with nicety the peculiar private opinions of their adherents."[43]

In many respects the legal culture of Virginia was still in a process of anglicization. The procedures, education, and centralized control of law dated from before the Revolution and continued beyond that event. In many ways, too, the lawyers and judges of Virginia had become an elite, an aristocracy of talent which grew out of and replaced the aristocracy of the Byrds, Carters, Ludwells, Nelsons, and Pages of the prerevolutionary era. Virginia's republican lawyers felt at home with the rhetoric of the Country tradition and believed themselves to be defenders of the virtue of the republican experiment. But their very success brought about renewed criticism of lawyers in Virginia. Theirs was the classic dilemma of the Country—how to take power without losing the very substance of what the Country had always been about.

Outside observers confirmed what some Virginians suspected by 1810: the state was changing into a modern society, run by merchants, bankers, judges, and lawyers. When J. K. Paulding published his *Letters from the South: Written during an Excursion in the Summer of 1816*, he affirmed those suspicions. Virginia used to be noted for its rural simplicity and its dedication to republican virtue, Paulding reported. But by 1816 the commonwealth had been "debauched with the sordid money-making spirit." The spectacle of "men selling their lands to become merchants and manufacturers, smitten by the imposing appearance of wealth and competency, exhibited by the dependants of banks," Paulding found repellent. Another aspect of the Country tradition had been violated if formerly virtuous, independent men had become "the dependants of banks." He acidly concluded that a statue ought to be erected as a testimony to their vulgarity—the statue of "Hermathena." "This statue," he explained, "represented Mercury, the god of thieves, lawyers, and merchants, and Minerva in the same body; alluding to the custom on Change, of making wealth and trickery synonymous with wisdom."[44]

Clearly, Paulding was no more convinced than were many Virginians that lawyers and a more modern judicial system could be easily reconciled with the Country traditions of the past. Part of the burden that fell on republican lawyers had been to argue that more professional law would actually help the moral tenor of society by expediting debt causes and securing predictable, rational, scientific procedures to deal with the chaotic disorder of the 1780s. They had succeeded in establishing a streamlined court system, and the luster of the superior court bench and

---

43. Randolph, *History of Virginia*, p. 183.
44. 2:126–28.

bar had attracted large numbers of young Virginians to seek their fortunes in the practice of law. But the lawyers had not quite succeeded in convincing Virginia farmers and planters that the older, moral vision of law rooted in concepts of natural justice had survived the rise of the legal profession.

One wonders as well how many ordinary practicing attorneys really cared. For a Wythe, a Jefferson, a Wirt, or a Tucker liberal learning and dedication to moral values were important parts of the legal mind. But the complaints of ordinary Virginians expressed in the newspapers and discovered by lawyers seeking election seem to suggest that the typical attorney cared very little about the moral bases of law.

Wirt claimed that he had founded his knowledge of law on the firmest base—that of natural law (although he never clearly explained what he meant by that). But the ordinary attorney could have found more in common with Edward Barradall, who had articulated the modern understanding of law as early as 1735. In the case of *Waddill* v. *Chamberlayne,* Barradall had scorned the old notions of law grounded in morality. "The Laws of Society and Civil Government are not founded upon the strict rules of natural Justice. Public Convenience oft requires they sho'd be dispensed with.... To make specious Harangues concerning the Morality or Immorality of an Action that is to be determined by the Laws of a particular Society is arguing neither like a Lawyer or a Politician."[45]

By 1810 many Virginians would have agreed—and added that lawyers who thought like politicians made very odd republicans. Here was another familiar dilemma—how to keep alive the private virtue of a people so that a republican social order could exist. Jefferson and his republicans fell back on the need for superior talent, education, and legal learning—a classical solution that demanded public virtue and deference to the aristocracy of talent. But the idealism of the judicial and philosophical elite of Virginia really had no answer to the charges leveled by their critics that pettifogging lawyers were bent more on avaricious aggrandizement of their own interests than on practicing law in a republican order. The republican lawyers could only reply that the solution lay in restricting practice to an elite; rout the pettifoggers by demanding higher standards at the bar. Yet in reality this argument was hardly any different from that which General Court lawyers had used in 1748 when they banished county lawyers from the bar in Williamsburg. What had such a "professional" and elitist argument to do with republicanism?

---

45. Jefferson includes *Anderson qui tam* v. *Winston,* Barradall's defense of charging interest, in his *Virginia Reports,* pp. 24–30. Barradall's statement is cited from *Waddill v. Chamberlayne,* Barton, ed., *Virginia Colonial Decisions,* 2:B 49.

In 1831 the French observer of American mores Alexis de Tocqueville wrote that the check on the excesses of American democracy would come from the aristocracy of talent that he believed existed in the American bar. Tocqueville had at least gotten the tradition straight—the lawyers were to be members of the Court once again. Virginia republican lawyers could never quite admit that to themselves, because to do so would have excommunicated them from the Country orthodoxy of Virginia's past. It had been possible during the colonial period for reformers to put the blame for corruption either on the county oligarchies or on the corrupt monarchism implicit in the dual role of the governor and councillors as General Court judges. But after 1776 those excuses were no longer valid. To be sure, Jefferson continued to lament the unreformed nature of the county courts. But by the 1780s those ancient institutions were mere semblances of their former selves. District courts, appellate structures, and the alliance of a professional bench and bar with the banking, mercantile elite of Virginia altered the terms of the debate, permanently.

Virginians perhaps did not know it, but Tocqueville had stolen his prescription which made lawyers the aristoi of America. The man who first formulated that idea called himself a republican, but was vilified by Virginians as the worst kind of Federalist—Joseph Story of Massachusetts. In drawing upon Story's *Commentaries on the Constitution*, Tocqueville permanently oriented the American bar's self-understanding toward the New Englander's outright bias in favor of legal aristocracy.

What Virginia jurisprudence would have offered that was fundamentally different from this is hard to say. In the political arena, of course, Spencer Roane, William Brockenbrough, and other Virginia judges condemned the nationalist implications behind John Marshall's decisions. The Virginia republicans had clearly hoped to keep internal improvements, banking, and the legal elite the preserve of the state, not the federal government. But such political considerations, though important for constitutional law, did not differ that much in their implications for legal culture in the broadest sense.

In both Massachusetts and Virginia the triumph of the legal profession was stunning. Story was never really threatened by Robert Rantoul or the proponents of codification. In Virginia the radicals never even found an effective voice. The reason, of course, was that the Jeffersonian aristocracy of talent would never admit that it was dangerously close to becoming an aristocracy in fact. Criticism was deflected toward federalism, and sectional loyalty, even as early as 1810, began to shape opinion, redirect suspicions, and set the stage for the tragedies of 1861–65.[46]

---

46. I am indebted to R. Kent Newmeyer of the University of Connecticut for pointing

The criticisms leveled against lawyers after 1810 were dispirited and ineffective in Virginia. Despite the potentially radical heritage of Country thought Virginia merely substituted for an aristocracy of family, wealth, and deference to acknowledged rank an aristocracy of legal expertise, an expertise which dominated politics while it acquired wealth and preached deference to republican rank. In 1832, Kennedy's *Swallow Barn* romanticized the squirearchy of Virginia, noting that "the solitary elevation of a country gentleman . . . begets some magnificent notions." Long-winded and "impatient of contradiction," the squire "becomes as infallible as the Pope. There is nothing more conclusive than a rich man's logic any where, but in the country, amongst his dependents, it flows with the smooth and unresisted course of a full stream irrigating a meadow, and depositing its mud in fertilizing luxuriance."[47]

Yet the hero of *Swallow Barn* was Philly Wart, the lawyer, not the country squire, Frank Meriwether. Kennedy was being faithful to contemporary reality in this characterization. The Country tradition was largely a myth in Virginia—not false, but beyond discussion, in the same way that Virginians could talk reassuringly about their past without confronting the enormous changes in legal culture that had swept over the Old Dominion. The changes made were in favor of a professional, liberal society. Jefferson was no radical. His attacks on the county courts had simply been in favor of judges who were lawyers. He was skeptical of the possibilities of a legal system in which laymen would continue to have a say in the proceedings. Jefferson's revolution in Virginia had in fact confirmed and strengthened the already existing process of anglicization that was moving Virginia toward a British system of judge-made common law directed by a profession of lawyers.

Such a system of law naturally promoted the interests of an elite profession of lawyers, but such a system had to justify itself within the Country tradition of Virginia's past, especially after the republican Revolution. What we have been tracing in our investigation of Virginia legal culture is the confluence of two of the major themes that Kenneth Lockridge identifies as the ways in which social change manifested itself in public, political life. What Lockridge calls "the latent mobilization of a profoundly reactionary rural world view" and the resultant need of a frightened "political elite . . . to justify its existence" applies as much to the history of lawyers and the Country in Virginia after 1783 as it does to more classic Court-Country confrontations during the colonial era.[48]

---

out this intellectual genealogy of Tocqueville's opinion. See also McClellan, *Joseph Story and the American Constitution*, pp. 287–89.

47. Kennedy, *Swallow Barn*, p. 35.
48. Lockridge, "Social Change and the Meaning of the American Revolution," p. 433.

Virginia, Southerners, and the Law

In many respects these researches into Virginia's legal history confirm Sydnor's opinion that the Revolution in Virginia was conservative and that little profound social or political change disrupted the Old Dominion. Yet Sydnor's version smoothed over both implicit and explicit tensions and conflicts that continued to plague Virginia life in the postrevolutionary era. To conclude that lawyers were the natural leaders of an emerging nation-state and to assume the basic correctness and inevitability of the world view of the "cosmopolitans," the "modernizers," the Jeffersonian moderates in Virginia, is simply to ratify a success story whose legatees we continue to be two hundred years later.

It is a truism among political theorists that for a modern state to emerge, the structures, relationships (both personal and public), and culture of local society must be rendered less politically potent than they formerly were. Whether one is speaking of medieval barons or county court justices, the process is essentially the same. The tension between Court and Country is an ancient one, and if the present account ends in ambiguity, it is precisely because the balance between tradition and innovation is constantly being redressed and because all Americans, not just Virginians, have ambivalent feelings about both aspects of their culture.

Where the law itself is concerned, Virginia's experience appears to be the paradigm for understanding the South and the West in general. The history of political and legal culture in those regions has been shaped by the county structures first developed in the Old Dominion. The ability of a few able lawyers to rise to the top of a frontier society and the accompanying resentment and hostility of their primitive communities are common themes in the history of westward expansion. The West temporarily aligned itself with New England against the slaveowners of the South, but that alignment did not alter the basic common heritage that increasingly pitted West and South against a Northeastern "Court" where the financial, educational, and legal institutions of the new nation were located. For all of the nineteenth and much of the twentieth century the underlying cultural patterns and values of most of the United States were rural. Attitudes toward the law and legal professionals remained cool and faintly suspicious, if not openly hostile. One can hardly argue with the Country feeling that, in the long run, the rise of lawyers and courts spells the end of the independent man's abilities to handle his own affairs responsibly. The Country tradition in the South and the West that distrusted lawyers and felt more at home with laymen administering the law declined after 1896 as a politically potent force in American life, though it was still capable of periodic challenges to the modern age.

The legacy of Country opposition thought in the old states north of the Mason-Dixon line was rather minimal. By the time a group of former Whigs, Nativists, Liberty party members, and abolitionists formed what they called the Republican party, the South could only conclude, as has one scholar, that the ideology of that party looked very much like an amalgam of people doing lip service to republican principles who nonetheless "had fallen in love with enterprise."[49] Given the later-nineteenth-century legacy of entrepreneurial capitalism, which was defended by a triumphant, northern version of law, we, too, as latter-day observers, can only wonder if perhaps the South was not correct in its analysis of what had happened to northern republicanism. The inability of the South to deal with the immorality of slavery probably vitiated for all time the capacity of the region's apologists to argue that the South's view of law, and of republicanism, was one inherently tied to the notion of virtue. But that, in fact, was what the South believed, and the reason for so believing sprang from the experience we have been tracing.

The final judgment one can offer about the nature of republican lawyers' reforms in Virginia is that they were necessary and inescapable, but somewhat unsatisfactory. The Jeffersonian argument in favor of an aristocracy of legal talent was not convincing when first offered and is not convincing today, because it failed, like the Court arguments on which it was based, to say what the criteria were upon which deference to that aristocracy should be based. The Country's vision of the law was one that saw law tied to tradition, to religious beliefs that proclaimed that man's laws should reflect God's. The pragmatic arguments in favor of instrumental law, whether made by Barradall or by later generations of lawyers, failed to take seriously the depth of the older, Country convictions. Law had operated in prerevolutionary Virginia as a forum where formal authority and familiar custom met. The rise of print culture, of a legal profession, and of an expanding economic and social horizon wrenched apart that union. Because of its Country past, Virginia could never celebrate fully the rise of lawyers, bankers, merchants, and other moderns, because the culture of the Old Dominion was one that had long been suspicious of such people. The complexity of southern views regarding formal law sprang from this ambivalence, a troubled sense that could never fully articulate exactly why economic and social "progress" seemed

49. Banning, *Jeffersonian Persuasion*, p. 302 (fn. 54). Joyce Appleby, "Social Origins of American Revolutionary Ideology," argues that economic liberalism of the nineteenth century cannot be reconciled with purported origins of American thought in Commonwealth and Bolingbrokeian ideology. On the contrary, I would argue that Country opposition thought had room for certain types of entrepreneurs even while criticizing the effect such people have on a virtuous society. Virginia's ambivalence is but one such example.

alien and threatening. Northern critics could only dismiss the fervid defenses of a southern way of life as hypocritical and increasingly saw each constitutional argument presented by the South as a mere blind which served to obscure the real issues—that the South was a slaveowning aristocracy which was bent on destroying the republican institutions of the free North.

Concentrating as they did on the structure of society, the framework within which law functioned, such external perceptions could not penetrate to the heart of Virginia's ancient culture. The law, whether of a constitutional or civil variety, could be regarded as legitimate for many southerners only if they felt it to be close to their way of life and to their values. The Country tradition in Virginia guaranteed that the leaders of the state would have to come to terms with the traditional, local culture, which still survived, despite all the legal reforms, despite all the wishes of modern lawyers for a more rational, competitive society. Those leaders increasingly ratified their claims to eminence by proclaiming a continuity with Virginia's past that in fact was somewhat difficult to prove. Nevertheless, if local, agrarian institutions had been found wanting and had been replaced by more streamlined structures and professional personnel, the old notions about law remained.

It would be easy and simple to conclude that we have merely traced a rather familiar story of the dialectic between tradition and modernity, between populism and professionalism. Yet the implications are more disturbing than that comforting and all too neat summary suggests. The Country tradition of a rural past may not hold many values that remain persuasive for an urban, technological present. Yet even in the face of pragmatic and professional law, Americans still demand that the legal culture of their nation be rooted in their own day-to-day experiences, that it link them with rather traditional demands for moral conduct on the part of officials, that the law still give each man what is his due. In the fragmented, pluralistic culture of America, however, consensus, even one formed around a local courthouse, is largely an absent quality. Many observers suggest that precisely because of this situation trust and deference must be paid to the professional lawyers, politicians, bureaucrats, and technicians who increasingly dominate America's public life. In the wake of a recent experience with a lawyer who would be king, however, this prescription seems equally out of date in our dangerous times.

It has been the peculiar but perhaps not wholly unique fate of Virginia to struggle with just such a dilemma. Undoubtedly, a continual redressing of the balance between local community norms and national needs and pluralistic tolerance must continue. Like Virginia, the nation possesses a tradition composed of both Court and Country elements. The Old Dominion still honors its Country past, even while training sons and daughters at Mr. Jefferson's law school for service at a Court on the very shores of the Potomac. Virginia's, and the nation's, legal culture remains one created by both faithful magistrates and republican lawyers.

Bibliography

Manuscripts, Rare Pamphlets, Newspapers, Almanacs, and Court Records

VIRGINIA STATE LIBRARY, RICHMOND

Court Order and Minute Books, Inventories, Wills, and Deeds:*
 Caroline County, 1732–70, 1777–91, 1799–1805
 Charles City County, 1737–57, 1757–62, 1769, 1788–89
 Essex County, 1716–43, 1745–1805
 Henrico County, 1719–32, 1737–46, 1752–69, 1781–99
 King George County, 1721–70, 1788–1805
 Lancaster County, 1713–43, 1750–70, 1778–1805
 Middlesex County, 1732–37, 1740–70, 1782–97, 1799–1805
 Northumberland County, 1719–70, 1773–97
 Richmond County, 1725–74, 1776–95
 Warwick County, 1749–62
 Westmoreland County, 1705–66, 1770–95, 1797–1805
 York County, 1705–54, 1759–70, 1783–1805
 Caroline County. Appeals and Land Causes, 1777–1807
 Fredericksburg District Court Orders, 1789–1805
 Northumberland District Court Orders, 1789–1805
 Register of Virginia Justices and County Officers, 1776–1815
 Richmond City Hustings Court Orders, 1782–1806
 Virginia Legislative Petitions, 1700–1810
 Yorktown Hustings Court Orders, 1788–1806
 Allason Letterbook, 1757–70
 Diary of William Cabell, Sr.
 William Nelson Letterbook, 1766–75
 Tazewell Papers, Correspondence, 1650–1793

AMERICAN ANTIQUARIAN SOCIETY, WORCESTER, MASSACHUSETTS

 Robert Carter Papers, 1772–93 (typescript of Library of Congress originals)
 Robert Wormeley Carter Diary for 1774 (in *Virginia Almanac* for 1774)
 Farmer's Repository (Charleston, Virginia)
 Richmond Enquirer (Richmond, Virginia)
 Robert Barraud Taylor Letterbook, 1813–14
 Virginia Gazette (Williamsburg, Virginia, 1736–76)
 Virginia Almanac Collection, 1742, 1748–90

*Wills, inventories, and deeds are recorded in separate books for some counties at certain periods. In other instances, these documents are included in the order and minute books. For details on the extant records, see Flaherty, "Select Guide."

THE COLLEGE OF WILLIAM AND MARY, EARL GREGG SWEM
LIBRARY, WILLIAMSBURG, VIRGINIA

Diary of Robert Wormeley Carter, 1769, 1777, 1780–91
Tucker-Coleman Collection. Correspondence and Notes on Cases; Manuscript copy of Tucker's Blackstone
Virginia Gazette or the Independent Chronicle (Richmond)
Virginia Independent Chronicle (Richmond)

THE COLONIAL WILLIAMSBURG FOUNDATION RESEARCH LIBRARY,
WILLIAMSBURG, VIRGINIA

Diary of Robert Wormeley Carter, 1776
Nicholas Cresswell Journal, 1774–1824
John Norton and Sons Papers, 1750–1902
Mann Page, Jr., Papers, 1765–1869
Charles Stewart Papers, 1762–89
Tazewell Papers, 1664–1805
Waller Family Papers, 1737–1912

THE JOHN CARTER BROWN LIBRARY, BROWN UNIVERSITY,
PROVIDENCE, RHODE ISLAND

[Gooch, Sir William]. *A Dialogue Between Thomas Sweet-Scented, William Oronoco, Planters, both Men of good Understanding, and Justice Love Country, Who can speak for himself; Recommended To the Reading of the Planters. By a Sincere Lover of Virginia.* Williamsburg, 1732

THE HOUGHTON LIBRARY, HARVARD UNIVERSITY, CAMBRIDGE,
MASSACHUSETTS

Ebeling Collection

THE LIBRARY OF CONGRESS, MANUSCRIPT DIVISION,
WASHINGTON, D. C.

Robert Carter Papers
Robert Honeyman Papers
Wilson Cary Nicholas Papers

THE SOUTHERN HISTORICAL COLLECTION, UNIVERSITY OF NORTH
CAROLINA AT CHAPEL HILL

Thomas Burke Papers

THE UNIVERSITY OF VIRGINIA, MANUSCRIPTS DEPARTMENT,
ALDERMAN LIBRARY, CHARLOTTESVILLE

Cabell Family Papers
Landon Carter Papers, Sabine Hall Collection
Latané Family Papers, 1667–1800 (number 6490)
Latané Family Papers (number 38–262)
Legal Papers of Nicholas and Wythe. Chancery Suits, 1740–59

Norfolk Gazette and Public Ledger
Stuart Family Papers
Virginia Herald (Fredericksburg)
Wormeley Family Papers:
  Ralph Wormeley Letterbook, 1783–1802
  Letters of Ralph Wormeley (miscellaneous)
  Charles Yates Letterbook, 1773–83

Published Original Sources

Alexander, Edward Porter, ed. *The Journal of John Fontaine: An Irish Huguenot Son in Spain and Virginia, 1710–1719*. Charlottesville, 1972.
Allen, D. H., ed. *Essex Quarter Sessions Order Book, 1652–1661*. Chelmsford, 1974.
Ames, Susie M., ed. *County Court Records of Accomack and Northampton, Virginia, 1640–1645*. Charlottesville, 1973.
Banks, Henry. *Observations Designed to shew the Propriety of Establishing an Independent System of Banking*. Richmond, 1811.
―――. *Propositions Designed to Simplify and Expedite the Administration of Justice*. Richmond, 1811.
Barton, R. T., ed. *Virginia Colonial Decisions: The Reports by Sir John Randolph and by Edward Barradall of Decisions of the General Court of Virginia, 1728–1741*. 2 vols. Boston, 1909.
Beverley, Robert. *The History and Present State of Virginia*. Edited by Louis B. Wright. Chapel Hill, 1947.
Billings, Warren M., ed. "Some Acts Not in Hening's *Statutes*: The Acts of Assembly, April 1652, November 1652, and July 1653." *Virginia Magazine of History and Biography* 83 (1975): 71.
Branch, John P. *John P. Branch Historical Papers of Randolph-Macon College*. Edited by W. E. Dodd. 1st ser. Richmond, 1901–18.
Brooke, Francis T. "Some Contemporary Accounts of Eminent Characters, from a Narrative of My Life for My Family." *William and Mary Quarterly*, 1st ser., 17–18 (1908–10): 1–8.
Burn, Richard. *Justice of the Peace and Parish Officer*. London, 1755.
Byrd, William, et al. *The Correspondence of the Three William Byrds of Westover, Virginia, 1684–1776*. Edited by Marion Tinling. 2 vols. Charlottesville, 1977.
Carman, Harry J., ed. *American Husbandry*. New York, 1939 and 1964.
Carroll, Charles. *Unpublished Letters of Charles Carroll of Carrollton*. Edited by Thomas M. Field. New York, 1902.
Carter, Robert. *Letters of Robert Carter, 1720–1727: The Commercial Interests of a Virginia Gentleman*. Edited by Louis B. Wright. San Marino, 1940.
Chamberlain, Richard. *The Complete Justice, Being a Compendious and Exact Collection out of All such Statutes and Authors as may any ways concern the Office of a Justice of Peace*. . . . London, 1681.
Chinard, Gilbert, ed. *The Commonplace Book of Thomas Jefferson: A Repertory of His Ideas on Government*. Baltimore, 1926.
Coke, Sir Edward. *The Fourth Part of the Institutes of the Laws of England*. [1642.] London, 1797.

Creecy, John Harvey, ed. *Virginia Antiquary: Princess Anne County Loose Papers, 1700–1789*. Vol. 1. Richmond, 1954.
Crevecoeur, Hector St. John de. *Letters from an American Farmer*. Edited by Warren Barton Blake. New York, 1957.
Dalton, Michael. *The Countrey Justice*. . . . [1619] London, 1697.
Dinwiddie, Robert. *The Official Records of Robert Dinwiddie*. Edited by R. A. Brock. 2 vols. Richmond, 1883.
[Durand of Dauphine.] *A Frenchman in Virginia: Being the Memoirs of a Huguenot Refugee in 1686*. Translated by Fairfax Harrison. N.p., 1924.
Eddis, William. *Letters from America*. Edited by Aubrey C. Land. Cambridge, Mass., 1969.
Farish, Hunter Dickinson, ed. *Journal and Letters of Philip Vickers Fithian, 1773–1774: A Plantation Tutor of the Old Dominion*. Williamsburg, 1943.
Fielding, Henry. *A History of Tom Jones, a Foundling*. Edited by Wilbur Cross. 2 vols. New York, 1924.
――――. *Joseph Andrews*. Edited by R. F. Brissenden. New York, 1977.
Fitzhugh, William. *William Fitzhugh and His Chesapeake World, 1676–1701: The Fitzhugh Letters and Other Documents*. Edited by Richard Beale Davis, Chapel Hill, 1963.
Gibbon, Edward. *The History of the Decline and Fall of the Roman Empire*. 6 vols. London, 1846.
Green, Roger. *Virginia's Cure: or an advisive Narrative Concerning Virginia, Discovering the True Ground of that Church's Unhappiness*. Vol. 3, tract 15 in *Tracts and Other Papers Relating . . . to the Origin . . . of the Colonies in North America . . . to the Year 1776*, edited by Peter Force. 4 vols. Washington, D.C., 1836–46.
Greene, Jack P., ed. *A Diary of Colonel Landon Carter of Sabine Hall, 1752–1778*. 2 vols. Charlottesville, 1965.
Hale, Sir Matthew. *History of the Common Law of England*. Edited by Charles M. Gray. Chicago, 1971.
Hartwell, Henry; Blair, James; Chilton, Edward. *The Present State of Virginia and the College*. Edited by Hunter Dickinson Farish. Williamsburg, 1940.
Hening, William Waller. *The Statutes at Large: Being a Collection of all the Laws of Virginia, From the First Session of the Legislature, in the Year 1619*. 13 vols. Richmond and Philadelphia, 1809–23.
――――. *The New Virginia Justice: Comprising the Office and Authority of a Justice of the Peace in the Commonwealth of Virginia, Etc*. 2nd edition. 1810.
Jarratt, Devereux. *The Life of Devereux Jarratt*. Baltimore, 1806.
Jefferson, Thomas. *The Papers of Thomas Jefferson*. Edited by Julian P. Boyd, et al. Princeton, 1950–.
――――. *Virginia Reports: Reports of Cases Determined in the General Court of Virginia From 1730 to 1740 and From 1768 to 1772*. Charlottesville, 1829.
――――. *The Writings of Thomas Jefferson*. Edited by H. A. Washington. 9 vols. Washington, D.C., 1854.
――――. *The Writings of Thomas Jefferson*. Edited by Paul Leicester Ford. 12 vols. New York, 1904–5.
Johnson, Alden, et al., eds. *Dictionary of American Biography*. 20 vols. and Index. New York, 1929–37.
Johnson, Samuel. *A Dictionary of the English Language*. . . . 2 vols. London, 1755.

Jones, Hugh. *The Present State of Virginia*. Edited by Richard J. Morton. Chapel Hill, 1956.
Jones, Joseph. *Letters of Joseph Jones of Virginia, 1777–1787*. Edited by Worthington C. Ford. Washington, D.C., 1889.
Kennedy, John Pendleton. *Swallow Barn, or a Sojourn in the Old Dominion*. 2nd ed. New York, 1852.
Koch, Adrienne, and Peden, William, eds. *Life and Selected Writings of Thomas Jefferson*. New York, 1944.
Kukla, Jon, ed. "Some Acts Not in Hening's *Statutes*: The Acts of Assembly, October 1660." *Virginia Magazine of History and Biography* 83 (1975): 77–97.
Labaree, Leonard W., ed. *Royal Instructions to British Colonial Governors, 1670–1776*. 2 vols. New York, 1935.
Lambarde, William. *Eirenarcha, or the Office of the Justices of Peace*. London, 1581.
Lemay, J. A. Leo, ed. *A Poem by John Markland of Virginia*. Williamsburg, 1965.
McIlwaine, H. R., et al., eds. *Executive Journals of the Council of Colonial Virginia*. 6 vols. Richmond, 1925–66.
──────. *Journals of the Virginia House of Burgesses, 1619–1776*. 13 vols. Richmond, 1905–16.
Madison, James. *The Papers of James Madison*. Edited by William T. Hutchinson, et al. Chicago, 1962–.
Manson, Charles William. *The Stranger in America, 1793–1806*. New York, 1935.
Marraro, Howard R., trans. *Memoirs of the Life and Peregrinations of the Florentine, Philip Mazzei, 1730–1816*. New York, 1942.
Marshall, John. *The Papers of John Marshall*. Edited by Herbert Johnson and Charles T. Cullen. Chapel Hill, 1974–.
Mason, George. *The Papers of George Mason, 1725–1792*. Edited by Robert Rutland. 3 vols. Chapel Hill, 1970.
Monroe, James. *Writings of James Monroe*. 7 vols. Edited by Stanislaus Murray Hamilton. New York, 1898–1903.
Munford, William. *Poems and Compositions in Prose on Several Occasions*. Richmond, 1798.
The Office and Duty of the Clerk of Assize . . . together with the Office of the Clerk of the Peace. London, [1676.] 1682.
Palmer, William P., et al., eds. *Calendar of Virginia State Papers and Other Manuscripts*. 11 vols. Richmond, 1875–93.
Parker, James. *Conductor Generalis*. . . . New Jersey, 1764.
Parry, Stanley, ed. *Thomas Aquinas: Treatise on Law*. Chicago, 1970.
[Paulding, J. K.] *Letters from the South: Written during an Excursion in the Summer of 1816*. . . . 2 vols. New York, 1817.
Pendleton, Edmund. *Letters and Papers of Edmund Pendleton, 1734–1803*. Edited by David John Mays. 2 vols. Charlottesville, 1967.
Randolph, Edmund. *History of Virginia*. Edited by H. Shaffer. Charlottesville, 1970.
Selden, John. *Table Talk*. . . . Edited by Frederick Pollock. London, 1927.
Shepherd, Samuel. *The Statutes at Large of Virginia, October 1792 to December 1806*. 3 vols. Richmond, 1835.
Smith, Joseph Henry, ed. *Appeals to the Privy Council from the American Plantations*. New York, 1950.

Smith, Joseph Henry, and Crowl, Philip A., eds. *Court Records of Prince Georges County, Maryland, 1646–1699*. Washington, D.C., 1964.

Spotswood, Alexander. *The Official Letters of Alexander Spotswood, Lieutenant-Governor of the Colony of Virginia, 1710–1722*. Edited by R. A. Brock. 3 vols. Richmond, 1932–35.

Staples, Waller R. "Presidential Address." In *Reports of the Sixth Annual Meeting of the Virginia Bar Association*, pp. 127–56. Richmond, 1894.

Starke, Richard. *The Office and Authority of a Justice of Peace*. Williamsburg, 1774.

Sweeny, William K. "Gleanings from the Records of (Old) Rappahannock County and Essex County, Virginia." *William and Mary Quarterly*, 2nd ser., 18 (1938): 297–313.

Swem, E. G., and Williams, J. W., compilers. *A Register of the General Assembly of Virginia, 1776–1918, and of the Constitutional Conventions*. Richmond, 1917.

Taylor, John. *An Enquiry into the Principals and the Tendency of Certain Public Measures*. Philadelphia, 1794.

Tucker, Henry St. George. *Commentaries on the Laws of Virginia, Comprising the Substance of a Course of Lectures. . . .* 2 vols. Winchester, Virginia, 1836.

Tucker, St. George. *Blackstone's Commentaries: . . . with . . . Reference to the . . . Commonwealth of Virginia*. 5 vols. Richmond, 1803.

Van Schreeven, William J., and Scribner, Robert L., eds. *Revolutionary Virginia: The Road to Independence*. 3 vols. Charlottesville, 1973.

Virginia General Assembly, 1776–1860: House of Delegates Journal, 1776–1790. 4 vols. Richmond, 1827–28.

Webb, George. *The Office and Authority of a Justice of Peace*. Williamsburg, 1736.

Winfree, Waverly, ed. *The Laws of Virginia: Being a Supplement to Hening's The Statutes at Large, 1700–1750*. Richmond, 1971.

Wirt, William. *The British Spy, or Letters, to a Member of the British Parliament*. Newburyport, Mass., 1804.

———. *The Old Bachelor*. Richmond, 1814.

Wright, Louis B., ed. *An Essay upon the Government of the English Plantations on the Continent of America*. San Marino, Ca., 1944.

Books, Articles, and Theses

Abel-Smith, Brian, and Stevens, Robert. *Lawyers and the Courts: A Sociological Study of the English Legal System, 1750–1965*. London, 1969.

Adams, Evelyn Taylor. *The Courthouse in Virginia Counties, 1634–1776*. Hamilton, Va., 1966.

Alden, John R. *The South in the Revolution, 1763–1787*. Baton Rouge, La., 1957.

Ambler, Charles Henry. *Thomas Ritchie: A Study in Virginia Politics*. Richmond, 1913.

———. *Sectionalism in Virginia from 1776 to 1861*. 1910. Reprint. New York, 1964.

Ames, Susie M. *Studies of the Virginia Eastern Shore in the Seventeenth Century*. Richmond, 1940.

Ammon, Harry. "James Monroe and the Election of 1808 in Virginia." *William and Mary Quarterly*, 3d ser., 20 (1963): 33–56.

———. "The Jeffersonian Republicans in Virginia: An Interpretation." *Virginia Magazine of History and Biography* 71 (1963): 153–67.

———. "The Richmond Junto, 1800–1824." *Virginia Magazine of History and Biography* 61 (1953): 395–418.

Anderson, James LaVerne. "The Virginia Councillors and the American Revolution: The Demise of an Aristocratic Clique." *Virginia Magazine of History and Biography* 82 (1974): 56–74.

Appleby, Joyce. "The Social Origins of American Revolutionary Ideology." *Journal of American History* 64 (1978): 935–58.

Bailey, Raymond C. *Popular Influences upon Public Policy: Petitioning in Eighteenth-Century Virginia.* Westport, Conn., 1979.

Bailyn, Bernard, "Politics and Social Structure in Virginia." In *Seventeenth Century America*, edited by James M. Smith, pp. 90–115. Chapel Hill, 1959.

Banning, Lance. *The Jeffersonian Persuasion: Evolution of a Party Ideology.* Ithaca, 1978.

———. "Republican Ideology and the Triumph of the Constitution, 1789 to 1793." *William and Mary Quarterly*, 3rd series, 31 (1974): 167–88.

Barnes, T. G. *The Clerk of the Peace in Caroline Somerset.* Leicester, 1961.

Beane, Wendell C., and Doty, William G., eds. *Myths, Rites, Symbols: A Mircea Eliade Reader.* 2 vols. New York, 1966.

Beeman, Richard R. "The New Social History and the Search for 'Community' in Colonial America." *American Quarterly* 29 (1977): 422–43.

———. *The Old Dominion and the New Nation, 1788–1801.* Chicago, 1968.

Berger, Peter L. *The Sacred Canopy: Elements of a Sociological Theory of Religion.* New York, 1969.

———, and Luckmann, Thomas. *The Social Construction of Reality: A Treatise in the Sociology of Knowledge.* New York, 1966.

Berthoff, Rowland, and Murrin, John. "Feudalism, Communalism, and the Yeoman Farmer: The American Revolution Considered as a Social Accident." In *Essays on the American Revolution*, edited by Stephen G. Kurtz and James H. Hutson, pp. 256–88. Chapel Hill, 1973.

Billias, George A., ed. *Law and Authority in Colonial America.* Barre, Mass., 1965.

Billings, Warren M. "The Growth of Political Institutions in Virginia, 1634–1676." *William and Mary Quarterly*, 3d ser., 31 (1974): 225–42.

———. "Virginia's Deploured Condition, 1660–1676: The Coming of Bacon's Rebellion." Ph.D. dissertation, Northern Illinois University, 1968.

———, ed. *The Old Dominion in the Seventeenth Century: A Documentary History of Virginia, 1606–1689.* Chapel Hill, 1975.

Birks, Michael. *Gentlemen of the Law.* London, 1960.

Black, Henry Campbell. *Black's Law Dictionary: Definitions of the Terms and Phrases of American and English Jurisprudence, Ancient and Modern.* 4th rev. ed. St. Paul, 1968.

Bledstein, Burton J. *The Culture of Professionalism: The Middle Class and the Development of Higher Education in America.* New York, 1976.

Bliss, Willard F. "The Rise of Tenancy in Virginia." *Virginia Magazine of History and Biography* 58 (1950): 427–41.

Bloomfield, Maxwell. *American Lawyers in a Changing Society, 1776–1876.* Cambridge, Mass., 1976.

Bohannon, Paul. *Justice and Judgment among the Tiv*. Oxford, 1957.
Boorstin, Daniel. *The Americans: The Colonial Experience*. New York, 1958.
Bouwsma, William J. "Lawyers and Early Modern Culture." *American Historical Review* 78 (1973): 303–27.
Brauer, George C., Jr. *The Education of a Gentleman: Theories of Gentlemanly Education in England, 1660–1775*. New York, 1959.
Brenner, Robert. "Agrarian Class Structure and Economic Development in Pre-Industrial Europe." *Past and Present* 78 (1976): 30–75.
Breuner, Robert Paul. "Commercial Change and Political Conflict: The Merchant Community in Civil War London." Ph.D. dissertation, Princeton University, 1970.
Bridenbaugh, Carl. *Vexed and Troubled Englishmen, 1590–1642*. New York, 1953.
———. "Violence and Virtue in Virginia, 1766: or, The Importance of the Trivial." *Proceedings of the Massachusetts Historical Society* 76 (1964): 3–29.
Brown, Richard D. *Modernization: The Transformation of American Life, 1600–1865*. New York, 1976.
Bruce, Philip Alexander. *Economic History of Virginia*. 2 vols. New York, 1896.
———. *Institutional History of Virginia in the Seventeenth Century*. . . . New York, 1910. Reprint. Gloucester, Mass., 1964.
Bryson, William Hamilton. *Census of Law Books in Colonial Virginia*. Charlottesville, 1978.
Buckley, Thomas E. *Church and State in Revolutionary Virginia, 1776–1787*.
Campbell, T. E. *Colonial Caroline: A History of Caroline County, Virginia*. Richmond, 1954.
Carr, E. H. *What is History?* New York, 1965.
Carr, Lois Green. "County Government in Maryland, 1689–1709." Ph.D. dissertation, Harvard University, 1968.
Chumbley, George Lewis. *Colonial Justice in Virginia*. Richmond, 1938.
Cockburn, J. S. *A History of English Assizes, 1558–1714*. Cambridge, 1972.
Cohen, Percy. "Theories of Myth." *Man: The Journal of the Royal Anthropological Institute* 4 (1969): 337–53.
Colbourn, H. Trevor. *The Lamp of Experience: Whig History and the Intellectual Origins of the American Revolution*. Chapel Hill, 1965.
Cooper, J. P. "In Search of Agrarian Capitalism." *Past and Present* 80 (1978): 20–65.
Corwin, Edward S. *The "Higher Law" Background of American Constitutional Law*. Ithaca, 1955.
Craven, Wesley Frank. *The Colonies in Transition, 1660–1713*. New York, 1968.
———. *The Southern Colonies in the Seventeenth Century, 1607–1689*. Baton Rouge, La., 1949.
———. *White, Red, and Black: The Seventeenth-Century Virginian*. Charlottesville, 1971.
Crowley, J. E. *This Sheba, Self: The Conceptualization of Economic Life in Eighteenth-Century America*. Baltimore, 1974.
Cullen, Charles T. "Completing the Revisal of the Laws in Post-Revolutionary Virginia." *Virginia Magazine of History and Biography* 82 (1974): 84–99.
———. "New Light on John Marshall's Legal Education and Admission to the Bar." *American Journal of Legal History* 16 (1972): 345–51.

―――. "St. George Tucker and Law in Virginia, 1772–1804." Ph.D. dissertation, University of Virginia, 1971.
Curtis, George M., III. "A Communication." *William and Mary Quarterly* 26 (1969): 636–38.
―――. "The Role of the Courts in the Making of the Revolution in Virginia." In *The Human Dimension of Nation-Making: Essays on Colonial and Revolutionary America*, edited by James Kirby Martin, pp. 121–46. Madison, 1976.
―――. "Virginia Courts During the Revolution." Ph.D. dissertation, University of Wisconsin, 1970.
Dabney, William N. "Letters from Norfolk: Scottish Merchants View the Revolutionary Crisis." In *The Old Dominion: Essays for Thomas Perkins Abernathy*, edited by Darrett Rutman, pp. 109–21. Charlottesville, 1964.
Davis, Richard Beale. *Francis Walker Gilmer: Life and Learning in Jefferson's Virginia*. Richmond, 1939.
―――. *Intellectual Life in Jefferson's Virginia, 1770–1830*. Knoxville, Tenn., 1972.
―――. *Intellectual Life in the Colonial South, 1585–1763*. 3 vols. Knoxville, Tenn., 1978.
Deen, James W., Jr. "Patterns of Testation: Four Tidewater Counties in Colonial Virginia." *American Journal of Legal History* 16 (1972): 152–76.
Dietze, Gottfried. *Magna Carta and Property*. Charlottesville, 1965.
Dodson, Leonidas. *Alexander Spotswood, Governor of Colonial Virginia, 1710–1722*. Philadelphia, 1932.
Dowdell, E. G. *A Hundred Years of Quarter Sessions: The Government of Middlesex from 1660 to 1760*. Cambridge, 1932.
Dowdey, Clifford. *The Virginia Dynasties: The Emergence of "King" Carter and the Golden Age*. Boston, 1969.
Drell, Bernard. "John Taylor of Caroline and the Preservation of an Old Social Order." *Virginia Magazine of History and Biography* 46 (1938): 285–98.
Egnal, Marc. "The Economic Development of the Thirteen Continental Colonies, 1720–1775." *William and Mary Quarterly*, 3d ser., 32 (1975): 191–222.
Egnal, Marc, and Ernst, Joseph. "An Economic Interpretation of the American Revolution." *William and Mary Quarterly*, 3d. ser., 29 (1972): 3–32.
Eliade, Mircea. *Images and Symbols*. Translated by Philip Mairet. New York, 1961.
Ellis, Richard E. *The Jeffersonian Crisis: Courts and Politics in the Young Republic*. New York, 1971.
Ernst, Joseph A. "Genesis of the Currency Act of 1764: Virginia Paper Money and the Protection of British Investments." *William and Mary Quarterly*, 3d ser., 22 (1965): 33–74.
―――. "The Robinson Scandal Redivivus: Money, Debts, and Politics in Revolutionary Virginia." *Virginia Magazine of History and Biography* 77 (1969): 146–73.
Evans, Emory. "The Rise and Decline of the Virginia Aristocracy in the Eighteenth Century: The Nelsons." In *The Old Dominion: Essays for Thomas Perkins Abernathy*, edited by Darret B. Rutman, pp. 62–78. Charlottesville, 1964.
―――. *Thomas Nelson of Yorktown: Revolutionary Virginian*. Charlottesville, 1975.

Fallers, Lloyd A. *Law without Precedent: Legal Ideas in Action in the Courts of Colonial Busoga*. Chicago, 1969.
Fiering, Norman S. "Benjamin Franklin and the Way to Virtue." *American Quarterly* 30 (1978): 199–223.
Fischer, David Hackett, and Stone, Lawrence. "Growing Old: An Exchange." *New York Review of Books*, September 15, 1977, pp. 47–49.
———. *Growing Old in America*. . . . New York, 1977.
Fishburne, Junius Rodes. "The Office of Secretary of State in Colonial Virginia." Ph.D. dissertation, Tulane University, 1971.
Fitz, Virginia White. "Ralph Wormeley: Anonymous Essayist." *William and Mary Quarterly*, 3d ser., 26 (1969): 586–95.
Flaherty, David H. "A Select Guide to the Manuscript Court Records of Colonial Virginia." *American Journal of Legal History* 19 (1975): 112–37.
Foord, Archibald S. *His Majesty's Opposition, 1714–1830*. Oxford, 1964.
Forman, Henry Chandlee. *Virginia Architecture in the Seventeenth Century*. Williamsburg, 1957.
Friedman, Lawrence M. *A History of American Law*. New York, 1973.
Fuller, Lon. *The Morality of Law*. New Haven, 1964.
Garland, Hugh. *The Life of John Randolph of Roanoke*. 2 vols. New York, 1851.
Gawalt, Gerald W. "Massachusetts Lawyers: A Historical Analysis of the Process of Professionalization, 1760–1840." Ph.D. dissertation, Clark University, 1969.
———. *The Promise of Power: The Emergence of the Legal Profession in Massachusetts, 1760–1840*. Westport, Conn., 1979.
Gay, Peter. *The Enlightenment: An Interpretation*. 2 vols. New York, 1966 and 1969.
Gee, Wilson, and Gorson, John J., III. *Rural Depopulation in Certain Tidewater and Piedmont Areas of Virginia*. Charlottesville, 1929.
Geertz, Clifford. "Centers, Kings and Charisma: Reflections on the Symbolics of Power." In *Culture and Its Creators: Essays in Honor of Edward Shils*, edited by Joseph Ben-David and Terry Nichols Clark, pp. 150–71. Chicago, 1977.
———. *The Interpretation of Cultures: Selected Essays*. New York, 1973.
Gierke, Otto Frederick von. *Natural Law and the Theory of Society, 1500 to 1800*. Translated and with an introduction by Ernest Barker. Boston, 1957.
———. *Political Theories of the Middle Age*. Translated and with an introduction by F. W. Maitland. Cambridge, 1900.
Gill, Howard. "Wheat Culture in Colonial Virginia." *Agricultural History* 52 (1978): 380–93.
Gipson, L. H. *The British Empire before the American Revolution*. 8 vols. Caldwell, Idaho, and New York, 1936–54.
Giseburt, Dirk J. "The Life of Loyalty: The Corbin, Tayloe, and Wormeley Families and the Revolution in Virginia, 1760–1820." Senior thesis, Princeton University, 1978.
Glassey, Lionel K. J. "The Commission of the Peace, 1675–1720." D. Phil. dissertation, Lincoln College, Oxford University, 1972.
———. *Politics and the Appointment of Justices of the Peace, 1675–1720*. Oxford, 1979.
Gluckman, Max. *The Ideas in Barotse Jurisprudence*. New Haven, 1965.
———. *The Judicial Process among the Barotse of Northern Rhodesia*. Manchester, 1955.

Goebel, Julius, Jr. "King's Law and Local Custom in Seventeenth Century New England." *Columbia Law Review* 31 (1931): 416–48.
Goffman, Erving. *Behavior in Public Places: Notes on the Social Organization of Gatherings*. New York, 1965.
———. *Interaction Ritual: Essays on Face-to-Face Behavior*. Chicago, 1967.
———. *The Presentation of Self in Everyday Life*. New York, 1973.
Gooch, G. P. *Political Thought from Bacon to Halifax*. London, 1914.
Gough, J. W. *Fundamental Law in English Constitutional History*. Oxford, 1961.
Gray, Lewis Cecil. *History of Agriculture in the Southern United States to 1860*. 2 vols. Washington, D.C., 1933.
Greene, E. B., and Harrington, Virginia D., eds. *American Population before the Federal Census of 1790*. New York, 1932.
Greene, Jack P. "Foundations of Political Power in the Virginia House of Burgesses, 1720–1776." *William and Mary Quarterly*, 3d ser., 16 (1959): 485–506.
———. *The Quest for Power: The Lower House of Assembly in the Southern Royal Colonies, 1689–1776*. New York, 1972.
———. "Search for Identity: An Interpretation of the Meaning of Selected Patterns of Social Response in Eighteenth-Century America." *Journal of Social History* 3 (1969–70): 196–205.
———. "Society, Ideology, and Politics: An Analysis of the Political Culture of Mid-Eighteenth-Century Virginia." In *Society, Freedom, and Conscience: The Coming of the Revolution in Virginia, Massachusetts, and New York*, edited by Richard M. Jellison, pp. 14–76. New York, 1976.
Griffin, Barbara J. "Thomas Ritchie and the Founding of the Richmond Lancastrian School." *Virginia Magazine of History and Biography* 86 (1978): 447–60.
Griffith, Lucille. *The Virginia House of Burgesses, 1750–1774*. University, Ala., 1968.
Gunderson, Joan. "The Anglican Ministry in Virginia, 1723–1776: A Study of a Social Class." Ph.D. dissertation, Notre Dame University, 1972.
———. "The Myth of the Independent Virginia Vestry." *Historical Magazine of the Protestant Episcopal Church* 44 (1975): 133–42.
Gwathmey, John H. *Justice John: Tales from the Courtroom of the Virginia Judge*. Richmond, 1934.
———. *Legends of Virginia Lawyers: Anecdotes and Whimsical Yarns of the Old Time Bench and Bar*. Richmond, 1934.
Halpern, Ben. " 'Myth' and 'Ideology' in Modern Usage." *History and Theory* 1 (1961): 129–49.
Hamilton, J. G. de Roulhac. "Southern Members of the Inns of Court." *North Carolina Historical Review* 10 (1933): 273–86.
Hanson, John R., II. "The Economic Development of the Thirteen Continental Colonies, 1720 to 1775: A Critique," and a response by Marc Egnal. *William and Mary Quarterly*, 3d ser., 37 (1980): 165–75.
Happel, Ralph. "Stafford and King George Courthouses and the Fate of Marlborough, Port of Entry." *Virginia Magazine of History and Biography* 66 (1958): 183–94.
Harrison, Joseph H., Jr. "Oligarchs and Democrats: The Richmond Junto." *Virginia Magazine of History and Biography* 78 (1970): 184–98.
Hart, H. L. A. *The Concept of Law*. Oxford, 1961.

Hartog, Hendrik. "The Public Law of a County Court: Judicial Government in Eighteenth Century Massachusetts." *American Journal of Legal History* 20 (1976): 282–329.
Hay, Douglas; Linebaugh, Peter; Rule, John G.; Thompson, E. P.; Winslow, Cal. *Albion's Fatal Tree: Crime and Society in Eighteenth-Century England.* New York, 1975.
Hayden, Horace Edwin. *Virginia Genealogies.* . . . Wilkes-Barre, Pa., 1893.
Heaton, Lynda Rees. "Littleton Waller Tazewell's Sketch of His Own Family . . . 1823, Transcribed and Edited." M.A. thesis, College of William and Mary, 1967.
Hemphill, John M., III. "John Wayles Rates His Neighbors." *Virginia Magazine of History and Biography* 66 (1958): 302–6.
———. "Virginia and the English Commercial System, 1689–1733: Studies in the Development and Fluctuation of a Colonial Economy under Imperial Control." Ph.D. dissertation, Princeton University, 1964.
Henretta, James A. *The Evolution of American Society, 1700–1815: An Interdisciplinary Analysis.* Lexington, Mass., 1973.
———. "'Modernization': Toward a False Synthesis." *Reviews in American History* 5 (1977): 445–52.
Herndon, Melville. *Tobacco in Colonial Virginia: "The Sovereign Remedy."* Williamsburg, 1957.
Hill, Christopher. *The World Turned Upside Down: Radical Ideas during the English Revolution.* New York, 1972.
Hirschman, Albert O. *The Passions and the Interests: Political Arguments for Capitalism before Its Triumph.* Princeton, 1977.
Holmes, G. E. *British Politics in the Age of Anne.* London, 1967.
Horne, Janis M. "The Opposition to the Virginia Tobacco Inspection Act of 1730." Master's thesis, College of William and Mary, 1977.
Horwitz, Morton J. *The Transformation of American Law, 1780–1860.* Cambridge, Mass., 1977.
Hurst, Gerald. *A Short History of Lincoln's Inn.* London, 1946.
Ireland, Robert M. *The County Courts in Antebellum Kentucky.* Lexington, 1972.
———. "The Place of the Justice of the Peace in the Legislature and Party System of Kentucky, 1792–1850." *American Journal of Legal History* 12 (1969): 202–22.
Isaac, Rhys. "Dramatizing the Ideology of Revolution: Popular Mobilization in Virginia, 1774 to 1776." *William and Mary Quarterly*, 3d ser., 33 (1976): 357–85.
———. "Evangelical Revolt: The Nature of the Baptists' Challenge to the Traditional Order in Virginia, 1765 to 1775." *William and Mary Quarterly* 3d ser., 31 (1974): 345–68.
———. "Preachers and Patriots: Popular Culture and the Revolution in Virginia." In *The American Revolution: Explorations in the History of American Radicalism*, edited by Alfred F. Young, pp. 125–56. Dekalb, Ill., 1976.
———. "Religion and Authority: Problems of the Anglican Establishment in Virginia in the Era of the Great Awakening and the Parsons' Cause." *William and Mary Quarterly*, 3d ser., 30 (1973): 3–36.
Johnson, Richard R. "Politics Redefined: An Assessment of Recent Writings on the Late Stuart Period of English History, 1640 to 1714." *William and Mary Quarterly*, 3d ser., 35 (1978): 691–732.

Jones, E. Alfred. *American Members of the Inns of Court*. London, 1924.
Jordan, Daniel P. "John Randolph of Roanoke and the Art of Winning Elections in Jeffersonian Virginia." *Virginia Magazine of History and Biography* 86 (1978): 389–407.
———. "Virginia Congressmen, 1801–1825." Ph.D. dissertation, University of Virginia, 1970.
Jordan, Winthrop D. *White over Black: American Attitudes toward the Negro, 1550–1812*. Chapel Hill, 1968.
Katz, Stanley N. "The Politics of Law in Colonial America: Controversies over Chancery Courts and Equity Law in the Eighteenth Century." *Perspectives in American History* 5 (1971): 257–86.
Keim, C. Ray. "Primogeniture and Entail in Colonial Virginia." *William and Mary Quarterly*, 3d ser., 25 (1968): 545–86.
Kelly, Kevin P. "Economic and Social Development of Seventeenth-Century Surry County, Virginia." Ph.D. dissertation, University of Washington, 1972.
Kerber, Linda K. "Daughters of Columbia: Educating Women for the Republic, 1787–1805." In *The Hofstadter Aegis: A Memorial*, edited by Stanley Elkins and Eric McKitrick, pp. 36–59. New York, 1974.
Kershaw, Robert Barnsley. "The Development of the Maryland Bar, 1715 to 1830: 'The Road to Riches and Ye Highest Honors.'" Senior thesis, Princeton University, 1974.
Kirk, G. S. *Myth: Its Meaning and Functions in Ancient and Other Cultures*. Berkeley, 1970.
Klingaman, David C. "The Development of the Coastwise Trade of Virginia in the Late Colonial Period." *Virginia Magazine of History and Biography* 77 (1969): 26–41.
———. "The Development of Virginia's Coastwise and Grain Trade in the Late Colonial Period." Ph.D. dissertation, University of Virginia, 1967.
Knafla, Louis A. *Law and Politics in Jacobean England: The Tracts of Lord Ellesmere*. Cambridge, 1977.
Koch, Adrienne, ed. *The American Enlightenment: The Shaping of the American Experiment and a Free Society*. New York, 1965.
Kramnick, Isaac. *Bolingbroke and His Circle: The Politics of Nostalgia in the Age of Walpole*. Cambridge, Mass., 1968.
Kuklick, Henrika. "The Organization of Social Science in the United States." *American Quarterly* 28 (1976): 124–41.
Kuroda, Tadahisa. "The County Court System of Virginia from the Revolution to the Civil War." Ph.D. dissertation, Columbia University, 1969.
Land, Aubrey C. *The Dulaneys of Maryland*. Baltimore, 1955.
———. "Economic Behavior in a Planting Society: The Eighteenth Century Chesapeake." *Journal of Southern History* 33 (1967): 469–85.
———, ed. *Bases of the Plantation Society*. New York, 1969.
Landau, Norma Beatrice. "Gentry and Gentlemen: The Justices of the Peace, 1680–1760." Ph.D. dissertation, University of California, 1974.
Landon, Michael. *The Triumph of the Lawyers: Their Role in English Politics, 1678–1689*. University, Ala., 1970.
Lemay, J. A. Leo. "Robert Bolling and the Bailent of Colonel Chiswell." *Early American Literature* 6 (1971): 99–142.
Liddle, William D. "'Virtue and Liberty': An Inquiry into the Role of the Agrarian Myth in the Rhetoric of the American Revolutionary Era." *South Atlantic Quarterly* 7 (1978): 15–38.

Little, David. *Religion, Order, and Law: A Study in Pre-Revolutionary England.* New York, 1969.
Lockridge, Kenneth. *Literacy in Colonial New England: An Enquiry into the Social Context of Literacy in the Early Modern West.* New York, 1974.
———. "Social Change and the Meaning of the American Revolution." *Journal of Social History* 6 (1973): 403–39.
Low, W. A. "Merchant and Planter Relations in Post-Revolutionary Virginia, 1783–1789." *Virginia Magazine of History and Biography* 61 (1953): 308–18.
McClellan, James. *Joseph Story and the American Constitution: A Study in Political and Legal Thought.* Norman, Okla., 1971.
McCoy, Drew Randall. "Republicanism and American Foreign Policy: James Madison and the Political Economy of Commercial Discrimination, 1789 to 1794." *William and Mary Quarterly*, 3d ser., 31 (1974): 631–46.
———. "The Republican Revolution: Political Economy in Jeffersonian America, 1776 to 1817." Ph.D. dissertation, University of Virginia, 1976.
———. "The Virginia Port Bill of 1784." *Virginia Magazine of History and Biography* 83 (1975): 288–303.
McLoughlin, William G., Jr. "The Role of Religion in the Revolution: Liberty of Conscience and Cultural Cohesion in the New Nation." In *Essays on the American Revolution*, edited by Stephen G. Kurtz and James H. Hutson, pp. 197–255. Chapel Hill, 1973.
Macpherson, C. B. *The Political Theory of Possessive Individualism, Hobbes to Locke.* Oxford, 1962.
Maddox, William Arthur. "The Free School Idea in Virginia before the Civil War: A Phase of Political and Social Evolution." Ph.D. dissertation, Columbia Teachers' College, New York, 1918.
Maier, Pauline. *From Resistance to Revolution: Colonial Radicals and the Development of American Opposition to Britain, 1765–1776.* New York, 1973.
Main, J. T. "The Distribution of Property in Post-Revolutionary Virginia." *Mississippi Valley Historical Review* 41 (1954): 241–58.
———. "The One Hundred." *William and Mary Quarterly*, 3d ser., 11 (1954): 354–84.
———. *Political Parties before the Constitution.* New York, 1974.
———. *The Upper House in Revolutionary America, 1763–1788.* Madison, 1967.
Maitland, F. W. *Constitutional History of England.* Cambridge, 1908. Paper edition, 1974.
Mays, David John. *Edmund Pendleton, A Biography, 1721–1803.* 2 vols. Cambridge, Mass., 1952.
Menard, Russell R. "Immigrants and Their Increase: The Process of Population Growth in Early Colonial Maryland," in Aubrey C. Land, et al., eds., *Law, Society, and Politics in Early Maryland*, pp. 88–110. Baltimore, 1977.
———. "Immigration to the Chesapeake Colonies in the Seventeenth Century." *Maryland Historical Magazine* 68 (1973): 323–29.
Merton, Robert K. "Patterns of Influence: Local and Cosmopolitan Influentials." In *Social Science and Social Structure*, pp. 441–74. Enlarged ed. New York, 1968.
———. "The Unanticipated Consequences of Purposeful Social Action." *American Sociological Review* 1 (1936): 894–904.

Miller, John C. *The Wolf By the Ears: Thomas Jefferson and Slavery.* New York, 1977.
Moir, Esther. *The Justice of the Peace.* New York, 1969.
———. *Local Government in Gloucestershire, 1775–1800: A Study of the Justice of the Peace.* Publications of the Bristol and Gloucestershire Archaeological Society, Records Section, vol. 8. Gloucester, 1969.
Molnar, John E. "Publication and Retail Book Advertisements in the *Virginia Gazette*, 1736–1780." Ph.D. dissertation, University of Michigan, 1978.
Morgan, Edmund S. *American Slavery, American Freedom: The Ordeal of Colonial Virginia.* New York, 1975.
———. "Headrights and Head Counts: A Review Article." *Virginia Magazine of History and Biography* 80 (1972): 361–71.
Morgan, Gwenda. "Virginia Law Revision of 1748–49." Master's thesis, College of William and Mary, 1968.
Morrill, John. *The Revolt of the Provinces: Conservatives and Radicals in the English Civil War, 1630–1650.* London, 1976.
Morton, Louis B. *Robert Carter of Nomini Hall.* Williamsburg, 1941.
Morton, Richard L. *Colonial Virginia.* 2 vols. Chapel Hill, 1960.
Mudge, Eugene Tenbroeck. *Social Philosophy of John Taylor of Caroline: A Study in Jeffersonian Democracy.* New York, 1939.
Mullett, Charles F. "Coke and the American Revolution." *Economica* 12 (1932): 457–71.
Mullin, Gerald W. *Flight and Rebellion: Slave Resistance in Eighteenth-Century Virginia.* New York, 1972.
Murrin, John M. "Anglicizing an American Colony: The Transformation of Provincial Massachusetts." Ph.D. dissertation, Yale University, 1966.
———. "The Legal Transformation: The Bench and Bar in Eighteenth-Century Massachusetts." In *Colonial America: Essays in Politics and Social Development*, edited by Stanley N. Katz, pp. 415–49. Boston, 1971.
Nenner, Howard. *By Colour of Law: Legal Culture and Constitutional Politics in England, 1600–1689.* Chicago, 1977.
Nicholls, Michael L. "Origins of the Virginia Southside, 1703–1753: A Social and Economic Study." Ph.D. dissertation. College of William and Mary, 1972.
Nichols, Frederick Doveton. "Palladio's Influence on American Architecture." In *Palladio in America*, pp. 101–25. Milano, 1976.
Olafson, Frederick A., ed. *Society, Law, and Morality.* Englewood Cliffs, N.J., 1961.
Ong, Walter J. *Interfaces of the Word: Studies in the Evolution of Consciousness and Culture.* Ithaca, 1977.
———. *The Presence of the Word: Some Prolegomena for Cultural and Religious History.* New Haven, 1967.
Otto, Rudolf. *The Idea of the Holy.* Translated by John W. Harvey. New York, 1950.
Pearce, Robert R. *A History of the Inns of Court and Chancery.* London, 1848.
Pearson, Charles Chilton. *The Readjuster Movement in Virginia.* New Haven, 1917.
Perkin, Harold. *The Origins of Modern English Society, 1780–1880.* Toronto, 1969.
Pilcher, George W. *Samuel Davies, Apostle of Dissent in Colonial Virginia.* Knoxville, Tenn., 1971.

Plumb, J. H. *The Growth of Political Stability in England, 1675–1725.* New York, 1967.
Pocock, J. G. A. *The Ancient Constitution and the Feudal Law.* Cambridge, 1957.
――――. *The Machiavellian Moment: Florentine Political Thought and the Atlantic Republican Tradition.* Princeton, 1975.
――――. "Machiavelli, Harrington, and English Political Ideologies in the Eighteenth Century." *William and Mary Quarterly*, 3 ser., 22 (1965): 550–83.
Porter, Albert O. *County Government in Virginia: A Legislative History.* New York, 1947.
Prall, Stuart E. *Agitation for Law Reform during the Puritan Revolution, 1640–1660.* The Hague, 1966.
Prest, Wilfrid. *The Inns of Court under Elizabeth I and the Early Stuarts, 1590–1640.* London, 1972.
――――. "Legal Education of the Gentry at the Inns of Court, 1560–1640." *Past and Present* 38 (1967): 20–39.
Price, Jacob M. *France and the Chesapeake: A History of the French Tobacco Monopoly, 1674–1791, and of Its Relationship to the British and American Tobacco Traders.* 2 vols. Ann Arbor, 1973.
――――. "The French Farmers-General in the Chesapeake: The MacKercher-Huber Mission of 1737–38." *William and Mary Quarterly*, 3d ser., 14 (1957): 125–53.
――――. "The Rise of Glasgow in the Chesapeake Tobacco Trade, 1707–1775." *William and Mary Quarterly*, 3d ser., 11 (1954): 179–99.
Quitt, Martin Herbert. "The Virginia House of Burgesses, 1660–1706: The Social, Educational and Economic Bases of Political Power." Ph.D. dissertation, Washington University, 1970.
Rainbolt, John C. "The Absence of Towns in Seventeenth-Century Virginia." *Journal of Southern History* 35 (1969): 434–61.
――――. *From Prescription to Persuasion: Manipulation of Seventeenth Century Virginia Economy.* New York, 1974.
Rankin, Hugh F. *Criminal Trial Proceedings in the General Court of Colonial Virginia.* Charlottesville, 1965.
Rheinstein, Max, ed. *Max Weber on Law and Economy and Society.* Translated by Edward Shils. New York, 1954.
Rich, Myra L. "Speculations of the Significance of Debt: Virginia, 1781–1789." *Virginia Magazine of History and Biography* 76 (1968): 301–17.
Ricoeur, Paul. "The Model of the Text: Meaningful Action Considered as a Text." *Social Research* 38 (1971): 529–62.
Risjord, Norman K. *Chesapeake Politics, 1781–1800.* New York, 1978.
――――. *The Old Republicans: Southern Conservatism in the Age of Jefferson.* New York, 1965.
――――. "The Virginia Federalists." *Journal of Southern History* 33 (1976): 486–517.
――――. "Virginians and the Constitution: A Multivariant Analysis." *William and Mary Quarterly*, 3d ser., 31 (1964): 613–32.
Ritchie, John. *The First Hundred Years: A Short History of the School of Law of the University of Virginia for the Period 1826–1926.* Charlottesville, 1979.
Robson, Robert. *The Attorney in Eighteenth Century England.* Cambridge, 1959.

Roeber. A. G. "Authority, Law, and Custom: The Rituals of Court Day in Tidewater Virginia, 1720 to 1750." *William and Mary Quarterly*, 3d ser., 37 (1980): 29–52.

Rosenblatt, Samuel Michael. "The House of John Norton and Sons: A Study of the Consignment Method of Marketing Tobacco from Virginia to England." Ph.D. dissertation, Rutgers University, 1960.

Rubini, Dennis. *Court and Country, 1688–1702*. London, 1967.

Rudé, George F. *Wilkes and Liberty: A Social Study of 1763 to 1774*. Oxford, 1962.

Schutz, Alfred. "Common-Sense and Scientific Interpretation of Human Action." In *Philosophy and the Social Sciences: A Reader*, edited by Maurice Natanson, pp. 302–46. New York, 1963.

———. "Concept and Theory Formation in the Social Sciences," In *Philosophy and the Social Sciences: A Reader*, edited by Maurice Natanson, pp. 231–49. New York, 1963.

Schwoerer, Lois G. "Propaganda in the Revolution of 1688–89." *American Historical Review* 82 (1977): 843–74.

Scott, Arthur P. *Criminal Law in Virginia*. Chicago, 1930.

Scott, Donald M. *From Office to Profession: The New England Ministry, 1750–1850*. Philadelphia, 1978.

Shammas, Carole. "Benjamin Harrison III and the Authorship of *An Essay upon the Government of the English Plantations on the Continent of America*." *Virginia Magazine of History and Biography* 84 (1976): 166–73.

———. "English-Born and Creole Elites in Turn-of-the-Century Virginia." In *The Chesapeake in the Seventeenth Century: Essays on Anglo-American Society and Politics*, edited by Thad W. Tate and David L. Ammerman, pp. 274–96. New York, 1979.

Shaviro, Daniel. "The Carters and the Byrds in Colonial Virginia: A Social and Biographical Study." Senior thesis, Princeton University, 1978.

Shepard, E. Lee. "Administration of Justice in Revolutionary Virginia: The Norfolk Courts, 1770–1790." Master's thesis, University of Virginia, 1974.

———. "Courts in Conflict: Town-County Relations in Post-Revolutionary Virginia." *Virginia Magazine of History and Biography* 85 (1977): 184–99.

Simms, Henry H. *Life of John Taylor*. Richmond, 1932.

Smith, Alan McKinley. "Virginia Lawyers, 1680–1776: The Birth of an American Profession." Ph.D. dissertation, Johns Hopkins University, 1967.

Smith, Daniel Blake. "Changing Patterns of Local Leadership: Justices of the Peace in Albemarle County, Virginia, 1760–1820." Master's thesis, University of Virginia, 1973.

———. "Mortality and Family in the Colonial Chesapeake." *Journal of Interdisciplinary History* 8 (1978): 403–28.

Smith, Stanley Phillips. "The Northern Neck's Role in American Legal History." *Virginia Magazine of History and Biography* 77 (1969): 277–90.

Speck, W. A. "Bernard Mandeville and the Middlesex Grand Jury" *Eighteenth-Century Studies* 11 (1978): 362–74.

———. *Tory and Whig: The Struggle in the Constituencies, 1701–1715*. London, 1970.

Starnes, George T. *Sixty Years of Branch Banking in Virginia*. New York, 1931.

Stone, Lawrence. *Crisis of the Aristocracy, 1558–1641*. Oxford, 1965. Abridged edition. New York, 1967.

---. *The Family, Sex and Marriage and England, 1500–1800*. New York, 1977.
Stourtz, Gerald. *Alexander Hamilton and the Idea of Republican Government*. Stanford, 1970.
Sutherland, Stella H. *Population Distribution in Colonial America*. New York, 1966.
Sutton, Robert P. "Nostalgia, Pessimism, and Malaise: The Doomed Aristocrat in Late-Jeffersonian Virginia." *Virginia Magazine of History and Biography* 76 (1968): 41–55.
Swem, Earl Gregg. *The Virginia Historical Index*. 2 vols. Roanoke, Va., 1934.
Sydnor, Charles S. *Gentleman Freeholders: Political Practices in Washington's Virginia*. Chapel Hill, 1952. Reprint edition. *American Revolutionaries in the Making*. New York, 1965.
---. "The Southerner and the Laws." *Journal of Southern History* 6 (1940): 3–23.
Thompson, E. P. *Whigs and Hunters: The Origins of the Black Act*. New York, 1975.
Thomson, Robert Polk. "The Reform of the College of William and Mary, 1763–1780." *Proceedings of the American Philosophical Society* 115 (1971): 187–213.
Turner, Victor W. *Dramas, Fields, and Metaphors: Symbolic Action in Human Society*. Ithaca, 1974.
---. *The Ritual Process: Structure and Anti-Structure*. Chicago, 1969.
Tyler, Lyon G., ed. *Encyclopedia of Virginia Biography*. 5 vols. New York, 1915.
Unger, Roberto Mangabeira. *Law in Modern Society: Toward a Criticism of Social Theory*. New York, 1976.
Upton, Anthony F. "The Road to Power in Virginia in the Early Nineteenth Century." *Virginia Magazine of History and Biography* 62 (1954): 259–80.
Veall, Donald. *The Popular Movement for Law Reform: 1640–1660*. Oxford, 1970.
Walcott, Robert, Jr. *British Politics in the Early Eighteenth Century*. Cambridge, Mass., 1956.
---. "The Idea of Party in the Writing of Stuart History." *Journal of British Studies* 1 (1962): 54–62.
Ward, W. R. *The English Land Tax in the Eighteenth Century*. Oxford, 1957.
Washburn, Wilcomb E. *The Governor and the Rebel: A History of Bacon's Rebellion in Virginia*. Chapel Hill, 1957.
Waterman, Julis S. "Thomas Jefferson and Blackstone's Commentaries." In *Essays in the History of Early American Law*, edited by David H. Flaherty, pp. 451–88. Chapel Hill, 1967.
Watkins, C. Malcolm. *The Cultural History of Marlborough, Virginia*. Washington, D.C., 1968.
Watlington, Patricia. *The Partisan Spirit: Kentucky Politics, 1779–1792*. New York, 1972.
Webb, Sidney, and Webb, Beatrice. *English Local Government from the Revolution to the Municipal Corporations Act*. 2 vols. Vol. 1, *The Parish and the County*. Vol. 2, *The Manor and the Borough*. London, 1906–8.
Webb, Stephen Saunders. *The Governors-General: The English Army and the Definition of Empire, 1569–1681*. Chapel Hill, 1979.
Wertenbaker, Thomas J. *Virginia under the Stuarts, 1607–1688*. New York, 1959.

Whiffen, Marcus. "The Early County Courthouses of Virginia." *Journal of the Society of Architectural Historians* 18 (1959): 2–10.
———. *The Public Buildings of Williamsburg, Colonial Capital of Virginia: An Architectural History*. Williamsburg, 1958.
White, Stephen D. *Edward Coke and the 'Grievances of the Commonwealth,' 1621–1628*. Chapel Hill, 1979.
Williams, David Alan. "Anglo-Virginia Politics, 1690–1735." In *Anglo-American Political Relations, 1675–1775*, edited by Alison G. Olson and Richard M. Brown, pp. 76–91. New Brunswick, N.J., 1970.
———. "Political Alignments in Colonial Virginia Politics, 1678–1750." Ph.D. dissertation, Northwestern University, 1959.
———. "The Small Farmer in Eighteenth-Century Virginia Politics." *Agricultural History* 42 (1969): 91–101.
Wills, Garry. *Inventing America: Jefferson's Declaration of Independence*. New York, 1978.
Winder, W. H. D. "The Court of Requests." *Law Quarterly Review* 52 (1936): 369–94.
Wood, Gordon S. *The Creation of the American Republic, 1776–1787*. Chapel Hill, 1969.
———. "The Democratization of Mind in the American Revolution." In *Leadership in the American Revolution*, pp. 63–88. Washington, D.C., 1974.
———. "Rhetoric and Reality in the American Revolution." *William and Mary Quarterly*, 3d ser., 23 (1966): 2–32.
Wroth, Lawrence C. *William Parks, Printer and Journalist of England and Colonial America*. Richmond, 1926.
Zagorin, Perez. *The Court and the Country: The Beginning of the English Revolution*. New York, 1969.

Index

Admiralty, Court of, 58
Ad quod damnum, writ of, 214
Age: significance of, 76
Agriculture: production rate of, 35
Allason, William, 131
Anderson qui tam against *Winston*, 106–7
Anglican church, 167
Anglicization: of courts, 133, 153–54; of culture, 254
Anthropology: methods of, xv, 74n
Antilawyer sentiment: English, 18–19; Virginia, 47–48, 53, 126–37, 151, 156–57, 231, 241–51
Appeals: to General Court, 44, 132; to District courts, 212. *See also* Assembly; Privy Council; Supreme Court of Appeals
Architecture: courthouse, 78–80
Aristocracy: attacked, 165–; of talent, 235, 244, 254–57
Assault, 128
Assembly, 41; as court of last resort, 44; laws passed by, 49, 150, 169, 171, 175, 179, 189, 190, 196–97, 199, 201, 203, 205–7, 216, 221, 223, 229, 240, 250. *See also* Burgesses, House of
Assize, Court of: English, 4, 12–16; Virginia, 153–54, 192–95. *See also* District court
Attachment, writ of, 220
Attorney general: English, 53, 61; Virginia, 52, 60–62, 64, 68, 96, 108
Attorneys: English, 16–18; licensing of (seventeenth century), 48–53; and printing, 49–50; emigré character of, 56n; where concentrated, 56, 57; control over, 67, 68; used *in forma pauperis*, 91; licensing of (1732), 108; forbidden exorbitant fees, 109; licensing repealed (1742), 109; licensing of, revived (1746), 109;

county and General Court, separated, 110; licensing of (1748), 110; training of, 58–59, 119, 121, 247; relation of, to language, 122; licensing pattern among, 122; examiners of, 122–25; English, in Virginia, 125; earnings of, 130n. *See also* Barristers; Lawyers; University of Virginia
Authority and deference, 11, 80–83; and property, 74; and unpropertied, 90–95 passim; and law, 92. *See also* Law; Property

Bacon's Rebellion, 44; causes of, 48–49; recalled, 99; view of, by Edmund Randolph, 164
Banking and lawyers, 232, 234
Bank of Virginia, 234, 240, 242
Banks, Henry, 241, 242, 243
Baptists, 112, 137
Bar: division of, 110–11, 121, 204, 255. *See also* Attorneys; General Court; Lawyers
Barradall, Edward, 100; view of law in Virginia of, 102; reports by, 102, 103, 106–7, 255. *See also* Randolph, Sir John
Barristers, English, 16–18; at court of Assizes, 17
Barristers, Virginia: how defined, 55n, 57, 58, 59, 60; number of, 76; practice of, 110n. *See also* Attorneys; County court; General Court; Lawyers
Bastardy: presentments for, 89–90. *See also* Grand Jury; Misdemeanors; Women
Battaley, Moseley, 119, 146n
Beckwith, Marmaduke, 146
Bentley, Rev. William, 218
Berkeiey, Edmund, 210
Berkeley, Governor Sir William, 45,

283

47, 48, 49, 50. *See also* Bacon's Rebellion; Justices of peace; Patronage
Beverley, Robert, Sr., 50, 51
Beverley, Robert, II, 57; views of, on courts, 62, 63; authorship of, 62n, 68
Bill: Reforming Courts of Justice, 145; For More Easy Administration of Justice, 153–55; Establishing General Court and Assize Court, 167–68; Better Regulating County Courts, 168; for Diffusion of Knowledge, 168; for Establishing Courts of Assize, 192–95; Reforming County Courts, 193; to Punish Delinquent Justices, 208. *See also* Revisals of laws
Blackstone, William, 151, 236
Blackstone's *Commentaries*, 164, 236, 237, 246. *See also* Tucker, St. George
Blair, John, Jr., 132
Bland, Richard, 149, 153, 154n
Blathwayt, William, 26
Bloomfield, Max, 241
Board of Trade, 61
Bolingbroke, Henry St. John, Lord, 22, 23, 252. *See also* Ideology
Bolling, John, 82
Book debt: method of proving, 40, 41; statute for proving attacked, 136
Borough English, 164, 165n
Bowyer, Luke, 116
Boyd, David, 119
Bradford, William, 147
Breckinridge, John, 235
Brent, George, 56
Breton, Nicholas, 7
Brockenbrough, William, 231
Brooke, Francis T., 234
Buckner, John, 49
Burgesses, House of, 37; laws passed by, 48, 49, 51, 52, 63, 108, 109–10, 115, 131, 132, 135, 140, 145–46, 149, 150, 153, 155, 160, 168; conflict of, with Spotswood, 65, 66, 67; and Gooch, 95, 96. *See also* Assembly; Attorneys; Council; Lawyers; Revisals of laws; Senate
Burke, Thomas, 150

Bylaws: of county courts, 114, 176
Byrd, William II, 24, 25, 26, 38; Court identity of, 70, 71; plan of, for supreme court, 70; death of, 109
Byrd, William III, 170

Cabell, Joseph, 231
Cabell, William, Sr., 170
Called courts: established, 42, 43n; decisions of, surveyed, 77n. *See also* Felony; Justices of peace; Misdemeanors; Oyer and Terminer, court of
Carr, E. H., xv
Carter, John, 24
Carter, Landon, 77; presented by grand jury, 89, 112; views of, on justices, 116, 120; views of, on lawyers, 120, 145; conflict with lawyers, 151; views of, on General Court, 152–53; views of, on court reform, 155
Carter, Robert, 25, 26, 28, 29, 30, 31, 62
Carter, Robert, III, 125
Carter, Robert Wormeley: presented by grand jury, 89; 116
Cary, Wilson, 132
Case: actions on, 16, 128; and debt recovery, 136, 225. *See also* Debt, action of; Detinue, action of; Wager of law
Cases agreed, 154n
Catholics, 20
Certiorari, writ of, 18, 197, 219, 220, 222
Chamberlain, Richard, 6, 7, 11; charge to grand jury by, 87; opinion of, on punishment, 93–94
Chancery, courts of, 225
Charter, Great (of Virginia), 41
Chaucer, Geoffrey, 18, 32
Chicheley, Henry, 49, 50
Chilton, Edward, 58, 59
Chiswell Affair, 149–50
Church: nonattendance at, 140–42
Circuit court, 45n; petition of merchants for, 130. *See also* Assize, Court of
Clayton, John, 68, 96, 100, 108

Clergy, 112; number of, in Virginia, 133n; letters of, about courts, 138, 148; historical role of, outlined by Jefferson, 165–66
Clerk of peace, 13, 14
Clerks: how appointed, 31, 47; relationship to lawyers, 31; control over, 69; ordered to report on Commission of Peace, 114, 173; of General Court, 105; letters of, 146; justices serve as, 174–75; of district court, 208–9. *See also* Attorneys; Lawyers, training of; Patronage; Secretary, colony
Club Law, 99, 100n
Coke, Sir Edward, 12, 19, 21, 27, 28, 32n; view of Commission of Peace, 94; learning of, 57; admired in Virginia, 236. *See also* Jefferson, Thomas; Law, republican, sources of
College of William and Mary: reforms at, 167
Commissioner of equity, 222–23
Commission of Peace: English, 12; Virginia, 46, 68, 76, 119, 122, 168, 182, 200. *See also* County court; Gentry; Justices of peace
Common law, 5, 36, 165, 166
Common Pleas, Court of (English), 44, 58
Commonwealth attorney, deputy, 184, 188, 213
Contempt of court, 80–83; lawyers in, 118, 119. *See also* Deference; Misdemeanors; Lawyers
Conway, Edwin, 76, 117
Corbin, Francis, 195
Corbin, Richard, 130, 198
Corrie, John, 115
Corruption, 28. *See also* Ideology; Virtue
Council, governor's, 26, 50, 60, 61, 63; and Oyer and Terminer dispute, 69, 70, 71, 102, 114, 116, 117, 120, 161. *See also* Attorneys; Oyer and Terminer, court of; General Court; Judges, tenure of
Counties, English, 3, 13, 20–21. *See also* Assize, Court of; Fielding, Henry; Justices of peace; Sheriff's Court
Counties, Virginia: Albemarle, 173–74; Amherst, 170; Brunswick, 209; Caroline, 38, 198, 199, 200, 219, 220, 221; Charles City, 41, 117, 128, 130; Dinwiddie, 137; Elizabeth City, 41, 110, 116, 148; Essex, 76, 115, 118, 128, 157, 158, 170, 174, 183, 185, 198, 199, 201, 205, 226, 231, 234; Fairfax, 188, 189, 191; Gloucester, 49, 51, 110, 198, 200; Halifax, 219; Hanover, 38, 98, 140, 148, 199; Henrico, 82, 84, 116, 117, 130, 173, 187, 198; James City, 53, 66, 68, 110; Jefferson, 249–50; King George, 39, 114, 129, 175, 183, 184, 185, 187; King and Queen, 190, 208; King William, 148; Lancaster, 76, 117, 118, 152, 176, 177, 182, 187, 209, 213; Madison, 227; Middlesex, 45, 85, 109, 130, 170, 185, 187, 198, 199; New Kent, 66, 95, 117, 119, 120, 191; Norfolk, 173–74, 190–91; Northumberland, 98, 114, 146, 172, 185, 213; Orange, 192, 226; Prince George, 200; Princess Anne, 169, 220; Richmond, 90, 112, 116, 120, 128, 151, 153, 172, 173, 176, 177, 183, 187, 214, 220; Rockbridge, 219; Spotsylvania, 200; Stafford, 32, 39, 53, 57, 109; Surry, 140; Warwick, 110; Westmoreland, 53, 87, 102, 114, 117, 129, 161, 172, 173, 174, 181, 185, 187, 213; York, 35, 53, 110, 176, 182, 183, 187
Country: definition of, 7, 8; real and official, xvii, 244, 252n; tradition, 10–11, 30–31, 258–59. *See also* Antilawyer sentiment; Court; Ideology
Country party, 66–71
County court (Virginia), xv, 64, 73, 100–130 passim, 211, 212, 226, 227. *See also* Attorneys; Clerks; Justices of peace; Lawyers
Court, xvii–xviii; definition of, as cultural term, 7, 24–27, 28, 29–31, 51n. *See also* Attorneys; Barristers;

286 Index

Country; General Court; Justices of peace; Lawyers; Patronage
Court day, 73–95, 114, 115–37, 172
Courthouses: descriptions of, 78, 79, 227, 229. *See also* Architecture
Court of Appeals, 206, 220, 221
Court of Commissioners, 169, 170
Courts: efficiency of certain, 121, 131; closure of, 160. *See also* Assembly; Privy Council; and various courts by name
Crown attorneys, deputy, 64, 65, 79; salary for, proposed and rejected, 109, 118; wages of, 130n. *See also* Attorney general
Culpeper, Governor Thomas, Lord, 49, 50
Currie, Ellyson, 211
Custom: in Virginia courts, 74n, 74–95 passim, 105, 106n

Dalton, Michael, 6, 118
Dandridge, Bartholomew, 191
Davies, Samuel, 137
Dawkins, William, 29
Debt, action of, 220, 221, 225
Debt: causes, 40–41; small amounts, how recovered, 84; number of causes, 85, 114, 127; and exchange rate, 130; collection of, suspended during Revolution, 169; causes resumed, 171. *See also* Case, action on; Detinue; Trover and conversion
Dedimus potestatem, writ of, 13
Deference, 3, 5, 29–31, 35, 36, 53; decline of, 174, 191. *See also* Authority; Property; Virtue
Delegates, House of, 178, 179, 188, 191, 192, 195, 231, 233. *See also* Assembly
Detinue, action of, 84n, 128, 213
District court, proposed, 134, 201; opposition to, 205; function, 207; jurisdiction of, 208; review of county court decisions by, 212, 213, 214. *See also* Appeals; Assize, Court of; Judges, tenure of; Judges' Remonstrance
Diversification: agricultural, 38, 39.

See also Agriculture; Towns
Dogs: control of, 140. *See also* Gentry; Grand jury, presentments of
Dower, waiver of, 43
Drama, court, 14, 74, 75, 78
Dual suits, 131n
Dulaney, Cawan, 119
Dunmore, Governor John Murray, Lord, 155, 160, 161, 170
Duval, Samuel, 117
Duval, William, 117, 130

Economy (Virginia), 28, 29, 35, 37, 38–41, 144n, 177n, 206, 232. *See also* Debt; Diversification; Merchants; Towns
Edwards, Thomas, 209
Effingham, Governor Howard, Lord, 51, 52
Ejectment, action of, 59
Ellis, John, 85
Enquiry of damages, writ of, 154, 155n
Entail, 166n
Equity, 19, 44, 222, 223, 224, 225. *See also* Chancery, courts of; Common law; Justices of peace, equity jurisdiction of
Error, writ of, 220
Escheat, traverse of, 58n
Exchequer, court of, 44, 58
Exclusion Crisis, 21
Executive Council, 191, 204

Factors, Scottish, 39
Farmer's Repository: letters to, 249, 250
Fee Act, 160
Fees, set for attorneys, 68
Felony, 14, 15–16, 42. *See also* Assize, Court of; Called courts; County courts; General Court; Misdemeanor
Fielding, Henry, 3, 23, 24
Fitzhugh, Henry, 109
Fitzhugh, William, 32, 49, 57–58
Fowler, Bartholomew, 60
Fredericksburg, District Court of, 210
Fundamental law, 5, 21. *See also*

Coke; Ideology; Natural law; Law, republican, sources of

Gaming, prohibited, 140n, 144n
Garland, Hugh, 203
Gavelkind, 164, 165n
General Court: jurisdiction of, 44; composition of, 44; procedure in, 56, 57, 102, 105, 106; term of, 196; salary increase for judges requested, 114n; docket of, 132, 136, 137, 150–52, 154, 160, 175; relation of, to district courts, 204, 219. *See also* Appeals; Council; County courts; Judges, tenure of; Privy Council
Gentry: English, 3, 4, 10, 17, 18, 22, 25; Virginia, 30–32, 35, 34–41, 45–49, 53, 56, 58, 59, 75–79, 81–83, 88, 89, 99, 100, 112, 113, 127, 137–45 passim, 147, 153, 173, 174, 177–79, 182–84. *See also* Country; Court day; Economy; Justices of peace
Giles, William Branch, 210
Gilmer, Francis Walker, 253
Glorious Revolution, 9, 10, 52, 53
Gooch, Governor Sir William, 71, 74, 95, 96–100, 106
Gordon v. Bates, 219
Grand jury, English: charge to, 14; at Assizes, 15, 16
Grand jury, Virginia: freeholders on, 86, 87; impaneling of, 86; members of, not justices, 86–87; presentments of, summarized, 88–90; courts fail to summon, 140; presentments of, summarized, 140–45; presentments of, against justices, 176, 177; presentments of, against nonvoters, 180–83; presentments of, surveyed, 184–88; presentments of, in City of Richmond, 186–87; district court, presentments of, 212, 215, 216

Habeas corpus, writ of, 64, 222
Hamilton, Alexander, 232
Hamilton, John, 129
Harrison, Benjamin, 24

Harrison, Benjamin, Jr., 60, 61
Hening, William Waller, 210, 217, 236
Henry, Patrick, 128, 149, 193, 199; biography of, 241, 244
High Court of Appeals, 207
High Court of Chancery, 205, 222, 223, 224, 225
Hobday, John, 38
Holloway, John, 59, 60, 68, 96, 100
Hopkins, William, 59, 60
Hustings Court, 131, 139

Ideology, xvi, 22, 23, 30. *See also* Country; Law, republican, sources of; Tory party; Whig party
Imparling, 84
Indictment, traverse of, 14
Injunction, 44n, 141, 142
Innes, James, 210
Innes, Robert, 209, 210
Inns of Court, 16, 17, 18; Virginians attending, 24, 25, 121. *See also* Attorneys; Barristers; Lawyers, training of
Isaac, Rhys, 94n, 148

Jarratt, Devereux, 78, 137
Jefferson, Field, 117
Jefferson, Thomas, xviii, xix; influenced by Country tradition, 160, 162, 163, 252; view of history of, 163–65; view of education and court reform of, 167, 168; on natural law, 224; views of, on banking, 233n; on county courts, 239–40. *See also* Law, republican, sources of; Revisals of laws, 1776–79, 1785
Jenings, Edmund, 52, 70
Jeofails: law of, 114n; Act concerning, 221
Jerdone, Francis, 143, 144
Jones, Hugh, 64
Jones, Joseph, 199, 200
Judges: independence and tenure of, 10n, 63, 218; district court, 204, 216. *See also* General Court; *Kamper v. Hawkins*
Judges' Remonstrance, 207, 222, 249

288 *Index*

Junto, Essex, 234
Juries: Act concerning, 115; county court, attacked, 132, 135, 213, 214; and Act concerning Jeofails, 221; increased reliance on, to be revived, 243
Jury trial: and debt causes, 85, 86; when denied in summary justice, 42, 104, 105, 191; increase in use of, 128; statistics on, 128
Justices of peace, English, 4, 13; powers of, 11–15; stipendiary, 13–14
Justices of peace, Virginia: powers of, 42–43; administrative duties of, 43; felony jurisdiction of, 42n, 43; ecclesiastical court jurisdiction of, 43; equity jurisdiction of, 44n; proposals to pay, 45, 134, 135, 136, 193; control of, 45–46; of quorum, 76; oath of, 78; dignity of, guarded, 81; duties of, reviewed, 97, 98; and tobacco inspectors, 98–100, 104; attacked, 98, 99, 103–4, 112, 113, 137–38, 190; absence from court of, 115, 173; forbidden legal practice, 121; Dunmore's view of, 160–61; new men as, 173–74, 183, 184, 202–3; in town, and rural courts, 190, 191; forbidden district court clerkships, 217; forbidden to be commissioners of equity, 223; description of, 228; number of, in assemblies, declines, 240

Kamper v. Hawkins, 218, 225, 249. *See also* District courts; Judges, independence of; Tucker, St. George
Kennan, William, 82, 119
Kennedy, John Pendleton, 228–30
Kentucky, 241n
Kerr, David, 130
King's Bench, Court of, 15, 18, 44, 58

Lamb, Mathew, 115
Lambarde, William, 11
Land: tenures of, in England, 36; and authority, in England, 36; availability in Virginia, 38. *See also* Borough English; Escheat, traverse of; Gavelkind; Primogeniture; Property

Law: basis of, 6, 10, 11, 246; administration of, 73; definition of, 74, 83; of England, how regarded in Virginia, 74; qualities of, 73, 74; uses of, contested, 107–8; private, 92–93; viewed as science, 113, 167, 236–37, 247; republican, sources of, 163–71; function of, stated, 216; southern views of, 258–60. *See also* Bylaws; Coke, Sir Edward; Common law; Custom; Ideology; Natural law
Lawyers: English, 16–24, 26; and merchants, 21, 27, 28, 101, 129, 156, 250; and printing, 32, 49–50, 56, 95; in General Court, 59, 60; cited for contempt, 82; attack justices, 96, 103–8; and revisals of laws, 95–96, 110, 115n; increase in numbers of, 95; around capital, 53, 100, 110n, 121, 131–32; rhetoric of, 113; training of, 121–25; social background of, 121; observations on, 125, 127, 131; ratio of, to population, 129; and politics, 145, 240; and local court practice, 203–9; in district courts, 210; as Country heroes, 228. *See also* Attorneys; Barristers; County courts; Country; Court; District courts; General Court; Gentry; Merchants
Lawyers' bench, 118
Lee, George, 82
Lee, Richard, 32
Legal culture: creation of, xvii; shaped by justices, 41; and lawyers, 48–71 passim; differing views on, 118–59 passim, 230, 251; district courts and, 203–30; legacy of, 231–61 passim
Legal profession, xvi, 48–71, 110, 113, 118, 128–29; definition of, 147n, 245, 256. *See also* Attorneys; Barristers; Lawyers
Literacy: in Virginia, 74n, 76–77, 125
Lords of Trade and Plantations, 28
Loyalists: in Virginia, 169, 170, 199, 200
Ludwell, Philip, 25, 51, 53
Ludwell, Thomas, 56

Madison, James, 147, 169, 192, 194, 195, 226
Mandamus, writ of, 175
Mansfield, Lord, 159, 248
Markland, John, 95, 96
Marshall, John, 192, 193, 211, 234, 245
Martin, John, 91
Maryland: land deeds, 38; courts, 136n
Mason, George, 166, 177–78, 188–89, 234
Mason, Thomson, 161, 162
Massachusetts: lawyers in, 145, 146
Maury, Reverend James, 148
Mazzei, Phillip, 166
Mercer, John, 119, 129, 146
Mercer, John F., 210
Merchants: and lawyers, 21, 24, 27, 28, 129, 156, 250
Militia, 30, 250
Milner, Thomas, 52
Misdemeanors, 42, 43. See also Felony; Grand jury, presentments of; Justices of peace
Mobs, 97, 169
Monroe, James, 193, 206, 207, 210
Monthly court, 41, 42
Morrill, John, xvii, 18
Mortality, 35, 129n. See also Population
Multiple offices, 46. See also Clerks; Justices of peace; Patronage; Sheriff
Myth: definition of, 11; and Common law, 36; and South, 228; and lawyers, 241; and Country, 257. See also Ideology

Natural law, 6n; and natural justice, 106, 107, 224, 255. See also Fundamental law; Ideology; Law, republican, sources of
Nelson family, 139
New York, equity courts in, 224n
Nicholas, Robert Carter, 132, 149
Nicholson, Governor Francis, 60, 61, 62, 63
Nisi prius court, 16, 192n, 224
Nonimportation, 156n
Norfolk, 190, 191

Northumberland District Court, attorneys in, 211
Nott, Governor Edward, 63
Nuthead, John, 49

Office: desire for, attacked, 248
Office judgments, 194
Oldum á Allerton and Pope, 102
Oratory, of lawyers, 107; praised, 245; attacked, 251
Order conditional, 114
Original process: in county courts, 44, 212n; in General Court, 44, 115; in Assize Court (1772), 153; in district courts, 212
Orphans: estates of, 80
Otway, Major Francis, 25
Oyer and Terminer: commission of, 43; court of, 65; dispute over judges of, 69–71

Page, Mann, 215
Park, John, 130
Parker, Richard, 151, 152
Parker, Sir Thomas, 70
Parliament, 8, 19, 20, 28
Parsons' Cause, 148
Patronage: described by Fielding, 3, 4; used in Virginia, 25–26, 45, 46, 47, 56n, 65, 96, 97
Paulding, J. K., 254
Pendleton, Edmund, 154n, 160, 162; conservative views of, 164–65; views on county courts, 201; opinions of, as judge of High Court of Appeals, 229n
Petition: small debt action by, 84n
Petitions: and legislation, 51n; against tobacco law of 1713, 66, 67; instigated by attorneys, 67; against 1730 tobacco law, 98; for more justices, 155; regarding Randolph family, 116; for new Commission of Peace, 116; regarding quarter sessions, 130; against irregular court days, 190; favoring salaries for justices, 190; for court reform, 188, 189; lack of, for schools, 239
Petty sessions, 13
Pinckard, Thomas, 117, 152

290 Index

Pinckard, Thomas, Jr., 211
Place Act, 47, 48
Placemen, opposition to, 25–26
Plant Cutters' Rebellion, 44, 50
Planters. *See* Gentry; Tobacco
Pocock, J. G. A., xviii, 9
Pole, Godfrey, 68
Poor: laws on, in England, 15; laws on, in Virginia, 44; justices serve as attorneys for, 48; actions of courts toward, 89; farmers, 96–97, 136
Population: of Virginia, 44n, 132
Ports: creation of, 234n
Posey, John Price, 191–92
Postea, writ of, 16
Prentis, Joseph, 195
Presbyterians, 137
Primogeniture, 164, 165, 166
Private law, 94
Privy Council, 13, 44, 51, 53
Procedendo, writ of, 222
Property, 15; right of, 32, 34, 74, 76; relation of, to authority, 36, 37, 40–41, 44n; of justices, 75n, 182; defined, 90n; attacks on, feared, 100, 164, 165n; larger amounts, for jurors, 213–14
Prosser, Thomas, 119

Quarterly Court, 42. *See also* General Court
Quarter Sessions, Court of: in England, 4, 12–15; petitions for, 130; proposed, 154; established, 194; rendered ineffective, 195
Quincy, Josiah, Jr., 204
Qui tam, action, 106

Randolph, Edmund, 34, 164
Randolph, John (of Roanoke), 203, 232
Randolph, Peter, 85
Randolph, Peyton, 149
Randolph, Richard, 116, 117
Randolph, Sir John, 25; on lawyers, 59–60, 96, 100; views of, on law procedures, 102; on county courts, 105–6
Records, court, 263n
Reporters, opinions of, 229

Republicans. *See* Ideology; Law, republican, sources of; Jefferson, Thomas; Mason, George; Pendleton, Edmund; Tucker, St. George; Wythe, George
Requests, Court of, 16n
Restoration era: litigiousness of, 16; role of lawyers during, 19, 20, 21
Revisals of laws: 1700–1705, 61; 1748, 110; 1776–79, 162, 169; 1785, 177n
Rhetoric, 145, 226, 250, 254. *See also* Oratory, of lawyers
Ritchie, Thomas, 244, 247n
Ritual, xix; of court day, 74n, 80n, 81–82, 74–95 passim
Roane, Spencer, 200
Robertson, William, 96
Robinson Scandal, 149
Rolfe, John, 37
Rose, Alexander, 129
Rust Family, 87

Sanction: use of, 88, 89
Scire facias, writ of, 85, 221
Secretary, colony, 47, 69
Selden, John, 19
Senate, 195, 196, 250, 251
Servants, 35, 36, 90–93
Settlement, Act of, 10n
Sexual offenses. *See* Grand jury, presentments of; Misdemeanors
Sheriff, in England, 13; in Virginia, 46, 47n, 79, 81, 83, 85, 181, 185, 200, 201
Sheriff's Court (English), 44
Sherwood, William, 54
Slaves, 36; how tried, 42n, 43, 93; age of, determined in court, 80; how regarded, 93n; illegally freed, 158; rebellion of, feared, 227
Smith, Meriwether, 117, 157, 199, 200, 205, 234
Social standards, 34–41; defined by sanctions and law, 73, 75, 79; and race, 91; and change, 257
Society of Gentlemen Practisers, 20
Solicitors (English), 16–18. *See also* Attorneys; Barristers, Lawyers
Special juries: proposals favoring, 135;

Index 291

and Parsons' Cause, 148, 149; Tucker, St. George, and, 213, 214
Special verdicts, 102, 154n
Spicer, Arthur, 56
Spotswood, Governor Alexander, 30, 64–71 passim
Stamp Act, and justices of peace, 161
Staples, Judge Waller R., 227, 228
Star Chamber, Court of, 19
Starke, Richard, 120
Story, Joseph, 256
Superior courts: replace district courts, 241–42
Superior Courts of Chancery, 222, 225, 249
Supersedeas, writ of, 18, 197, 208, 213
Supreme Court of Appeals, 207
Sydnor, Charles S., xv, xviii–xix, 258

Tarpley, John, 129
Tarpley, Travers, 129
Taverns: licenses of held by justices, 139
Tax commissioners, 178
Taylor, John (of Caroline), 232, 233, 235, 240
Tazewell, Henry, 209
Tazewell, John, 150
Tazewell, Littleton Waller, 238
Tertium Quids, 232
Tidewater, region of: defined, 37–38; voting patterns in, 198–99, 205; population of, declines, 217
Tithables: failure to list, 140, 143, 144, 180
Tobacco: and society, 37, 39–41; variety of marketing patterns, 39–41. See also Economy; Gentry; Land
Tobacco Law: of 1713, 65–69; of 1730, 96–97
Tocqueville, Alexis de, 256
Tory party, 21–22
Towns: absence of, in Virginia, 37; New England, admired by Thomas Jefferson, 163; attorneys' view of, 247
Trespass, action of, 102, 103
Trover and conversion, action of, 128
Tucker, St. George: view of circuit courts, 176, 204, 208; view of county practice, 209–10, 211, 215; view of Virginia Constitution, 218–19; "Notes on Cases," 219–20; adapts Blackstones' *Commentaries*, 236; views on law as science, 236–37; educational scheme of, 237–38. See also *Kamper* v. *Hawkins*; Law, republican, sources of
Turberville, John, 85
Twopenny Acts, 148
Tyler, John, 213

University: plans for, 238–39
University of Virginia, 252–53

Venire facias, writ of, 14
Virginia Almanac, 126, 135, 231
Virginia Gazette: letters to, 73, 133–34, 135, 136, 139–40, 150, 151, 153, 155, 156–57, 158, 167
Virginia Independent Chronicle: letters to, 196, 205
Virtue: defined, 8–9; related to deference, 26; and lawyers, 137, 156–57, 166; demanded of justices, 138; upheld against loyalists, 169; and politics, 176; and voting habits, 179–80; and law, 179–80; republican definition, 196–97, 240n, 246n, 248
Voting: penalty for not, 179–83; pattern of Tidewater, on court reform, 198–99, 205. See also Grand jury, presentments of; Virtue

Waddill against *Chamberlayne*, 106–7, 255
Wager of law, 136n
Walke, Anthony, 119
Waller, Benjamin, 149, 152
Walpole, Sir Robert, 10, 22
Warranty, law of, 107
Warrington, Reverend Thomas, 148
Washington, Augustine, 92
Washington, Bushrod, 210
Washington, George, 195–96
Washington, Martha Custis, 191
Wayles, John, 127, 130
Webb, George, 119

Whig party, 20–23 passim
White, Reverend Alexander, 148
Wilkes, John, 152, 153
Wirt, William, 241, 244, 246
Women, 15; waiver of dower by, 43; offenses of women presented, 90; sue in courts, 91; and virtue, 240n
Wood, Gordon S., xvi
Wormeley, Ralph, I, 58
Wormeley, Ralph, III, 85, 170, 177
Writs: in Assize Courts (English), 14; in *Nisi prius* court, 16; in Virginia, 59. See also *Ad quod damnum, Certiorari, Dedimus potestatem,* Error, *Mandamus, Postea, Procedendo, Supersedeas*
Wythe, George, xix, 150, 162, 166; opinions of, as chancellor, 229–30; and Judges' Remonstrance, 249

Yates, Charles, 171–72
York County Court: efficiency of, 132; opinion of, on equity and debt procedures, 225–26
Yorktown, 131, 143

Zagorin, Perez, 7

www.ingramcontent.com/pod-product-compliance
Lightning Source LLC
Chambersburg PA
CBHW021355290426
44108CB00010B/251